The Artistry of Aeschylus and Zeami

MAE J. SMETHURST

The Artistry of Aeschylus and Zeami

A Comparative Study of

Greek Tragedy and Nō

PRINCETON UNIVERSITY PRESS

Published by Princeton University Press, 41 William Street,
Princeton, New Jersey 08540
In the United Kingdom: Princeton University Press, Guildford, Surrey

This book has been composed in Linotron Sabon type

Clothbound editions of Princeton University Press books are printed
on acid-free paper, and binding materials are chosen for strength
and durability. Paperbacks, although satisfactory for personal
collections, are not usually suitable for library rebinding

Printed in the United States of America by Princeton University
Press, Princeton, New Jersey

Library of Congress Cataloging-in-Publication Data
Smethurst, Mae J., 1935-
The artistry of Aeschylus and Zeami: a comparative study of Greek
tragedy and nō / Mae J. Smethurst.
p.   cm.
Bibliography: p.
Includes index.
ISBN 0-691-06752-X (alk. paper)
1. Aeschylus—Criticism and interpretation. 2. Zeami, 1363-1443
—Criticism and interpretation. 3. Tragedy. 4. Nō plays—History and
criticism. 5. Literature, Comparative—Greek and Japanese. 6. Literature,
Comparative—Japanese and Greek. I. Title.
PA3829.S49   1988
882'.01—dc19   88-25418

τῷ φιλτάτῳ πόσει

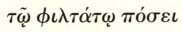

Contents

List of Abbreviations

AJP	*American Journal of Philology*
BICS	*Bulletin of the Institute of Classical Studies*
Camb. Phil. Proc.	*Proceedings of the Cambridge Philological Society*
Class. et Med.	*Classica et Mediaevalia*
CP	*Classical Philology*
CQ	*Classical Quarterly*
CW	*Classical World*
FEQ	*Far Eastern Quarterly*
GR	*Greece and Rome*
GRBS	*Greek, Roman and Byzantine Studies*
HJAS	*Harvard Journal of Asiatic Studies*
HSCP	*Harvard Studies in Classical Philology*
HThR	*Harvard Theological Review*
Heike	*Heike monogatari*
JATJ	*Journal of the Association of Teachers of Japanese*
JHS	*Journal of Hellenic Studies*
JJS	*Journal of Japanese Studies*
Koyama	Koyama Hiroshi, Satō Kikuo, and Satō Ken'ichirō, eds., *Yōkyokushū*, vol. 1, *Nihon koten bungaku zenshū*, vol. 33 (Tokyo: Shōgakkan, 1973)
MH	*Museum Helveticum*
MN	*Monumenta Nipponica*
NGS	Nippon Gakujutsu Shinkōkai, *The Noh Drama*, 3 vols. (Tokyo and Vermont, 1955–1960)
OCT	Oxford Classical Text
P-C	Pickard-Cambridge
Rh. Mus.	*Rheinische Museum*

Rimer   J. Thomas Rimer and Yamazaki Masakazu, *On the Art of the Nō Drama: The Major Treatises of Zeami* (Princeton, 1984)

TAPA   *Transactions and Proceedings of the American Philological Association*

WS   *Wiener Studien*

YKS   Yokomichi Mario and Omote Akira, eds., *Yōkyokushū*, vol. 1, *Nihon koten bungaku taikei*, vol. 40 (Tokyo: Iwanami, 1972)

ZZ   Omote Akira and Katō Shūichi, eds., *Zeami: Zenchiku*, *Nihon shisō taikei*, vol. 24 (Tokyo: Iwanami, 1974)

Acknowledgments

In the year 1961, Kubo Masaaki, Professor of Classics at Tokyo University, kindly invited me to join the *Girishahigeki kenkyūkai* (Greek Tragedy Research Seminar) for its discussions of Sophocles' *Philoctetes*, held in conjunction with preparations for a translation of the play into Japanese and a production at Tokyo's outdoor theater located in Hibiya Park. This experience, coupled with an introduction to performances of nō in Japan, kindled my interest in a comparison of Greek tragedy and Japanese nō, an interest that was then nurtured by Gerald F. Else of the University of Michigan, who actively encouraged me in my pursuit of the present project.

I regret deeply that Gerald Else died before he had the opportunity to see a draft of the manuscript in anything close to its present form, for my gratitude to him as a mentor is great: he first taught me how to read ancient Greek, he introduced me to the works of Aeschylus and to Aristotle's *Poetics*, and he took concrete measures to support my comparative study by providing financial backing for a Workshop on the Comparison of Nō and Greek Tragedy under the auspices of the Center for the Coordination of Studies Ancient and Modern at the University of Michigan.

On the Japanese side, I am especially indebted to Shimazaki Chifumi, a teacher and translator of nō, above all for the hours she spent discussing passages from a wide variety of nō texts with me and performing sections of song, dance, and drum accompaniment, but also for her introductions to actors, teachers, and scholars of nō, including Nishino Haruo of Hōsei University's Nō Research Center, who graciously answered my numerous questions about *Sanemori*.

I was able to develop my ideas for this book during the year spent at The Center for Hellenic Studies in Washington, D.C., under the auspices of the Board of Trustees of Harvard University. Both during that year and after, I profited greatly from conversations with Bernard M. W. Knox, who was the Director of the Center, and from his remarks on parts of the manuscript. Near the final stages of my study, the comments of Andrew Miller of the University of Pittsburgh encouraged me and significantly enhanced the presentation of my argument.

I am grateful to a number of other scholars for their suggestions at various stages in the genesis of this study. Discussions with Karen Brazell of Cornell University led me to important bibliographical materials with which I as a classicist was not familiar. Her invitation for me to join a series of seminars on the subject of *Time and Space: Japanese Aesthetics*, sponsored by the Social Science Research Council and American Council of Learned Societies, provided me with the opportunity to test some of my ideas with such scholars as William LaFleur of UCLA, Susan Matisoff of Stanford University, and Frank Hoff of the University of Toronto. Frank, trained as both a classicist and a Japanologist and with an extensive knowledge of the work of Japanese scholars and members of the Japanese theatrical world, gave me advice about how to draw connections between structure and performance in nō. An exchange of letters with Thomas B. Hare of Stanford University was especially useful in helping me gain a more nearly accurate understanding of Zeami's style and thought; his specific comments on parts of the manuscript were invaluable. J. Thomas Rimer of the University of Maryland had the uncanny talent of encouraging me at opportune moments. Joan Steiner of Drew University provided me with useful suggestions on the written style of an early version of the manuscript. I also want to thank Oliver Taplin of Oxford University, Magdalen College, for his incisive remarks on the manuscript as a whole, and John Herington of Duke University and Donald Keene of Columbia University for their specific comments on certain portions of the manuscript.

I am grateful to these people, to Carol Harada, and to my several editors at Princeton University Press for their help, but assume full responsibility for any errors that may appear in the manuscript. I also wish to thank the Japan Iron and Steel Federation and Mitsubishi Endowment Funds of the University of Pittsburgh for financial assistance. To these acknowledgments I add the name of Rachel C. Unkovic, who at the ages of three and four provided very real, if unintended, help by rousing my Muse when she was sleeping.

And finally I want to thank my husband, the dedicatee of this book, Richard J. Smethurst of the University of Pittsburgh, a scholar of Japanese history. His willingness to assist me in reading modern Japanese was essential to my undertaking of this comparative study. His understanding, continued moral support, and practical help at home, even when he too was in the throes of preparing his own manuscript for publication by Princeton University Press, ensured the successful completion of this book.

The Artistry of Aeschylus and Zeami

Introduction

Anyone choosing at random and reading the texts of a Japanese nō play and an ancient Greek tragedy cannot help being struck by the differences between them: the former will most likely be a play short in length, lyric in tone, and lacking in dramatic conflict; the latter will probably be long and involve dramatic action and confrontation between characters. And yet, one continues to see references of a comparative nature to nō and Greek tragedy by scholars both of Japanese and of Greek theater and of the theater in general.[1] The reason is that most of these scholars have observed, and correctly, that some features of the productions of the two theaters are similar. Firsthand evidence dating from the Muromachi period in the fourteenth and fifteenth centuries, when nō reached its artistic peak, as well as vestiges of early performances in present-day practice, taken with the existing evidence on the subject of Greek theatrical productions in the classical period of the fifth century B.C., when tragedy reached its artistic peak, assure us that, in spite of some obvious differences, performances of nō share a number of similarities with those of Greek tragedy. There is no question, for example, that early productions of both nō and Greek tragedy involved outdoor theaters, small all-male casts of actors, choruses, instrumentalists, masks, dancing, and other strikingly similar features. And yet, a lack of evidence about the circumstances of Greek performances, such as the nature of the audiences, theater structures, musical accompaniment, choreography, costumes, and props, makes a detailed comparison with performances of nō difficult. This lack

[1] See, for example, Arthur Waley, *The Nō Plays of Japan* (London, 1921); Peter Arnott, *Greek Scenic Conventions in the Fifth Century B.C.* (Oxford, 1962) and *The Theatres of Japan* (London, 1969).

of evidence on the Greek side may explain in part why no book devoted solely to a comparison of nō and Greek tragedy has ever been published.[2]

The many differences apparent in translated versions of the texts and the difficulty of reading the Greek and Japanese languages in their early poetic forms help to explain why no one has so far attempted a detailed comparison of important similarities and differences between the poetic texts of nō and Greek tragedy either. And yet, the texts do exist and provide ample material on which a comparison may be based—a comparison that can be of value in increasing our appreciation not only of nō and of Greek tragedy, but also of other poetic dramas. For whatever the real differences between nō and Greek tragedy may be, a close scrutiny of the texts of one dramatic form in the light of the other does provide the scholar with a gauge against which to measure the unique features of each. Moreover, as I shall attempt to show in this study, there are also similarities between the structures and the styles in the works of two playwrights, Zeami and Aeschylus, which when analyzed carefully in the light of each other can provide a fresh perspective on both.[3]

There are at least two approaches that can be taken in a study based primarily on the texts of plays, as is necessarily the case for the Greek side. One is to compare those nō which involve "plot," that is, action unfolding contemporaneously with the dramatic time, with the majority of Greek tragedies; the other is to compare those tragedies which lack such action with the majority of nō. The former approach involves a larger number of texts on the Greek side; however, the latter is clearly the more informative

---

[2] To my knowledge the only works of length devoted to this subject are two dissertations: "A Comparative Study of Some Aspects of Greek Theatre and Nō Theatre: Aesthetic Values Arising from the Quest for the Meaning of Life," by Ono Shinichi (Diss., University of Texas, 1975), and "The Mask in Ancient Greek Tragedy: A Reexamination Based on the Principles and Practices of the Noh Theater of Japan," by Martha Bancroft Johnson (Diss., University of Wisconsin, 1984). (I follow the normal practice in this work of giving the surname first and the given name second for Japanese names, unless they appear in the other order in the author's published work itself.) Martha Johnson writes on the subject of the types, the use, and the function of masks in Greek tragedy and nō. In "Apples and Oranges: The Construction of Character in Greek Tragedy and Noh Drama," *Par Rapport: A Journal of the Humanities* 5–6 (1982–1983):3–12, Thomas B. Hare points out the differences in portrayal of character between Sophocles' *Oedipus the King* and Zeami's *Izutsu*. The illustrations that she includes should be of interest to those who want to compare the differences and similarities between the masks of Greek tragedy and nō. Jason Roussos summarizes the similarities between the performances of nō and Greek tragedy in a short article, "Ancient Greek Tragedy and Noh," *Diotima* 13 (1985): 121–128.

[3] Within his books on the subject of nō, Nogami Toyoichirō, a Japanese scholar of literature, compared Greek tragedy and nō very effectively; however, his conviction that nō is unique led him to emphasize the differences, at the expense of the similarities, between the two. In particular, see his article, "Nō to girishageki" (Nō and Greek Drama), in *Shisō* (Tokyo, 1938), in which he refutes H. B. Chamberlain, who listed similarities between the two dramatic forms in his work *Things Japanese*, 5th ed. (London and Yokohama, 1905).

about the distinctive features of nō that were developed by Zeami. More importantly for the present study, the latter approach is also a better means by which to illuminate Greek tragedy from a new perspective and to direct the reader's attention to features of works written by Aeschylus, especially his *Persians*, that may not have been sufficiently appreciated heretofore. In addition, this approach allows us to concentrate attention on plays that Zeami, one of the most important playwrights, actors, critics, and teachers of nō, treats as the best of the genre, and to profit from the evidence of his fifteenth-century treatises on the art of nō.

The second approach, which is that adopted in the present study of Aeschylus's and Zeami's works, can be helpful to the classicist, who has very little external evidence about dramatic texts or performances in Greek antiquity. Beyond the exaggerated remarks of comic playwrights and the criticisms of Plato, little written evidence dating from the fifth century B.C. on the subject of Greek tragedy exists. We know that Sophocles wrote a treatise on the chorus, but it has not survived. Thus we must draw conclusions from the texts of the tragedies themselves and from what later critics and writers said when different fashions were in vogue than existed in the fifth century B.C. Aristotle, who is the author of our only existing theoretical work on the subject of Greek tragedy from the ancient period, wrote in the fourth century B.C., and he was not a playwright, actor, or teacher of actors, as Zeami was. In the *Poetics*, he does not focus on the subject of Aeschylus, questions of performance, or ways to engage the audience's attention in the theater. Although he addresses such matters as plot, character, diction, thought, and length of plays, he says nothing about the timing of the dramatic action, demotes the visual effects of the costumes and the masks to the lowest level of the playwright's art, assumes that his readers know about music composition, and often treats structure and style as if these pertained to a work intended for a reading rather than for a performance in the theater. In sum, Aristotle is less interested in questions of performance than he is in a theoretical discussion of the nature of poetry, especially dramatic poetry (although Aristotle shows that he is not unaware of the effect of performances on audiences in the theater; see the end of his *Politics*). Therefore, we must draw conclusions about Aeschylean performance, as we do about Sophoclean or Euripidean performance, from both the limited evidence of the extant texts and the external sources that do exist, that is, the vase paintings dating from the fifth century B.C. and later, and the remarks of such writers as Aristophanes and Plato, and of those who, like Athenaeus, Plutarch, and Pollux, wrote hundreds of years after Greek tragedy flourished.

The external evidence for nō, on the other hand, is by comparison quite extensive. Not only do we have vestiges of early nō preserved in performances today, but we also have Zeami's treatises, which are both theoretical and practical. (It is because Zeami wrote treatises that his nō serve as a better basis for this comparison than those written by his father Kan'ami, although he was equally important as a playwright and actor.) In these treatises, the playwright, actor, and teacher discusses or comments not only on length, structure, character, composition, and the aesthetics of nō, but also on dance, gestures, posture, music, prosody, special verbal effects, acting, the delivery of lines (even of single words and syllables), actor training, use of poetic sources, masks and costumes, use of the theater structure and props, attaining the desired effect of a performance on an audience, and so forth. When the plays he mentions are extant, such as the nō *Sanemori*, on which much of this comparison concentrates, we can find examples to illustrate precisely what he means. In other words, Zeami's treatises remove some of the guesswork from the study of nō.[4]

Unfortunately, no one can claim that a comparison with nō will remove all the guesswork from a study of Greek tragedy. However, at the very least, a comparison of nō and Greek tragedy can provide for those familiar with only one of these theaters a meaningful introduction to the other, and an examination of the similarities and the differences between early Greek tragedy and Japanese nō can yield a sharper delineation of each form than is possible when each is taken in isolation from the other. In addition, because Zeami's treatises on the subject of performance are extant, because the secrets of the profession have been handed down since Zeami's day from one generation of actors to another, and because nō is still alive in theaters throughout Japan, in those areas in which the performances of tragedy and nō are similar it is possible to use the example of nō in an attempt to illustrate how the poetry of Aeschylean drama must have been brought alive by performers, musicians, and visual props. And most importantly, in spite of the obvious differences between the contents of the texts of nō and Greek tragedy, Zeami's treatises and plays can usefully contribute to an analysis of the structure and the style of Aeschylus's plays by providing material, such as does not exist from ancient Greece, to illustrate how the structure of a play written in poetic language is reflected in performance and how verbal techniques and literary allusions can be used in the theater. These are the areas that will be investigated in detail in this, a classicist's preliminary, comparison of nō and Greek tragedy.

[4] For a discussion of the treatises in the English language, see, for example, Richard N. McKinnon, "Zeami on the Nō: A Study of Fifteenth-Century Japanese Dramatic Criticism" (Diss., Harvard University, 1951); Yamazaki Masakazu, "The Aesthetics of Transformation: Zeami's Dramatic Theories," trans. Susan Matisoff, in *JJS* 7 (1981): 218–257; and Thomas B. Hare, *Zeami's Style: The Noh Plays of Zeami Motokiyo* (Stanford, 1986).

THE ORIGINS, the physical ambience of the productions, and the cultural, intellectual, and aesthetic milieu of nō and tragedy are not the subjects of this comparative study, which is focused instead on the structure and the style of dramatic texts and on the relationship of these to performance. However, a brief summary of the important similarities and differences in these areas is in order as background for anyone unfamiliar with either of the two theaters. On the subject of the origins or very early history of both nō and Greek tragedy,[5] the observations of Takebe Rinsyo at the conclusion to his article "Die griechische Tragödie und das japanische Noh-Drama" should suffice to illustrate one form a comparison can take.[6] Nō, Takebe says, developed from *dengaku*, field and harvest dances and songs, and from *sarugaku*, literally meaning "monkey songs and dances," connected with Shinto shrines and Buddhist temples. Both of these were early improvisational forms of entertainment—playful and roughly hewn at first—of which traces survive in *kyōgen*, the comic-relief pieces still performed during a day's program of three or more nō. Nō itself developed into a serious, noncomic, refined form of theater. Takebe argues that the history of nō might be comparable to that of tragedy in that, according to Aristotle, tragedy also sprang from improvisational beginnings, the *dithyrambos* and *satyrikon*, connected with the worship of the god Dionysus, and in that elements of these survived in the comic satyr plays performed after a day's program of three tragedies. Tragedy, like nō, only later developed into a formal and serious theater.

Takebe suggests that because nō was called *sarugaku nō*, "the performance of monkey music," long after the theater had dispensed with its original humorous and coarse elements, there could be an analogue here to the Greek name *tragōidia*. Since the name, which literally means "goat song," persisted after tragedy became fully developed, that name, like sarugaku nō, may point to origins in comic and informal entertainment named after crude and laughable animals. Whether Takebe is correct or not in this particular conjecture, with which many scholars would disagree,[7] he does draw attention to aspects of nō and tragedy that are relevant to the present comparison of both theaters. First, he observes that both nō

---

[5] A study of the origins and early histories of Greek tragedy and nō and their connections with performed and written poetry, with dance, songs, and skits performed in religious and nonreligious precincts, and with entertainment and ritual performances at religious festivals might well prove valuable to a study of Greek tragedy, since the evidence is more nearly complete on the Japanese than on the Greek side. But even there, as on the Greek side, the evidence is often obscure and confusing.

[6] *Wiener humanistische Blätter* 3, 2nd ser., no. 5 (1960): 25–31. The article contains an epilogue by Albin Lesky, a classical scholar of Greek tragedy.

[7] See, for example, the arguments of Gerald F. Else in *The Origin and Early Form of Greek Tragedy* (Cambridge, Mass., 1965).

and tragedy developed out of improvisational forms of entertainment into artistic forms of theater. That they are artistic forms, rather than improvised, refined, rather than crude, is both true and important; we are not dealing with primitive theater. Secondly, he observes that both were connected with religious performances and festivals. Indeed, the religious content of both Greek tragedies and nō and the ambience of the religious festivals at which the plays (in the case of nō, some plays) were performed throughout their histories distinguish Greek tragedy and nō from much theater of the world.

One can treat the similarities between the theater structures and the performances, which Takebe also discusses in his article, for all Greek tragedy and all nō once they had developed into artistic forms of theater. At the same time, a close look at these similarities helps to explain why the present study is limited to tragedy of the early, rather than late, fifth century B.C., and to nō of the fourteenth and early fifteenth century A.D., rather than to that of later centuries and of the present day. (Since the evidence is difficult to assess, fragmentary, and in many cases unreliable on the Greek side, this summary is limited to only that information which can be presented with any degree of certainty.)

The most important theater arena, the one used for performances of Greek tragedy during the festival in honor of the god Dionysus, was located on the side of the Acropolis in Athens. In Aeschylus's day, the structures of this theater were not permanent, as they were in the fourth century B.C. For most of the period during which Aeschylus was writing and performing, the slope of the Acropolis hill, either the ground itself or temporary wooden stands, served as the auditorium for the audience, and the flat area in front of it, later called the *orkhēstra*, served as an acting and dancing area for both actors and chorus. At one end of this orkhēstra stood a temporary wooden structure that may have served as a stage (called a *skēnē*), or merely as a place in which the actors changed their costumes.[8]

---

[8] On the Greek theater in Athens and its history, see A. Pickard-Cambridge, *The Theatre of Dionysus at Athens* (Oxford, 1946) and of the stage in Aeschylus's day, see N.G.L. Hammond, "The Conditions of Dramatic Production to the Death of Aeschylus," *GRBS* 13 (1972): 387–450, and Oliver Taplin, *The Stagecraft of Aeschylus* (Oxford, 1977), 452–459. On the evidence for rectangular-shaped acting areas, the differences between the theaters of the fifth century B.C. and those of the fourth century B.C., the size of the Greek theaters, and so forth, see the more recent work of E. Pöhlmann, "Die Proedrie des Dionysostheaters im 5. Jahrhundert und das Bühnenspiel der Klassik," *MH* 38, fasc.3 (1981):129–146. For information about the Festival of Dionysus, consult A. Pickard-Cambridge, *The Dramatic Festivals of Athens*, 2nd ed., rev. by John Gould and D. M. Lewis (Oxford, 1968), 57–125. Albin Lesky's article, "Noh-Bühne und griechische Theatre," *Maia*, n.s. 15 (1963): 38–44, which summarizes some of the similarities between nō and Greek tragedy, suggests that evidence for the use of resonators in the Greek theaters might be elucidated by the example of nō and the presence of

Outdoor nō theaters at religious sanctuaries, such as at Kōfukuji in Nara where performances are held today as they were in the past, were similar to this Greek theater in a number of respects. Evidence suggests that the audiences sat on temporary wooden benches or on the ground itself, around three sides of a flat area where the actors performed and the chorus sang, at one end of which there sometimes stood a temporary structure that was used as a stage, or sometimes a part of a temple or shrine building that was used as a viewing place for dignitaries. These theatrical arenas were smaller than their Greek counterparts. However, the arenas used for *kanjin nō*, "subscription nō," were at least as large, if not larger. Temporary wooden stands, boxes open to the sky, were built around an arena, which measured between ninety to one hundred and thirty-three feet or more in diameter—that is, more than three hundred feet in perimeter (sixty-three *ken* at five feet per *ken*)—and in which a temporary platform was constructed for the performances of the actors, chorus, and instrumentalists.[9] (In the fourteenth and fifteenth centuries, the one *hashigakari*, a bridge by which the actors entered the stage from center back, or the two, on either side of the stage back, were comparable to the *parodoi*, "passageways," used in the Greek theater.)

In the fifth century B.C., the Greek theaters evolved from temporary structures, which included an orkhēstra where actors, chorus, and instrumentalists alike performed, to more solidly built structures, which included orkhēstras and stages that could separate the chorus from the actors. The structures were made of wood during the earlier period; later these structures were made of stone. (Remains of a later stone theater still exist today at Epidaurus.) By the middle of the Tokugawa era in the eight-

---

thirteen pottery resonators used under the polished floors of nō stages today. His suggestion serves as an incentive for us to look further for other parallels.

[9] There is evidence that Sophocles had to stop acting in his own plays because his voice was too weak for the large theater; there is evidence that because the voice of Kiami, a *dengaku* performer, was not strong enough to fill a normal-sized arena for kanjin nō, the size of the stands was decreased especially for his performance to 54 sections or to an acting arena with a perimeter of 270 feet as opposed to the normal 300 plus feet. There is one notice for a performance of the year 1349 for which the nō theater featured at least 83 sections of boxes, or a perimeter of 415 feet. See P. G. O'Neill, *Early Nō Drama: Its Background, Character and Development 1300–1450* (London, 1958), 79.

Nō are still being performed at both the Buddhist temple Kōfukuji and at the nearby Shinto Kasuga shrine on the occasion of the Kasuga Wakamiya Onmatsuri, a religious festival. On the subject of this festival, of the subscription nō, and of the theater structure, see O'Neill, *Early Nō*, who thinks (78) that the stage itself, which was used in kanjin nō, was roofed. The ancient Greek *proskēnion* ("stage") seems not to have been covered with a roof during any period of its history. On the subject of kanjin nō, see also Jacob Raz, *Audience and Actors: A Study of Their Interaction in the Japanese Traditional Theatre* (Leiden, 1983), 76–85.

eenth century, the conventional nō theaters had evolved into intimate indoor auditoria with raised and roofed wooden stages measuring approximately twenty feet square. (These stages are used for performances throughout Japan today.) In nō theaters, there seems at first to have been no backdrop; later the painting of a pine tree was and still is used in all performances. On the Greek side, for a performance of Aeschylus's *Persians* (472 B.C.), no scene painting or backdrop was needed; however, by the time the *Oresteia* (458 B.C.) was staged, some representation of a building that could serve as a palace and temple must have been used.[10] In other words, in antiquity until the time that Greek tragedy was no longer a viable form of entertainment, the theater structures in Greece changed from temporary to permanent structures, and from one acting arena for both actors and chorus to a separation of some of their functions between the skēnē and the orkhēstra; in Japan, public nō theaters of Zeami's day were not permanent structures, but the later indoor theaters, which have remained essentially the same from the eighteenth century on to the present day, were. Throughout the history of nō the actors and chorus have performed together on the same surface. Thus, since Greek tragedy was always performed outdoors, but only *early* nō was with any frequency, and since nō has always featured one acting arena for the chorus, actors, and instrumentalists, but only the *early* classical Greek theater did, the Greek theater of the fifth century B.C., especially the early theater of Aeschylus's day in which a stage with a backdrop was not needed, is most nearly comparable to that of Muromachi period nō.[11] In fact, because they accommodated a variety of props and mechanical devices,[12] later Greek

[10] Comparable to the painting of the pine in nō is the presence of a religious marker, an altar, in ancient Greek theaters. The pine tree represents the Yōgō pine at the Kasuga Shrine in Nara in front of which the god of the shrine was first said to dance. Even today, once a year during the festival there, a nō actor regularly stands at the pine so that "the god may descend into the actor and make him his reflection." See Donald Keene, *Nō: The Classical Theatre of Japan* (Palo Alto, 1973), 13; this book, as well as the original hardback edition published in 1966 with many illustrations, is a good general introduction in the English language to the subject of nō. See also the appropriate pages of E. Miner, Hiroko Odagiri, and Robert E. Morrell, *The Princeton Companion to Classical Japanese Literature* (Princeton, 1985), esp. 307–316. In Japanese, almost all facets of nō are discussed in *Nōgaku zensho*, ed. Nogami Toyoichirō, 7 vols. The new edition (Tokyo, 1984) was edited by Nishino Haruo and Matsumoto Yasushi.

For diagrams of the changes that took place in the physical nō theater, see Earle Ernst, *The Kabuki Theatre* (New York, 1956), 33. It is likely that even lines 140–141 of the *Persians*, which refer to a place for taking counsel, do not point to the need for scene painting or a backdrop. See below, Chapter Two, note 40.

[11] Pöhlmann, "Die Proedrie," has suggested that there was greater flexibility with respect to the playwrights' use of the acting area in the fifth century B.C. than there was in the next century.

[12] Certainly by the fourth century B.C., productions of tragedy included a number of mechanical devices, such as the *mēkhanē* used for the *deus ex machina*. One of the ex-

theaters dating from the end of the fifth and from the fourth centuries B.C. are more nearly comparable to the present-day kabuki theater.

In both early tragedy and fourteenth- and fifteenth-century nō, the uncluttered acting arena in which few props were needed allowed the performers in their costumes and their masks to be visually prominent and serve as the focus of the plays. The costumes were elaborate, perhaps stylized, and reflected the function and the class of the character that an actor depicted.[13] To judge from the lists in Pollux's *Onomasticon* of the second century A.D., and from the collection of the Kanze school of nō, masks fell into similar categories in both countries.[14] Perhaps because there are only so many types of characters that can appear in myth and legend and history, the material on which the writers of tragedy and nō drew, the masks in both theaters were similarly typed by sex, age, and class. Coloration of the skin and the style of the hair indicated certain distinctions between the types, such as the degree of suffering of the character. To the extent that masks were used and the masks of the two theaters fell into similar categories—character types, famous people out of legend, divinities, and monsters or supernatural beings—Greek tragedy and nō were alike.

Unfortunately, none of the masks survives from the Greek classical period, but on the basis of inferences drawn from the texts of the plays and

---

ceptions to the absence of such devices in nō today is the use of a large bell dropped to the stage by means of a pulley in the play *Dōjōji* written by Nobumitsu in the late fifteenth or early sixteenth century. See Keene, *Nō*, 76–78. On the use of realistic props in nō, see Raz, *Audience and Actors*, 115. In kabuki many such devices are featured. On the subject of the paucity of stage resources required for the performance of Aeschylus's plays, see Taplin, *Stagecraft*, 434–451. The *Life* of Aeschylus (14) states that the playwright outdid his predecessors and adorned the skēnē and amazed the spectators in a number of ways, including the use of painting, devices, altars, tombs, musical instruments. To my mind, this and similar late evidence can be interpreted in two ways. It may reflect the practices of a period later than Aeschylus during which the prop managers and set designers translated scenes from Aeschylus's texts into spectacular productions. Or, this evidence may suggest that Aeschylus amazed the audiences because his use of painting, costumes, props, musical instruments, etc., was more in evidence and more effective than that of his predecessors. However, I do not think that we should interpret it to mean that in Aeschylus's day productions of his plays were filled with spectacle or that many props and elaborate sets were required for them.

[13] For tragedy, see Pickard-Cambridge, hereafter P-C, *Dramatic Festivals*, 197–209; for nō, see Keene, *Nō*, 65–66. The actors and chorus members of nō usually carry fans; those of Greek tragedy do not.

[14] See Pollux 4. 133–142. On the problems involved in using Pollux as a source for costumes and masks in Greek tragedy, specifically, in determining which period of tragedy he means, see P-C, *Dramatic Festivals*, 177–179. The collection of the Kanze school is a major collection of masks, but not the only one. See Katayama Kuroemon, ed., *Kanzeke denrai nōmenshū* (translated at the end of the book as "Noh Masks Treasured in the Kwanze Family") (Tokyo, 1954), whose book was chosen for citation because it includes at the end a short description in English of each mask illustrated.

from Greek vase paintings dating from the fifth century B.C., it seems likely that the masks of tragedy from the early rather than the late periods are more like those of nō.[15] In the fourteenth century, there is evidence to show that nō masks could be expressive and realistic compared to those of later centuries. All these later masks, and many of the earlier masks as well, including those Zeami used, were more elegantly carved and more subtle in their depiction of differences in facial expression than the earliest versions. The same degree of subtlety of expression is not apparent for those masks represented on Greek vase paintings and in later sculpted models. In fact, along with the changes that took place in the development of the theaters, the Greeks, like the Romans, moved toward greater distortion of facial expression on the masks and larger masks than we find in the nō theater.[16]

The kinetic elements—the dances, movements, and gestures—made it possible for the actors who wore masks to display emotions.[17] We know little about dance and movements, important features of performances of tragedy at least in early fifth-century B.C. Greece, for the Greek texts do not contain choreographic directions, as the nō texts do.[18] However, to

[15] According to P-C, *Dramatic Festivals*, 191, the *early* masks seem to cover the face alone, but later masks include full heads of hair. (The Japanese nō mask covers the face alone; the wig is a separate piece.)

[16] See the discussion of the young woman mask painted on a fragment of a vase that probably dates from Aeschylus's time in Lucy Talcott, "Kourimos Parthenos," *Hesperia* 8 (1939): 267–273. This mask is not naturalistic, nor does it exhibit a distorted facial expression. It is compared to a young woman's mask (*magojirō*) in nō by Johnson, "The Mask in Ancient Greek Tragedy," 272. Johnson includes illustrations of these masks in figs. 1 and 44 respectively.

[17] Since those nō actors who did not and do not wear masks maintain expressionless faces throughout a performance, the effect is very much as if they had donned masks. Only those nō actors who are playing the roles of a woman, old person, demon, monster, or deity wear masks. By contrast, all members of the cast in tragedy wore masks.

[18] See P-C, *Dramatic Festivals*, 246–254, and U. v. Wilamowitz-Möllendorff, *Aeschyli tragoediae* (Berlin, 1958), 12–13. On pp. 250–251, P-C quotes evidence on the subject of the importance of dance to the tragedians Phrynichus, Aeschylus, and Sophocles and gives the evidence for Aeschylus's invention of many dance figures. Even though we cannot reconstruct the choreography, we know that dance was an important aspect of early, if not later, Greek tragedy. See Lillian B. Lawler, *The Dance of the Ancient Greek Theatre* (Iowa City, 1964). Famee Lorene Shisler, "The Technique of the Portrayal of Joy in Greek Tragedy," *TAPA* 73 (1942), discusses on pages 286–288 some gestures and movements that seem to be required in the light of the texts of Greek tragedies. On the subject of imitation in the arts, Aristotle (*Poetics*, 1447a27) says that dancers imitate character, feeling, and action by means of rhythms that are embodied in gestures.

Zeami speaks to the importance of dance and gestures in his treatises. For example, at the beginning of his *Nōsakushō* (On the Composition of Nō), he says that dance and song, which includes poetry, are the two arts of greatest importance to consider in one's choice of a subject for nō. For a detailed discussion in the English language of dance in nō, see Monica Bethe and Karen Brazell, *Dance in the Nō Theatre*, Cornell University East Asia Papers, no. 29 (Ithaca, N.Y., 1982).

judge from Greek vase paintings, late evidence, and the texts themselves, the gestures and the dances were more flamboyant in the Greek theater than in the Japanese nō theater.[19] Yet this difference, like the others, is less pronounced if we compare the nō of the early period rather than that of the present day with Greek tragedy. During the earliest period, and again when we enter the second half of the fifteenth century and the sixteenth century, many of the nō performances were melodramatic. But government sanctions in the sixteenth and seventeenth centuries produced a permanent change, and the dances, not to mention the speeches and songs, became very solemn and slow in tempo. The effect of this change can be seen in the slow-moving and dignified performances today in which the words of the songs and the speeches are sometimes so muffled that they are unintelligible.[20] In Greece, on the other hand, vase paintings strongly suggest that there was flamboyant acting during every period of tragedy. This vital element, dances and movements by the actors on stage, even more vital in nō than in tragedy, is comparable only if we limit ourselves to the early period of nō.

Thus the particular aspects of the theaters and the performances mentioned above recommend a comparison, not of late tragedy or nō, but of the theater of the early part of the fifth century B.C., especially that of Aeschylus, with that of late fourteenth- and early fifteenth-century nō. In sum, there are significant parallels between the performances of nō and tragedy that set them apart from other theaters. In both, three or more serious plays, often with a religious message, and the comic *kyōgen* or satyr plays were performed on religious and/or public occasions for all classes of people, [21] in outdoor theaters that contained few props or architectural structures compared with much of later Greek tragedy and other types of Japanese and Western drama. From the three sides of these outdoor auditoria, the audience's attention was directed toward the small, all-male casts, with primary roles limited to two or three actors, one of whom

---

[19] See the evidence of T.B.L. Webster, *Greek Theatre Production*, 2nd ed. (London, 1970), and A. D. Trendall and T.B.L. Webster, *Illustrations of Greek Drama* (London, 1971).

[20] See Keene, *Nō*, 39–41. When nō became the official entertainment of the courts, the public turned its attention to the more melodramatic kabuki and bunraku performances.

[21] On the presence of "commoners" at the performances of nō during the Muromachi period, see Raz, *Audience and Actors*, and Watsuji Tetsurō, "Yōkyoku ni arawareta rinri shisō" (Japanese Ethical Thought in the Noh Plays of the Muromachi Period), trans. David A. Dilworth, *MN* 24 (1969): 467–498.

One difference between nō and Greek tragedy is that Zeami, like other playwrights of nō, also put on productions of plays for the shogun in his palace. These were performed for a more elite audience and in smaller theaters both than his productions of kanjin nō or those nō put on at religious festivals, and than productions of Greek tragedy.

was the playwright himself. These actors were supplemented in some cases by mute extras, but always in both theaters by choruses and musical instrumentalists, a flutist and two or three drummers in nō, and a player of a double-reed instrument (*aulos*) and perhaps a lyre player in Greek tragedy.[22] In both forms the dances, movements, and gestures enhanced the appearance of those members of the cast who were dressed in masks and costumes, and also complemented the words of the texts. Finally, in both, the texts, which were poetic, were delivered in a variety of ways: sung to the accompaniment of instruments, recitative, narration, and speech.[23]

The similarities summarized above, which as a whole apply to the theaters of Aeschylus and Zeami and which in many cases apply to nō and Greek tragedy throughout their histories, in themselves provide a basis for a comparison. At the very least, the similarities allow us to posit one conclusion about nō and Greek tragedy that sets them apart from many theaters. They prevent members of an audience from mistaking a performance not only for everyday reality, as is true of other theaters, but also for the degree of realism even, for example, of a Shakespearean or kabuki play.[24] Various elements, such as the masks, the small number of male actors, and the presence "on stage" of the chorus and the instrumentalists throughout a performance, create a special aesthetic relationship between the plays and the audiences. The use of masks or expressionless faces not only disguises the fact that males are playing female roles, but also submerges the personalities of the actors. The words, because they are for the most part poetic, the stage, because it is devoid of sets and many props, and the movements, because they are arranged by a choreographer (the playwright himself), do not reproduce their counterparts in the real world. The scarcity, but importance, of the visual features helps the playwright in turn to place the focus on that which in his mind is essential for the audience to appreciate in any given play.

The special aesthetic relationship between actors and audience in both nō and Greek tragedy is achieved in part because the casts of both are limited to a small number of actors. The masks make it possible for an actor in nō or in tragedy to assume two roles and even more than two roles

[22] See P-C, *Dramatic Festivals*, 165–167.

[23] On delivery in Greek tragedy, see P-C, *Dramatic Festivals*, 156–167. On the subject of vocal music and chant, see the work of the nō performer (drum player) Kunio Komparu, *The Noh Theater: Principles and Perspectives*, trans. Jane Corddry (text) and Stephen Comee (the nō plays) (Tokyo and New York, 1983), a translation of *Noh e no izanai* (Invitation to the Noh). On the musical dimensions of Aeschylean tragedy, see William C. Scott, *Musical Design in Aeschylean Theater* (Hanover, N.H. and London, 1984).

[24] See John Gould, "Dramatic Character and 'Human Intelligibility' in Greek Tragedy," *Camb. Phil. Proc.*, n.s. 24, no. 204 (1978): 43–67, on the subject of actions and characters in tragedy. See his note 56 on nō.

in tragedy. To be sure, there can be more than three actors with speaking roles in nō, as there cannot be in tragedy, but the effect is similar—one actor, presumably the main actor and the playwright, is the center of attention. In nō, predictably, there is the *shite*, the main actor, and the *waki*, the adjacent actor who prepares for and draws out the story from the shite. Each of these actors can be attended by *tsure*. The attendant of the shite is called simply *tsure*, of the waki *wakizure*. The former may, but need not, play important roles; the latter are often attendant priests or courtiers who, whatever their number, do not have a dramatic character of their own but assume a function literally as attendants of the waki priest or courtier. (The waki and wakizure do not wear masks.) Thus the total number of significant actors in nō is three: shite, tsure, and waki (although often there are only a shite and a waki).

In tragedy, the main actor (sometimes called the *tragōidos*), and the one or two other actors (called *hypokritai*), later called the protagonist, deuteragonist, and tritagonist respectively,[25] all can play more than one role, but in many tragedies, in which the main character appears in the beginning, middle, and end, the same actor presumably plays this role throughout. Of the three actors in tragedy, one often plays the role of a nameless character, such as a messenger. In nō, the *kyōgen*, often playing the part of an ordinary and nameless inhabitant of the place in which the play is set, is an additional actor. Some tragedies and nō feature, in addition to the actors mentioned above, children and mutes and walk-ons, but for the most part, the limitation of two or three significant actors in both theaters helps to create a setting in which the audience's attention is attracted to, rather than distracted from, the words, movements, and visual appurtenances, the props, and the costumes of the few actors. In Aeschylus's *Persians*, for example, there are only two actors; in Zeami's *Sanemori*, there are two actors plus the kyōgen.[26]

[25] P-C, *Dramatic Festivals*, 129–135, presents the evidence for the use of these names in Greek tragedy. It may be the case that in early Greek tragedy a distinction by name was not drawn between the main actor and the one or two others, as Gerald F. Else had suggested there was in "The Case of the Third Actor," *TAPA* 76 (1945): 1–10, and "HYPOKRITES," *WS* 72 (1959): 75–107. However, Else's suggestion is one for which the example of nō provides a parallel.

[26] Nogami, in "Nō to girishageki," discusses the differences in the deployment of roles in nō and tragedy, saying that there may be many more actors on stage in nō than in Greek tragedy. However, such is true only when there are a number of wakizure or tsure or attendants of the kyōgen, that is, actors who play relatively insignificant parts and are often not individual characters in their own right. Nogami also states that the shite is the only important character, the one on whom the play is focused. On this point, see his article, "Nō no shuyaku ichinin shugi" (The Principle of the One-actor Leading Role in Nō), in *Nō: kenkyū to hakken* (Nō: Research and Discovery) (Tokyo, 1930 [originally published in 1909?]), parts of which have been translated into English by Chieko Irie Mulhern under the title "The Monodramatic Principle of the Noh Theatre," *JATJ* 16,

The constant presence on stage of a chorus of eight to ten men in nō and twelve to fifteen men in tragedy is another distinctive, if not unique, feature of these theaters that enhances the special aesthetic relationship between the actors and the audience. In opera, for example, there may be a chorus; however, it does not remain on stage throughout the performance, and the ensemble is externally directed by a conductor, often standing on a podium above the instrumentalists, who are not in full view of the audience. In nō and tragedy, on the other hand, the chorus, as well as the instrumentalists, remains on stage, and both groups perform without the assistance of a conductor.

The choruses, like the masks and the number of actors, differ in important particulars between nō and Greek tragedy. In nō, the chorus is neither masked nor dressed in costumes that depict a character, because the chorus is not a character in its own right. In fact, it only rarely expresses an opinion of its own, never stands up from its seated position, and does not become involved in the movements during the course of a performance. The chorus assumes the part of characters in a different manner: it speaks for the playwright, as in the tragedies, and serves as a mouthpiece for the characters. The nō chorus assumes more than one identity during a play by becoming the voice of the main actor (shite) or of the second actor (waki). (There is a tendency in many nō for the chorus to sing on behalf of the shite so that he can dance when the audience's attention is directed toward him.) The result is an interaction between the chorus and the actor, between the group and the individual for whom it speaks, such that often the distinctions between them disappear. In Greek tragedy, the chorus has a fixed identity. Not only do the members of the choruses wear masks and costumes that distinguish the group as a group of old men or of maidens, for example, but they also function as a group of characters in their own right. The chorus speaks in its own voice, participates actively in dialogues, sings, moves around, and even dances. It may advise, give information, express emotion in the first person, on occasion display differences of opinion within the group, and take part in the action.

The presence of a chorus is a feature that nō and tragedy share in common; the function of the chorus is different. And yet, if the chorus is to be considered in a comparison between nō and tragedy, that comparison is best made between the works of Aeschylus and Zeami rather than between those of Sophocles or Euripides and Zeami. In many of the works of the

---

no. 1 (April 1981): 72–86. At the end of this article (pp. 80–83 in the translated version), there is a summary of some differences—the number of actors, the function of the choruses, and the use and types of masks—that Nogami found between nō and Greek tragedy.

latter two tragedians, the choruses act as objective observers or commentators upon the action of the play; by contrast, the choruses of Aeschylus's tragedies can become so involved in the action that in two of his tragedies, the *Suppliants* and the *Eumenides*, the chorus functions as a major character. These choruses engage in a degree of physical action, which most probably included a vigorous dance in the original productions of the *Eumenides*, that is antithetical to the lack of motion on the part of the seated choruses of nō. However, the choruses in Aeschylus's works can serve, if not as the mouthpiece for other actors, at least as a main character in some plays, as an important but secondary actor (like the waki) in others, and in all plays as a spokesman for the author (like the choruses of nō). In addition, the function of the Aeschylean chorus as an actor provides a third or fourth actor to his tragedies as tsure provide extra actors in nō. It is therefore possible to draw a comparison between the Aeschylean chorus and that of nō. Nogami, who takes into account the differences in the choruses of Aeschylus's, Sophocles', and Euripides' plays as well as the relative importance of the chorus in Aeschylus's works as opposed to his successors, makes a particularly important point when he argues that the idea of a one-man show is intrinsic to nō, whereas the contraposition of actor and chorus at first, and later of actor and actor, creates a tension in tragedy that one does not find in nō. The lack of confrontation between actors and between actor and chorus in the *Persians* is one of the primary reasons why the analysis of structure in Chapter Two focuses on this Aeschylean work.[27]

A point-by-point correspondence does not present itself in a comparison of the choruses of nō and tragedy any more than it does in other areas of the comparison. We should not expect it to do so. Yet again and again there emerges in Aeschylus's works some quality that makes them, more than the works of Sophocles and Euripides, seem like Japanese nō—a fact that reflects the times in which Aeschylus wrote and the difference between the first and second halves of the fifth century B.C. The differences among the tragedians is in part due to the influence of formal rhetoric and sophistical modes of thought that began to be taught and practiced extensively in Athens during the latter half of that century; their influence is clearly

[27] See Nogami, "Nō no shuyaku ichinin shugi," 29–36 (pp. 80–83 in Mulhern's translation), on this difference between nō and Greek tragedy. Nogami's "Gasshōka no higikyokuteki seishitsu: Nō to girishageki to no hikaku" (The Tragic Quality of Choral Songs: A Comparison of Nō and Greek Drama), in *Nō no saisei* (The Rebirth of Nō) (Tokyo, 1935), is devoted to the subject of the chorus. The article begins with a caveat against seeing a similarity between the choruses of nō and of tragedy. But his observation (139) that the chorus is the onlooker in tragedy and that similarly the waki is not part of the action in nō is one of many that are helpful in a formulation of the differences and the similarities between the roles of the choruses and actors in nō and Greek tragedy.

visible in the plays of Sophocles and Euripides, but less so in those of Aeschylus. The reasoned exposition of Sophocles' plays and the dissection of arguments common in Euripides' plays hardly appear at all in the works of Aeschylus. A syllogistic and expository style does not characterize nō either. The Japanese did have a "philosophy and a rhetoric" in the fifteenth century, but the nō theater, not to mention the literature, exhibited neither the kind of rhetoric that could be used in courtrooms and assemblies nor the kind of philosophy that led to the development of Western logic, science, and mathematics. "Abstract" thinking in Japan lay instead in the realms of religion, study of historical change, and aesthetics.

It can be argued that Sophocles and Euripides appeal intellectually to their audiences in a way that Aeschylus and Zeami do not. The audiences of later Greek tragedy could feel flattered when invited to exercise their wits and to realize that they knew better than some character what another meant to say to him. In Euripides' *Medea*, for example, the audience knows, as Jason does not, that Medea is lying when she begs his forgiveness, and it may take delight in her sophistical methods of persuasion. Or when Oedipus, in Sophocles' *Oedipus the King*, says that he is as fully committed to finding Laius's killer as if Laius were his father, the audience knows that he is in fact both the son and the killer of Laius. It enjoys its superior knowledge and speculates on the possibilities that this knowledge offers to the development in the plot of a well-known story.

In the *Agamemnon* and the *Libation Bearers*, Clytemnestra and Orestes also practice deceit, but this is not the case with characters in Aeschylus's *Persians*, where the emotional mood and the atmosphere of the words, music, movements, and costumes engage the audience's attention instead. In his model plays, Zeami does not depend for success on the impact of a logical argument as much as on the emotional or poetic or aesthetic impact of the characters' words, music, movements, and appearance. His characters are not sarcastic, do not intend to deceive. They are unlike Medea, who pretends to be weak when she lies in her speech to Jason, or Oedipus, whose words depend on a fallacy created by the author for their effectiveness. As a result, the styles of Aeschylus in his *Persians* and of Zeami allow the audiences to concentrate on the words themselves and thus to grasp the literal, the emotional, the religious, the moral, and the aesthetic significances directly. The richness, depth of tone, and significance of the statements and songs of the characters and chorus often derive from allusions to ritual forms or to poetry and song that provide an added religious, spiritual, and aesthetic dimension. In other words, the playwrights appeal to the audiences' familiarity with and knowledge of poetry, song, and the techniques of poetic language. This type of appeal to knowledge is very different from the irony found in the plays of Sophocles, and even more in the plays of Euripides.

Among the aesthetic ideals that do apply to nō and that had developed by the fifteenth century is *yūgen*. The term is almost impossible to define inasmuch as its meaning changed, even within Zeami's lifetime;[28] but as a working definition I offer "half-revealed or suggested grace, tinged with wistful sadness."[29] Part of what is involved in this aesthetic in nō is the veiling in mystery of that which is to be perceived or grasped by the audiences so that it cannot be appreciated by reason alone, but engages other faculties as well, that is, the senses, the heart, and the spirit. Zeami's plays all show marks of the subtle more than the obvious, of suggestion more than explicit statement, and of restraint more than prolixity of expression. Zeami recommended above all that the actors display yūgen (grace and elegance) in their acting. With his poetry as well, especially in the woman nō, which are the most lyric plays, Zeami succeeds both in creating an atmosphere of grace tinged with wistful sadness and in representing what is regarded in Buddhist thought, which so strongly influenced him, as the fragile world in which we live.

Suggestion and subtlety of expression are not unknown qualities of style in ancient Greek writings. Suggestion rather than explicit statement characterizes the style of Aeschylus's older contemporary, Heraclitus, who seemed to allude to his own method in a famous fragment: "The lord whose mantic office is in Delphi does not speak out or conceal, but gives signs."[30] Beauty tinged with wistful sadness is eminently descriptive of the lyric poetry of Sappho, a poetess of the seventh and sixth centuries B.C. Aeschylus's style, in many respects comparable to that of Heraclitus, often hints and suggests rather than states explicitly. It is often highly lyric, if not in Sappho's mode. But even in the *Persians*, the aggregate definition of yūgen does not apply. Wistful sadness does not tinge Aeschylus's work; the emotions he expresses in his plays are fear and grief. Nor does he represent to his audience a fragile and elusive world; rather, his world of gods and human beings is solidly planted on earth. A longing for someone or a regret about some experience during his or her lifetime is often the character's "tragedy" in nō, especially when he is a ghost or spirit. The successful resolution of this tragedy is release from the world and from the punishment of remaining attached to it. In Aeschylean works, fear and

[28] See Andrew A. Tsubaki, "Zeami and the Transition of the Concept of Yūgen: A Note on Japanese Aesthetics," *The Journal of Aesthetics and Art Criticism* 30, no. 1 (Fall 1971): 55–67.
[29] This definition is suggested in *The Noh Drama*, NGS, vol. 1 (Tokyo and Vermont, 1955), x.
[30] Diels-Kranz no. 93.

grief, two tragic emotions that can also, though less frequently, be found in nō, spring not so much from a character's experience or relationship with another person as from some violent act in which the main character, a living person, is involved and for which he or she suffers the consequences from divine and human retribution on earth.

Nō is a world of comparatively ephemeral beings; Greek tragedy, a world of substantial beings. And yet, when Herington says that Aeschylus "stands on the other side of a gulf both from us and from the extant works of Sophocles and Euripides," he points to an important and substantive reason for a comparison of Aeschylus's plays with those of Zeami: there is a "spiritual force" that pervades the works of both.[31] That is, gods and spirits interact with human beings and the two worlds interpenetrate both on the stage and in the word without the rationalism found in the works of Sophocles and Euripides. (This rationalism is found even in those plays of Sophocles and Euripides, such as the *Oedipus at Colonus* and the *Bacchae*, in which the worlds of men and gods are interrelated.) In addition, it is important for the reader to bear in mind that Zeami was not as esoteric in practice as an application of the concept of yūgen to his works might suggest. Zeami himself wrote treatises not only on the subject of aesthetics, but even more on matters, such as acting, that reveal him to have been a practical man of the theater. We know that he wrote his plays with the theater in mind, that he acted in them, that he directed them, and that he trained other actors. Although there is no evidence to suggest that Aeschylus wrote treatises on the dramatic art, we do know that he also acted in the plays he wrote, directed them, and trained the choruses for dances, and that, like Zeami, he was successful in the theater.[32] For these reasons and, as I said, because both playwrights produced ethically, spiritually, and emotionally stirring performances rather than those which appealed primarily to the intellect, I am convinced that a comparison of their plays is valuable.

The purpose of the present comparative study, recommended by the similarities mentioned above, is in part to support the view that Aeschy-

[31] John Herington, *Poetry into Drama: Early Tragedy and the Greek Poetic Tradition* (Berkeley, 1985), 131, confirms some of my observations about early Greek tragedy. R. N. McKinnon's remark about nō, in "The Nō and Zeami," *FEQ* 11, no. 3 (May 1952): 357, is typical, "It is the coexistence and free communication between the phantom world and the present world in the *Mugen* Nō [nō in which a ghost or spirit appears in the second half] which makes the Nō an especially distinctive form of dramatic art."

[32] At least we know that Aeschylus won first prizes in dramatic contests. On the dramatic festivals, see P-C, *Dramatic Festivals*, 79–82 and 93–100. Dramatic contests as such were not held in Japan, but the guilds and actors competed with each other for the favor of the ruling class. On patronage, see O'Neill, *Early Nō*, 41 and Keene, *Nō*, 30–31. On the competitions, see Masaru Sekine, *Ze-ami and His Theories of Noh Drama* (Gerrards Cross, 1985), 115–117.

lus's works, although they represent a significant breakthrough in the history of drama in ancient Greece, still belong to the tradition of recited and performed poetry that preceded and was contemporaneous with his day. Specifically, this study will attempt to show that our earliest extant tragedy, the *Persians*, in many respects unique among Greek tragedies, as well as other parts of Aeschylus's work, are, like many nō, drama that can be defined as verbal and visual poetry rather than drama that is characterized by its plot and action.[33] But this study also has a wider purpose: to show how nō and tragedy, with the similarities and differences they share, are informative and suggestive about each other, and thus to point to features of dramatic style that, when understood, can benefit any student of the theater. Through a detailed examination of the texts of Aeschylus and of Zeami, and through reference to Zeami's treatises and present-day performances of nō, this study will try to demonstrate how dramatic structure, words, and allusions to other poetry can be understood in the theater, how words are related to visual and kinetic features in a performance, and how the meaning of a play is revealed through all of these. Because the examples presented here are drawn primarily from plays written by Aeschylus and Zeami, and especially from the *Persians* and *Sanemori*, the conclusions are limited to a significant few; however, it is my belief that an understanding of the methods applied to these examples can be illuminating to the scholar of any theater.

THIS WORK is arranged in such a manner that the analysis of structure in nō, Chapter One, is presented before the analysis of structure in tragedy, Chapter Two, and the conclusions drawn on the basis of the comparison are relegated for the most part to Chapter Two. My own translation of the entire nō *Sanemori* appears within the text of Chapter One, and a summary of the *Persians* as a whole, for which published translations are readily available, is included in Chapter Two.[34] In Chapter Three, after intro-

[33] In *Poetry into Drama*, Herington says, "By some means Aeschylus has already acquired a truly unique mastery in the blending of verbal and visual poetry—a mastery that I cannot parallel in any other poet-dramatist known to me, of any date" (145). Nō provides a parallel.

[34] For those who would like to become familiar with Aeschylus's tragedies before reading this comparative study, translations are readily available. Among them are the Penguin Classics translations of *The Oresteia* by Robert Fagles and of the other Aeschylean tragedies by Philip Vellacott, the University of Chicago Press series translations of *The Oresteia* by Richmond Lattimore and of the other Aeschylean tragedies by Seth G. Benardete, and Hugh Lloyd-Jones, translation and commentary, *Aeschylus: Agamemnon*, *Aeschylus: The Libation Bearers*, and *Aeschylus: The Eumenides* (Englewood Cliffs: 1970). For English translations of the *Persians*, I recommend both A. J. Podlecki, *Aeschylus: The Persians* (Englewood Cliffs, N.J., 1970), and Janet Lembke and C. J. Herington, *Aeschylus: Persians* (New York and London, 1981); for a Japanese transla-

ducing the reader to stylistic features in Japanese poetry through a close examination of a passage from the nō *Matsukaze*, then comparing it with a passage from the tragedy *Agamemnon*, I analyze the style of Zeami's *Sanemori* and compare it with passages from Aeschylus's *Oresteia*. In Chapter Four, I first discuss Aeschylus's poetic style in general, the affinities it bears with the style of Zeami, and how these apply to a theater performance; then, with a view to identifying not only some essential similarities, but also some differences between the styles of Aeschylus's tragedy and Zeami's nō, and in order to show how the comparative dimension can enhance our appreciation of style in Aeschylus's work, I examine the *Persians* in terms of specific themes, verbal techniques, and literary allusions.

Japanese and Greek terms that are defined in the two Glossaries appearing after Chapter Four are italicized on their first occurrence only. For the benefit of Japanologists and of classicists, the text of *Sanemori*, excluding the *ai-kyōgen* section, and the Japanese and Greek texts of the passages that I have analyzed closely in Chapters Three and Four are printed in Appendices Three and Four respectively.

---

tion of the *Persians*, see Kubo Masaaki, "Perushanohitobito," in *Girishahigeki zenshū* (The Complete Greek Tragedies), ed. Kure Shigeichi, vol. 1 (Tokyo, 1979), 121–152.

ONE

Structure in Nō

The successful playwright of nō constructs his work in such a way that he engages the audience's attention by means of a progression that controls the mood of the play from beginning to end and that focuses onto the main character the visual appeal of costume, mask, and props; the meaning of the nō; the story on which the author has drawn; and the modes of presentation—the music, the words, the stage action. Because the number of characters is limited; the visual effects—costumes, masks, and stage props—are used economically in most nō; the subject is chosen on the basis of its adaptability to a performance, and then, in the best nō, is integrated fully into that performance, the audience's attention is seldom distracted in various directions, as in some theaters, away from the main character and the mood that the author purposefully creates.

In his treatises, Zeami gives specific and general advice that is a key to understanding how he achieved the kind of focus one finds in many of his nō. And from these works, it is clear that, like any good playwright, actor, teacher, or writer about drama, Zeami does not think a nō will be successful if, though well written, it is poorly performed, and also that he considers the audience's reaction important—the reaction to visual effects, to acting, to music, to language, to literary and historical sources, to "structure," and to subject, and not to any one of these alone. He writes about how one should choose subjects as the basis of nō; how one should organize a nō; how one should fill out a nō verbally, musically, and kinetically; how the actors should be trained; and how they should perform. At its best and in Zeami's hands, nō is a theater that engages the audience's attention fully, is entertaining, emotionally compelling, and at the same time, aesthetically and spiritually uplifting.

Zeami's views on the aesthetic and practical matters involved in the composition and performance of nō contain advice relevant for almost any playwright or actor and pertain to the appreciation of much theater. However, when they are understood at their most fundamental level, his views pertain especially well to theater in which there are dance or patterned movements and both vocal and instrumental music, in which a mood or certain emotions are developed, and in which characters and visual effects are used economically—that is, as I shall argue, the kind of theater Aeschylus created. In fact, in a number of ways Zeami's views are suggestive of how one can appreciate certain features of the emotionally compelling and religiously and ethically instructive play, the *Persians*. However, for an analysis of Aeschylus's works in terms of nō to be meaningful, one needs to understand some of the principles that Zeami recommended to the playwright composing nō.

In the treatise called both *Sandō* (Three Ways) and *Nōsakusho* (The Composition of Nō), Zeami's views on the composition of nō reveal how, when he maps out and fills in the details of a play, he has the performance in mind. He says at the beginning of the *Sandō* that there are three elements required for the composition of a nō: *shu* ("seed"), *saku* ("construction"), and *sho* ("writing of words").[1] In section one of the *Sandō*, Zeami treats the first of these, the seed, which he says entails an author's thorough knowledge of his sources and his choice of subject. That subject, he advises, should be a character whose actions are "especially effective in terms of the Two Arts of dance and song."[2] (By "song," Zeami means both music and poetry.) Zeami explains that even if a character is a famous person from the past or highly gifted, unless he or she can be presented in terms of the two arts, the theatrical effect appropriate to nō is not possible. His examples include female gods, deities, and other characters who would be naturally associated with the performance of sacred songs and dance; men who are highly cultivated, such as poets; and women accomplished in poetry and dance. Zeami adds that even for subjects who are unknown, roles

[1] For the text of Zeami's treatises I have used *Zeami: Zenchiku, Nihon shisō taikei*, vol. 24, ed. Omote Akira and Katō Shūichi (Tokyo, 1974), hereafter ZZ. The *Sandō* (Three Ways) appears on pages 133–144. The *Sandō* has been translated by J. Thomas Rimer in conjunction with Yamazaki Masakazu in *On the Art of the Nō Drama: The Major Treatises of Zeami* (Princeton, 1984), hereafter Rimer. They base their translation on *Nōgakuronshū, Nihon koten bungaku taikei*, vol. 65, ed. Nishio Minoru (Tokyo, 1961). The reader will be continually referred to the Rimer and Yamazaki translation, the only English translation available in one volume of a substantial number of treatises written by Zeami. In French, there are the translations of René Sieffert, *La tradition secrète du Nô* (Paris, 1960). For an excellent discussion of many parts of the treatises that pertain to Zeami's style, the reader is encouraged to read Thomas B. Hare's *Zeami's Style: The Noh Plays of Zeami Motokiyo*. Unless otherwise noted, the summaries, translations, and interpretations of sections from Zeami's *Sandō*, *Fūshikaden*, *Kakyō*, and *Sarugaku dangi* offered here are my own.

[2] Translation by Rimer, 148.

should be created so that "the characters can be rendered suitable for the arts of song and dance."[3]

From among early nō and part of the present-day repertory, one can see that by choosing the appropriate character as subject, the playwright is able to integrate subject and performance effectively. For example, the main character of *Hyakuman* is a dancer whom the author skillfully, yet naturally, integrates into the performance of her story, which is accompanied by dance and song.[4] Since the warrior Yorimasa was as well known to the audience for his poetry as for his prowess on the battlefield, Zeami was able to conclude his nō *Yorimasa* with a finale appropriate to the source, the character, and the theater: the quotation of a poem composed by the epico-historical Yorimasa and delivered by his dramatic counterpart. To these two examples, drawn from many, I add the nō *Atsumori*, written about the young warrior Atsumori, who was not a poet or artist, but who, according to the epico-historical accounts of his death, was said to have played his flute at dawn on the day he was killed in battle.[5] A high point in performances of *Atsumori* today is created quite naturally at the moment when, in the context of verbal references to flutes, the instrumentalist on stage plays his flute.[6] In each of these three examples, source, character, and an art appropriate to the theater are integral and interrelated parts of the nō.

If Aeschylus in his Achilleid trilogy had based a scene on the ninth book of the *Iliad*, the source he knew so well, and had portrayed the character Achilles playing his lyre and singing at one of the musical peaks of the performance, he could have gained an effect comparable to that which one enjoys in *Atsumori*. But he did not. In extant Greek tragedy there seem not to have been character roles directly connected with the arts of song,

---

[3] Rimer, 149. See Hare, *Zeami's Style*, 50.

[4] On this play and Zeami's views, see *Sandō* in *ZZ*, 193, and Rimer, 154. There is some question as to whether Zeami wrote this play—Yokomichi Mario and Omote Akira in *Yōkyokushū*, vol. 1, *Nihon koten bungaku taikei*, vol. 40 (Tokyo, 1960), 57, hereafter *YKS*, suggest that it was written either by Zeami or by his father. Zeami specifically mentions the play in the *Sandō* as one that includes the *kusemai* style, a particular dance style that Zeami's father, Kan'ami, adapted into nō. On the performance of kusemai in another nō, *Yamamba*, see Monica Bethe and Karen Brazell, *Nō as Performance: An Analysis of the Kuse Scene of Yamamba*, in Cornell University East Asia Papers, no. 16 (Ithaca, N.Y., 1978).

[5] The nō *Yorimasa* has been translated by René Sieffert, *Nô et Kyôgen: Théâtre du Moyen Âge*, vol. 1 (Paris, 1979), 532–547. *Atsumori* has been translated by Noël Peri in *Le Nô* (Tokyo, 1944), 116–160.

[6] In a letter, Shimazaki Chifumi informed me that during modern performances of *Atsumori*, the flute music enters at this point for reasons of musical structure, not because of the words. In addition, since instrumental musical notations dating from Zeami's day do not exist, it is impossible to know with certainty whether the words and the flute music were meant to go hand-in-hand at this particular point in *Atsumori*. And yet, the idea seems to be in the spirit of what Zeami wrote.

25

dance, instrumental music, or literature.[7] Instead, prefiguring the advice of Aristotle, who gave plot priority over character and text priority over performance, the Greek playwrights often chose as the subject of their tragedies an event or an action for which the character of a play was famous, rather than a character known for an artistic skill. Any degree of comparability in this realm lies instead between those nō in which a deity or spirit dances and sings (for example, in the nō *Takasago*) and those tragedies in which there exists a natural connection between the character and a song or dance (for example, the song and dance of enchantment enacted by the Furies in Aeschylus's *Eumenides*, or the sacred hymns and dances to Dionysus, enacted by the chorus of his adherents in Euripides' archaizing play, the *Bacchae*).

Even when the main character of a nō is not an artist, but is familiar to the audience as a subject of poetry, history, or literature, the playwright tries to integrate character and literary source with the arts of song and dance. Zeami features this type of character in his nō *Sanemori*, a play to which this analysis will turn later. Sanemori was not an artist but a famous warrior, drawn from epico-historical accounts of the fighting between the Heike and Genji "families" who vied for control of Japan.[8] In the nō, Zeami organizes and uses his source materials in such a way that, without transforming the warrior into an artist, he presents the warrior's story effectively in performance on stage. To this extent, I shall argue, his approach is comparable to Aeschylus's. In addition, *Sanemori* was a topical play in which Zeami was able to capitalize on an event that occurred within seven years of his composition of the nō and thus use the arts of song and dance quite naturally in it. It was known to the audience that Sanemori had appeared as a ghost to a priest in the year 1414, when that priest was traveling about the countryside and proselytizing at services that included not only his sermons, but also religious songs and dances, *odori nembutsu*.[9] The nō features both a waki (second actor) who plays

[7] The title of a tragedy ascribed to Sophocles, *Thamyris* (*Thamyras?*), suggests the possibility that the character Thamyris, a Thracian bard, appeared in the play. According to Athenaeus 1.20 f and the *Life* of Sophocles 4, Sophocles played the lyre in this tragedy; see A. C. Pearson, *The Fragments of Sophocles*, vol. 1 (Amsterdam, 1963), 178. However, only a small fragment of the play remains, and that is uninformative about the character.

[8] The Heike were at first victorious, but were utterly defeated by the Genji in 1185. The events are narrated in the *Heike monogatari* (The Tale of the Heike), hereafter *Heike*, and the *Gempei jōsuiki* (An Account of the Rise and Fall of the Genji and the Heike). For a brief introduction to and a translation of the former, see *The Tale of the Heike*, trans. Hiroshi Kitagawa and Bruce T. Tsuchida (Tokyo, 1977).

[9] According to Kōsai Tsutomu, "Sakuhin kenkyū: Sanemori" (Research on the Production of Sanemori), *Kanze* (January 1970): 3–9, reprinted in *Nōyōshinkō: Zeami ni terasu* (New Thoughts on Nō Texts: In the Light of Zeami) (Tokyo, 1972, reprinted 1980), 274–282, since *Sanemori* is mentioned in Zeami's treatise, the *Sandō*, we know

the part of that itinerant priest and the performance of religious music. There is a kind of analogue in tragedy, if Aeschylus intentionally alluded to parts of the Panathenaic festival parade with his inclusion of a procession enacted by metics and the women of Athens at the end of the *Eumenides*. The allusion to this festival is suggested because it was regularly held in Athens, which is a setting of the play, in honor of Athena, who is a main character of the tragedy, and included metics dressed in crimson robes, in which the metic Eumenides of Aeschylus's play are also dressed. (About plays not based on a specific literary source, but related to a famous place or historical site, as the *Eumenides* is in part, Zeami says at the end of the first section of the *Sandō* that they are the achievements of the talent of a supreme expert.)

In the second section of the *Sandō*, Zeami discusses saku ("construction"), the next element of composition, which I have called structure. This structure is not so much a *desis* ("tying up") and *lusis* ("untying") in Aristotle's terms (*Poetics* 1455b24–32), if indeed such terms are relevant, as it is an aesthetic progression toward various peaks in which words, music, and action on stage reinforce each other. The construction is not an Aristotelian plot fashioned out of characters' actions and arranged in terms of logical and probable relationships, but the arrangement of the parts of a play in terms of a principle called *jo-ha-kyū*, a principle that a playwright should bear in mind if he wants to engage successfully the full attention of all members of the audience and provide them with a feeling of satisfaction at the end of a performance.

According to Zeami in this second section of the *Sandō*, jo-ha-kyū is divided into five parts—*jo* is comprised of the first, *ha* the next three, and *kyū* the last part.[10] (The three parts into which ha is divided are also called a jo and a ha and a kyū.) We might define jo-ha-kyū as a beginning, a middle, and an end; but, because it applies to performance, it is more accurate to call it an opening, a development, and a finale. The quiet opening section is jo; the developing middle section ha (literally meaning "break open"); and the climactic, quickened final section the kyū. Since this principle originated in performances of dance and music, it is understandable that Zeami advises against thinking of it in terms of text alone. Section

---

that it was written before 1423. An account of the visitation of the ghost appears in a diary, the *Mansai jungo nikki*, under May 11, 1414, to the effect that the incident took place on March 11. This evidence gives us a *terminus post quem* and a *terminus ante quem* for the date of *Sanemori*. Kōsai also believes that Zeami wrote the words and the music for, acted in, and directed this warrior play.

[10] On jo-ha-kyū, see, for example, Hare, *Zeami's Style*, 50–51; Frank Hoff, "Zeami on Jo-Ha-Kyū Theory," *Proceedings of the Fourth ISCRCP* (1981): 217–228; Nogami Toyoichirō, *Yōkyoku geijutsu* (The Art of Nō) (Tokyo, 1936), 42–46.

fifteen of the late work *Sarugaku dangi* (An Account of Reflections on the Art of Sarugaku [nō was called sarugaku in Zeami's day]), in which Zeami's son Motoyoshi wrote down his father's views, says that to think of jo-ha-kyū mechanically or only in terms of the text is an inferior way of composing nō.[11] One should compose in terms of a performance in which the jo mood progresses to the ha, which "breaks it open," that is, elaborates upon it. He adds that the jo-ha-kyū of the words of the text only may be entertaining to listen to during a performance, but he also says that one should not separate words and action in performance. It is clear from a section on the relationship between performance and text in an earlier treatise of his, the *Fūshikaden* (Teachings on Style and the Flower),[12] that Zeami or his father Kan'ami, whose views we are told are recorded in this treatise, thought the movements of the actor's body should depend on the text and that the actor should make his feelings conform to the written word. For example, Zeami says that when the text reads "look," the actor should make the gesture of looking; "point" or "pull," he should point with his finger or pull his hand back; "listen," he should assume the attitude of listening; and so forth. In other words, the movements of the body depend on what is written in the text and not the other way around.

Finally, in section three of the *Sandō*, Zeami discusses the third element of composition: sho ("writing of words"). In this section of the treatise he advises that one choose words appropriate to the nō and to the character who is the subject of the nō—the poems and songs should correspond to the types of emotions and moods to be expressed. To this extent his views are compatible with those of most, if not all, playwrights. But he continues with more specific advice suited especially for nō, namely that one should include a quotation from a famous poetic source for the shite (main actor) to recite and that, if the play focuses on a famous place or historic site, a well-known song or poem about the place should be included in important places in the ha section. I will turn to the subject of the words in Chapter Three.

Zeami's advice on the three elements—the choice of subject, the construction, and the writing of words—reveals the high degree of mutual integration he intended them to exhibit. But essential to an understanding of how and why the elements of composition and performance are coordinated is an understanding of the second of Zeami's elements, construction according to the jo-ha-kyū principle. This principle, Zeami tells us, is

[11] ZZ, 287–288, and Rimer, 216.
[12] *Fūshikaden* 3.7, in ZZ, 34–35, and Rimer, 27. On the meaning of the word, "Flower," Richard N. McKinnon ("The Nō and Zeami," 359–360) says, "According to his [Zeami's] works, *hana* [flower] can be broadly defined as the quality of a performance which gives to the audience a sense of novelty and charm."

a process toward completion that involves a sense of fulfillment in every-thing.[13] In nō, it applies to the broadest and the most specific aspects—it is the means by which a playwright can satisfy the members of an audience and make them feel that the opening, development, and finale of a nō pro-gram, of a nō play, or of one part of a nō—a dance, a section of recitation, a gesture, or even the pronunciation of one syllable—is just right. For ex-ample, Zeami informs us that the utterance of the sound o ("yes") in re-sponse to a question, if too quick, does not observe this principle. Timing is an important part of jo-ha-kyū. The moment before a person utters the sound, says Zeami, is the jo, the word itself constitutes the ha, and the moment after the actor stops is the kyū.[14]

In the *Fūshikaden*, Zeami speaks of the jo-ha-kyū of nō on a broad scale, in a full program of four or more plays.[15] The distribution of the plays into each of the four or more positions on a program, he says, will be deter-mined according to the artistic content of the performances. Without ex-plaining in detail what he means, Zeami says that the first play serves as the jo portion of a program and should be based on an authoritative classic or well-known legend, should be dignified without too much complexity of style in the movements and songs of the actor, and should be executed smoothly. Words of blessing, such as prayers for the long life of the em-peror or the well-being of the nation, are essential to this first play, which is termed *waki sarugaku*, that is, waki nō, literally meaning "adjacent nō," so called because it is placed next to a religious piece in song and dance, called *Okina*, with which a program is introduced (today on festive occa-sions in particular). In other words, the first play in the jo position of a program sets the proper tone for the day and therefore must contain con-gratulations and felicitations. The second and third plays in a program, Zeami says, should be fine productions, well-composed plays more intrin-sically interesting to the audience in terms of the actor's skills than the play that preceded. Finally, the play in the kyū position, often (but not always) the last piece of the day, will include especially vigorous movements by the actor and the full degree of concentrated acting skill at his disposal.

It is clear that Zeami's suggestions are meant to be understood in terms of audience reaction and the securing of a successful performance, for he adds that the waki nō, when presented on a day after the first day of dra-matic performances, should have a different appeal from the waki nō cho-sen for the first day, and that the plays that are particularly moving, in the sense of exciting feelings of pity or sadness, should be placed in the middle

[13] See *Shūgyoku tokka* (Finding the Gems and Gaining the Flower) 5, in ZZ, 190–192 and Rimer, 137–140.
[14] *Sarugaku dangi*, sec. 12, in ZZ, 281, and Rimer, 205.
[15] *Fūshikaden*, sec. 3.2, in ZZ, 29, and Rimer, 21.

part of a program on those successive days.[16] Zeami's advice is not merely theoretical, but practical. His works are full of such advice—for example, in the context of emphasizing that the playwright and actor must be one and the same person, he warns that it is important to choose plays that differ from those of one's rivals.[17] One can see that playwrights of nō had an advantage over their Greek counterparts, who were required, preliminary to the actual performance days, to enter a *proagōn* ("something before the dramatic contest"), in which they probably announced the subjects of their plays to a panel of judges.[18] Thus it would seem that the Greek tragedians could not switch their programs on the basis of what a competitor had produced the day before.

In the section on language in his *Poetics*, Aristotle considers details of poetry as specific as letters and syllables in words (1456b20–21). He also treats tragedy in terms as broad as those in Zeami's discussion of jo-ha-kyū, that is, the relationship of tragedy to other branches of art, history, and philosophy.[19] But, in the *Poetics*, Aristotle does not focus on performance or on how an actor creates a rapport with his audience through his delivery of words and his movements. In this respect, he differs noticeably from Zeami.

From other statements Zeami makes about jo-ha-kyū and the programming of nō, it is apparent that performance is paramount in his mind.[20] In the *Kakyō* (Mirror Held to the Flower), a treatise written one year after the *Sandō*, he recommends how one should distribute the plays of a program into the five divisions of jo-ha-kyū.[21] In the jo part of the program, Zeami says, the fundamental style of the first of the plays is song and dance. This first play, the waki nō, is often called a "god play" and is

[16] Ibid. My interpretation of this passage is based on Rimer's translation.

[17] Ibid., 3.3, in ZZ, 30, and Rimer, 21–22.

[18] See P-C, *Dramatic Festivals*, 67.

[19] For example, in 1456a34–35, in his discussion of thought in tragedy, Aristotle refers the reader to his work on rhetoric.

[20] On the form this relationship takes, see Mark J. Nearman, "Feeling in Relation to Acting: An Outline of Zeami's Views," *Asian Theatre Journal* 1, no. 1 (Spring 1984): 49–51.

[21] Section 8, in ZZ, 90–92, and Rimer, 83–87. For a good analysis and translation with footnotes of the *Kakyō*, see Mark J. Nearman, "Kakyō: Zeami's Fundamental Principles of Acting," *MN* 37, no. 3 (1982): 332–374; no. 4 (1982): 461–496; and vol. 38, no. 1 (1983): 49–71. On jo-ha-kyū, see also *Shūdōsho* (Learning the Way), in ZZ, 239–240, and Rimer, 170–171. Zeami says that during religious festivals and subscription nō, both in the past and in the present, there are usually three nō and two kyōgen, comic-relief pieces, performed on a program. However, when nō are performed at the request of nobility, the programs can include as many as ten plays. On programming, see O'Neill, *Early Nō*, 88–89. On the implications of jo-ha-kyū to good programming, see, for example, Kenneth K. Yasuda, "The Structure of *Hagoromo*, a Nō Play," *HJAS* 33 (1973): 8–10.

characteristically divided into two "halves": in the former, called the *maeba*, one or two persons, sometimes aged, appear in the form of human beings; in the latter, called the *nochiba*, one or both characters appear again, but this time in the form of deities or spirits. Because the atmosphere of these waki nō is religious, specifically Shinto, and because most of them are better thought of as celebrations than as dramatic pieces, there is nothing precisely comparable to them on a program of Greek tragedy. The closest parallel, perhaps, is to be found in the dithyrambic choral presentations in song and dance on the two days preceding the three days of tragic performances at the Festival of Dionysus. Concerning the waki nō, Zeami repeats in the *Kakyō* much that he says in the *Sandō*: "Its basic, direct theme is not overly detailed; although it is celebratory [in nature], it should have an aesthetic effect that is direct and flowing."[22] Thus, the program of nō begins quietly with a play that prepares the audience for the more elaborate theater that will follow later in the day.

After the waki nō, the next plays, says Zeami, who continues to bear the performance in mind, have different qualities from the first. The second play of a program, the *shura nō*, usually deals with the hell in which warriors who have died continue to exist after death and thus is called "warrior nō"; it regularly features a warrior who appears as an ordinary character in the first half, the maeba, and is revealed as the ghost of the warrior dressed in armor in the second half, the nochiba. Zeami says about plays that appear in the second position of a program that they should be based on a straightforward source, be powerful, and have grace. Zeami adds that although these plays, positioned at the beginning of the ha section of a program, differ from the waki nō, yet even these are not too complex nor do they require the degree of refined acting skills on the part of the actor found later on a program. Zeami's shura nō fit these prescriptions well: they preserve traces of the jo, but are more powerful than a waki nō and more straightforward in execution than the plays that follow on a program. It is to this category of nō that *Sanemori* belongs, the play I will be discussing below.

After the waki and shura nō come several nō, more complex than the first two, that fall squarely into the ha section of the program. A play from the ha section, today called *sanbanmemono*, "third category piece," is highly lyrical; poetry and grace dominate, and a woman is usually featured as the main character. In *Nonomiya*,[23] for example, as in many of these "woman nō," there are two parts—in the first, the maeba, the main actor

---

[22] This is the translation by Nearman, "Kakyō," 464.
[23] For an analysis of *Nonomiya*, see Kenneth K. Yasuda, "On the *Nonomiya* of Zeami," in *Asien Tradition und Fortschritt: Festschrift für Horst Hammitzsch* (Wiesbaden, 1971), 680–703.

appears as an ordinary woman; in the second, the nochiba, he appears again as a woman, but as a ghost attached to her lover and thus not yet freed from her attachment to the world. There are also one-part woman nō, but Zeami advises that, if possible, these should be performed and constructed in such a way as to provide variation within them, almost giving the illusion of two parts.[24] In the *Kakyō* Zeami says that whereas the nō in the jo section is simple and straightforward in its execution, the plays in the ha category are more complex and require more *monomane no fūtei*, "manifestation of imitation," that is, more naturalistic representation of the character portrayed. The plays of the ha section are central to a day's program, he adds.

The fourth and (when there are six nō on a program) the fifth plays require greater artistic efforts on the part of the actors. These plays at the end of the ha section of a program are today a miscellaneous group that includes, for example, revenge pieces (often featuring characters who are like demons in form, but humans in mind), historical pieces, "realistic pieces," mad woman plays, and such nō as are more true to life than the plays in the jo and first two parts of the ha sections. Since some of these nō even feature a degree of dramatic confrontation between characters, they are closer in terms of "plot" to Greek tragedy than the other nō.[25] For example, in *Shunkan*, written by an unknown author, a play like most tragedies in that it does not feature a ghost or spirit in the second half, the exiled Shunkan's initial happy reaction to the news of pardon for the exiles who plotted against the Heike changes to despair when he realizes that he will not be pardoned with the other two exiles and will be forced to remain on the island.[26] The play ends as he watches his two companions leave for the capital. The situation is not unlike that in Sophocles' *Philoctetes*, in which an exiled Philoctetes is fetched by Odysseus and Neoptolemus, but his joy at the possibility of returning home turns to despair when he realizes that his enemy Odysseus has used Neoptolemus to trick him into returning to the battlefront at Troy. Even though the ending of the *Philoctetes* is happy to the extent that Sophocles brings in the god Heracles and resolves the problem of whether Philoctetes should go home, where he wants to go, or to Troy, where he must go, whereas the conclusion of

[24] *Sarugaku dangi*, sec. 15, in ZZ, 288–289, and Rimer, 217–218.

[25] The nō *Koi no omoni* (The Burden of Love), belonging to this group of nō, is unusual among Zeami's plays. In the narrated report of the interlude scene, a scene comparable to messenger scenes in tragedy, there is a reference to a death occurring contemporaneously with the dramatic time. For a translation of this play, see P. G. O'Neill, "Translations: The Nô Plays Koi no Omoni and Yuya," *MN* 10, nos. 1–2 (1954): 203–266.

[26] Translations appear in Sieffert, *Nô et Kyôgen*, 2: 330–342, and Kunio Komparu, *Noh Theater*, 326–342.

Shunkan is unhappy, the subject matter and plot of the two plays are similar enough to invite a comparison. However, a comparison of Sophocles'
plays with nō is inappropriate here for the reasons outlined in the Introduction, particularly since, in his discussions of nō in the *Kakyō* and elsewhere, Zeami reveals a preference for the other types of nō. In other
words, what we learn about his ideas on the composition and performance
of the best types of nō pertains to those that can fall into the jo and into
the first divisions of the ha part of a program.

Last on a modern program of five nō plays, in the kyū section, is an
abbreviated form of a play pared down to little more than the dance of a
spirit or a demon, who is a demon in both form and mind, or a nō in two
parts that culminates in a dance at the end of the second part. (The ending
piece, the *kiri nō*, literally meaning "cut off," as in "to bring to an end,"
can also be a celebratory piece of the sort found in the jo section and added
to the kyū in order to relax the mood.) In the *Kakyō*, Zeami says that while
the ha "breaks up" the mood of jo and brings with it the complex and
great artistic skill of the actors, the kyū augments the mood of the ha by
pushing acting techniques as far as possible—there is a concentrated effect
of powerful, rapid movement, and dance, as well as pronounced and
strong gestures. The kyū is the part of the program that "dazzles the eyes
of the spectator," says Zeami.[27] Zeami also advises that a kyū that lasts for
a long time is not a kyū at all; the ha is the part to prolong.

In sum, if there are five plays on a program, the first is the jo, the second
is still part of the jo but begins the ha, the third and the fourth are the
second and third parts of the ha, and the fifth or last play is the kyū. (Sometimes, as I mentioned, a *shūgen* or congratulatory piece of the jo type may
end a program.)[28] Plays used regularly in these five positions are now
called first, second, third, fourth, and fifth category plays, but individual
examples of these, with the exception of shura nō, may belong to more
than one category and, depending on the day's performances and attending circumstances in the theater, may be switched from one position to
another.

From this summary of Zeami's views about the application of jo-ha-kyū
to the programming of nō, it is apparent that he was concerned with timing and acting, as well as the mood and the effect of a play on his audience.
In fact, in the *Kakyō*, he continues with a discussion of what happens when

[27] Rimer, 84.
[28] A program of nō does not conform to inflexible rules, as Zeami himself says in the
Kakyō. In *Sarugaku dangi* sec. 15, he compares different types of plays, each of which
might belong to the first (jo) position on a program. It is important to remember that
the program consisting of five categories of plays that I have used in this discussion was
not fully developed in practice until the seventeenth century.

a dignitary arrives late to a performance and the program has already progressed to the ha or kyū stage. He says that, although the nō program is already at the finale, the mood of the arriving person is appropriate to the jo, and he will not respond to a nō that belongs to the kyū. In addition, since the audience, which has seen the performance from the beginning, will have its attention distracted by the entrance of the important person, the atmosphere in the theater will again assume the mood of jo so that the nō cannot succeed. Zeami does give some advice to the actor under these constraints—he says that an actor may think that he should revert to the jo style, but should not, for the effect will then be inferior. He recommends instead that the actor cope with this kind of eventuality by attempting to capture the attention of the important spectator and performing a good nō belonging to the ha stage with grace and a quality directed a little toward the jo. In this way, he says, capturing the heart of the dignitary, one should try to make a smooth transition for the audience back to the atmosphere of the ha or the kyū. But even so, he adds, the results will not be entirely satisfactory. From these comments one can perceive that Zeami was acutely aware of the need for a rapport between actor and audience and of the importance of jo-ha-kyū.

To translate such characteristics as mood, tempo, stage action, acting techniques, and types of source used in the programming of nō into terms applicable to the programming of Greek tragedy is very difficult. Not only do we not have firsthand or much early information about Greek performances, but also the text of only one program of tragedies, namely Aeschylus's Oresteian trilogy, exists against which to test the comparison.[29] And that is a program in which the plays are connected thematically, as the plays of a nō program are not. (At best, references to the same season, the season of the performance, might serve as a connecting link among nō presented on the same program.) Yet in some respects we could say that the *Oresteia* shares characteristics with the program Zeami prescribes in terms of jo-ha-kyū.

Although the Greek plays are presented on one of the three days following the dithyrambic performances of songs and dances in honor of gods by choruses of men and boys, and not on the same day, yet, as suggested above, the dithyrambs might be compared to *Okina* or a waki nō, the congratulatory god play at the beginning of a day's program of nō. The beginning of the *Agamemnon*, the first play of the *Oresteia* trilogy, is

---

[29] The evidence for the reconstruction of full programs of tragedy by Sophocles and Euripides has been amassed and discussed by T.B.L. Webster. See his *An Introduction to Sophocles* (Oxford, 1936) and *The Tragedies of Euripides* (London, 1967). However, Webster's findings do not encourage one to compare the programs of Sophocles or Euripides with those of nō.

within its own milieu comparable to a nō in the jo position of a program. It begins with songs and speeches and without any indication of complicated action on the part of the actors. At most there are the entrances of two actors and the movements of the chorus that accompany their songs. The first major action of the tragedy is the arrival home in a chariot, or a prop representing a chariot, of the Greek general Agamemnon with his Trojan mistress Cassandra, followed by his entrance into the palace upon purple-red carpets. In addition, the sources of the beginning of the play are less ambiguous than those of the later part of the *Agamemnon* or the second and third plays of the trilogy—stories and poems of the epic cycle, including Homer's work, and most probably Stesichorus's *Oresteia*, a long poem, which tell of the sacrifice of Iphigenia, the Greek expedition to Troy, the crime of Paris, and the return of the Greeks from Troy. In fact, the first half of the *Agamemnon* is in some respects comparable to a shura nō (warrior nō), usually falling at the end of the jo or beginning of the ha position of a program—it is not too complicated in stage action, yet it is emotionally compelling and straightforward (that is, orthodox) in the construction of the plot, as I shall explain in the next chapter, and is based on sources that are familiar to the audience.

There is nothing represented in the *Oresteia*, indeed in the entire repertoire of Greek tragedy, that resembles a woman play. For a parallel, one would have to imagine the dramatization of the Atthis poem or of another work written by Sappho on the subject of the memories of loved ones. The Cassandra scene of the *Agamemnon*, a scene in which the prophetess raves madly about the crimes of the past, present, and future before she is led off to her death, might correspond to a mad woman nō, which occasionally is found in the third position on a program, but more often in the fourth.[30] Moreover, given the movement and agitation featured at the end of the *Agamemnon* where the chorus and Aegisthus fight; in the second half of the *Libation Bearers*, the next play of the trilogy, where Orestes confronts his mother in preparation for killing her and then is driven mad; and in much of the *Eumenides*, the third play, where there is a confrontation between the Furies and Apollo and a decided divergence from the traditional version of the legend of the house of Atreus, one might suggest that these all satisfy *some* of Zeami's prescriptions for the late ha section in a program of nō, the section in which the historical, revenge, and realistic plays appear. And finally, parts of the *Eumenides*, including the appearance of the ghost of Clytemnestra, the dance of the Furies, and their pursuit of Orestes, which might have required that the actor use every skill at his disposal, could be said to satisfy some of the requirements of plays

[30] On mad woman nō, see *Sandō* 2.2, in ZZ, 138, and Rimer, 154.

positioned at the end of the ha section and those of the kyū in a program of nō. Perhaps the end of the *Eumenides*, in which Aeschylus introduces the pomp of lanterns, red robes, and an adjunct chorus parading offstage, might serve as a grand finale that dazzles the eyes of the audience with a spectacle. However, there is no indication that this procession included a vigorous dance, such as one finds at the end of some programs of nō. In its own milieu, the procession is celebratory and thus functions like a shūgen piece placed after the kyū in a program of nō.

Some of the problems involved in a comparison of the programming of nō with that of tragedy do not occur when we consider the application of Zeami's jo-ha-kyū progression to individual plays and compare these with the *Persians*, a play chosen as the focus of the discussion of structure in Greek tragedy because it alone among Aeschylus's extant works is not connected thematically with the play that preceded it (the *Phineus*) or the one that followed it on the program (the *Glaucus*).[31] In fact, although the *Persians* differs from an ideal warrior nō in that Zeami's word "graceful or refined" does not seem to apply, the play does share similarities with a warrior nō in that it is powerful in its emotional content, it appears to be orthodox in its structure (that is, one that Aeschylus seems to have favored at the beginning of three of his extant plays), it is not too complex, and it is based on a straightforward and familiar source, the history of the Persian Wars (which, as far as we know, Aeschylus used as the theme of his play without benefit of a specific text). Indeed, like many nō, the *Persians* lacks action—it begins with almost no action at all and does not require, until the finale, anything approximating vigorous and extensive acting skills. But to the subject of this play I will turn in the next chapter.

In the second section of the *Sandō*,[32] Zeami considers the construction of nō plays in terms both of performance and of the composition of the texts. After saying that jo-ha-kyū in each nō is divided into five parts called *dan* (comparable to episodes and attendant odes in tragedy), so that jo represents dan one, ha represents dan two, three, and four, and kyū represents dan five, Zeami distinguishes these within a nō in terms of some of

---

[31] On this subject, see H. D. Broadhead, *The Persae of Aeschylus* (Cambridge, 1960), lv–lix. Very little is known about the *Phineus* and the *Glaucus*. From among the other extant plays of Aeschylus, the *Agamemnon*, *Libation Bearers*, and *Eumenides* make up the Oresteian trilogy; the *Suppliants* is the first play of the Danaid trilogy; and *The Seven against Thebes* is the final play of an Oedipus trilogy. I exclude the *Seven* from my discussion of structure. Although we are certain that the first two plays were thematically connected to the *Seven*, we do not know enough about them from the existing fragments to justify a discussion of the *Seven* in this comparative study. Here, as elsewhere, I leave out of consideration the *Prometheus Bound*, which I do not think was written by Aeschylus. On this view, see, e.g., Mark Griffith, *The Authenticity of Prometheus Bound* (Cambridge, 1970).

[32] *ZZ*, 135, and Rimer, 149–150. See also Hare, *Zeami's Style*, 50–51.

the actors' movements, including their entrances, and in terms of the musical and rhythmic units of which the dan are composed. A general outline of these divisions in a nō is as follows: dan one (the jo) begins with the entrance of the waki (second actor) and wakizure (his attendants) and continues to the end of a song shared by the waki and wakizure. Dan two, the beginning of the ha section, continues from the entrance of the shite (main actor) through a song sung by him. Dan three, the middle of the ha section, includes the meeting of the waki and the shite, a verbal exchange between them, and the first choral passage of consequence in the play. Dan four, the end of the ha section, is a musical section that may include a *kusemai*, the part of a play that is musically, rhythmically, verbally, sometimes kinetically, and thematically especially important.[33] Dan five, the kyū, is the "quickened" part in which there may be a dance or vigorous movements to a fast beat performed by the shite. Ordinarily there is a sequence of five dan, but Zeami says that there may be four or six, depending on the nature of the material used for a play—the quality of the story and what an author adds or subtracts. Zeami concludes this second section of the *Sandō*, on the discussion of jo-ha-kyū, with advice that one should determine what kind of and how much music is appropriate to each section of the jo, ha, and kyū parts of a nō.

One can illustrate the bare outline of Zeami's jo-ha-kyū and his deployment of dan as follows:

Jo, dan one, begins with the entrance of the waki and the wakizure
    and continues through their song.
The first part of the ha, dan two, begins with the entrance of the shite
    and continues through his song.
The second part of the ha, dan three, contains a verbal exchange between
    the waki and the shite and the first choral song.
The third part of the ha, dan four, contains the rhythmically interesting
    section, the kusemai. The revelation of the shite's name, as well as
    vigorous movements or a dance, often occurs here.
In all two-part nō, the shite exits within or at the end of the third part of
    the ha for a change of costume. During the interim, there is an interlude scene, called *ai-kyōgen*, which is not part of the jo-ha-kyū development. In this scene, the kyōgen actor, one of those who play a role in
    the kyōgen comic-relief pieces performed between some of the nō plays

---

[33] The *kuse* tends to deviate from the regular meter; a *tadautai*, another type of song that may replace the kuse, is more regular: the rhythm follows the formal prosodic units of Japanese lines of verse, five and seven syllables. In Japanese poetry, five- and seven-syllable sequences, plus or minus one or two syllables in each line, represent one verse or unit. *Waka*, for example, consist of two units: an introductory three lines of five, seven, and five syllables respectively, and an additional two lines of seven syllables each.

on a program (kyōgen refers to both a play and the actor), enters and, in accordance with Zeami's views on the function of the kyōgen in these scenes,[34] tells the background of the main character's story. He then retires to his position on stage at the back left corner.

The kyū, dan five, which includes the reappearance of the shite, might be thought of as the entire second half of the play. However, because in practice the second halves of nō contain more than a dance or the active movements of the shite, the core of the kyū section, they represent a continuation of the ha plus the whole of the kyū section.

For the sake of convenience, the nochiba, second halves, can in turn be divided, as Yokomichi has interpreted the spirit of Zeami's discussions, into subdivisions that reveal their own jo-ha-kyū, rather than according to what Zeami says specifically.[35] Using Yokomichi's schema, we can divide the nochiba, not into one or two dan, but, like the maeba, into five dan as follows (each of these concludes with a song):

In the jo section, dan one, the waki waits.

In the beginning of the ha, dan two, the shite appears as the ghost of the character represented.

In the second part of the ha, dan three, a dialogue takes place between the two actors, the waki and the shite.

At the end of the ha section, dan four, highly poetic passages are featured and accompanied by dance.

In the kyū and final section, dan five, there occur the most vigorous movements of the shite and the most insistent beat of the drums.[36]

The structure of nō is fairly predictable, but only as predictable as the number of episodes or the position of choral odes between episodes is in tragedy. One finds, for example, that each play differs from the structure of other nō on a program of five plays and from plays in the same position on a program as well. The variety is not surprising, given the flexibility Zeami allows in the planning of a program and given his own recommendations for varying the structures of plays. In fact, after his discussion of the three elements in the composition of nō, Zeami continues in the *Sandō* with the subject of the structure of specific types of plays. He arranges this discussion around the three basic roles found in the types of nō to which he attached the greatest importance and out of which other types develop,

[34] In the *Shūdōsho*, 6, in ZZ, 239, and Rimer, 170.

[35] See the introduction to YKS, 18–20. For an explication of the analysis in English, see Frank Hoff and Willi Flindt, "The Life Structure of Noh," *Concerned Theatre Japan* 2, nos. 3 and 4 (1973): 210–256.

[36] In the nochiba outlined here, sections jo (dan one) through ha (dan four) belong to the end of the ha section of the nō as a whole; the remainder, kyū (dan five), belongs to the kyū of the whole.

namely the roles of old person, woman, and warrior, in that order. He gives advice about jo-ha-kyū in the nō featuring these characters, including recommendations about quality, tone, sources, character, deployment of parts of dan (called *shōdan*), and such specific matters—too specific to consider in this comparative study—as the number of lines the waki and shite should exchange and the number of syllables one should use in some lines of certain shōdan.

In the section on old person nō (by which he means generally the celebratory plays of the first category), the waki nō, and a few plays in the woman category, Zeami sets out the ideal and orthodox structure of nō in greater detail than he has done earlier.[37] Here, although the plays he considers feature a jo-ha-kyū structure and deployment of dan similar to what Zeami recommended earlier and to what one finds in the example above, he makes specific recommendations that distinguish these old person plays from the warrior nō. For example, he recommends that the nochiba be short in the old person nō, but that in the warrior play, the maeba be as brief as possible and the second half be prolonged.[38] Zeami's recommendations on the placement of the various types of units within a dan (shōdan) also differ between the two types of plays.

Inasmuch as the analysis of the structure of nō in this chapter is focused on the warrior nō and on *Sanemori* in particular, a discussion of the structure of woman nō is unnecessary.[39] Nor will I treat at length the structure of waki nō, the celebratory and nontragic pieces featuring song and dance, although the basic characteristics of jo-ha-kyū do apply to these types of plays. However, to insure that the warrior nō, which I will compare with Aeschylus's work, is not treated in isolation from its own genre, I will summarize for the reader unfamiliar with the conventions of nō some of the ways in which jo-ha-kyū is revealed within the structure of *Takasago* and how these agree with and differ from the structure of *Sanemori*.[40]

[37] In ZZ, 136–137, and Rimer, 151–152.

[38] In ZZ, 138–139, and Rimer, 155.

[39] One of the attractions of choosing the warrior plays as a focus of this comparison is that, as Shimazaki pointed out to me, the characterization and representation on stage of these seem not to have suffered from as many changes between the Muromachi and later periods as other categories of plays. See Kōsai, "Sakuhin kenkyū: Sanemori," 4, and his conviction that the *Sanemori* that we have now is virtually the same as the original in which Zeami acted.

Zeami calls woman nō graceful and refined pieces, the highest level of the art (ZZ, 137–138, and Rimer, 152–155). For a discussion of plays in the woman "mode" (*nyotai*), see Hare, *Zeami's Style*, 131–182. Zeami concentrates his discussion of woman nō more on the character chosen for the main role than on the structure; yet jo-ha-kyū applies to these nō as well as it does to others.

[40] For a discussion of why *Takasago* represents well the *rōtai* ("old person") nō, a translation and analysis of it, and a discussion of other plays in this mode, see Hare, *Zeami's Style*, 65–128.

Takasago is divided into two halves, a maeba and a nochiba, and as a whole into five dan, representing the jo, three parts of the ha, and the kyū. When one divides the maeba and nochiba each into its own dan according to Yokomichi's method, the nochiba contains fewer dan than the example schematized above. The deployment of dan in *Takasago* reveals that there is a progressive increase in the amount of stage action between the shite's entrance at the beginning of the ha and his dances in the kyū. Moreover, each dan tends to begin with prose, recitative, or a song that does not follow the beat, and concludes with a melodic song in rhythm that does follow the beat.[41] The final dan ends with the most insistent and explicit beat. In addition, the development of the nō from beginning to end discloses the identity of the shite and tsure—at first they appear as an old couple, the spirits of pine trees; after connecting them with poetry, Zeami reveals one of them visually in the form of a deity. The similarities that *Takasago* and warrior plays share are crucial to an understanding of the basic progression of jo-ha-kyū. In both there is a development toward more action and stage business by the shite, more explicitness in the presentation of the themes, and more melody and dominant beat in the music. These similarities, which are fundamental to jo-ha-kyū, are not altered by the differences between waki nō and shura nō. However, there are differences.

The difference in source alone guarantees that the warrior nō is more interesting theater and provides a more gripping verbal account than one finds in *Takasago*, which features the legend, drawn from poetry anthologies, of two pines. In speaking about shura nō, the type of nō that he seems to have developed, Zeami says that if the main character is a famous Heike or Genji warrior, as the shite tends to be, then one should compose the play according to the account of his story as given in the *Tale of the Heike*,[42] following the narrative line of this "epic" source.[43] In *Sanemori*,

---

[41] In a song in rhythm that follows the regular beat, called *hiranori*, there are eight beats to the twelve-syllable line. Today they are arranged in the following manner (the beats are numbered):

$$\text{hi/—/to/\underline{na}/to/—/ga/\underline{me}/so/—/ka/\underline{ri}/so/\underline{me}/ni/—.}$$
$$\quad\ 1\quad\ \ 2\quad\ \ 3\quad\ \ 4\quad\ \ 5\quad\ \ 6\quad\ 7\quad\ \ 8$$

[42] *Sandō*, in ZZ, 138–139 and Rimer, 155. References to Zeami's words about shura nō are all taken from this section of the *Sandō*, unless otherwise indicated. On warrior nō, see Hare, *Zeami's Style*, 185–224; on this passage from the *Sandō*, see pp. 186–187 specifically. On Zeami's role in the development of the shura nō, see Yashima Masaharu, "Sanemorikan no hensen: shudai ishiki kara mita nōsaku no suii" (Changes in the Views of Sanemori: Transitions in the Composition of Noh Plays, Based on an Awareness of Their Subject Matter), in *Zeami no nō to geiron* (Theories on Zeami's Nō) (Tokyo, 1985), 660.

[43] See note 8 above. Zeami probably drew on the best-known epico-historical source, the *Heike* or a version of it, for shura nō. The account of the wars between the Heike and the Genji had been written down by Zeami's day—the most authoritative account

the main character (shite) is the warrior Saitō Bettō Sanemori, who was distinguished in his later life as a famous Heike warrior. Zeami bases the nō on the warrior's story from the *Tale of the Heike* and specifically on the section connected with the warrior's last battle and death.[44]

The appeal of warrior nō also derives from a different placement of shōdan, spoken and sung units, within dan, from that of *Takasago*, for example. After Zeami gives specific advice in the *Sandō* about the careful regulation of the five dan by the length of the musical pieces in each of them, he says that near the end of the second half (nochiba) of a warrior nō, there should be a kusemai if the nō is one in which the shite of the first half exits, and reappears in the second half transformed into a different manifestation of the same character. (The later shite is called *nochijite*; the former *maejite*.) In *Sanemori*, Zeami delays all dancing and the kusemai until the second half, as he does not in *Takasago*. There, even though the play features a nochijite, the kusemai is positioned within the fourth dan of the *first* half of the play.

Zeami also suggests that the kusemai be placed specifically in the last part of the ha section, since he continues by saying that the ha will extend into the kyū. (This means that the kusemai occurs in the nochiba.) The result is that the ha part of the warrior nō is lengthened in terms of the number of dan. In fact, Zeami says that there will be four dan in the ha section, rather than three, and six dan in the warrior nō as a whole. (If the nō is not in two parts, he adds, there will be only four dan. The number of dan depends on the play.) It is in accordance with this advice that Zeami says, as I mentioned above, that the beginning of the warrior play must be brief; the kyū is then prolonged.

In the continuation of his discussion of shura nō, after adding that there are variations among them since the sources from which the subjects are drawn differ, Zeami says that in the kyū section, the final exit of the shite should involve a rapid tempo appropriate to a warrior suffering the agonies of "hell"; that the shite's musical passages should display bravery and

---

is that of the Kakuichi text of 1371—but it continued to be narrated by bards orally to the accompaniment of the *biwa*, a type of lute. Since the narrative is epic-like, I shall use the word "epic" for convenience. However, the *Heike* differs from the Homeric epic poems: the narrative is in prose to which the *biwa* adds rhythm, not in verse as in the Homeric epics; the events covered are more easily verifiable historically than those in the *Iliad*; and the degree of religious and moral teaching is more nearly comparable to that found in the works of Hesiod or Herodotus than that of Homer. On the transmission of the text and the historicity of the contents, see Kenneth D. Butler, "The Textual Evolution of the 'Heike Monogatari,' " *HJAS* 26 (1966): 5–51.

44 The story is found in book 7, chapter 8. I have used as a version against which to compare Zeami's text Takagi Ichinosuke's edition, *Heike monogatari*, vol. 2, in *Nihon koten bungaku taikei*, vol. 33 (Tokyo, 1960), 79–82.

strength and provide for vigorous physical movement; that his songs and recitations should be kept short; and that when the shite appears in the second half as a warrior, a section of chant should be included in which he reveals his true identity. Faithful to this advice, Zeami wrote *Sanemori* in such a way that it, like many other warrior plays, ends with the shite's performance of a battle scene in a rapid tempo and a display of the bravery and strength of the warrior. The nō also develops on a verbal level toward the identification of the shite, not only in the first half, but also in the nochiba. Finally, during the nochiba, the shite's songs and recitations are kept short, and he is given ample opportunity to display the qualities of a warrior. The result is a performance more vigorous in the execution of its dance and movements, more forceful in its music, and more engrossing in its story than a performance of *Takasago*.

Sanemori, a play that was considered exemplary,[45] conforms in many ways to Zeami's prescriptions for shura nō in the *Sandō*. At the same time, in a number of respects it is different from other two-part warrior plays written by Zeami—*Atsumori*, *Tadanori*, and *Yorimasa*—which also conform to his prescriptions.[46] In these four shura nō, the nochiba is prolonged; in all but *Tadanori*, which has no kusemai, the kusemai is placed in the nochiba; the warrior is identified not only in the maeba, but also in the nochiba; and the main character and his story are drawn from the tales about the Heike and the Genji. To be sure, in three out of the four plays, the main character is connected with the arts as Sanemori is not: Atsumori is a flute player; Tadanori and Yorimasa are poets, whose poetry is quoted

---

[45] See *Sarugaku dangi*, sec. 16, in *ZZ*, 291, and Rimer, 222. See also Yashima, "Sanemorikan no hensen."

[46] That *Sanemori* and *Yorimasa* have a similar structure, see Yashima, "Sanemorikan no hensen," 663. *Kiyotsune*, another shura nō written by Zeami, is a "one-act" play. The play is also different from the other four shura nō in the type of character roles it features: although, as in the other four nō, the shite is the warrior after whom the nō is named, the waki is not a priest, as in those four, but a retainer of the Heike warrior Kiyotsune; and the tsure is not merely an attendant of the shite as in *Atsumori*, but a second important actor, the warrior's wife. The play dramatizes the moment after Kiyotsune drowns himself, when his retainer returns to the capital and gives a lock of hair to his wife, who is both angry and grief-stricken over her husband's suicide. The ghost of Kiyotsune appears and tells his story to her. The play has been translated by René Sieffert, *Nô et Kyôgen*, 2: 157–170. *Tadanori* is translated by Sieffert in the same work, 1: 309–324, and is the focus of Hare's analysis of warrior plays, what he calls "The Martial Mode," in *Zeami's Style*, 188–211. See note 5 above for translations of *Yorimasa* and *Atsumori*. On the subject of two other shura nō, *Ebira* and *Michimori*, see William Ritchie Wilson, "Two Shuramono *Ebira* and *Michimori*," *MN* 24, no. 4 (1967): 415–465. His introduction to the translations and notes of these two nō plays includes a discussion of the historical context of shura nō. Also of interest are Wilson's comments on the need for Zeami to appeal to the warrior patrons and to the common people in the audience and on the competition Zeami faced with other actors and playwrights. Wilson refers his reader to the work of Kanai Kiyomitsu, "Zeami to shuramono" (Zeami and Warrior Pieces), in *Kokugo to kokubungaku* 31, no. 9 (September 1954): 27–36.

in the nō. And yet, even in *Atsumori* and *Yorimasa*, as in *Sanemori*, Zeami concludes with the strong, vigorous movements of the warrior's enactment of his last battle.[47] Only the call for prayers on behalf of each warrior lightens the musical and kinetic intensity of their finales. *Tadanori* is different; it concludes with the text of the warrior's poetry, an ending appropriate for this poet.

The differences among these warrior nō are closely related to the importance that Zeami places on jo-ha-kyū. In fact, one finds that whereas in *Tadanori* and *Yorimasa*, which deal with poet warriors, Zeami follows the narrative story line of the source on which he drew, he varies the structure of *Atsumori* and *Sanemori* in this respect because, as it stands, the narrative line of the original source is not amenable to the jo-ha-kyū of the nō. In the *Tale of the Heike*, Atsumori's flute-playing is mentioned only after the young warrior's head is cut off by his grief-stricken opponent, Kumagae, who thinks of the pain Atsumori's father will feel when he hears that his son has been killed. In the *Heike* there follows after this scene a history of Atsumori's flute, in much the same way that Homer provides the listener with the history of Agamemnon's scepter in the *Iliad*.[48] In the nō, the names of flutes, including the one belonging to Atsumori, are enumerated at the beginning and again later in the first half; Atsumori's flute-playing is mentioned after the kusemai scene of the second half. But none of these references to the flute appears *after* the narration of the battle scene, as in the original. With this variation from the narrative source, the jo-ha-kyū structure appropriate to a shura nō remains intact—the most active section, the battle scene, is delayed until the end of *Atsumori*. This, at least, is the explanation suggested by Zeami's words for his alteration in the source of *Sanemori*.

In the *Sarugaku dangi*, Zeami says, in the context of his discussion of jo-ha-kyū and the composition of nō: "In *Sanemori*, after the washing of the beard [the scene in which the warrior's dyed hair and beard are washed], if you follow the regular order [of the narrative line in the *Heike*], you should compose the battle scene; however, by expressing the words, 'then again, Sanemori,' and so forth [that is, by adding at this point another element, the kuse, and the story from the *Heike* about Sanemori wearing a brocade robe into battle], the fighting scene can occur at the very end of the play and you can observe the shape of jo-ha-kyū."[49] From these views of Zeami written down by his son we know for certain that he reversed the order of the narration in the *Heike* for the sake of the structure

---

[47] In *Yorimasa*, the battle scene is near, but not at the very end of, the nō.
[48] Book 9, chapter 16 of the *Heike*; *Iliad*, 2.100–108.
[49] Section 15, in ZZ, 288, and Rimer, 217.

of the play, and that an important ingredient of jo-ha-kyū in warrior nō is the inclusion of the engrossing battle scene at the end.[50]

A TRANSLATION AND ANALYSIS OF STRUCTURE IN *SANEMORI*

By taking into account Zeami's recommended alteration in the narrative order of events in *Sanemori* and his advice pertaining to warrior nō, one can use the example of *Sanemori* to illustrate the shape of jo-ha-kyū. I have already compared the structure of *Sanemori* in general terms and will continue to compare it in specific terms with other nō, in particular with *Takasago*, in many respects a structurally orthodox waki nō, and with the three warrior nō written by Zeami that are mentioned above. In this way the structure of *Sanemori* can be understood within its own milieu, and it will be clear when elements of *Sanemori* deviate from the norms found in other nō. It is important that the reader familiar with Greek tragedy set aside preconceived notions about drama and ignore the obvious differences between tragedy and nō so that the jo-ha-kyū development of the nō can be appreciated on its own terms. For this reason I have postponed the bulk of a comparison with Greek tragedy, particularly Aeschylean works, to the next chapters. However, comments of a comparative nature are scattered throughout this chapter, as well as remarks that place jo-ha-kyū within a context of the thematic development of the nō, so that *Sanemori* may simultaneously be appreciated from a point of view familiar to Westerners (and one not discussed by Zeami).

This analysis of *Sanemori*, into which is incorporated my full and literal translation of the play,[51] includes as many comments on that translation as are needed to convey the spirit of jo-ha-kyū in the nō, to reveal the progression from prose or recitative to song following the beat in each dan, from anonymity toward the identification of the shite in each half, and from relatively quiet and uncomplicated movements of the shite to more vigorous action over the course of the play. To these aspects of jo-ha-kyū, which Zeami mentions explicitly, I add other elements that contribute to the overall development within the structure of *Sanemori*, namely, the pro-

[50] This point and the ensuing structural analysis of *Sanemori* is greatly indebted to the unpublished work of Frank Hoff and Jean Hoff, "Staging Epic: Theory and Practice. A Study of *Sanemori*" (1976).

[51] The translation of *Sanemori* throughout is my own and based for the most part on the text of Yokomichi and Omote, *YKS* 1: 265–273. Their text is my major source for the stage directions. I have also consulted Koyama Hiroshi et al., *Yōkyokushū*, vol. 1, *Nihon koten bungaku zenshū*, vol. 33 (Tokyo, 1973), 183–197; Sanari Kentarō, *Yōkyoku taikan*, vol. 2 (Tokyo, 1931; reprinted 1982), 1243–1263; Nogami Toyoichirō, *Kaichū yōkyoku zenshū*, vol. 2 (Tokyo, 1935), 115–130; Itō Masayoshi, *Yōkyokushū*, in *Shinchō Nihon koten shūsei*, vol. 2 (Tokyo, 1986), 106–117; and for stage directions, "Sanemori," *Kanze* (1970): 17–19.

gression from less explicit language to explication and comment and from less to more focus on the main character and his "tragedy." The first half of the play progresses from the introduction and words of the waki to the revelation of the shite as the warrior Sanemori. After the kyōgen's narration of the background of the warrior and his last battle, the second half progresses from the introductory song of the waki to the convergence of the themes, music, costume, dance, and rhythm in the finale. There Zeami reveals the reason for the attachment of the ghost of Sanemori to this world from which he has not been freed, his warrior hell.

Sanemori begins, as is the practice in many nō, with the silent entrance of the waki and his attendants, the wakizure, all of whom are dressed as priests. However, the nō does not continue with the standard short introductory song, as does *Takasago*, for example. Instead, in a *nanori*, "naming speech," delivered in informal prose, the kyōgen, the unnamed character who is dressed as an ordinary person, introduces himself as an inhabitant of Shinowara, the setting of the play. He also introduces the waki as His Reverence Taami. (The nanori is comparable in its position within the play to the prologue of the *Agamemnon* delivered by the nameless watchman.)

KYŌGEN: Such as he is, this person [I][52] lives in the village of Shinowara, in the province of Kaga. Now then, the successor to Yugyō, His Reverence Taami, who traveled here in accordance with the practice of that itinerant priest, offers sermons here everyday. But there is something strange about this: before or after the noontime services he carries on a monologue. Everyone says that this is strange. Because this person [I] regularly approaches the place from which he delivers sermons, everyone asks that he [I] inquire about the matter. Everyone, please stand informed of this. Everyone, please stand informed of this.

Contrary to the normal practice in warrior nō, Zeami uses the kyōgen rather than the waki for the delivery of the nanori, and he gives the waki's name. (In fact, it is unusual for a kyōgen to enter the stage at this point in a nō that features a ghost in the second half, as *Sanemori* does.) Thus the playwright attracts attention to the first words of the play and places more focus here on the waki than in other types of nō.[53] That does not mean

[52] The kyōgen speaks of himself as "this person," which of course means "I." No one in the audience would think otherwise. However, I translate literally the use of the pronouns in the Japanese text so that when a word designating the first-person pronoun and nothing else is used, as in the English "I," it will have its full impact.

[53] As it happens, the waki is also named in *Takasago*, but is not as essential to the development of the play as the waki is in *Sanemori* or in other warrior nō. In *Yorimasa*, for example, the nanori is of a type more characteristic of nō. In it, the waki, a priest, without naming himself, says that he has made pilgrimages through various provinces

that the kyōgen addresses the waki, for, although he is seated stage left, during the nanori he is not part of the dramatic action. Instead, the kyōgen addresses his remarks in the second person to an imaginary audience, as is suggested by his final words, "Everyone, please stand informed of this." And, like the watchman who at the end of the prologue of the *Agamemnon* (39) says, "I speak to those who understand . . . ," the kyōgen seems to address the audience of the theater.[54]

In this nanori, Zeami anticipates two later scenes within the nō. One is near the end of the maeba, the first half, where it is revealed that the waki's monologues are in reality conversations with Sanemori's ghost who cannot be seen by the other people at Shinowara. (This revelation is emphasized in the interlude scene.) The other scene is near the beginning of the nochiba, the second half of the nō. Because of the connection drawn in the nanori between the priest Taami and Yugyō, the founding priest of the Ji sect of Amida Buddhism, which the waki espouses,[55] the audience would realize that, like his predecessor Yugyō, Taami is traveling around Japan, proselytizing to rich and poor, giving sermons, and carrying out special religious services, odori nembutsu, which include music, song, and dance. Given Zeami's interest in connecting the main character of a nō with the arts appropriate to the theater, it seems highly likely that he prepares in the nanori for an element of performance: the suggestion of an odori nembutsu. Near the beginning of the nochiba, the *taiko*, a large drum used in all waki nō, but not in all warrior nō, accompanies the entrance of the shite in the form of the ghost of Sanemori. The use of the drum and the words of the text, which mention a service, suggest, in the light of the priest's connection with Yugyō mentioned only in the nanori, that a special religious service, the odori nembutsu, is taking place on behalf of Sanemori.[56] The choice of the priest Taami and the performance of the service on behalf of the warrior, who is the main character of the nō, are Zeami's additions to the epic version of Sanemori's tale. These are also the elements that help to integrate the dramatic characters into the performance of this

---

and is now on his way to Nara after his visit to the capital city and its temples and shrines.

[54] There is a difference of opinion among scholars as to whether the watchman addresses the audience or not. See E. Fraenkel, *Aeschylus Agamemnon*, 3 vols. (Oxford, 1962), 2: 24. All translations from the Greek are mine unless otherwise indicated. The text used for Aeschylus's works is the OCT, *Aeschyli septem quae supersunt tragoediae*, ed. Denys Page (Oxford, 1972).

[55] For the importance of Buddhism to nō, especially to warrior nō, see G. Renondeau, *Le bouddhisme dans les Nō* (Tokyo, 1950); on *Sanemori* see esp. 98–107. See also William R. LaFleur, *The Karma of Words: Buddhism and the Literary Arts in Medieval Japan* (Berkeley and Los Angeles, 1983), 116–132.

[56] On this point, see Kōsai, "Sakuhin kenkyū: Sanemori," 8.

nō, which is unique to the extent that the warrior nō featuring an old man as the shite is simultaneously a "ghost" nō and a topical nō.

After the kyōgen's speech and his withdrawal to a designated spot, stage back right, the first dan of *Sanemori* begins with a *sashi*, a song that does not follow a beat and is delivered in a smooth recitative by the waki and wakizure, who remain seated.[57] Within this sashi, the words, consonant with the priest's hieratic function, are not directed at a specific person, but are intended for anyone.

WAKI: Although Paradise is a place millions of miles away,
  A long way for one to be reborn,
  Here too in one's heart is Amida's country.
  The voices of people, both high and low,
  Are heard reciting the *nembutsu* [the prayer to Amida Buddha],
WAKIZURE: Both day and night in the garden of the Law,
WAKI: Truly the glory of Amida saves all—
WAKIZURE: By virtue of this Vow of His, who is there
WAKI: Who would be excluded!

The waki priest, beginning with quotations from Buddhist sutras,[58] says that Paradise is far away, a long way to be reborn, but then specifies with the word "here" that Amida's home is in one's heart. In content, the movement from one sutra to the other is from the distant Paradise to the proximate here, which is then defined more concretely by the mention of the voices of people in the congregation, both rich and poor, reciting the nembutsu. This reference to the congregation is connected in turn to the continuation of the sashi shared by the waki and the wakizure, where the priests' words clearly apply not only to the imaginary congregation, but because of Zeami's use of the word "all," to everyone. One learns that "the glory of Amida saves all," for according to the Ji sect of Buddhism, among others, the Vow assures that one nembutsu, invocation of Amida Buddha, is sufficient for salvation. The play begins on this optimistic and highly religious note, applicable to anyone in the audience, and comparable in importance to the dictum *pathei mathos*, "suffering entails learning," which appears near the beginning of the *Agamemnon* (177) and which

---

[57] Sanari (*Yōkyoku taikan*, 1246), with whom I agree, does not consider the nanori a part of the first dan, but separate from it; Nogami (*Kaichū yōkyoku zenshū*, 117), thinks that the nanori is dan one and that the sashi introduces the second dan; Yokomichi and Omote (*Yōkyokushū*, 266) also begin the second section of the nō with the sashi. This nanori and the presence of the kyōgen in the first part of the nō is unusual in a two-part "ghost" nō; see Kōsai, "Sakuhin kenkyū: Sanemori," 7. See further Sieffert, *La tradition secrète*, 352 n. 1, on the possibility that the nanori is a later addition to the nō.
[58] See *YKS*, 441 nn. 107 and 105.

Aeschylus does not apply to any dramatic character specifically when the dictum is first expressed.

The first dan of *Sanemori*, the jo section, concludes with the next sub-unit (shōdan), an *ageuta*, a high-pitched song sung by the waki and waki-zure, in a regular rhythm. The song, following a beat set by the two drummers, functions as a musical conclusion to the first dan, which was introduced with a speech and began with a recitative; the ageuta is like the kyū part of the dan. Because the first three lines of the ageuta are borrowed from the words of His Reverence Ippen (the Yugyō mentioned by the kyōgen and the founder of the Ji sect),[59] they are closely connected with Ta-ami's priestly function.

WAKI AND WAKIZURE: Just one person even if alone,
    Let him pursue Buddha's holy name,
    Let him pursue Buddha's holy name,
    When everyone leaves the garden of the Law.
    Both hearts that believe and those that do not
    His Vow draws in: will anyone pass through the net? No.
    Both people who believe and those who do not—
    He will help them take passage
    And go to that country aboard the ship of the Law
    That floats along the Way easily, as it is said.
    That floats along the Way easily, as it is said.

Ordinarily in nō the ageuta, appearing at the end of dan one, is a *michi-yuki* or "travel" song enumerating places visited by the waki (as priest or courtier) in his wanderings, culminating in the place in which the play is set.[60] In *Sanemori*, to the extent that Amida's Vow is compared to a ship that takes souls to Paradise, the ageuta contains a reference to travel. In performance, however, the song serves more as a verbal introduction to the shite's entrance than as a reference to the waki's travels. (The waki's function is introduced in this play by the kyōgen.) With the words "take passage and go to that country," the shite appears on the hashigakari, the bridge leading to the stage.

Since there is no special entrance music or call to announce the shite, as in many nō, dan one flows visually into dan two with greater smoothness than in many nō and, I would suggest, creates a special effect—the inclu-

[59] See ibid., 266 n. 13.

[60] In *Takasago*, for example, there is a michiyuki. In *Yorimasa*, the waki mentions places, some of them famous for their association with poetry and poets. The *tsukizerifu*, the "arrival speech" following the michiyuki, is formulaic in nō; the waki says that he has hastened, and he has reached such and such a place, which is the setting of the play. In *Yorimasa*, the waki says that he has reached Uji.

sion of the shite in the saving power of Buddha. (The notation of instrumental music does not date from Zeami's time, but I work on the assumption that there is continuity in the music he wrote for this play and the music used today.) The words "help them take passage" in the waki's song are, to be sure, not directed at anyone in particular in their reference; however, since the shite becomes visible to the audience at this point, the words become associated in the audience's mind with the shite. Furthermore, since later in the nō, after the shite instructs the waki to send the other people away, Sanemori becomes one person in the "garden" (that is, one consonant with the meaning of Ippen's words, "Just one person even if alone"), the words are brought to bear upon the main character. At the end of dan one, the shite is one of many who have come to listen to the priest's sermons; later, the play sharpens its focus on the identity of that one person and his salvation.

The second dan at the beginning of the first part of the ha section is in three parts, each delivered by the shite. These are a sashi in melody, a section in speech, and finally another section in melody. There is no special entrance music or announcement of the shite, as I mentioned, nor is there an entrance song for the shite to sing, as there is in *Takasago*. Instead, the shite already implicated in the performance by the waki's words is drawn further in through an integration of his words and the instrumental music—his first words, "the sound of the flutes," may point to the flute that was played on stage during the preceding ageuta and while the shite was entering.

SHITE: (*Sashi in melody*)
The sound of the flutes is heard in the distance above a lone cloud,
A holy multitude comes before the setting sun to receive [me].[61]
(*The shite, still on the hashigakari, turns toward the stage and joins
his hands in prayer. He is dressed in the costume of an old man,
wears an "old-man" mask and carries prayer beads.*)[62]
Ah, on this holy day as well a purple cloud hovers above.
(*In speech*)
The sound of the bell and of voices reciting the nembutsu are heard.
Ah, well, it is now time to listen to the sermons,
(*The shite faces forward.*)

[61] This translation, which is literal like the others, is punctuated in such a way that when one line flows into another, even though the result is a run-on sentence, the syntax in my English reflects that fluidity of style.
[62] There are many more stage directions written into the actors' texts today than I present in this chapter. However, that there is a consistent progression toward more extensive and more vigorous movement on the part of the shite is not undermined by my omissions.

49

But, even if he [I] were not trying to hurry, [as he is,]
Waves of old age would make the going difficult
And he cannot approach those in the garden of the Law.
Yet, he will listen from outside.
  (In melody)
With one sincere invocation of Buddha's name
The hope of enlightenment that comes from Buddha's glory shines
  forth without clouds,
But the path for one whose vision is impaired by old age is not clear.
  (The shite enters the stage, sits down, and joins his hands in prayer
  once again.)
Come now, although he [I] is a little late,
The distance from here is not far.
Namu Amida Butsu [the nembutsu, a prayer invoking Amida Buddha].

The first two lines that are spoken by the shite in the nō are, like the first words of the waki, a quotation, from the words of Jakushō, an eleventh-century monk.[63] In the third line of this important shōdan, Zeami uses his own words again, rather than a quotation, and turns to the dramatic present time "on this . . . day." Appropriately, in the spoken section of the dan, the words, more prosaic in content, are directed to the shite's own thought, namely that he too should attend the sermons, but that he is too old. (The reference to old age draws attention to the appearance of the shite playing the role of an old man, to his wig and mask, as well as to his posture and movements.) In the final and melodic section at the end of the dan, the shite adds that he has not yet reached enlightenment: he says that the path is not clear. Ostensibly the words refer to the path into the "garden" that he cannot see because his eyes are blurred; however, they are also intended to suggest the path to enlightenment, which the audience discovers that the old man takes during the course of the nō. This second dan, important as an introduction of the shite's "tragedy" to the play, concludes on an optimistic note when the shite says that the distance is not far and repeats the nembutsu—Namu Amida Butsu—a prayer that he himself has said one needs to intone but once to be saved. His words prepare for the ending of the nō where he prays and repents and the audience is assured that he will be saved.

The jo-ha-kyū of the second dan is manifest in the movement of the shite from the hashigakari to a position in front of the waki, who is seated stage left, and from a spoken to a sung delivery. (The sashi, also in melody, serves as an introduction.) In terms of content, there is a transition from

----

[63] See *YKS*, 267 n. 19. The next to the last line of the sashi is also a quotation, from the *Kammuryōju* sutra.

quotation to Zeami's own words and from the suggestion of the old man's tragedy to a solution for it, namely that Buddha's grace will save him. The preparatory function of the content of the first two dan in *Sanemori* becomes increasingly apparent as the nō develops; in this respect they are comparable to the first choral song in the *Agamemnon* and its preparatory, indeed proleptic, function.[64] To put it simply, there the chorus of elders hints at the defeat of Troy and presents an account of the sacrifice of Iphigenia, both causes for the tragedies that ensue; repeats the dictum that one learns through suffering; and expresses the hope that all will turn out well, as it does by the end of the *Eumenides*.

The third dan of *Sanemori*, like the first two, progresses from speech to song: it contains a *mondō*, speeches and a dialogue, first; a *kakeai*, a sung exchange, second; and an ageuta, a song, third. Specifically, it progresses from unmetered speech to unmetered song to metered song and finally to metered song that follows a beat. At first the waki and the shite speak, then they recite melodically in a section that begins as the shite lowers his joined hands and, seated, listens to the waki.

WAKI: Well now, old man, indeed you are not negligent about the daily invocations. Therefore, this person [I][65] thinks you are a devout person. As it is, other people cannot see your presence and all the people are wondering among themselves whom he [I] meets and what he says. Now [literally, today], give your name.

SHITE: *(He looks at the waki.)*
This is an unexpected question you ask!
Let him [me] inform you from the start that he comes from faraway and is but a country person. So he does not necessarily have a name. If he had a name worth mentioning, he *would* give his name.[66]
Only, your Reverence's arrival is utterly as if Amida had come to receive him.
(At this point in the dialogue, the shite faces forward and sings one line in a melody that, like a sashi, does not follow a beat, but is delivered more insistently than the words that preceded.)
It is fortunate that he has lived long enough
(In speech)

[64] See A. Lebeck, *The Oresteia: A Study in Language and Structure* (Washington, D.C., 1971), for a detailed discussion of prolepsis in the trilogy.

[65] The waki and the shite use the third person both of themselves and of each other. Although a Japanese audience would have no difficulty in distinguishing the one as a first person and the other as a second, I translate the former in the third person, the latter in the second person.

[66] As Shimazaki pointed out, the Japanese text here suggests that the priest thinks that the old man is somebody, but the old man, being from the country, thinks he is not worthy of being considered as even an ordinary person.

To experience the occasion of these recitations.
   (In melody)
It has the feeling of a blind turtle's discovery of a log floating in the
ocean or of one eagerly awaiting and seeing the bloom of the udonge.[67]
The happiness of one who has had a rare experience in his old age is
exceedingly great. Tears of joy on his sleeves are abundant.
   (*The shite looks down and then up.*)
Even as he is, can he be reborn in the land of peace and happiness?—
this thought causes incomparable joy. On such an occasion, to have to
give his name [as if it were important], a name that belongs to this
world of blindness and continual cycles of rebirth, is regrettable.

Although the revelation of the main character's name is common in nō and
in mondō, Zeami places special emphasis on it here and in the continuation of the dialogue. In fact, in the *Sarugaku dangi*[68] we are told that it is
difficult to deliver lines that are spoken and not sung and that few can
master the technique, which demands that an actor truly imitate the character he is portraying and not be distracted. Zeami's son mentions his father's talents in this regard. The example cited is *seme*, meaning "would,"
in the shite's line of *Sanemori*—"he *would* give his name." The words of
the nō text and the emphasis on the line in the treatise suggest that the
revelation of the name is particularly important, perhaps even a first step
toward the old man's salvation, the main issue of the play.

As the dialogue continues, the priest, sympathetic toward the old man,
claims that he can repent and be saved, but the old man, who has expressed his hesitation both in gesture and in words, delays the disclosure
of his identity. The dialogue, the only occasion in the play in which there
is any verbal confrontation between two characters on stage, becomes increasingly engrossing as it focuses on the old man, who asks that the other
people be sent away, and who, although he does not identify himself at
first, mentions the name of Sanemori for the first time. This dialogue, a
mondō, is not unlike sections of tragedy in iambic trimeter, the most prosaic meter, which at certain points assume the form of a stichomythy, sin-
gle- or double-line exchanges. The difference is that in the nō, the prose
dialogue and single-line exchange progress in the direction of melody as
the stichomythy does not.[69]

   [67] The lines refer to parables of Buddhist origin; see Sieffert, *La tradition secrète*, 353
n. 13. The udonge flower blooms but once every three thousand years. Thus seeing its
bloom is as likely to occur as that a blind turtle, who surfaces once every one hundred
years, should discover in the ocean a floating log with a hole in it and pass his head
through that hole.
   [68] *ZZ*, 285, and Rimer, 212.
   [69] In the mondō of *Yorimasa*, names and parts of the setting at Uji are mentioned; in

(The shite looks forward.)

WAKI: Indeed, what the old man says is exceedingly reasonable; however, you could be saved through repentance of your sins. Just name your name.

(The shite looks at the waki.)

SHITE: Then he cannot avoid giving his name?

WAKI: That is right. Quickly give your name.

SHITE: In that case have the people before you sent away. And he will approach you and give his name.

(The shite stands up, goes to the middle of the stage, and sits down.)

WAKI: Of course, the appearance of the old man is not seen by the eyes of the other people. And yet, if that is your wish, he shall have the people move away. And you come near and name your name.

SHITE: In the past Saitō Bettō Sanemori of Nagai was defeated and killed in the battle here at Shinowara. Word of it has no doubt reached you.

WAKI: He was a Heike samurai, a famous warrior of the bow. But the story of that battle is of no benefit. Just name your name.

SHITE: Ah, but it is relevant. It is said that in the water of the pond before you

(The shite faces forward.)

Sanemori's hair and beard were washed.

(The shite faces the waki.)

Therefore, it may be that an attachment on his part stays behind.[70] Even today among the people of this area it is said that the form of the ghost is seen.

WAKI: Then is it seen by people even now?

Inasmuch as news of the appearance of the ghost of Sanemori to the priest had first reached the capital city within a few years before the play's production and the ghost continued to be seen in Shinowara, the audience's attention might be attracted to the words, "even today it is said," and might be prepared for the identification of the old man as Sanemori. Zeami capitalizes on the contemporary event for dramatic effect in this section[71] and uses it to prepare for the appearance of the ghost of Sanemori

---

Atsumori, different kinds of flutes; and in *Tadanori*, an identification of the shite's dwelling.

[70] This line refers to the belief, according to Buddhist thought, that the attachment of part of the dead person's spirit to the world of the living is a hell, that is, part of the karma or cycles of rebirth that living creatures experience.

[71] "The idea of such supernatural manifestation was not incredible or unfamiliar to the Japanese of the Middle Ages" (Wilson, "Two Shuramono," 415). Kōsai, "Sakuhin kenkyū: Sanemori," 7, discusses how *Sanemori* is like both other *genzai nō* (contemporary event pieces) and *mugen nō* (ghost nō) and thus has a double structure. See also

as the nochijite, the shite of the nochiba, to the Yugyō priest, just as he was reported to have actually appeared to the Yugyō priest in the village of Shinowara. But first Zeami further engages the audience's attention with a scene in which a dramatic character, the priest, learns what the audience knows. The effect is, within its own context, comparable to the creation of suspense built into the *Persians*. There Aeschylus withholds until the second episode of the play news of an event that the audience knows from history, but the characters in the play do not, namely, the Persians' defeat. The revelation of that news to the queen of Persia is an important turning point in the dramatic development. In *Sanemori*, Zeami maintains suspense by delaying the moment in which the warrior's name is disclosed.

The mondō continues with the shite's recitation in melody of a poem written by the warrior Yorimasa, which Zeami uses as preparation for the revelation of the old man's identity:

SHITE: A tree not seen among the many other treetops on a mountain
　　When in bloom betrays itself as a cherry tree.[72]
　　Observe the same thing in the old tree.

The waki, upon hearing the shite's words, draws an inference from the comparison that he has been talking to Sanemori.

WAKI: (*In melody*)
　　How strange! The story about Sanemori's past
　　Which he heard, he thought was about another person.
　　But how strange, it was about you.
　　So then, you are the ghost of Sanemori, are you?

At this climactic moment of revelation, the shite looks at the waki and in speech says:

SHITE: *I* am the ghost of Sanemori.
　　While the soul is in the other world,
　　A part of the spirit remains in this world.

This response contains the only appearance in the play of an explicitly first person pronoun, *ware*, which one assumes would be noticeable because in Japanese texts it is not used frequently and because in present-day perfor-

---

Yokomichi Mario, "Sanemori no hanashi" (Discussion of Sanemori), in *Yōkyoku kyō-gen* (Nō and Kyōgen), *Nihon bungaku kenkyū shiryōhankōkai* (Tokyo, 1981), 170. My discussion is indebted to this article, pages 169–178, in which Yokomichi discusses the structure of the nō and compares it to other warrior nō.
72 Yorimasa's poem is found in the anthology *Shikashū* and in the *Heike*, book 1, chapter 15.

mances, at least, the shite assumes a very expressive tone in his voice to deliver the line as he turns his body and faces the waki.[73] The language approaches a high point in the ha part of the dan, as the melody begins to dominate over speech, and it reaches that high point when the melody is interrupted by the one line of speech in which the waki asks whether the old man is the ghost of Sanemori and the speech in which the shite identifies himself.

After the revelation of the old man's identity, a verbal climax in the nō, Zeami increases the rhythmic intensity. The dan now progresses from unmetered speech and unmetered song at the beginning to metered song that, after one line spoken by the shite, is not interrupted by speech as the dialogue was. This part of the dialogue is the kakeai, comparable to an epirrhematic exchange in tragedy in that there is some alternation between speech and song, but different from it in that melody dominates. The shite and waki, who have been talking to and at each other, in the kakeai continue each other's thought, so that by the end, one cannot distinguish either character from the other.

WAKI: (*In melody*)
  In sinful attachment to this transient world
SHITE: (*In speech*)
  More than two hundred years have elapsed
WAKI: (*In melody, which continues to the end of the dan.*)
  But still he cannot be saved, floating on Shinowara's
SHITE: Pond, in vain, waves wash against the shore at night
WAKI: And by day without distinction in the darkness of the soul
SHITE: Whether in a state of dreams
WAKI: Or in a state of wakefulness
SHITE: He is obsessed with this thought.[74]

---

[73] In *Yorimasa*, the waki uses "I" of himself at the beginning of the nō; the shite uses *waga*, another explicitly first-person pronoun, to refer to a poet other than himself; and the chorus, in the ageuta at the end of the maeba, identifies Yorimasa, when speaking for him, with the first-person pronoun in the line, "I am the ghost of Yorimasa"—the line is both similar in itself and analogous in its position to the line in which Sanemori identifies himself. In *Tadanori*, the first-person pronoun is used differently, but just as effectively—it is the first word of the shite's narration of his story. In *Atsumori*, the shite uses "I" to identify himself in the mondō; it is used also by the shite and the tsure in the second dan of the maeba. The choice of one pronoun over another in the Japanese language is usually determined by an interest in marking the status of the speaker. I am suggesting that the limited use of the straightforward "I" in these nō marks an important juncture in the development of the plays.

[74] A prose rendering of this passage might read as follows: "He has been bound to this world for more than two hundred years and still is lost at Shinowara. There like impermanent waves that wash against the shore of the pond, both day and night without distinguishing between them, his darkened soul, whether asleep or awake [that is, in a dream world or reality], thinks of this only."

The syntax of the sung exchange is as fluid as the melody and as the semantic content, in which Zeami draws a parallel between the waves rolling against the shore of the pond at Shinowara and the soul being tossed by an obsession. Furthermore, Sanemori's spirit, because it is compared to the waves in the pond, is related to the historical site at Shinowara where Sanemori's head was washed; in the play this is the dramatic setting. Finally, Zeami expands upon and is explicit about the old man's tragic condition, only alluded to earlier: the ghost remains attached to the world.

Before the third dan and the first half of the nō end, Zeami allows the kakeai to flow into a metered song, an ageuta, which follows the musical beat of the drummers. The ageuta is introduced by the shite's line in which Zeami begins to allude to a poem.

SHITE: At Shinowara very much like hoarfrost on the grass is
    the old man
CHORUS: Like hoarfrost on the grass is the old man.
    With him let no one find fault,
    Temporarily revealed—
    Sanemori appears.
    (The shite looks eagerly at the waki.)
    Please, he asks, do not let his name leak out.
    Talk about his past will bring shame.
    (The shite looks down and then forward. He stands up.)
    When one thought he was rising
    And leaving his holy presence,
    At the edge of Shinowara's pond,
    (The shite moves forward on the stage.)
    His shape faded into an apparition and disappeared.
    His shape faded into an apparition and disappeared.

At the end of the song, the shite leaves the stage and exits along the hashigakari—that is, he "disappears" from view, as if to follow a stage direction suggested in the chorus's last words.[75] In fact, in this part of the nō, the words and action converge to the extent that even the content of the poem quoted is descriptive of what is seen.[76] In it the reference to hoarfrost on the grass is a poetic expression for the gray hair of an old man. In the original context of the poem, an old man goes out in a robe tempo-

---

[75] The words are almost formulaic at the end of maeba in shura nō, as well as in other nō featuring a spirit in the nochiba. In *Yorimasa*, the chorus sings, "But hardly had he given his name before he disappeared"; in *Atsumori*, the chorus sings, "His form disappeared out of sight"; and in *Tadanori*, "It disappears." In each of the nō, the last line is repeated and in each the shite leaves the stage.

[76] The poem, written by Ariwara no Yukihira, comes from the *Ise monogatari* (The Tales of Ise), no. 114.

rarily worn for a hunting expedition; in the nō, the shite, playing the role of an old man, has appeared, only temporarily dressed in ordinary clothes. (In the nochiba, the second half, he returns dressed in the armor of a warrior.) It is in the final ageuta of the maeba that Zeami focuses most sharply on the old man's appearance, his name, and his expression of shame.

Through the first three dan, representing the maeba, the structure of *Sanemori* is both similar to and different from that of *Takasago*, for example, and of the other shura nō. In fact, up to the end of the third dan the similarities approach in number those found in the three plays of Aeschylus that I shall consider in the next chapter, the *Suppliants*, the *Agamemnon*, and the *Persians*. It is as if Aeschylus, like Zeami, had a dramatic structure in mind, which he varied in view of the purposes of the particular plays. The jo-ha-kyū structure is the reason Zeami gives for altering the specific arrangement of shōdan within the dan of his plays. And yet, that same progression accounts for the similarities among his nō. For example, *Takasago* and the four shura nō all move in the direction of more melody, more movement on stage, a revelation of the shite's identity, and more straightforward explication of the main character's tragedy as the play progresses.[77]

Before the nochiba of the warrior nō begins, the jo-ha-kyū progression is interrupted by an ai-kyōgen, an interlude scene.[78] In *Sanemori*, the kyōgen, the same character and actor who delivered the nanori, moves forward on stage and, in conversational, prose-style speech, begins as if speaking to someone who has witnessed the action of the play, but could not see the shite.[79]

KYŌGEN: What? Are you saying that His Reverence was speaking to himself? In that case, I think I will go right to him and make an inquiry.

[77] For a comparison of the structure of the maeba of these five plays, see Appendix One, part 1. For a comparison of the structure of warrior plays, see Kobayashi Yasuji, "Heike monogatari to shura nō: Yōkyoku Tadanori, Sanemori o chūshin ni" (The Tale of the Heike and Warrior Nō: Centering on *Tadanori* and *Sanemori*), in *Gunkimono to sono shūhen* (Military Stories and Related Subjects) (Tokyo, 1969), 683–714.

[78] The kyōgen scenes are not discussed by Zeami in the context of jo-ha-kyū and thus present some problem in a discussion of the structure. However, since we know from his treatise *Shūdōsho* that Zeami used some sort of kyōgen interlude in two-part nō, that such a scene appears in the holograph of the nō *Eguchi*, and that these scenes are well attested in the eighteenth-century texts, I include them. On this subject, see Hare, *Zeami's Style*, 69. On the importance of the ai-kyōgen in the play *Takasago*, see ibid., 98.

[79] The text of the kyōgen section that follows, not included in Yokomichi and Omote's edition, is taken from Sanari, *Yōkyoku taikan*. It is the Ōkuraryū koshahon, a text dating from 1789. The first- and second-person pronouns do not appear in the Japanese text; however, I use them here in order to convey the colloquial tone of the language.

(He goes to stage center, turns to the waki, and sits down.)
Today I fear that I am late.

WAKI: Why have you been negligent?

KYŌGEN: I wanted to come much more quickly, but am late because of
many obligations. Now, I want to make an inquiry of Your Reverence.
Every day at the noon services you carry on a dialogue with yourself
and I hear that everyone at Shinowara is wondering about this. Since
they know that I am a person who customarily approaches you, they
have asked me to make inquiry. What is this all about?

WAKI: How is that? The people at Shinowara are wondering about my
carrying on a monologue at the time of the noon-hour invocations?

KYŌGEN: That's exactly right.

WAKI: Pertaining to that subject, I want to pose a question. What I am
going to ask is unexpected, but tell me, if you know, about the way in
which Saitō Bettō Sanemori of Nagai died long ago at the battle here in
Shinowara.

KYŌGEN: This is an unexpected question you ask. I do not know much
about the matter, but will tell you the story as it reached me through
hearsay.

WAKI: I appreciate your kind consideration.

At this point the kyōgen turns toward the audience as if to narrate a
story for its benefit, rather than to answer the waki's question. The narrative mode of this scene, not unlike the mode of messenger scenes in
Greek tragedy, includes both past and historical present tense verbs.

KYŌGEN: Well then, the person called Saitō Bettō Sanemori was from
a Northern province, a person who in the middle of his career went to
the Minamoto [Genji] side. It is said that he received the domain of
Nagai in Musashi province and gave himself the name Nagai no Saitō
Bettō. At the time of the battle at Ishibashiyama he again goes to serve
the Taira [Heike].

The battle at Shinowara here, it is said, took place well over two
hundred years ago. However, the Taira, wanting to fight Kiso Yoshi-
naka [the Genji leader] and further to destroy Yoritomo, sends a force
of more than 100,000 cavalry to the Northern province. Lord Kiso
with 50,000 cavalry went to meet them. They say various encounters
took place.

Sanemori was an extraordinary old warrior. His hair and beard were
white. So wanting to die in battle attired like a young person, he dyed
his hair and beard with black ink. His armor plaques were made for
him of tanned leather. The protector at his throat was made of the
plant *saikachi*. They say that he looked like a first-class young warrior.

58

However, during the encounter, when the Taira were defeated in the battle and when Sanemori held back and waited for a good rival, one of Lord Kiso's quicker men came forward and cut off his [Sanemori's] head beneath the ears. In the presence of Lord Kiso [to whom the soldier presented the head] it was said, "There is something special about this head." During various discussions, there were some who say that it is Sanemori's head and others that it is not. "At any rate," someone said, "have it washed and we shall see."

When he had it washed in the water of the pond here at Shinowara and looked at it, it was the head of no one other than Saitō Bettō. Then moved by Sanemori's example, it is said, everyone, saying that any warrior who carries a bow like him should try to be true to his aspirations, shed tears.

(The kyōgen turns toward the waki.)
Anyhow, that's the sort of thing I learned through hearsay. But why was it you asked? I wonder because it is an unusual inquiry.
WAKI: You have related this story in detail. I asked for no other reason than that recently on the occasion of the noon-hour invocations an old man appears out of nowhere [and as usual came again today]. When I asked him who he was he related the story of a battle of long ago and had scarcely said that he is the ghost of Sanemori when I lost sight of his figure at the edge of the pond!
KYŌGEN: Oh. Around the time of the noon-hour services you [seem to] carry on a dialogue with yourself because the spirit of Sanemori appears. Therefore [since he does appear], I hope you will pray for the repose of Sanemori.
WAKI: As I too think that way, let me go to the edge of the pond and hold a special odori nembutsu service. Let us pray for his repose. Make an announcement of this to the people of Shinowara.
KYŌGEN: Leave it to me.
(The kyōgen rises, moves to the right, faces the audience, and makes the announcement.)
Everyone, listen. In order to pray for the repose of Sanemori, His Reverence will hold a special odori nembutsu service at the edge of the pond at Shinowara. So all and everyone at Shinowara please attend and stand informed, stand informed.
(The kyōgen returns to the waki and faces him.)
I have made the announcement.
WAKI: I appreciate your special attention [to this matter].
(The kyōgen exits to his seat at stage back right.)[80]

[80] The kyōgen's long narration is slightly different in Koyama's edition, pages 189–

Although a kyōgen scene has not always been treated by audiences in the nō theaters with respect and although it does interrupt the jo-ha-kyū of the nō, at the same time it often, as in the case of *Sanemori*, provides background about the main character in a more straightforward manner than anywhere else in the play, verifies what the audience has seen enacted in the maeba, and prepares for the shite's appearance in the nochiba. For some of these reasons, the kyōgen scenes can be compared to messenger scenes in Greek tragedy.

Verification of what has preceded is not the normal function of a messenger in Greek tragedy; however, in Aeschylus's *Agamemnon* the herald does confirm what Clytemnestra has already claimed to be true, namely that the Greeks have won the Trojan War; in *Sanemori*, the kyōgen and the waki verify the fact that the priest has been talking to the ghost of Sanemori and resolve one issue pertaining to the dramatic action. The former verifies the truth of an event that took place outside the dramatic time and setting; the latter verifies an "event" that is contemporaneous with the dramatic time and setting. In addition, just as the kyōgen presents infor-

---

190. A translation of his text is as follows: "First of all, Sanemori was a person from a Northern province who went to the Minamoto [Genji] side and was granted as his feudal domain Nagai in Musashi. That's why he called himself Nagai no Saitō Bettō Sanemori. After the battle at Ishibashiyama he went to the capital and served Munemori of the Taira [Heike]. Now, thinking that he would surely be killed in the battle of the North, he pleaded with Munemori. His wish granted, he traveled day and night away from the capital [and went North].

"At the battle of Shinowara here the Taira were defeated. When everyone else withdrew, Sanemori, thinking, 'Oh, for a good opponent whom I could fight in battle to the point of death,' alone turned back. While he was engaged in battle, a soldier came forth from the side of Lord Kiso, at least that's what I heard, and from behind cut off his head and let it fall. Now, when he took the head before Lord Kiso, Lord Kiso, looking at it, asked, 'Whose head is this?' Some people said, 'That is the head of Sanemori.' And others said, 'No, that is not so.' It is quite understandable that he [Lord Kiso] could not tell. Since Sanemori was a very old warrior who wanted to make himself look like a young man and die in battle, he dyed his hair and beard with black ink. It is said the black ink ran down and dirtied his face so his identity was difficult to determine.

"Someone suggested, 'At any rate, wash it and see.' When they washed it in that pond at Shinowara, lo, it was actually Nagai no Saitō Bettō Sanemori. 'How amazing! A warrior of the bow should try to be true to his ideals.' These were the words of praise."

After the waki reacts to the kyōgen's tale and tells him about the appearance of the ghost of Sanemori in words that are the same as those of the Sanari text, the kyōgen's response, according to Koyama, is as follows: "This is amazing! How extraordinary it is! Then there is no doubt. It must be the spirit of Sanemori. Why do I say so?—Since Your Reverence gives blessed sermons every day, he, thinking that by listening to them he will be saved, has made an appearance every day. That is what I think. If you think so too, I hope you will pray for the repose of Sanemori."

After this speech the texts of Sanari and Koyama are the same again. Itō Masayoshi's version of the long kyōgen speech is again different, *Yōkyoku*, 111–112. Unlike the versions of Sanari and Koyama, Itō includes the kyōgen's reference to Sanemori's request that he be permitted to wear a brocade robe.

mation about the battle at Shinowara in the past and Sanemori's role in it and prepares for the ghost's arrival and the priest's prayers on his behalf, the herald in the *Agamemnon* provides an account of what happened at Troy and, with a narration of the travels home of the Greeks, a preparation for Agamemnon's arrival on stage. Furthermore, both scenes are self-contained: the herald rounds off his final speech with the formulaic-sounding words,[81] "Be assured that all the things you have heard are true" (680); after a request that the priest pray for the repose of the warrior Sanemori, a formula itself in kyōgen scenes, the kyōgen concludes that he has made an announcement and the waki thanks him.[82] In neither scene does the playwright suggest that there is anything more for the nameless character to say.

There are, as might be expected, differences between messenger and kyōgen scenes. Many, if not all, two-part nō could be viewed or read and make sense without the interlude scenes, for the kyōgen does not bring news; there could just as well be an intermission in place of a kyōgen scene to allow the shite time to change costume. (There are more than a half dozen two-part nō that do not have a kyōgen scene. In one-part nō, in the warrior play *Kiyotsune*, for example, there is no kyōgen scene at all; however, kyōgen actors may appear in these. Three of Aeschylus's plays, the *Libation Bearers, Suppliants,* and *Eumenides,* do not feature messenger scenes involving long narrative speeches.) One could say that the herald scene of the *Agamemnon* and the messenger scene of the *Persians* are not indispensable, inasmuch as the audience is told in the former by Agamemnon and Cassandra about the outcome of the war and in the latter by the queen and Xerxes, and in neither of these is the messenger scene required so that an actor may change costume. However, important additions to the development of the two tragedies are contained within these scenes, as is not always the case in kyōgen scenes of nō. I shall discuss the messenger scene of the *Persians* in the next chapter; in the *Agamemnon,* the specific

---

[81] On the formulaic expressions in messenger speeches, see Bernard M. W. Knox, "Traditional Structure and Formula in the Tragic Narrative Speech" (Diss., Yale University, 1948).

[82] There is much of a formulaic nature in the kyōgen scenes. For example, we find that in *Atsumori* after the kyōgen and the waki introduce themselves to each other, the waki says that he wants to ask the kyōgen a question that is extraordinary—namely, to ask him to tell the story of Atsumori. The kyōgen says, as in *Sanemori,* that the question is unexpected and that he does not know the details, but then turns to the audience and tells the story. Afterward he claims puzzlement over the question. In the scene the waki admits that he was the one who killed Atsumori and says that he will pray for the warrior's soul. The ending of the scene is of a more common type than the kyōgen's announcement to the people in *Sanemori.* In *Atsumori,* the kyōgen invites the waki to call on him if he needs anything. In another nō, *Miwa,* the kyōgen, like the one in *Sanemori,* apologizes for being late.

details of the king's role in the war, of the gods' punishment of the Greeks on their return home, and of the fate of Menelaus are among the subjects treated by the herald, but not elsewhere in the play. In the *Seven against Thebes*, a play that, like those of Sophocles and Euripides, includes a report of a tragic event contemporaneous with the dramatic time, there would be no justification for the lament at the end without the news that the war is over and the two brothers have died.

Even in those nō in which the kyōgen have an important role to play—for example, in *Funa Benkei*, which features the kyōgen as a boatman who provides passage for Benkei, or in *Dōjōji*, which features a group of kyōgen actors who set up a bell to be dedicated at the temple, Dōjōji, and under which the shite is transformed from a dancer to a serpent[83]—the scenes are not so much a part of the jo-ha-kyū as they are the playwright's opportunity to entertain the audience with a touch of humor or down-to-earth talk and action. The nurse scene in the *Libation Bearers* provides the closest parallel to these from among Aeschylus's plays. In the scene, an ordinary character comments on the falseness of Clytemnestra's tears and Aegisthus's probable pleasure at hearing the news that Orestes is dead, and tells how she reared the child Orestes from the time he was born. None of the information is absolutely essential to the development of the play;[84] the scene relaxes the tension, is down-to-earth, and, like some kyōgen scenes, serves as a break, about two-thirds of the way through the play, before a major action: in the tragedy, the arrival of Aegisthus and the deaths of him and Clytemnestra; in the nō, the reappearance of the shite and an account of his or her story. The nurse's speech is not necessary to Aegisthus's arrival any more than the kyōgen speech is necessary to introduce the nochijite. Both scenes prepare.

In *Sanemori*, the kyōgen scene assumes unusual importance in being the only place in which the odori nembutsu is mentioned explicitly in the play. (In *Michimori*, a warrior nō not written by Zeami, the kyōgen announces prayers on behalf of the warrior and these are realized, as in *Sanemori*, with the playing of the taiko. In other nō, such as the warrior play *Tsunemasa*, which also was not written by Zeami, there is an announcement of a *kangenkō*, a musical Buddhist service. Sometimes the "service" is real-

---

[83] Neither of these plays was written by Zeami; in fact, they both are probably late nō, written by Kanze Kojirō Nobumitsu (1435–1516). The translation of the former can be found in *The Noh Drama*, vol. I, under the auspices of the Nippon Gakujutsu Shinkōkai (The Japan Society for the Promotion of Science), hereafter NGS (Tokyo and Vermont, 1955), 161–182, and the latter in Donald Keene, *20 Plays of the Nō Theatre* (New York and London, 1970), 241–252.

[84] One might argue, however, that when Apollo says in the *Eumenides* that a mother is not a true parent, as a father is (658–661), his arguments are strengthened by the nurse's tale of how she, not Clytemnestra, cared for the baby Orestes.

ized with musical accompaniment, in *Tsunemasa* with flute music.) Without the kyōgen scene and the kyōgen's specific reference to the service, the
waki's first words in the nochiba, "Come now, let us pray for that ghost
with a special recitation of prayers"; his mention of a bell, of voices of
prayer, and of the prayers themselves; and the arrival of the shite to the
accompaniment of the taiko drum and other instruments, might very well
have evoked a hint of the odori nembutsu, the special service performed
by priests of the Ji sect. But with the interlude scene, Zeami prepares fully
for its enactment and removes any ambiguity about the form he intends it
to take. At the beginning of the nochiba, the playing of the three drums
and the flute and the singing of the waki and the wakizure to their accompaniment provide a dramatic version of the religious memorial service,
part of the milieu of priests who follow the example of Yugyō. To be sure,
Sanemori is not a poet or an instrumentalist; however, he attends the
priest's services, and the priest is a character especially well-suited to the
performance of these services, which historically involve entertainment.
Therefore, the connection between the waki, the performance, and the
shite is a natural one. Zeami has chosen his subject well for this play.[85]

In accordance with Zeami's division of nō into dan, *Sanemori* continues
in the nochiba, the second half, with the ha section and dan four, five, and
six. However, as Yokomichi has interpreted the spirit of Zeami's construction of a nō, the nochiba has its own dan one, two, and so forth. For the
sake of analysis, I shall divide the nochiba into six dan, that is, the customary five found in the structure of a full nochiba, plus the extra dan that
represents Zeami's lengthening of the second half of this particular nō. In
effect, dan one, two, and three of the nochiba are actually dan four of the
nō as a whole and represent a continuation of the middle part of the ha
section.

Dan one of the nochiba begins as the waki stands up and calls for special
prayers:

WAKI: Let them [us] pray for that ghost with a special recitation
    of prayers.

Then he and his attendants, the wakizure, go to the center of the stage and
sing an ageuta, here, as elsewhere at the beginning of the nochiba, called a
machiutai, "a waiting song." It comprises the whole of the first dan, which
is shorter than dan one of the maeba.

---

[85] Aeschylus achieves a similar relationship between character and performance, as I
shall argue in the next chapter, in the *Persians*: the messenger, in the wake of reporting
the details of battles in which the Persians were defeated, calls for a lament. As is natural
for those defeated in war and those who have lost their loved ones, the Persian elders
who make up the chorus engage in a lament, the most important musical element in
Aeschylus's tragedy.

WAKI AND WAKIZURE: At Shinowara
  At the edge of the pond, over the water of the Law
  At the edge of the pond, over the water of the Law
  Deep in invocation,
  In recitation of prayers,
  The clear voices cross.
  Hold a memorial service
  From the first to the last
  Watch of night.
  The heart also Westward
  Goes with the moon
  Light cloudless, clear.
  They [we] ring the bell through the length of the night.

At the end of the song, the wakizure sit down and the waki, standing, faces forward and joins his hands in prayer while he invokes Amida twice with a nembutsu, the prayer to Amida Buddha. The taiko drum begins playing at this point.

WAKI: *Namuamidabu. Namuamidabu.*

In this ageuta, the waki repeats, from his first sashi in the maeba, a reference to the voices reciting prayers, but in somewhat greater detail. (He also mentions here, as he does not in the first ageuta, the pond at Shinowara, the setting of the play, which, by means of verbal interaction to be discussed in the third chapter, is further associated with the waters of the Law, that is, Paradise.[86]) But whereas at the beginning of the nō the prayers were not recited on behalf of anyone in particular, here the audience knows from the kyōgen scene and the identification of the ghost in the maeba that the service is intended for the ghost of Sanemori specifically. In other words, the nō becomes more focused on the shite in accordance with what Nogami called "the principle of the one actor."[87]

The second dan of the nochiba begins with the arrival of that one most important actor, the shite, to the accompaniment of special instrumental music, including that of the taiko, which is played throughout the dan. (The waki sits down before the shite enters.) The dan consists of two shōdan, the shite's recitative (a sashi), followed by the more melodious *issei*, which he shares with the chorus.

[86] Verbal interaction between the name of the setting and something of religious significance is common in nō. In *Yorimasa*, for example, the name of the temple Byōdōin, which literally means "all people without discrimination," leads to the words in the fifth ageuta, *byōdōdaie*, meaning "equal in His great mercy."
[87] Nogami, "Nō no shuyaku ichinin shugi."

SHITE: When one has reached Paradise,
   He has left the world of suffering forever
   And the seat of transmigration is far away.
      (He looks toward the hashigakari.)
   How great is the joy in his [my] heart!
   That Place is a place from which one does not return.
      (He turns to the waki.)
   Life [there] is without end, Amida Buddha. He [I] is filled with hope.
      (He faces forward.)

In this sashi the shite again expresses his hope: not the dim hope expressed in the second dan of the maeba, but rather the joy and hope that he can indeed be saved. This sashi, recited smoothly and in a rhythm that does not follow a beat, is sung *tsuyogin*, "in a strong tone." In the next shōdan, the issei, a dignified and melodious piece that, like the sashi, does not follow the beat of the drums, Zeami treats the prayer, *Namuamidabu*, in a special and an explicit manner. The emphasis is achieved when the rhythm of the issei changes, with the exception of a single line, to a regular beat appropriate to the end of a dan, which this is; with the delivery of the word, *namu*; and with the chorus's definition of the meanings of the two important words in the prayer, namely, *namu* and *Amida*. The jo-ha-kyū of the dan and of the nō as a whole is revealed in the progression toward the regular beat, in the explication of meaning, and in the fact that the shite is engaged in a greater amount of stage action than in any part of the nō that preceded.[88]

SHITE: *(The shite turns to the waki.)*
   Every time a person repeats the name of Amida Buddha,
CHORUS: Then, every time he is saved.
SHITE: As for *namu*—
   (The shite stamps with his left foot and moves forward two steps.)
CHORUS: That is, to submit one's destiny to Buddha.
SHITE: As for *Amida*—
   (The shite stamps with his right foot and moves forward one step.)
CHORUS: By virtue of righteous acts[89]
   (The shite turns left and flips his sleeve over his arm.)

---

[88] Here again I include only as many stage directions as pertain to the meanings of the words and as are sufficient to illustrate the increase in kinetic interest. It is important to remember that these directions come from present-day texts. They probably reflect, but do not necessarily reproduce, the movements used in Zeami's productions. The waki takes two steps forward once or twice within this section.

[89] According to *YKS*, 270 n. 2, the Sanskrit for *namu* and *Amida*, translated into the Chinese in a work by the priest Shantao, means that if one carries out religious acts and

SHITE: One should without fail be saved.
(The shite brings his sleeve back.)
CHORUS: It makes him [me] thankful.
(The shite, with his hands folded in prayer, turns to the waki.)

In the next dan, the third, the waki's acknowledgment of the shite "as the old man he has just seen" connects verbally the first and second halves of the nō, specifically the third dan of each. However, in view of the jo-ha-kyū, there is more rhythm in this dan than in the corresponding dan of the maeba. There the mondō, the dialogue between the waki and the shite, begins with speech; here, except for one line in which the shite says that he is visible to the eyes of the priest only, the dan is in melody. Earlier the kakeai, an exchange by the end of which the two actors are singing as one person, followed the spoken mondō; in the nochiba, the kakeai begins the dan.

(The shite looks forward.)
WAKI: Amazing!
On the surface of the pond growing white from the light of dawn,
The one faintly floating into view
Is the old man he [I] just saw,
But he is dressed in armor. It is amazing.
(The shite looks at the waki.)
SHITE: A fossil tree
That no one knows
Submerged.
Fom the depths of the heart
It is difficult to express
The innumerable agonies of the warrior hell.
Release him [me] from these.
(As the kakeai continues, the shite looks forward and then at the waki several times.)
WAKI: So then, your appearance before his [my] eyes and your words [are]
Not seen nor heard by the others
SHITE: *(In speech)*
Only evident to Your Reverence.
WAKI: *(In melody)*
He [I] sees a form, the traces of snow,
SHITE: White hair and beard of the old warrior, but

---

submits himself to Buddha, Buddha listens to his prayers and saves him. Zeami took the Japanese version from the Chinese.

WAKI: Brilliant is the appearance
SHITE: Of his outfit, bright
WAKI: In the moon's radiance
SHITE: In the burning light of the lantern.

The words and the rhythm of the kakeai progress smoothly and directly into the choral song, the ageuta, at the end of the third dan, in which the chorus takes over and sings for both the shite and the waki.[90]

CHORUS: Not dark
(The shite moves to the right and to the left.)
Is the night's mantle
A brocade robe
Is the night's mantle
A brocade robe
He wears green armor
(The shite turns to the left and looks at his sword.)
And swords with sheaths decorated in gold.
(The shite faces forward and makes the gesture of thrusting with a sword.)
But, he asks, under the present conditions,
What kind of treasures are these?
(The shite moves forward and looks intently at the waki.)
In the Lake of Treasures [Buddha's Lake in Paradise], there is
a lotus calyx.
This should be the real treasure.
(The shite flips his sleeve over and moves to the left.)
Indeed, there is no doubt
The teaching of the Law does not tarnish.
(The shite makes a small turn.)
If the golden words you respect,
(The shite turns toward the waki.)
Why should you not be There?
Why should you not be There?

In the kakeai, the waki acknowledges the presence of the shite, as he has done at the same juncture of the maeba, and as is customary in two-part nō. In addition, since the shite appears in a more distinctive costume than earlier (the shite here carries swords and is dressed in armor and a brocade

90 The words of an ageuta are usually connected closely with the preceding kakeai. In the libretto, the direction *sueru* is written next to the last of the shite's words, "light." The direction means that the actor is to sing in such a way that he "hands over" (*watasu*) the singing to the chorus. This is always the case when the rhythm changes from free to regular rhythm, as in this passage.

robe, while the white hair and old–man mask are the same as those of the maeba), as is the norm in two-part nō, the waki refers to the costume of the shite, specifically the armor, the white hair and beard appropriate to the old man, and the brilliant outfit. In the ageuta, the chorus mentions the brocade robe, the green armor, and the swords.

The explicit verbal articulation of what is simultaneously a visual presentation need not be focused in nō on the costume to the extent that it is in *Sanemori*; a prop, a part of the shite's costume, or a movement can serve as well. However, it is not unusual at this juncture in the nochiba of two-part nō to find some connection made between the verbal and the visual, along with an increase in the melody, specifically in the form of an ageuta, and in the number of the shite's movements. The result is that the audience's attention is engaged and attracted to the words that assume special importance. This is not the final "eye-opening" section of the nō, to be sure, but one that prepares for it. In *Sanemori*, with the kakeai and ageuta, Zeami artistically creates a close relationship between the shite's appearance (he wears brocade), the story of the warrior Sanemori (the epic warrior was known for wearing red brocade into battle), and the moral lesson of the nō, and thus achieves a focus of the contributing parts that surely helps to account for the success of *Sanemori* in performance.

Through verbal interaction, to be discussed in Chapter Three, Zeami connects the costume of the shite with the night sky, in which the moon is a symbol of enlightenment, and states clearly that the treasures of Buddha's Lake are the real treasures, not earthly treasures such as the outfit and swords. As we learn later in the nochiba, and as the audience may know from the *Heike*, Sanemori had requested permission to return home and to fight wearing a red brocade robe, a sign of his valor. However, Zeami adds that the golden words of Buddha are unfading, but the gold on the sheaths of swords tarnish, and that the star-studded sky, although brocade-like and brilliant, is the proper goal of one's aspirations, not the outfit worn by the warrior.[91] This does not mean that the brocade robe is denigrated in the nō; on the contrary, Zeami extols Sanemori's spirit, for, although he was an old man who expected to die, he wanted to go to battle in his homeland and to fight, dressed in a brocade robe. However, the religious lesson stated in the ageuta, namely that one should reach Paradise through the repetition of Buddha's golden words, takes precedence over the moral lesson, inasmuch as the ghost of Sanemori has no use for earthly riches.

[91] This caveat against worldly riches is familiar to the reader of Greek tragedy. See, for example, *Agamemnon* 779–780. However, whereas Zeami contrasts earthly with heavenly treasures in *Sanemori*, Aeschylus contrasts wealth justly gained with that which is not.

The moral is stated very explicitly by the waki in his last speech of the play, after which the nō becomes shite-centered and focuses on the relinquishment of the warrior's earthly attachment.

WAKI: When he [I] looks at you, you are in the form of one still in the world of transmigration. You should relinquish your attachment and reach the calyx of Amida who destroys all sins.[92]
(The waki retires to the stage front right.)

As I mentioned above, in his discussion of two-part warrior nō in the *Sandō*, Zeami advises that the important kusemai scene be placed near the end of the nochiba. As a result, the kusemai, which is usually placed in the third dan of the ha section, will extend into the kyū and lengthen that part. The ha would then contain four dan and the play as a whole six dan. In *Sanemori*, Zeami follows this advice: there are three dan in the maeba and three in the nochiba. If in turn we divide the nochiba into dan, as in the model sketch of the nō structure, there are six dan of which the jo comprises one dan, the ha four, and the kyū one.[93] The kusemai scene of *Sanemori* accounts for both dan four and five of the second half.

Within a kusemai scene, the most interesting in the nō both musically and thematically, the normal sequence of shōdan units is a *kuri*, a high-pitched and melodious short song in a free rhythm not following a beat; a *sashi*, a song again in free rhythm delivered smoothly as a recitative; and a *kuse*, a long song in a regulated rhythm that begins slowly at a low pitch and ends like an ageuta on a high pitch. (In the kuse a main actor, usually the shite, delivers one or two lines.) In *Sanemori*, there is a variation on this pattern that creates a special effect. The scene begins with a kuri and a sashi, but then the sequence is interrupted by a *katari*, the shite's long epic-like narration, by a kind of *sageuta*, a low-pitched song, and by a choral ageuta, before Zeami continues with the kuse itself. The themes and the music of the kuse then flow naturally into the kyū section, which includes a *rongi*, a sung exchange, and a *chūnori* section, a continuation of the singing in a rhythm found especially, but not exclusively, in warrior nō. In sum, the deployment of shōdan, the parts of the dan, at the end of *Sanemori* is as follows: dan four and five, kuri, sashi, katari, "sageuta," ageuta, kuse; dan six, rongi and chūnori.[94]

[92] This speech is not found in all texts. *YKS* prints it in small letters. Texts of the shite actors fall into two groups: the Kamigakari texts (those of the Kanze and Hōshō schools of nō), and the Shimogakari texts (those of the Kongō, Komparu, and Kita schools of nō). (There are a total of these five schools today.) The lines in question are from the Shimogakarihōsho waki school of nō.

[93] My divisions follow those of Nogami. See pages 123–130 of his text, *Kaichū yō-kyoku zenshū.*

[94] Consult part 2 of Appendix 1 for a chart of the differences in dan four, five, and six of the nochiba of *Sanemori*, *Atsumori*, and *Yorimasa*.

The kuri and sashi, both shared by the shite and the chorus, which sings for the waki in the former and for the shite in the latter, establish in the fourth dan of the nochiba, still a part of the ha section, the religious framework for the remainder of the nō and define the task that the ghost of Sanemori faces.[95]

(The shite sits down on a stool placed in the middle of the stage.)

Kuri

SHITE: One invocation of Amida abolishes innumerable sins.[96]

CHORUS: That is, a heart blessed with its own virtue turns [to Buddha] and aspires [to Paradise].

Do not leave your heart behind in attachment.

Sashi

SHITE: The time has arrived; this evening he [I] has received the teachings difficult to encounter.[97]

CHORUS: The tale of shame and repentance—

Still he cannot forget the past and recollects how at Shinowara He died like dew on the grassy plain.[98]

He will tell his tale.

(The shite looks at the waki.)

The katari that follows is both a "tale"told by the shite in narrative form and the first part of the warrior's confession. It is drawn from the *Heike*, as Zeami advised for warrior nō, and follows the source closely. However, in accordance with his views in the *Sarugaku dangi* about jo-ha-kyū and about *Sanemori* specifically, he changes the narrative sequence by delaying the account of the warrior's death, which in the *Heike* is told at the beginning, until the end of the play. The katari begins like the corresponding part of the *Heike*: the shite tells what happened in the enemy camp of the Genji after Sanemori's side, the Heike, were defeated in a battle at Shinowara. The narration is spoken in the third person, often in the historical present tense, and in prose such as a bard, chanting the *Heike*, might use. In fact, the shite speaks for Tezuka, the man who cut off Sanemori's head. He also tells how Kiso, the Genji leader of the enemy, sent for Higuchi, a former friend of Sanemori, to identify the head of the old warrior, which had been disguised by the black ink with which he had dyed his hair and beard. (This is the scene in which occurs the washing and the identification

---

[95] See Hoff and Hoff, "Staging Epic," 33.

[96] It is not unusual for Zeami to quote lines from the same source in more than one play; this line from the *Kammuryōju* sutra appears in *Atsumori* also.

[97] This line comes from the *rokudō kōshiki*, a religious service.

[98] In Buddhist thought life is merely a temporary dwelling place in which we are as long-lived as dew.

of the dead warrior's head, as mentioned by Zeami.) Then the shite adds an account in the voice of Higuchi of what Sanemori had said in the past.[99]

This katari appears at a juncture comparable to the moment in the *Agamemnon* when the king returns and the action of the tragedy begins. There the two main characters, Agamemnon and Clytemnestra, carry on a spoken exchange. The tragic event, the murder of Agamemnon, takes place soon after, contemporaneous with the dramatic time. In *Sanemori*, Zeami removes the action from the dramatic time and concentrates instead on the shite's verbal account both of an event and of spoken exchanges between characters. In some, if not most theaters, this scene and the following would call for two actors; however, Zeami creates a one-man show in which the shite plays the part not only of himself, but of these other characters as well. Aeschylus's addition of a second actor and the later addition of a third, facilitated by the fact that some actors played multiple roles in a single play, created a means of stepping out of the narrative mode of epic. Zeami, who had the same resources at his disposal, does not change the narrative mode in this scene but creates interest with a story, as he does in other nō, especially the shura nō. The interest for the audience lies in the words and the content, and is kindled in part by its awareness of how Zeami adapts the epic account.

During the katari, there are no gestures or melody until the shite narrates the part of the epic story about the identification of the head. At this point, which presumably corresponds to Zeami's recommended identification of the shite in nochiba, the shite looks down and the melody begins.[100] With this first line of melody Zeami evokes compassion for the warrior not only by verbal and musical/rhythmical means, but by kinetic means as well. It is at this point that the shite moves for the first time during the katari.

(*The shite looks forward toward the audience.*)
SHITE: Now then, when the battle of Shinowara was lost [by us],
Tezuka no Tarō Mitsumori, a Genji, came before Lord Kiso and said,
"Mitsumori [I], fighting a strange character, has cut off his head. He looks, I[101] said at the time, like a great leader, but he has not the forces

[99] In the katari of other warrior nō, the shite also tell a tale, often an account of the last battle in which the warrior died.

[100] The form this identification takes varies among the warrior plays. *Tadanori* is similar to *Sanemori*—there we hear that Rokuyata sees how young and noble his opponent is, but does not recognize him until he finds a poem stuck in the warrior's quiver. The shite, representing the ghost of Tadanori, tells the tale in the katari, performs a dance, and after reciting the poem, divulges the name of its author, that is, Tadanori himself.

[101] In the translation of the katari, I have used the first-person pronoun where appropriate, although it does not appear as such in the Japanese text. The different characters about whom the shite speaks and for whom he speaks are difficult enough to distinguish

behind him [to be one]. And again, if you think he is an ordinary warrior, he wears a brocade robe. I insist that he name his name, but to the end he refuses to give it." His accent was that of the Kantō dialect.[102] Lord Kiso said, "Ah, this must be Saitō Bettō Sanemori. If so, his hair and beard should be white, but it is strange that they are black. It may be that Higuchi no Jirō is acquainted with him." When he had Higuchi sent for, on arrival and with but one glance,

(The shite looks down.)

Higuchi shed tears and said,

(The melody begins.)

"Alas, how piteous! This is indeed Saitō Bettō!

(The shite looks up again.)

Sanemori was accustomed to say that, if at sixty years of age or more one goes to battle, to compete with young warriors in order to advance first would be childish. And again, to be looked down upon by people as an old warrior would be mortifying. He would choose to dye his hair and beard with black ink and be killed fighting just like a young man. That is what he always said.

(The shite looks down.)

Indeed he has dyed them

(The shite looks up.)

Have his head washed and look for yourselves."

(The shite opens the fan that he holds.)

Scarcely had he spoken when holding the head—

(The shite rises from the stool, then kneels and with both hands on his fan makes the gesture of lifting a head.)

In this scene, Zeami creates an interesting relationship between the source, the *Heike*, and the dramatic performance: the shite, who has been narrating the *Heike* in the manner of a bard and with the words of the epic account, delivers a melodic version of the words of his former friend, and then, rising, carries out the gestures of washing the head of his epic counterpart while the chorus takes over the singing for the shite in a "sageuta."

(The shite moves forward.)

CHORUS: He leaves the lord's presence and faces the shore of the pond close-by

(The shite rises and moves forward.)

---

without adding the confusion that can arise from the use of the third person for all of them.

[102] The Kantō area is where Tokyo is located.

in whose green waters are reflected the leaves of willow branches
hanging [above].
(The shite stops, brings the fan to his right hand, and looks down.)

At this point the melody changes to the regular beat and the prosodic
rhythm to the regulated form of an ageuta, the song found most often at
the end of dan. This is a highly lyric moment in which Zeami creatively
diverges from the epic account—in the *Heike*, the washing of the head is
mentioned, but that is all.[103] In the choral song, Zeami begins by quoting
a poem that describes the washing.[104]

CHORUS: The weather is clearing, the wind combs the young
  willows' hair.
The ice is melted, the waves wash the old moss's beard.
  *(During the singing of the poem, the shite extends his left hand for-
  ward, kneels, looks at his right side, and with his fan makes the ges-
  ture of dipping water two or three times.)*
When one looked,
  (The shite lowers his fan and looks.)
the black ink flowed away and there was the original gray hair.
  (The shite returns to the pillar at stage back right.)
"Truly any warrior of the bow who is concerned about his name
should be like this.
  (The shite faces forward.)
Ah, what a noble warrior!" said everyone, shedding tears.

With the words of the chorus and with the gestures of the shite, playing
the role of the warrior's ghost miming his friend's identification of the epic
Sanemori's head, Zeami might well have evoked from the audience a response of compassion, even pity, for the warrior. The praise of the warrior
also elevates the main character to the level of an example worthy of the
audience's esteem and emulation, and thus justifies the feeling of compassion ethically as well as aesthetically. The justification is enhanced by references to clearing of the weather, which might suggest by analogy that
the ghost's mind is being cleared of its accumulated impurities and that the
warrior may attain salvation. The effect of the passage is very much the
product of the compositional skill with which Zeami develops the scene
from speech to song, from the epic to the lyric mood, from close adherence

---

[103] On Zeami's creative genius in this nō, see Yashima Masaharu, "Zeami ni okeru
shura no keifu" (Lineage Warrior Nō in Zeami), in *Geinōshi kenkyū* (Research on the
History of the Performing Arts) 43 (1973): 14–26, esp. 25.

[104] As before, I include only those gestures and motions which are closely connected
with the meanings of words. Many of the gestures employing the fan and the movements
around the stage have become conventional today, as they were not in Zeami's time.

to the *Heike* to free addition of new elements—a poetic quotation and praise of the warrior—and from a lack of movement to the gestures and the motions of the shite. This development continues in the next scene, the kuse, and in the rongi and chūnori sections with which the nō concludes.

The kuse, representing the fifth dan of the nochiba and both the end of the ha and beginning of the kyū sections of the play as a whole, has been duly anticipated by the performance of the kuri and sashi. However, it is clearly marked as a separate dan inasmuch as the presence of the katari, "sageuta," and ageuta interrupts the normal sequence of shōdan (kuri, sashi, kuse). In addition, Zeami does not continue with an account of the final battle, but with the words, "And then, Sanemori," and the story of Sanemori's wearing a red brocade robe, in accordance with his advice in the *Sarugaku dangi* about the composition of *Sanemori* specifically. The story of the robe is anticipated in the earlier parts of the nochiba where Zeami places emphasis on the warrior's outfit, but does not elaborate upon it. By delaying the battle scene once again, Zeami avoids an anticlimax in the performance and a disruption of the jo-ha-kyū progression.

In the katari, "sageuta," and ageuta of the fourth dan, Zeami presents the warrior as a person worthy of the audience's admiration. In the kuse, a significant section of the nō in which he alludes to the authoritative words of other authors, Zeami justifies the admiration by suppressing the epic warrior's reason for wearing the brocade robe, which was to compensate for his cowardly action in an earlier battle when he fled with the other men. Zeami alters the epic version and says that Sanemori wears the robe not for selfish reasons, but in the spirit of Shubaijin, the Chinese paragon of virtue, who is mentioned in the epic version as well. This kuse section is central to the characterization of Sanemori in the nō: the epic Sanemori was a noble warrior, the dramatic Sanemori is nobler still.

Zeami's alteration of the *Heike* provides some of the interest in the scene. In addition, the movements of the shite are numerous; from this point on they become more and more rapid and display more and more the vigor and strength appropriate to a warrior. Throughout the kuse, the shite continues to dance while the chorus, as is customary in a kuse scene, takes over the singing for him. The shite's recitation of a few words, called an *ageha*, is customary in kuse. The melody also develops—from a slow tempo and a low pitch at the beginning to a faster pace and a higher pitch at the end.[105] In addition, although in the katari, the shite has spoken in the person of Sanemori's enemy and killer, Tezuka; the enemy leader, Lord Kiso; and his former friend, Higuchi, in the kuse he speaks, albeit still in

---

[105] See Hare, *Zeami's Style*, 296.

the third person and with reference to the beginning of a poem, for Sanemori himself.[106]

CHORUS: And then,
    Sanemori's wearing a brocade robe
    Was not out of a wish to be selfish.
    Sanemori, when he left the capital,
    Said to Lord Munemori [his commanding officer],
    "There is a saying in the classics,
    'Wearing brocade one returns to his birthplace.'
    Sanemori was from Echizen,
    But in recent years was awarded a domain
    And took residence in Nagai of Musashi.
    Now if he leaves and goes North,
    He will surely be killed in battle.
    In his old age, nothing would make him happier to remember
    Than being granted this permission [to wear a brocade robe]."
    Since that was his wish,
    Munemori bestowed upon him a red brocade robe.
SHITE: Now, in an old poem as well [there appear the words]—
    "Maple leaves,
CHORUS: While brushing them aside he returns home wearing brocade
    And the people see him."
    That is what a poet wrote.
    It is in the spirit of the original saying.
    Shubaijin [Chu Mai-ch'en] of old let his brocade sleeves
    Flutter [in the wind] on Mount Kaikei [K'uai-chi shan, a mountain in
    China].
    (The shite flips his sleeve over his arm.)
    Now, Sanemori
    Has brought fame to the four corners of the Northern province
    And the celebrated warrior's name has lasted through generations,
    Visible to all.
    Till dawn
    Throughout the moonlit night
    He will relate his tale of repentance.

    In terms of the nō as a whole and the jo-ha-kyū development, the kuse
is not only thematically, musically, kinetically, and visually one of the

---

[106] I shall include only one stage direction in this section, that which is most closely
related to the words. Actually the reader should bear in mind that the shite is dancing as
the chorus sings.

most engrossing scenes, but also in terms of the authority of literary precedents that Zeami brings explicitly to the surface. Except that he has changed the order of the sequence of events and omits mention of Sanemori's cowardly flight from the enemy, Zeami again follows the *Heike* account, as he has done in the katari. From the *Heike*, Zeami alludes to a proverb, which he specifically labels "a saying in the classics." Furthermore, in the shite's line of the kuse, Zeami begins to quote a poem that is not found in the *Heike* and in which there is an allusion to the already quoted proverb.[107] The poem, to which Zeami attracts attention with mention of both the "old poem" and the "poet" and which the shite begins and the chorus finishes, contains the gist of Sanemori's request—his wish that people will see him in a brocade robe when he returns to the Northern province. The shite's movement of his sleeve as the chorus sings the words "sleeves flutter" draws attention not only to the words, but to the shite's costume, which may include a red brocade robe like that of Shubaijin, the Chinese scholar Chu Mai-ch'en who waved the sleeves of his red brocade robe on Mount Kaikei.[108] (This does not mean that the shite flips his sleeve over his arm at this point only in the nō. But, like a dead metaphor, the gesture is brought to life by the verbal context in which it is performed. In the Kanze performance of *Sanemori* that I saw, the shite twirled the sleeve of his red and gold brocade costume tightly and deliberately over his arm. The gesture was very noticeable inasmuch as, when the words "red brocade robe" were sung, the shite extended the brocade sleeve and kept it extended until he flipped it over his arm. The gesture was further emphasized by the stomp of his foot.) In other words, Sanemori's actions are granted authority by virtue of three literary precedents: the *Heike*, the proverb, and the poem. (The red color of the maple leaves, mentioned in the poem, is appropriate to the color of the brocade robe and to autumn, the season in which the play is meant to be performed.) For this reason alone the kuse, which concludes the ha section of the play, is important as the penultimate section of the nō.

The kuse ends with a return to the present dramatic time, both with the adverb "now" and the reference to the eternal fame of the warrior made

---

[107] The poem, an autumn poem, is found in the anthology *Gosenshū*. According to *YKS*, 272 n. 16, it may have been written by Isse.

[108] This Chinese scholar was persuaded by the Emperor Wu, second century B.C., with the words of the proverb, to return home attired in robes of the court, because the emperor respected Chu Mai-ch'en, who had overcome poverty and suffering, for his wisdom. He then became an official in his homeland. See Itō, *Yōkyokushū*, 116 n. 7. The kinds of costumes used in particular nō are not absolutely fixed; however, in all present-day performances of *Sanemori* with which I am familiar the nochijite wears armor and a brocade robe. In a 1985 performance of the Kanze school, that I saw, the shite wore a red and gold brocade robe.

manifest to all, and with an explicit statement that the warrior ghost will tell his tale of repentance, the tale that constitutes the remainder of the nō and the character's "action" toward which the plot of the play, unlike the epic, has developed. In the rongi and the chūnori sections at the end of the nō, which is the kyū proper of the play, the account of the battle between Sanemori and his adversaries at Shinowara, drawn from the *Heike*, serves as the tale of repentance. It is here that the audience finally learns why the warrior's soul remains attached to this world: he wanted to fight Lord Kiso himself but was prevented by the intervention of Tezuka. The battle scene is described in the *Heike*, as I mentioned, before the account of the identification of the head and the account of the brocade robe; however, Sanemori's desire to fight Lord Kiso is not mentioned there. Nor is it mentioned in the nō outside the rongi. (In the kyōgen scene we are told only that Sanemori looked for a good adversary.) Sanemori's resolve to fight the best adversary and his inability to do so cause the resentment that lies at the root of his attachment. Zeami delays the most action-packed part of the tale, the account of the battle, mentioned briefly at the beginning of the katari[109] and in the kyōgen scene, until the end of the nō, where he makes it the content of the warrior ghost's confession, the culmination of the "plot" contemporaneous with the dramatic time, and he introduces there the most vigorous stage action and insistent rhythmic beat. Thus Zeami creates a great theater performance out of epic in the "eye-opening" section of the nō.

Speaking for the waki, the chorus begins the rongi, which follows a beat and is in a regular rhythm.

CHORUS: Indeed, with a tale of repentance
    Purify to the bottom the water in your heart;
    Leave no impurities behind.

The shite responds by stating in the voice of Sanemori the cause of his resentment, a statement that in terms of the play's development, is the verbal climax. It is also economically expressed—the words "has come" and the first syllable of Kiso's name are both expressed in the Japanese text with the one syllable *ki*.

SHITE: That deep-rooted attachment of warrior hell,
    (The shite moves forward.)
    Moving around and around again to this place
    Has come. Kiso—

[109] Yashima, "Zeami ni okeru," 23, thinks that because the death of the warrior is treated at the beginning of the katari and then repeated at the end of the nō, the structure of *Sanemori* is not linear.

*(The shite stamps his foot both before and after expressing
the name Kiso.)*
He [I] intended to grapple with him,
But Tezuka intervened.
Even now that resentment persists.
(The shite mimes a thrust and a parry.)

The rongi then continues with an exchange between the chorus and the
shite in which they describe the fight.

CHORUS: Among Kiso's followers,
    Who one by one gave their names, the first to advance was
    (The shite appears to be looking for the enemy.)
SHITE: Tezuka no Tarō Mitsumori.
CHORUS: A retainer fearing lest his lord be killed
    *(The shite moves around to the right and goes to the center
    of the stage.)*
SHITE: On his horse interceded [between Tezuka and Sanemori]
    (The shite moves to the right.)
    And to the side of Sanemori
CHORUS: He came. And as he grappled with him,
SHITE: Sanemori said, "Ah, you want to grapple
    With the best warrior in Japan."

In the last line Sanemori speaks in his own Kantō dialect,[110] which, because
it is also used in the line of the *Heike* that Zeami quotes, helps to focus the
nō on the warrior of the epic, the warrior of the nō, and the shite simultaneously. In this line the Sanemori of the nō expresses pride and spirit in
his own voice, which are further expressed in the "action," that is, both
the epic language describing action and the vigorous movements display-
ing the bravery of Sanemori.

SHITE: Against the front of the saddle he [Sanemori] pressed him
    And cut off and threw away the [retainer's] head.
    *(During the delivery of these two lines, the shite thrusts and after a
    number of motions mimes the beheading with his fan. He then
    pretends to look at an imaginary head held in his hand by its long
    hair and to drop it to the ground.)*

Once this moment of glory for Sanemori has been enacted in the chūnori
section, which features the strong beat at the rate of two syllables per beat,

---

[110] See *YKS*, 273 nn. 28 and 30. Hare, *Zeami's Style*, 217, says that Zeami not only
imitates the Eastern dialect, but includes a mild form of vulgarity in Sanemori's speech.
Hare's translation of the rongi (218) brings out this element of Sanemori's speech.

and the rapid tempo that Zeami recommends for the end of warrior nō, the chorus takes over all but one line for the shite.

CHORUS: After that, Tezuka no Tarō
  Circled around Sanemori on the left,
  Pulled up the skirt of his armor,
  And stabbed him twice with his sword.
    (The shite moves about the stage and looks at his
    left upper thigh. He then sits down.)
  They grappled at close quarters and between the two horses
  Fell down with a crash.
SHITE: Alas, he was an old warrior
  (The shite stands.)
CHORUS: Exhausted from battle
  An old tree crumpled by the wind,
  Whose strength is broken
  Beneath Tezuka. As he fell,
    (The shite sits down and mimes a fall with his fan.)
  Retainers came to the spot.
  Finally his head was cut off.
    (The shite stands.)

At this point there is a relaxation in the intensity as the beat returns to the hiranori, the regular beat found in ageuta at the end of dan.

CHORUS: He became one with the earth at Shinowara.
  His form and shadow leave no traces.
  His form and shadow—*Namuamidabu.*

In this final and kyū section of the nō, the ensemble of the instruments (drums and flute), the driving beat, the words of the songs, and the movements of the shite, present the final battle and death of Sanemori in a manner that, if well performed, brings to the audience the sense of satisfaction, which is the aim of jo-ha-kyū. Here, the arts that make their equal, but diverse, contributions to the play converge.

Among the epic themes of the play, the warrior's tale, altered slightly from the *Heike* version so that the jo-ha-kyū structure is arranged most effectively, comes to a fitting conclusion with the death of the warrior. This ending is intrinsically better suited to performance than the subject of the brocade robe or the washing of Sanemori's head. Among the lyric themes, Sanemori's association with trees in Zeami's quotation of and allusion to the poems of other authors comes to a fitting conclusion in Zeami's comparison of the warrior's demise to the crumpling of an old tree in a poetic line that he adds to the *Heike* account. (On this subject I shall say more in

Chapter Three.) In terms of the visual appeal of the nō, the numerous references to the armor and to the old age within the play (that is, to the costume and the mask of the shite) become fully significant in the battle scene, in which the warrior is said to use his sword and to be stabbed beneath the skirt of his armor, and in which one learns that because he is an old man he cannot be victorious. From another standpoint, the shite's expression of pain and sorrow in the line, "Alas, he was an old warrior," is an emotional peak in the play, more emotionally loaded than the similar line of the katari and one poignantly made visible by the actor who, as he falls, must act as the old man Sanemori who wants to act as if he were young and brave. The shite tries to maintain the rapid and vigorous movements appropriate to a young man on the battlefield, but like the old warrior falls slightly behind the rhythmic beat.[111]

Zeami presents the warrior in the best light, both in spite of and because of his old age: he puts up a good fight, looks for the most able opponent, and displays bravery and spirit. Zeami enhances his image further by comparing him to Shubaijin and by suppressing the warrior's flight on an earlier occasion and so makes him a model worthy of emulation. Added to this characterization is the confession that concludes the dramatic action. At the end of the nō, the chorus says the nembutsu, the prayer, which is intended to ensure the salvation of the warrior who has asserted his desire to be saved and who has admitted the cause of his attachment to the world. The sincerity of the admission is visually underscored by the warrior's turn toward the priest in an attitude of prayer before he exits from the stage. It is made religiously legitimate by the chorus's request for prayers—the audience hears behind the words echoes of the earlier Buddhistic ritual and service. It is emotionally charged by the shite's expression of sorrow in the only line he sings in the chūnori section. Zeami integrates the religious, ethical, and emotional levels with the most personal level of expression by the shite, the most rhythmic music, the most original lyrics, the most exciting part of the epic story, the most driving beat of the instrumental music, the most vigorous movements on stage, and the most flamboyant display of the costume. In the finale, the salvation of the warrior seems assured—not because Zeami says so explicitly, but as a result of the jo-ha-kyū structure that focuses attention on the shite alone and creates the sense of completion at which Zeami aimed in the composition both of the text and of the performance.

[111] When the actor himself is old, the best age for playing the role of Sanemori, then it is appropriate that he, like the character Sanemori, try to act like a young man who is really old. A performance of parts of *Sanemori* by Shimazaki Chifumi, now advanced in age, brought out the difficulty of executing the dances in this play, which is not taught to the novice or intermediate level students of the shite role. Zeami himself discusses the role of an old man in the *Fūshikaden*, in ZZ, 58, and Rimer, 56. On this subject, see Hare, *Zeami's Style*, 65–66, and Hoff and Hoff, "Staging Epic," 35.

TWO

Structure in Aeschylean Tragedy

Aeschylus's *Persians* is longer, has more dialogue, and employs a larger number of major characters and theatrical effects than Zeami's *Sanemori*. And yet, because the overall structure of Aeschylus's play is more nearly comparable to that of the warrior nō written by Zeami than are the tragedies written by Sophocles and Euripides, or for that matter, others written by Aeschylus himself, I have chosen the *Persians* as the focus of this chapter. To be sure, many of these other tragedies, like plays from other theaters, are composed so that they develop from implicit to explicit, from less to more intense, from verbal to visual; but the degree of concentration on such development in both language and theatrical effects is extraordinary in nō written by Zeami. Its nearest equal in Greek drama is to be found in the *Persians*, our earliest extant tragedy. This play, like other tragedies and nō, is artistically and aesthetically conceived; but unlike other tragedies and like nō, it is constructed without a display of animated dialogue and persuasive argument, without conflict between characters on stage, without tragic acts taking place within the time frame of the play, and without numerous characters and many entrances and exits, that is, without such features as would distract the audience's attention.[1] The *Persians* is not realistic drama, and its structural organization depends less on the logic of a "necessary or probable" plot sequence that exercises the audience's intellect and wit than it does on the gradual intensification of verbal, rhythmic, and theatrical effects that reach a crescendo at significant moments within the play. The finale of the *Persians*, like that of *Sanemori*, is the most intense of these peaks. There the full impact of the drama

[1] Jacqueline Duchemin, "Du lyrisme à la tragédie: Réflexions sur l'Agamemnon et les Perses d'Eschyle," in *Serta Turyniana*, ed. John L. Heller (Urbana, Ill., 1974), 132, says, "Il y a encore moins d'action dans les *Perses*. Mieux: aucune action directe n'est présentée au cours de ce drame."

emerges out of the movements, costumes, and song attending the main actor's performance, and these are combined with the words for an overall effect that is striking, not only to the mind, but also to the eyes, the ears, the heart, and the spirit of the audience simultaneously.

We do not have Aeschylus's own comments, as we do Zeami's, about which elements of composition he considered important or about how he constructed his play. His text must speak for itself. From it we can discern easily that although he has not chosen characters connected with the arts, as Zeami recommended, he has chosen characters—the Persian people and Xerxes—from history, a "source" that he knew well and that was familiar to his audience, and he has linked their roles and their emotional responses closely with a lament, which constitutes the most important musical and kinetic feature in a performance of the play. We can also discern that he has written the text with careful attention to the language and to the "literary" resonance beneath the surface meaning.[2] Moreover, the structure, the overall conception of text, reveals analogies with Zeami's warrior nō. However, Aeschylus's text does not tell us as explicitly as Zeami's own words and present-day performances can for his nō how Aeschylus visualized and mapped out a performance of his play, an understanding of which is a prerequisite to the full appreciation of his, and any playwright/actor's, work.

From his *Poetics*, our oldest extant theoretical source that is devoted to the subject of poetry in general and of tragedy in particular, we know that Aristotle considered *muthos* ("plot"), *ēthos* ("character"), *dianoia* ("thought"), and *lexis* ("diction") to be, in that order, the most important elements in the composition of a tragedy. (Three of these are roughly comparable to Zeami's saku, shu, and sho. Aristotle also mentions, but unfortunately does not treat at length, the two elements that especially pertain to performance: *opsis* ("visual effects") and *melopoiia* ("composition of song"). Instead, Aristotle emphasizes the importance of plot, which he says is "the soul as it were of tragedy."

Aristotle defines plot as the imitation of action (*praxis*), which, in the construction of tragedy, means the arrangement of actions *qua* events (*pragmata*), both contemporaneous and not contemporaneous with the time frame of the play.[3] The overall progression that Aristotle has in mind

---

[2] The "literary" tradition lying behind Aeschylus's works is not a sophisticated written tradition of the same sort Zeami drew on.

[3] See *Poetics*, 1449b31–50b20, where Aristotle lists and explains his priorities and defines each element in greater or lesser detail. On plot in particular, see 1450a3–5, 15–23, and 38–39. On the types of events that can be included, both contemporaneous and not contemporaneous with the time frame of the play, see the example of Aristotle's outline of the *Iphigenia at Tauris*, 1455b2–12. The translations and paraphrases of Aristotle's text, based on *Aristotelis de arte poetica liber*, ed. Rudolf Kassell (Oxford, 1965), like those of all Greek texts, are my own unless otherwise indicated.

for both simple and complex plots is a "tying up" (desis) and an "untying" (lusis). The former, which may include incidents preceding the action of the play as well as those within, extends from the beginning up to that point in the tragedy at which a change to good or bad fortune is about to occur; the latter extends from the beginning of the change to the end.[4] The best kind of plot, says Aristotle, is a complex plot, one in which a character's change in fortune entails a recognition (anagnōrisis), or reversal (peripeteia), or both, and one in which these develop out of the arrangement of the plot itself in such a way that they follow on the preceding events either by necessity or in accordance with what is probable.[5] To recognition and peripety, he adds the component pathos, that is, a destructive or painful act, found in simple and complex plots alike.[6]

Aristotle's prescriptions are not entirely irrelevant to a discussion of the Persians inasmuch as one could say, for example, that in this simple plot a change from good to bad fortune takes place when the queen of the Persians learns the painful truth that the Persian army has been defeated. However, we find that in many respects the Persians does not satisfy the Aristotelian prescriptions, or even the norms discernible in other tragedies. I have already mentioned the lack of overt argumentation in the Persians, such as we find in the Eumenides and the plays written by Sophocles and Euripides—part of what Aristotle calls dianoia ("thought"), which includes proofs and refutations. No "destructive or terrifying act" takes place in the Persians contemporaneously with the dramatic action, as it does or threatens to do in all other Greek tragedies. (The battles of Salamis and Psyttaleia and the Persian defeat reported in the Persians, like the Trojan War and Greek victory reported in the Agamemnon, are near in time to, but are not contemporaneous with, the dramatic action, as the murders of Agamemnon and Cassandra are in the latter play.) Furthermore, the act that is reported in the Persians is not perpetrated against kin or dear ones, as it is in the Seven against Thebes, for example; nor is it one that is carried out unknowingly, as Aristotle recommends for good tragedy—Xerxes, the king of Persia, planned to take revenge on the Greeks for his father's defeat. Therefore, Aristotle would probably have said that the two tragic emotions, pity and fear, are not built into the action or construction of the Persians in a manner that he would have considered best.[7]

Nor is the plot of the Persians the kind that Aristotle prefers, a complex

---

[4] See Poetics, 1455b24–29.

[5] See ibid., 1452a16–20. Aristotle defines and gives examples of peripety and reversal at 1452a22–52b8.

[6] See ibid., 1452b11–13.

[7] See ibid., 1453b14–22 and 54a2–9. At 1453b1–8, Aristotle says that fear and pity can arise out of opsis ("visual elements"), but it is better when they arise out of the structuring of the incidents, which is the plot as Aristotle defines it.

plot, in which the change of fortune involves a peripeteia and an ana-gnōrisis. The Persian people and Xerxes experience a change from good to bad fortune, from prosperity to defeat; however, Xerxes' recognition of what he has done and the unexpected shift—Xerxes' learning that the Greek enemy is not leaving the battle site when he thought they would—are both first reported by the messenger. There is no "recognition scene" enacted on stage by the dramatic characters, as there is in the *Libation Bearers*, for example. Nor does the major event itself involve a character who has been on stage, as it does in every other Greek tragedy, or one with whom the audience would identify as an undeserving victim or like them-selves, as Aristotle recommended. (Xerxes, who does not appear until the end of the play, is, after all, the Greeks' former enemy.) For these two reasons the structure of the play would seem not to evoke pity or fear for the main character.[8]

What pity and fear Aeschylus does evoke are first articulated and trans-mitted by other characters, namely the chorus and the queen, mother of Xerxes. Although these characters may strike an emotional chord for some members of the audience, they are not involved directly in the tragic event. If any feeling for Xerxes is aroused in the audience, it is most probably satisfaction that justice has been done, and perhaps the sort of sympathy that can be felt for anyone who suffers misfortune, even when the sufferer is one's former enemy. But again, these feelings do not occur as a result of the messenger's report of the event; they are delayed, and they arise out of the *performance*. The second half of the play features song, dance, stage action, and changes in costume: laments are heard; the queen enters with-out her former accoutrements of luxury; and Xerxes, appearing in rags, cries out that he was both a victim of and personally responsible for the disaster.

In a number of the particulars mentioned above, Zeami's warrior nō are similar to the *Persians*, as they are not to other tragedies. In these nō, as in *Sanemori*, there is little spoken argument. There is no tragic event contem-poraneous with the dramatic time. The event in warrior nō usually in-volves enemies, not loved ones or kin—in *Sanemori* there is not even the

---

[8] See Aristotle's views on complex plots in *Poetics* 1452a16–52b3 and on the relation-ship between the change of fortune and type of character in *Poetics* 1452b34–53a17. A. F. Garvie ("Aeschylus' Simple Plots," *Dionysiaca: Nine Studies in Greek Poetry by Former Pupils, Presented to Sir Denys Page on His Seventieth Birthday*, ed. R. D. Dawe, J. Diggle, and P. E. Easterling [Cambridge, 1978], 64) thinks that even the recognition scene in the *Libation Bearers* is less central to the plot than the similar scene in Sopho-cles' *Electra*. Similarly, he thinks that the peripeteia in the *Agamemnon*, whether that term means to us "reversal of situation or frustration of intention [or any variation on these]" (64), is not central to the structure in the way that it is to the plot of Sophocles' *Oedipus*.

presence of kin on stage. Furthermore, the act is perpetrated knowingly by the victim—like Xerxes' attempt to conquer Greece, Sanemori's desire to kill Kiso is unsuccessful. For these and other reasons, in Aristotle's terms, fear and pity are not properly built into the "plot" of *Sanemori*, or even into the tragic event that occurred during Sanemori's lifetime. In the kata-ri, when the shite reports Higuchi's recognition of Sanemori's head and sorrowful reaction, I assume that, since the character on stage is reporting what another said and felt about him, even though the character is sympathetic and the audience may be affected by the actor and his expression of sorrow, that expression is too far removed from the dramatic action to be properly effective in Aristotle's terms. What pity one may feel with respect to the tragic event is instead relegated to the end of the play, when Sanemori cries out on behalf of the old warrior who is himself. However, because the event is reenacted in dance and song and by an actor playing the role of a ghost, again pity does not arise out of the dramatic action in a manner that Aristotle would probably have considered best. Because Sanemori is a ghost, the pity—or the sympathy—he evokes pertains not to an event or the action (his death in battle, for example), but instead to his attachment to this world. This is the issue raised in the middle of the play and intensified, until it is brought to a peak at the finale in the warrior's (the actor's) *performance* of the tale of repentance, which is simultaneously the narration of the event.

To the extent that Aristotle's ideas reflect a direction in which Greek tragedy developed, they are important. However, since he shows a clear preference for complex plots over simple ones, for the plots of Sophocles and Euripides over those of Aeschylus, and for tragedies that can arouse the emotions of pity and fear as much from a reading as from a performance, Aristotle's views on the qualitative parts of Greek tragedy do not provide an adequate framework for an analysis of the structure of the *Persians*.

The *Poetics* also presents a list of quantitative parts, the basic units out of which any Greek tragedy can be divided and which are comparable to the division of nō into dan and shōdan. The parts common to all tragedies, we are told in the *Poetics*, are prologue, episode, *exodos*, and choral part, which includes *parodos* and *stasimon*; those parts only found in some tragedies are actor's solos and *kommoi*.[9] According to the *Poetics*, the pro-

---

[9] These parts are listed and then defined in the *Poetics* at 1452b14–27, but are not fully integrated into Aristotle's argument; nor are they on the same level as his discussion of other parts, such as pathos, immediately preceding. This section may represent a later addition to Aristotle's work. On this point, see Gerald F. Else, *Aristotle's Poetics: The Argument* (Cambridge, Mass., 1963), 359–363. For the view that it is part of Aristotle's original work, see the arguments of Richard Janko, *Aristotle on Comedy: Towards a Reconstruction of Poetics II* (Berkeley, 1984), 239–241.

[handwritten margin note: But see Taplin]

logue, a speech delivered in iambic trimeters, the verse pattern closest to the rhythm of ordinary Greek, is "the entire part of the tragedy before the choral parodos"; an episode is "the whole section of a tragedy between whole choral songs"; and the exodos is "the whole part of a tragedy after which there is not a song by the chorus." Of the choral parts, we are told that the parodos is "the first whole speech by the chorus"; the stasimon is "a choral song without anapaestic or trochaic rhythm"; and the kommos is "a *thrēnos* [literally, a lament] shared by the chorus and an actor."

In practice, we find that the *Poetics'* definition of these parts with respect to each other is accurately represented in the tragedies as we know them. However, the list is not entirely satisfactory, for not all these parts appear in every tragedy, and the description of some parts is not true to the evidence of all extant plays.[10] Anapaests are often used in transitional recitatives, like *shidai* in nō for example, and are found in the choral introductions to episodes or songs; trochees are recitative meters of dialogue, like *issei*, often found within episodes. However, both are also found in the stasima (choral songs). Further, the kommos may be a lament, but need not be; in form it is like a *rongi*, a lyric dialogue.

Among Aeschylus's plays one finds that the *Persians* and the *Suppliants* begin with a parodos, the section sung by the chorus in anapaestic rhythm as it enters the orkhēstra; his other tragedies begin with spoken prologues.[11] The exodos of the *Suppliants* is a choral song; that of the *Agamemnon*, an excited, spoken exchange in trochaic meter; those of the *Libation Bearers* and the *Eumenides*, anapaestic songs sung by the chorus; that of the *Seven against Thebes*, a kommos sung as a lament by two actors;[12] and that of the *Persians*, a kommos, again a lament, sung by the chorus and an actor. All of these are exodoi, but they differ in ways not mentioned in the *Poetics*. The episodes, consisting of spoken dialogue, speeches, and *epirrhēmata* (exchanges in which one party speaks and the other sings in the manner of a kakeai), vary in both form and number

---

[10] For a fuller discussion of these parts and their meaning in the fifth century B.C., see Taplin, *Stagecraft*, Appendix E.

[11] In both the *Seven against Thebes* and the *Libation Bearers*, a main character (Eteocles and Orestes, respectively) delivers the prologue; in both the *Agamemnon* and the *Eumenides*, it is given by a nameless character (the watchman and priestess, respectively), who does not return to the stage after the exit at the end of the prologue.

[12] Like many others (e.g., E. Fraenkel, "Zum Schluss der 'Sieben gegen Theben,' " *MH* 21 [1964]: 58–64), I consider line 1004 to be the end of the Aeschylean *Seven against Thebes*. According to our manuscripts, after the kommos (line 1004), a herald arrives, delivers a speech, and converses with Antigone; the play ends with a choral song in anapaests. There is also a possibility that the play ended with the choral song, at line 960; see T. Bergk, *Griechische Literaturgeschichte* 3 (Berlin, 1884), 302–305. For a discussion of the problems connected with the end of the play and the scholarship on the subject, see H. Lloyd-Jones, "The End of the *Seven against Thebes*," *CQ*, n.s. 9 (1959): 80–115.

within individual plays. The constant among all tragedies is their divisibility into episodes.

Among Aeschylus's extant works, two, the *Agamemnon* and the *Persians*, exhibit some parts of tragedy mentioned in the *Poetics* and others that are not mentioned. The plays also serve as evidence that Aeschylus wrote at least two tragedies about returning military leaders with a similar, if not fixed, structure in mind,[13] a structure that begins to show that the divisions of tragedy are comparable to those of dan and shōdan in nō. In these two plays, for example, Aeschylus presents a chorus singing a parodos as it marches on stage: in the *Persians*, this entrance occurs at the beginning; in the *Agamemnon*, after the nameless watchman delivers a prologue. The difference between the beginning of the two works approximates that between *Takasago*, which begins with a shidai, an entrance song sung by the waki and wakizure, followed by the nanori ("naming speech"), and *Sanemori*, which is abbreviated and begins with a nanori spoken by the nameless kyōgen. After the parodos, each tragedy continues with a lyric parodos, the first choral ode, sung by a chorus of elders,[14] in which Aeschylus reveals the identity of the chorus, as in the nanori the playwright identifies the waki.[15]

The choruses of the *Persians* and the *Agamemnon* next acknowledge a character and her identity, a queen in both cases, and speak with her in what is the first episode; prominent in this section of both plays are two extended speeches and a *stichomythia*, a dialogue between the chorus and actor in which each speaks in alternate lines.[16] (In nō, the shite usually delivers a monologue before he engages in a mondō "dialogue" with the waki.) Next in the *Persians*, a messenger, the second nameless character of this tragedy, arrives, utters a short speech, and engages the chorus in an epirrhēma—he speaks and the chorus sings—and finally enters into a dialogue with the queen, in the course of which he delivers four long speeches. In the *Agamemnon*, the second episode begins only after an anapaestic

[13] On the similarity between the structure of these two, see, for example, Thomas G. Rosenmeyer, *The Art of Aeschylus* (Berkeley, 1982), 42–43. H. G. Edinger, "Vocabulary and Imagery in Aeschylus' 'Persians' " (Diss., Princeton University, 1961), 76–82, has pointed out similarities between the end of the *Persians* and the end of the *Eumenides*, the third play of the trilogy of which the *Agamemnon* is the first play.

[14] The choruses of Greek tragedy are sometimes a group of elders. In Aeschylus's other extant works, they are females.

[15] The first long choral song usually does not occur until the end of dan three in nō. At best one hears a brief introductory song sung by the chorus at the beginning of nō. Songs of significant length do not appear at all before the end of dan one.

[16] The two speeches occur before the stichomythy in the *Persians*, after it in the *Agamemnon*. There are other variations as well; e.g., in the *Persians*, the chorus sings in anapaests before addressing the queen; in the *Agamemnon*, the anapaests occur at the end of the parodos and before the lyric parodos.

87

introduction and the first stasimon; it consists of a short speech by the queen, a comment by the chorus, and, once the herald arrives, some dialogue and four long speeches—three spoken by the herald and one by Clytemnestra. There is no epirrhematic passage. After the messenger exits in the *Persians*, the chorus and the queen speak; after the queen exits, the chorus sings an anapaestic introduction and the first stasimon. In the *Agamemnon*, with the exit of the herald, the chorus sings the second stasimon.

Up to and including the messenger/herald episodes and the choral songs that follow—that is, for approximately half of each play—the *Persians* and the *Agamemnon* exhibit a significant number of structural similarities. The major difference between them is the presence in the *Agamemnon* of a prologue and extra stasimon that are missing in the *Persians*.[17] After the stasima that follow the messenger/herald scenes of the *Persians* and the *Agamemnon*, the differences in structure become greater. In the table below, the plays are schematically outlined from beginning to end in terms of the larger components.[18]

THE STRUCTURAL PARTS OF THE *PERSIANS* AND THE *AGAMEMNON*

Persians	*Agamemnon*
—	Prologue
Parodos	Parodos
Lyric parodos	Lyric parodos
Episode 1 (queen)	Episode 1 (queen)
—	Stasimon 1
Episode 2 with an epirrhēma (queen and messenger)	Episode 2 (herald and queen)
Stasimon 1	Stasimon 2
Short episode 3 (queen)	Episode 3 (king and queen)
Stasimon 2	Stasimon 3
Episode 4 with a short epirrhēma (Darius and queen)	Episode 4 with a long epirrhēma (queen and Cassandra)
Stasimon 3	Speeches, epirrhēma and kommos (queen)
Kommos [exodos] (Xerxes)	Episode 5 [exodos] (Aegisthus and queen)

[17] As I pointed out in the last chapter, in nō there are fewer dan in the first halves of shura nō than in the first halves of waki nō. Even among the warrior plays there are differences; in *Yorimasa*, for example, there is no second dan; that is to say, after the first dan in which the waki and wakizure appear, the shite is not allotted a dan of his own. He enters and immediately engages in a dialogue with the waki.

[18] For a chart of the episodes appearing in the extant plays written by all three tragedians, see Klaus Aichele, "Das Epeisodion," in *Die Bauformen der griechischen Tragödie*, ed. Walter Jens (Munich, 1971), 50–51.

In a closer examination of the structure of the second halves of the *Persians* and the *Agamemnon*, one finds differences in the number, length, and position of smaller units as well. The *Agamemnon* is considerably longer than the *Persians* and features two more characters. And yet there is a recognizable pattern underlying the arrangement of both tragedies. The similar components include a parodos and lyric parodos at or near the beginning, three stasima, two epirrhēmata, a kommos, a messenger/herald episode near the middle, and two episodes in which the queen appears alone with the chorus. These similarities are comparable to those identified in the four warrior plays considered in the last chapter: each contains a nanori at the beginning; three ageuta "songs"; two sung exchanges, either kakeai or rongi; a kyōgen scene near the middle; and two dan in which the waki and wakizure appear alone with the chorus, without the shite. The similarities between the *Persians* and the *Agamemnon* point to a pattern in the division of these two, like other tragedies, into episodes divided and marked by stasima sung by the chorus or by songs shared by the chorus and an actor. These songs are comparable to the musical shōdan appearing at the end of, rather than between, dan in nō.

The method of dividing tragedies by means of whole strophic choral odes, odes in which each stanza is matched by another in the same meter, was initiated by the *Poetics* and serves as the basis for a majority of approaches used to divide tragedies into discrete parts. However, as Oliver Taplin has observed, this method is not valid. Not only does one strophic ode (*Suppliants* 418–437) not serve as a divider, but there are "acts" that divide in accordance with other types of songs.[19] Taplin has suggested a way of dividing tragedies that would complement the traditional method: he views the patterns in terms of the sequence of exits and entries. Taplin writes, "The alternation of speech and song in Greek tragedy is integrally bound up with the rearrangement of the action by means of actors' exits before songs and entries after them."[20] The underlying structure, then, is determined by the entrances[21] (which as in nō are usually announced mu-

---

[19] These songs include astrophic anapaests and astrophic dochmiac lyrics (dochmiacs are meters particularly well suited to expressions of strong emotion), "epirrhematic lyric structures and irregular lyric dialogue," and, outside of Aeschylus's works, actor's monodies. Taplin, *Stagecraft*, 51–52. In Aeschylus's works these exceptions occur at *Agamemnon* 1331–1342, *Libation Bearers* 719–729 and 855–868, and *Suppliants* 966–979. Actor's monodies do not appear in Aeschylus's plays, as they do in Zeami's and other nō. On the subject of monody in Greek tragedy, see Wilfried Barner's "Die Monodie," in *Die Bauformen der griechischen Tragödie*, ed. Walter Jens (Munich, 1971), 277–320.

[20] Taplin, *Stagecraft*, 54–55. On the subject of entrances and exits in the works of all three Greek tragedians, see Taplin, *Greek Tragedy in Action* (Berkeley and Los Angeles, 1978), 31–57.

[21] John Herington, in *Aeschylus* (New Haven and London, 1986), 39–40, appreciates well the importance of "entrances" in Aeschylean performances.

sically or verbally), the exits, and the songs, in that order. When a structural variant occurs, he says, it suggests that the playwright had some special effect in mind. In his discussion of the *Persians*, Taplin compares the beginning of that play with the beginning of the *Suppliants* and finds similarities that suggest "a certain continuity and care in Aeschylus's control of his structural techniques."[22] For example, both tragedies begin with an anapaestic parodos and a long lyric parodos; these are followed by the entry of a major character, the queen in the *Persians* and Danaus in the *Suppliants*. (In the *Agamemnon*, the queen enters into the dramatic "action" at this point.) Each of the ensuing scenes contains speeches and stichomythy, as does the comparable scene in the *Agamemnon*. Next a character enters from outside (a messenger and King Pelasgus, respectively), and a long scene ensues in which there is an epirrhematic exchange. (In the *Agamemnon* the herald scene occurs after a choral stasimon.) The second character then leaves and the first character "goes on a mission" before the chorus sings a song expressing disquiet. (This sequence is followed in the *Agamemnon*.) The first character returns. Next, in the *Persians*, there is a brief speech (*rhēsis*), followed by a song; in the *Suppliants*, a short exchange of speeches followed by a song in anapaestic, rather than in lyric, meter. Taplin points out that in neither play is there the expected exit before the song.[23] The absence of an exit creates a special effect: in the *Suppliants*, there is a sudden shift in mood from the maidens' song of blessing to their father's announcement that enemy ships have been sighted, the first verbally explicit turn toward a disaster that is realized later with the arrival of the Egyptians; in the *Persians*, the choral song is the first scene of kinetic interest in the play and prepares for the appearance of Darius's ghost, who both offers the most explicit verbal statement of the play's "moral" and, because he is dressed in royal attire, provides an important visual contrast to the queen's and Xerxes' appearance. In both tragedies, as in nō where it is the norm for the waki to remain on stage from beginning to end, the absence of a character's exit from the stage makes room for and avoids distraction from the entrance of a more important character or an important scene.

The relationship between entrances and exits of actors on the one hand and speeches and songs on the other is different in nō and tragedy inasmuch as nō actors do not consistently enter after songs and exit before them, and songs are generally considered a part of dan rather than separate from them. Yet there are exceptions to this tendency in nō that resemble the norm in tragedy as analyzed by Taplin. The first entrance of each char-

[22] Taplin, *Stagecraft*, 109.
[23] Ibid., 109.

acter, especially that of the shite and kyōgen, tends to follow a song; the kyōgen exits before a song. Special songs such as the shidai, issei, machi-utai, ageuta, or rongi, although they are part of dan, like songs or speeches in tragedy, usually mark the entrances and the exits of the waki and the shite. (Sometimes the entrance of the shite is announced by a call, *yobi-kake*, or by instrumental music, rather than by a song.) In addition, there seems to be a degree of predictability in the arrangement of the entrances and exits in some nō, such as we infer exists in at least some of Aeschylus's plays. The first and second dan in both the maeba and the nochiba regu-larly feature the entrance, or the movement from one side to the center of the stage, of the waki and shite respectively; the third or fourth dan usually contains the retirement of the waki to the side of the stage after a song, a virtual exit; the kyōgen scene has the entrance of the kyōgen after a song and his exit before a song; and the last dan features the exit of the shite, after or during a song. In the *Persians*, the two entrances and exits of the queen (like the first two entrances and exits of Danaus) and the entrance and exit of the messenger and of Darius, if played by the same actor, occur in the first and the second halves in a manner analogous to those of the waki and shite actors respectively in the maeba and nochiba. Like the kyō-gen, the messenger (and the herald in the *Agamemnon*) exits before a song; at the end, Xerxes' exit, like the shite's, follows or accompanies a song. (The *Persians* is unusual in that a song is not sung before the arrival of the messenger; however, the trochaic tetrameters preceding the entrance are more musical than the alternative meter of dialogue, iambic trimeters. In *Sanemori*, the kyōgen, like the herald of the *Agamemnon*, arrives after a song.)

In fact, a pattern emerges in the *Persians* that is easily compared to the pattern of entrances and exits of the two actors, the shite and the waki, in a nō performance. (For the purpose of this discussion of actors' entrances and exits, we separate the choral parodos and lyric parodos from the rest of the *Persians*, as we would the shidai that are often presented at the beginning of nō today, and consider the chorus in the light of the strictly choral function that it serves in nō, as a body of men who remain on stage from beginning to end and provide continuity rather than as a participant character as, of course, it also is.[24]) In the *Persians*, as well as in the *Aga-memnon* and the *Suppliants*, the chorus sings the parodos and lyric paro-

[24] In "The Chorus of Greek Drama within the Light of the Person and Number Used," *Commentiones Humanarum Litterarum* 46 (Helsinki, 1970), Maarit Kaimio concludes that the choruses of Aeschylean tragedy function like a dramatic character; on the other hand, in *Untersuchungen zur Form des aischyleischen Chorliedes* (Diss., Tübingen, 1965), 72, Jürgen Rode argues that the logical structure of the odes implies few mimetic features; that is, the choral odes, as poetry, are set apart from actors' roles.

dos (*Persians* 1–137) before the entrance of a major character. The first actor to appear plays the role of the queen. In the first scene (140–248) he is allotted speeches and a dialogue with the chorus, but without the presence of another actor. In nō, dan one is allotted to the waki and wakizure's recitations and songs.[25] In the next scene (249–289), without an exit from the stage by the actor who plays the role of the queen, the messenger enters, speaks (like the shite), then engages in an epirrhēma with the chorus. He does not speak to the queen. (It is the norm in Aeschylus's works for an actor to address the chorus first, rather than another actor, although this is not the case in the plays of Sophocles and Euripides.[26]) The queen, like the waki who in dan two allows the shite to speak in *Sanemori*, stands aside, remains outside the dramatic "action," and says nothing, as her first words when she does speak, "I have been silent for a long time, struck in my misery by the evils . . ." (290–291), suggest.[27] Although Aeschylus may have intended the queen's words to be psychologically motivated by the news of the Persian defeat, the analogy with nō suggests that he also uses them to mark a new section of the play (290–597). The queen acknowledges that she has heard the bad news, but does not make an explicit reference to the messenger's speech.[28]

[25] As I have said, the wakizure are often not considered characters in their own right any more than the extras, the mutes, such as may attend the queen's first entrance in the *Persians*, are thought of as characters in tragedy.

[26] See Taplin, *Stagecraft*, 86–87. According to Ann N. Michelini, *Tradition and Dramatic Form in the Persians of Aeschylus*, Cincinnati Classical Studies, n.s., vol. 4 (Leiden, 1982), 29, the second actor has a better claim than the chorus to be the interlocutor, but as a vestige of one-actor tragedy this custom of actor addressing chorus first persists.

[27] I place emphasis here on Aeschylus's use of these words to bring the queen back from the sidelines and to begin the dramatic "action" anew. I disagree with Taplin, *Stagecraft*, 288–290, on the comparable scene in the *Agamemnon*, for I do not think, as he does, that Clytemnestra exits before the stasimon (355–487), which precedes the herald scene. With the analogy of nō, it is easy to imagine that the queen remains on stage "totally unnoticed" and without being a "distracting irrelevance." In fact, according to J. D. Denniston and D. Page, *Aeschylus Agamemnon* (Oxford, 1957), 117, Clytemnestra may remain on stage from her entry at line 40 or 83 down to 1068. However, I agree with Taplin that lines 489–502, the first address to the herald, are spoken by the chorus, rather than by the queen. In the plays of Sophocles we might think about what the "imagined reaction" of the silent character is, but not in those of Aeschylus. See Charles Segal, "Visual Symbolism and Visual Effects in Sophocles," *CW* 74, no. 2 (1980/81): 125–142 (p. 140), also published in Charles Segal, *Interpreting Greek Tragedy: Myth, Poetry, Text* (Ithaca, N.Y., 1986): 113–136 (p. 133).

[28] In *Sanemori*, as he moves toward the waki, the shite, who has been speaking to himself despite the waki's presence on stage, mentions in the sashi that he is a little late and then prays. His reference to a delay is comparable to the queen's reference to her silence. At the beginning of dan three the waki acknowledges the presence of the shite and his devotion, but does not make an explicit reference to his speech. Similarly, the kyōgen of *Sanemori*, who has been physically present on stage from the time the nō began, starts off in the kyōgen scene with an apology to the waki for being late. Since he has been present on stage, there is every reason in terms of the requirements of dramatic

In terms of the overall structure of the *Persians*, the messenger in the scene that follows corresponds to both a shite and a kyōgen in nō: in the first half of some nō, such as *Takasago*, the shite delivers a katari (a narrative) that, in terms of its content, is more important than a kyōgen's speech to the structure of a play; the kyōgen, on the other hand, appears in warrior nō and delivers his set narrative speech to the audience in a mode of delivery not unlike that of the messenger's speeches in lines 302–514 of the *Persians* and of the herald in lines 503–680 of the *Agamemnon*. In the *Persians*, the messenger exits after his concluding remark, "This is the truth, and in speaking I leave out many of the evils which god cast down upon the Persians (513–514)," but before the queen exits and before the song is sung in reaction to his news (the structure of the *Agamemnon* is similar at this point);[29] the kyōgen similarly exits after his concluding remark, before another character exits and before a song. The chorus and the queen, like the waki in the kyōgen scene of *Sanemori*, respond directly to the words they have heard. Then, we assume, the queen exits; the waki "exits" by moving to a new position on stage.

At the beginning of the second half of the tragedy, after the messenger scene and the stasimon that follows, the queen enters alone and speaks with no other characters present. This short scene (598–680), which includes a choral song, is comparable to the short first dan of the nochiba in which the waki appears without the shite in *Sanemori*. The queen does not exit during the choral stasimon, as she did not during the epirrhēma in the messenger scene, and as the waki, who is singing the song, did not exit before the second entrance of the shite. In nō, it is usual for actors to remain on stage during the final song of a dan. In Aeschylus's works there are at least two other places in which the actor does not exit during a song, at *Suppliants* 625–709 and *Eumenides* 254–275.[30] In addition to these examples and the stasimon before the herald scene in the *Agamemnon*, there is the likelihood that Clytemnestra does not exit with Agamemnon into the palace (957).[31] In the *Persians*, during the song, the chorus sings

unity for him to apologize; however, the self-conscious remark also alerts the audience to a new scene. In the nō *Sesshōseki*, the kyōgen sits quietly on stage after delivering a speech at the beginning, then introduces the kyōgen scene with a self-conscious speech expressing his wish to talk to the priest (the waki). The play, not written by Zeami, has been translated by Sieffert, *La tradition secrète*, 294–307.

[29] On the messenger's exit, see Taplin, *Stagecraft*, 88–91.

[30] Taplin discusses the scene in the *Persians* and others like it, *Stagecraft*, 108–114.

[31] The dramatic effect of Agamemnon's exit is enhanced if all eyes are focused on the king alone (958–974). Then, while the chorus sings a stasimon, the queen, like a waki, stands aside in silence; after the stasimon, she turns to the chorus and takes care of the unfinished business, Agamemnon's Trojan mistress. When Cassandra speaks, she does so with the chorus, not with Clytemnestra, who has made her exit alone and in triumph.

and the queen makes the gestures of pouring libations. This division of labor resembles that in nō, where an important function of the chorus is to take over a song for the actor, in a kuse for example, so that he can dance or move about freely.

Although the queen is present on stage when Darius appears, he speaks at first with the chorus only, in a scene (681–702) comparable to that in which the nochijite appears and at first recites or speaks as if the waki were not present on stage. (In *Sanemori*, the shite first recites and then engages in an issei with the chorus.) Next, at the same point in both the *Persians* and nō, the two main actors engage in dialogue with one another. Before the end of this section (703–906), the queen leaves the stage, and does not return; the waki leaves the center of the stage to which he does not return. The chorus takes over for both of them so that the performance is focused on the main character in the last section (907–1077), which ends with his exit. An outline of the sections of the tragedy as enumerated above is as follows:

First Half of the *Persians*
      Lines 1–139: Introductory Section
      Lines 140–248: First Section
      Lines 249–289: Second Section
      Lines 290–597: Third Section
Second Half of the *Persians*
      Lines 598–680: First Section
      Lines 681–702: Second Section
      Lines 703–906: Third Section
      Lines 907–1077: Fourth Section

The major differences between the *Persians* and *Sanemori* in my analysis above are that in the former the messenger's role is more important than the kyōgen's and is most likely played by the first actor, and this first actor playing the role of Darius in the second half of the tragedy exits before the choral song and then reenters in the role of Xerxes; in the latter, the shite remains on stage in the second half of the nō as the ghost of Sanemori, another aspect of the shite's role in the first half.[32] And yet, in spite of the

---

The effect is quite different from and less distracting than what one imagines the *Agamemnon* would be like if Clytemnestra left the stage with Agamemnon and then came back again to talk to Cassandra. For arguments to the contrary, namely that Clytemnestra exits with Agamemnon, see Taplin, *Stagecraft*, 308–310.

[32] In Zeami's *Kiyotsune*, there is a third actor, the tsure, who plays the role of the warrior Kiyotsune's wife. He appears both in the first part with the waki, who plays the part of Kiyotsune's retainer, and in the second with the shite, who plays the part of ghost of Kiyotsune. But he does not play more than one role. This nō is unusual in that

two extra roles played by the main actor in the *Persians*, there are similarities between this tragedy and Zeami's nō which, when fully grasped, may be instructive to an appreciation of the performance of the former. To be sure, Nogami Toyoichirō was correct when he said that the invention of the second actor took Greek tragedy outside the bounds of epic and lyric into that of dramatic expression, making way for a confrontation between characters such as one does not find in nō, where even from its inception there could be more than three actors in a single play.[33] However, there is not in the *Persians*, any more than in nō, a confrontation between characters on stage; there is not even a confrontation between actor and chorus, such as one finds in *Seven against Thebes*. The confrontation occurs in the content of the words of the narrative speeches instead. The main actor, appearing successively as the messenger, Darius, and Xerxes, remains in each role the focal point of the performance; the second actor, always the queen, elicits and gives information; and the chorus both serves as counselor and, more importantly, expresses emotion in company with and on behalf of both actors. Each actor and character, moreover, is given the opportunity to appear alone with the chorus. In addition, although in the course of the *Persians* a single actor must change masks twice in order to depict his several roles, whereas in *Sanemori* the shite changes costume once to play two aspects of one character, an old man and the ghost of a warrior, the single actor in the tragedy appears in scenes that, in terms of content, are comparable to the last three dan of nō, the scenes that are the most demanding of the actor's skills. In the katari, the shite, like the messenger, narrates an event from the past in the third person, and on occasion quotes or speaks in the voice of another; in the kusemai, the chorus speaks for the shite who, like Darius, states a moral lesson of the play on the basis of examples and authority drawn from the past; and in the rongi, the shite, like Xerxes, in conjunction with the chorus, presents to the audience a vivid enactment of his tragedy.

In our earliest extant Greek tragedy, which as I have already mentioned is in many respects both like other tragedies and also unique,[34] the audience's attention is drawn to a single leading actor, probably the playwright, without a presentation of conflict between characters and with but

---

the shite does not appear in the first part, nor the waki in the second. The play has been translated by Sieffert in *Nô et Kyôgen*, 2: 157–170. Many characters appear in realistic nō and later nō, but normally only the shite changes costume.

[33] Nogami, "Nō no shuyaku ichinin shugi," 31.

[34] See L.J.D. Richardson, "The Inner Conflict in the *Persae*: Athenian Dramatist and Persian Characters," in *Studies in Honour of Gilbert Norwood*, ed. Mary E. White, *The Phoenix*, suppl. vol. 1 (Toronto, 1952), 55–67, on the effect of the unique aspect of the *Persians*—its treatment of recent Athenian history.

two exits by the second actor, one in each half of the play. This lack of conflict and of stage action is as close as the performance of tragedy comes to the example of nō. And the analogy with nō surely makes attractive the hypothesis that characters are left on stage whenever possible and virtual exits are used during stasima, especially in the *Persians* and in the beginnings of the *Agamemnon* and the *Suppliants*, so that extra real entrances and exits do not detract from the flow of the performance toward the climactic moment in which the main character is featured, and so that the entrances and exits of characters, when they do occur, help to direct attention to that climactic moment. That in the *Persians* Aeschylus consistently has actors first speak exclusively with the chorus, and only later engage in a dialogue with others, suggests that at the end, when Xerxes appears alone with the chorus and is the only character not to appear with another actor, the tragedy is poignantly focused on him.

Many approaches besides that of Taplin have been applied to the analysis of structure in the *Persians*.[35] Gerald F. Else, for example, divides the

[35] For example, Demetrius Detscheff, *De tragoediarum Graecarum conformatione scaenica ac dramatica* (Diss., Göttingen, 1904), 132, divides the play into eight parts— the parodos (1–142), three episodes (143–550, divided into two at line 248 where the messenger appears, 601–635, and 683–853), three stasima (551–600, 636–682, and 854–910), and an exodos (911–1077); these eight divisions almost coincide in their positions to those of Gustav Adolf Seeck, *Dramatische Strukturen der griechischen Tragödie: Untersuchungen zu Aischylos*, Zetemata 8 (Munich, 1984), 11, who, however, divides the play into four choral parts (1–139, 532–597, 633–680, and 852–907) and four scenes (A, divided into A¹ shared by the chorus and the queen and A² shared by the chorus, the messenger, and the queen; B, enacted by the queen alone; C, shared by Darius, the chorus, and the queen; and D, shared by Xerxes and the chorus). Seeck's division of A into two parts indicates that he, like others, sees a break at the point where the messenger arrives. Although his analysis of the *Persians*, unlike mine, is guided in part by the structural variations that he thinks Aeschylus takes from a "Grundstruktur," which applies in some respects to all Greek tragedy (5–6), some of my conclusions are similar to his. For example, he thinks that Aeschylus's variations isolate the characters of Darius and Xerxes and thus add an enriching complexity to the former and an emphasis on Xerxes himself in the latter. Thomas D. Goodell, "Structural Variety in Attic Tragedy," *TAPA* 41 (1910): 75–76, divides the play into four parts between the parodos and the exodos—episode one (155–547) with transitional anapaests (532–547), stasimon one (548–597), episode two (598–851), and stasimon two (852–908). Erling B. Holtsmark, "Ring Composition and the *Persae* of Aeschylus," *Symbolae Osloenses* 45 (1970): 5–23, sees four divisions (1–149, 150–531, 532–906, and 907–1077). Richmond Lattimore, "Aeschylus on the Defeat of Xerxes," in *Classical Studies in Honor of Wm. Abbott Oldfather* (Urbana, Ill., 1943), 82–93, divides the play into four parts— everything up to the messenger scene is the first part (1–248), the messenger scene (249–514) is the second, the Darius scene (515–908) is the third, and the Xerxes scene is the fourth. U. v. Wilamowitz-Möllendorff, *Aischylos Interpretationen* (Dublin and Zürich, 1966), 42–50, is among those who divide the tragedy into three acts; he says that the first begins with the entrance of the chorus, the second with the second entrance of the queen, and the third with the entrance of Xerxes. All the divisions of the *Persians* listed above, except that of Wilamowitz, treat the stasima as separate parts or place at least one stasimon, that is, a choral song within the play, at the beginning rather than at the

play into four parts on the basis of its "action," by which he does not mean the movements of actors on stage.[36] Instead, his views are closely related to his discussion of the early history of tragedy and his perception of the *Persians* as a play in which there is not conflict but rather the presentation of the effect of a disaster that has already taken place and the meaning of which Aeschylus "brings home" to us. According to Else, the phases of action are first, apprehension by the chorus and the queen; second, verification of defeat by the messenger; third, an explanation of it by Darius; and fourth, the emotional realization of it by the chorus and the defeated king, Xerxes. The pathos itself divides into two: the report, prepared for by apprehension, and the presentation, anticipated by explanation. Else's four-part analysis is thus reducible to a two-fold division of the tragedy that resembles the division of a warrior nō into maeba and nochiba. In *Sanemori*, the identity of the main character is revealed after preparation in the maeba; the "tragic event" is enacted in the nochiba once background has been provided. In both the nō and the tragedy, the fullest emotional realization of the tragic event occurs in the second half.

However, there is also an important difference between the *Persians* and nō: the function of the tragic event within the construction of the play. The second half of the tragedy provides Darius's explanation of the causes and the consequences of the Persian defeat reported earlier in the *Persians*, as well as the chorus's and Xerxes' emotional reactions to the event; the nochiba of *Sanemori* provides an explanation of the event reported by the kyōgen (that is, why Sanemori, though an old man, chose to fight) and the chorus's and Sanemori's emotional reaction to it. However, the battle event is described most vividly with the shite's *performance* of a battle scene at the finale. Thus the strongest expression of emotion for the main character Sanemori is tied directly to the stage enactment of the tragic event. On the other hand, because the tragic event reported in the *Persians* dictates the course of the "plot," that event is literally more central to the

---

end of a section. According to Wilamowitz's divisions, all three acts end with song, a stasimon or a thrēnos.

[36] Else, *Origin and Early Form*, 87. Similar to the four divisions posited by Else are those of D. J. Conacher, "Aeschylus' *Persae*: A Literary Commentary," *Serta Turyniana*, ed. John L. Heller (Urbana, Ill., 1974), 143–168, who divides the play into stages: first, anticipation; second, fulfillment (the report); third, retrospection, including an account of what will happen in the future; and fourth, Xerxes' appearance (149). Seeck, *Dramatische Strukturen der griechischen Tragödie*, 5–7, introduces a "Grundstruktur" inspired by, but different from, those of Schadewaldt and Jens, that divides tragedy into three basic parts—"Spannungssituation" (S), "Krisis" (K), and "Reaktion" (R). Seeck analyzes Aeschylus's plays in terms of this structure. By treating variations on it he shows how Aeschylus enriches the structure, the presentation of character, and the form of even this relatively straightforward play, the *Persians*, 11–21.

play. In this regard Aeschylus anticipates the importance that Aristotle places on the tragic event in the *composition* of tragedy, and the importance of a tragic event to the structure of later tragedies.

In addition, there is a difference in the kind of character each playwright chooses to feature. In the nō, Sanemori is a noble warrior, a character such as Aristotle might have chosen, but, because he is a ghost, he is set at some distance from the audience. In the tragedy, Xerxes is a negative model of immediate emotional concern to the Greeks, who won a war against him, and a living character, set at some distance because he is a foreign potentate and former enemy. One needs to be reminded that during the performance of the tragedy the Athenian audience might have enjoyed rather than feared a report of the Persian defeat and would not have considered Xerxes a person like themselves, let alone one undeserving in his misfortune. Yet Aeschylus has made first the Persian people and then Xerxes himself the focus of laments. And further, it seems unlikely that the Greeks would have pictured Darius, father of Xerxes and their former enemy, as a good and wise leader, the teacher of the best of Greek traditional morality; yet that is how Aeschylus has altered history to present the ghost of Darius. Therefore, the reason for Aeschylus's success with this play seems to lie not with his choice of characters per se, but with what he does with them. And this is one area of our investigation for which in spite of the differences nō is instructive. There is a development built into the *Persians*, as there is in the best of Zeami's nō, that connects the characters naturally to elements of performance. This in turn elicits the proper reactions in the Greek audience: if not pity, at least a feeling of satisfaction that those who do wrong are punished.

In one sense of the word, the "events" contemporaneous with the dramatic time of both the *Persians* and *Sanemori* are not destructive or terrifying events of the sort that Aristotle had in mind, but rather performances, which in these two plays are enacted rituals—in the *Persians*, a libation performed by the queen to raise the ghost of Darius from the dead and laments performed by the chorus and Xerxes; and in *Sanemori*, a special service performed by the priest on behalf of the ghost of Sanemori, the repeated invocations of Amida Buddha by the chorus and Sanemori, and the tale of repentance. We assume that in the *Persians* the performance of a ritual to raise up the ghost of Darius, based on elements of a ritual probably familiar to the Greeks, could affect the audience inasmuch as in his play, the *Frogs* (1028–1029 and 1030–1031 respectively), Aristophanes alludes to the appeal of and suggests a moral purpose for this scene. The laments, mentioned several times in the first half of the tragedy and finally performed at the beginning of the second half of the play, within the second part, and most effectively at the end, affect the audience emotionally, inasmuch as the laments increase in intensity through the course of the play and peak at the finale. The name of a specific person to serve as the object of special religious services is lacking at the beginning of *Sanemori*, but is supplied by the middle; the enactment of the special services on behalf of Sanemori's ghost affects the audience spiritually by the beginning of the second half. The repeated references to invocations of Amida Buddha throughout the nō and the preparation for the warrior's repentance come to fruition at the end, when Sanemori tells his tale and the chorus concludes with the nembutsu; this is both a spiritually and emotionally loaded moment, the kyū part of the kyū of the play. These spiritually loaded "events," as I call the most intense moments in the performances of the plays, are infused with the dramatic characters' feelings of grief for Xerxes and the defeated Persians and with hope for Sanemori's salvation respectively. They are effective in moving the audiences, I submit, because the plays in which they appear, both of which happen to dramatize events contemporary with the time of the audience, are constructed such that there is a gradual, emotional development closely connected with the performance that reaches the most intense verbal, kinetic, visual, musical, and rhythmic peak only at the end.

The tragedy and the nō both contain reports about tragic events that are not contemporary with the dramatic action, even though the two differ in the direction the respective chronologies of those reports take—the one moves forward, the other backward in time. And each unfolds toward a revelation of what is more significant than the tragic event or the choice of the specific character, namely, the presentation of human responsibility vis-à-vis the divine, which Aristotle does not mention in his discussion of tragedy. Delusion entices and traps a person, we are told in the *Persians*, so that he cannot escape; but we learn that Xerxes *also* is responsible for his actions. One invocation of Amida Buddha, we are told in *Sanemori*, is sufficient for salvation, but we learn during the course of the nō that the ghost of Sanemori *also* must save himself through repentance. Aeschylus places the event in which Xerxes erred in the middle, rather than at the end, of this tragedy, and he features two main characters, both the noble Darius and the ignoble Xerxes; thus all contributing parts converge with less focus at the end than in Zeami's play.[37] However, Aeschylus places the most striking performance event, the lament, at the end of his play, when the main character first appears and after the penultimate Darius scene has set off and established the culpability of Xerxes. Zeami presents a performance of the tale of repentance, which contains the warrior's assumption of responsibility for his own destiny, at the end of the nō, after he has established the warrior's nobility in the penultimate katari and kusemai

---

[37] In the *Seven against Thebes* there is only one main character, Eteocles. A report of his death is immediately followed by a lament at or near the end of the tragedy.

scenes. The structural similarity that the *Persians* shares with the warrior nō is that the religious and moral significance of the event to the main character, and through him to the audience, is gradually revealed by the language and with the help of the performance.

The structure that is at the basis of Zeami's work, as I discussed in the preceding chapter, is jo-ha-kyū, a structure not irrelevant to a discussion of the *Persians*. In this tragedy, the gradual movement toward more and more striking verbal, visual, kinetic, rhythmic, and thus emotional peaks is not only what makes the work comparable to nō, but also, given its religious provenance, the reason it is well constructed. I do not suggest that Zeami's organizing principle, jo-ha-kyū, can be applied indiscriminately or in its entirety to an analysis of the *Persians*. However, this approach to the play's structure, in conjunction with others,[38] reveals not only a correspondence between structure and content, but also a relationship between these and the performance. In spite of our lack of evidence about music and dance in the performance of the *Persians*, elements that are at the heart of jo-ha-kyū, I suggest that this principle underlying Zeami's saku ("construction"), based as it is more on natural and aesthetic considerations than on intellectually reasoned ones, can be helpful not in the reconstruction of details of choreography and musical accompaniment in the *Persians*, but in uncovering some of the methods Aeschylus used to organize and to map out the *Persians* as a *performance*, and in testing conclusions of others against the practice of a living theater. It is highly likely that this principle can also reveal clues to the further appreciation of other tragedies, even those in which there is a complex plot, dramatic and verbal conflict, or frequent entrances and exits.

In nō, although the structure is far from predictable, one form that jo-ha-kyū assumes is the subdivision of the maeba and nochiba into dan, and of the dan into shōdan. As it turns out, we find that a similar pattern is the basis of Aeschylus's construction of the *Persians* as two halves divided into smaller sections. Within Zeami's nō, spoken dialogues tend to appear in the third dan of each half to provide expository material before musical conclusions, and musical dialogues at the end of dan following the second dan. It is significant to this comparison that in the structure of the *Persians*, spoken dialogue between two actors is entirely absent from the first and last section of each half, but is present between these in the middle of each half. The epirrhematic exchanges that appear in the messenger and Darius

---

[38] E.g., the approach of Jacqueline Duchemin, who says of the *Persians*, "On pourrait dire que tout s'organise en *crescendo*" ("Du lyrisme à la tragédie," 134). Among the many others who have recognized the unfolding of the play in the direction of explicitness, see, for example, K. Deichgräber, *Die Perser des Aischylos* (Göttingen, 1941), 161; Maurice Croiset, *Eschyle: Études sur l'invention dramatique dans son théâtre* (Paris, 1928), 81–82; Holtsmark, "Ring Composition"; and Evangelos Petrounias, *Funktion und Thematik der Bilder bei Aischylos*, Hypomnemata 48 (Göttingen, 1976).

scenes conclude the respective actors' engagements with the chorus before they turn to the second actor. Zeami usually points explicitly to a written source for a nō in the thematically most important section, that is, the fourth dan; at the penultimate point in the *Persians*, Aeschylus presents the words of Darius drawn from history, from Solon, and from other writers of traditional wisdom, his comments on past, future, and present, and the prediction of Persian defeat at Plataea. Zeami specifically advises in the name of jo-ha-kyū that the narrative line of the "epic" source for *Sanemori*, the *Heike*, be rearranged in the nō; in addition, by adding to and subtracting from the *Heike* account, he enhances the nobility of the warrior. Although the *Persians* is not based on a written source, it is clear that Aeschylus's alteration of history for the sake of his depiction of Xerxes, and for the sake of the moral that he presents in the play, is also intricately bound up with the visualization of the performance. The most vigorous dance and movements of the shite occur in the final dan, the kyū section of the nō, in which he and the chorus sing; at the end of the *Persians*, the excited sung lament of the chorus and of Xerxes calls for vigorous gestures and motions.

There are other indications from the text of the *Persians* that Aeschylus, like Zeami, wrote his play with a gradual crescendo in mind. He often moves from the less to the more focused—for example, from his initial use of the third-person pronoun in a scene to his subsequent use of the first person for the same character; from hints to open articulation, explanation, and visualization; from veiled references to costume to the presentation of characters in costumes that are more and more closely tied to the moral of the play; from intimations of human along with divine responsibility for the defeat of the Persians to placing open blame on Xerxes. There is, to be sure, no expression of fear in *Sanemori*, no hint, prophecy, or foreboding of disasters to come, as there is in the *Persians* (and in Greek tragedy in general); preparation and suspense lie instead in *Sanemori* in the expression of hope, the hints and promises of salvation. This is in the nature of Zeami's highly hieratic play, which features a priest, religious services, and words derived from Buddhist texts. However, these differences, which should not be ignored, also should not be allowed to obscure the fact that the structure of nō, based as it is on a progression that Zeami considered inherent in everything in life, can open our eyes to significant structural features in the *Persians*.

AN ANALYSIS OF STRUCTURE IN THE *PERSIANS*

Within my detailed analysis of the structure of the *Persians* I shall argue that in this play the progression within scenes and between them—a progression connected closely with the depiction of the main character, the

101

alteration of history, and the presentation of the religious moral of the play—gradually evolves into a finale that is verbally, rhythmically, visually, and kinetically striking in a manner comparable to the progression in *Sanemori*. Nowhere is it my intention to suggest that divisions in nō are the same as those in tragedy. I refer to them in order to keep the comparative dimension in the reader's mind. My intention is instead to suggest that the overall effect and success of a performance of the *Persians*, a play lacking dramatic conflict, is in part the result of a progression that is illuminated by an understanding of jo-ha-kyū.

In the first section (1–139) of the *Persians*, the parodos and lyric parodos, Aeschylus begins the first part (1–64) with self-identification by the chorus, which one should be reminded functions differently from a chorus in nō—it is *both* a group and an actor. The chorus says in anapaestic recitative:

> These [are called] the trusted of [i.e., from among] the Persians who
> are gone. . . .[39]

By referring to itself as trusted Persians and identifying its role as guardian of the royal seat, the chorus establishes its credentials. One method by which Aeschylus delays a focus on the particular, specifically on personal expression, is his use of the third-person pronoun in the parodos, rather than the first-person pronoun, as is usual in Greek tragedy. In fact, this use of the third person as a substitute for the first in the parodos is unique in Greek tragedy. In the other anapaestic parodoi of Aeschylus's plays as well, the chorus characteristically refers to itself with collective nouns or in the first-person plural, rather than in the first-person singular typical of the plays of Sophocles and Euripides.[40] Thus the works of Aeschylus are more amenable than those of the other Greek tragedians to a comparison with nō, in which the third person is used throughout and almost to the exclusion of the other persons.[41]

In the *Persians*, Aeschylus contributes to the impersonal quality sug-

[39] The text of the *Persians* used is Denys Page's edition of the Oxford Classical Text of Aeschylus, *Aeschyli septem quae supersunt tragoediae* (Oxford, 1972). The translations of the text are mine unless otherwise indicated and, like those of nō, are made as literal as the English language allows.

[40] See Kaimio, "The Chorus of Greek Drama," 194, for a summary of his findings on the first-person usage in anapaestic parodoi. In the *Agamemnon*, the chorus does not refer to itself in the first-person plural until line 72, as it does again at line 74. After line 75 the chorus refers to itself in the third person. At line 104, it uses the first-person singular, "I have the authority to sing. . . ." At this point it begins to speak for Calchas and report his prophecy.

[41] Although there is no more doubt in the mind of the Greek audience who is meant when it hears a neuter plural pronoun than there is in the mind of the Japanese audience when it hears *kono hito*, "this person," the playwright's choice of a less straightforward pronoun sets a certain distance between character and audience.

gested by the third-person neuter pronoun in the first line of the parodos with an allusion to words from a play written by Phrynichus on the subject of the Persian defeat. Phrynichus had introduced his play with a prologue in iambic trimeters spoken by a eunuch and beginning, "These are, of the Persians who left long ago. . . ."[42] The quotation here functions like that of sutras at the beginning of the waki's first speech delivered in recitative in *Sanemori*: both the chorus and the waki speak words originated by someone other than the author.

Near the beginning of the parodos (5–6), the chorus names and identifies the character on whom the play eventually focuses, Xerxes, with his patronym, title, and rank. Similarly, the waki in his first speech of the warrior play *Atsumori* mentions the name of the warrior. However, in both works the second mention of the name and the appearance of the main character are delayed. In many of his nō, including *Sanemori, Tadanori,* and *Yorimasa*, Zeami delays the identification of the shite until the revelation scene. In tragedy, especially in the works of Sophocles and Euripides, the case is different: a main character usually identifies himself or is identified by someone else at or near the beginning of a play.[43] In fact, every example of delay in the appearance or identification of characters,

[42] The ancient argument to the *Persians* provides this information about a play, there called *The Phoenician Women*, which is not extant; see Page, OCT, 2. In Phrynichus's play, the chorus was made up of women who mourned over the defeat of the Persians. In the *Persians*, Aeschylus has transferred the chorus to elders so as to create an effect of the citizenry as a whole. See Gottfried Hermann, *De Aeschyli Persis dissertatio, Opuscula*, 2 (Leipzig, 1827–1877; reprinted, New York and Hildesheim, 1970), 93. This change is important to the development of the play inasmuch as the laments of the women mentioned frequently never materialize. Instead, the most striking lament is left for the main character, Xerxes, and the chorus, representing all the people.

[43] In none of Sophocles' extant plays is the name of the main character delayed; rather, the location of the setting and the persons on stage are identified at the beginning. The same can be said for Euripides' plays, excluding the unusual *Rhesus* and the satyr play, the *Cyclops*. Among Aeschylus's works, the main character of the *Seven against Thebes*, Eteocles, identifies himself in the prologue and refers to himself in both the third and the first person. The main character of the *Libation Bearers*, Orestes, identifies himself in the first person. (Orestes does not give his name in the fragments of the prologue that exist. It is possible that in the missing part he does. At the very least, he makes clear who he is when he calls to his father, says he has come home, and names his sister Electra.) The main character of the *Suppliants*, the chorus, identifies itself in the first-person plural and the third person. In these three examples, Aeschylus's practice resembles that of other playwrights, but differs from the norm in Zeami's nō. Closer than the *Persians* to the example of *Sanemori* are the *Agamemnon* and the *Eumenides*, in which a nameless character, rather than a main character, speaks the prologue and does not meet another character on stage. After the prologue of the *Eumenides*, in which the Furies are described, there are many references to the Furies; but they do not identify themselves by name until line 331. In the *Agamemnon*, the watchman mentions the wife of Agamemnon, but her name is left unstated until line 84. The chorus addresses her on her arrival at line 258. Agamemnon is mentioned in the prologue, the parodos, and the messenger scene, but does not appear until line 810. The delay in Agamemnon's appearance is like that of Xerxes'.

such as we find built into the structure of warrior nō, occurs in Greek tragedies written by Aeschylus.[44]

Aeschylus also delays a report of the event, news of the defeat, with only the slightest hint of trouble in the chorus's third-person expression of concern for the king and the Persian expedition to Greece—it does not say, "We are troubled," or, "Our spirit is troubled," but, "The spirit is troubled" (10–11). Instead of announcing the outcome of the expedition to Greece early in his play, as Phrynichus had, Aeschylus lists by name the leaders and the peoples who left Asia, the means by which they traveled, and the weapons they carried.[45] The specific designation, like the chorus's explicit reference to Xerxes, quickly becomes submerged by the generic. At the end of the list, names give way to such locutions as "crowd" (53) and "throng from all of Asia" (56–57); Xerxes' name is replaced with the word "king" (58). Aeschylus rounds off the parodos by repeating part of the content of the Phrynichean line, namely, "the flower of men from the Persian land has gone" (59–60), to which he appends in a relative clause a reference to the mourning. The chorus says:

> With ravenous longing the entire Asian land
> Mourns for the men she brought up
> And as they count the days,
> Both parents and wives
> Tremble over the time that has passed. (61–64)

The people of Asia to whom the chorus refers are not identified. Instead, the parodos (1–64), of which the contents are very specific like those of the nanori of nō, ends on a general note.

In the second part (65–114) of this first section of the *Persians*, the rhythm changes from the marching anapaests to the more melodic ionic meter, and the chorus continues to use generic appellations for the king and the Persian host. Xerxes is called the "impetuous ruler" (74), "a man like a god" (80), "one who looks a dark glance in his eyes, that of a murderous serpent" (83), and "one who pursues a Syrian chariot" (84–85), but he is not named. The chorus refers to the army as "the city-destroying army" (65–66), "the awesome flock" (75), two contingents, "on foot and by sea" (76), "the great torrent of men" (89), "the unconquerable wave of

---

[44] For a summary of announced entrances by characters in tragedy, see Richard Hamilton's "Announced Entrances in Greek Tragedy," *HSCP* 82 (1978): 63–82. For further discussion, see W. Nestle, *Die Struktur des Eingangs in der attischen Tragödie* (Stuttgart, 1930).

[45] In terms of the structure of the *Persians* as a whole, an important function of the list of names in the parodos is to prepare for the report of the expedition's failure and the death of many men; a similar list is twice repeated, as a list of the dead—once with the news of defeat, and once with the appearance of Xerxes.

the sea" (90), "the Persian army" (91), and "strong-willed people" (91), but does not refer to the leaders by name. The avoidance of proper names and of the chorus's use of the first person throughout the parodos and most of the lyric parodos maintains the same lack of personal expression and focus on a particular person that is found in the first two lines of the play.

The important religious dictum toward which the indirection leads is stated in the form of a question at first. The chorus asks:

What mortal man will flee the deceitful treachery of god?
Who is the one who is swift-footed and can master an easy jump?
For, at first friendly, Atē [Delusion] leads
A man into her nets by means of flattery,
Out of which it is not possible for a mortal, even one who has fled, to
    escape. (94–100)[46]

Introduced approximately at the same point as the *pathei mathos* dictum in the *Agamemnon* and as the religious message of the waki's first sashi in *Sanemori*, like them, this question is familiar to the audience and applicable to anyone. However, as the chorus continues, it turns to the somewhat more specific case of the Persians—from long ago they were ordered by god to pursue wars on land, but they learned to look to the sea. This is a reason for their defeat, only hinted at here, but articulated later in specific connection with Xerxes. The movement is not unlike that from the waki's first sashi to the ageuta that follows—the waki, quoting sutras, says first that Paradise is far away, yet here too in one's heart is Amida's Country, and then directs the religious dictum to the one person in the "garden," who, we learn later, is Sanemori. Near the beginning of both plays, there is given the first, but only slight, hint that one is responsible for his actions.

The third part (116–139) of this first section of the *Persians* is marked by another metrical change, from the ionic meters to the faster-moving trochaics, which complements the shift on the verbal level to the first use of the first person. This metrical shift is comparable to the shift in the first dan of *Sanemori* from prose to recitative to song. (The noticeable difference between the works is that the nō moves toward more regular rhythms, the tragedy toward more irregular and excited meters; however, in both, the movement is in the direction of expressing progressively greater emotion within its context.) In the continuation of the song, the

---

[46] On the position of this mesode within the text, which entails a problem outside the scope of this study, see H. D. Broadhead, *The Persae of Aeschylus* (Cambridge, 1960), 53–54 and W. C. Scott, "The Mesode at *Persae* 93–100," *GRBS* 9. no. 3 (1968): 259–266.

chorus, earlier concerned that no message had arrived about the departed king and army, expresses fear at the Persian infringement of god's will:

> About these my heart, clothed in black, is rent with fear;
> "O, for the Persian army!" May the city, the great capital of Susa
>   Empty of men, not hear this [cry]:[47]
> And the citadel of Cissians will sing in echoing reply,
> "O," with large throngs of women crying out this word, and rend the
>   Linen robes upon which they fall. (115–125)

The emotional progression that Aeschylus creates is clear. Earlier the chorus has mentioned the Susans and the Cissian citadel and articulated its concern in the third person for the men who left Persia—"the spirit is troubled." Here, in the lyric parodos, it says, in the first person, *"my* heart is rent with fear." Earlier the chorus has mentioned only that the Asian land mourns and that parents and wives tremble; here it expresses the hope that the capital of Susa will not hear the cry "O" and, with a repetition of that cry, that the citadel of Cissians will not sing "O" in reply. Both the repetition of the cry and the description of the women's lament are explicit manifestations of the elders' concern.

The focus is further intensified in the final lines of the lyric parodos. There Aeschylus turns from the generic "women" to the poetic description of the effect of the expedition on each woman. He writes:

> Beds are filled with tears of longing for men,
> And the Persian women, delicate in their grief, each with
>   A longing for her dear husband,
> Having sent off her warlike, impetuous bedmate,
> Is left singly yoked. (134–139)

Shifting focus from the public mourning described earlier to the private, Aeschylus changes the number from the plural to the singular, from beds to bedmate, from women to each woman. The movement is again analogous to that between the sashi and the ageuta of *Sanemori*, where there is a shift from the mention of people high and low reciting prayers to one person repeating Amida Buddha's name in the garden. Both playwrights prepare for the arrival of a character on stage—Zeami for the shite, Aeschylus for the queen.

In recognition of the importance of the visual dimension to a performance of the *Persians*, Aeschylus may allude in line 115 to the costume of

---

[47] The word "this" is a translation of *touto*, which I read instead of *toude*, which also means "this." The use of *touto* in the antistrophe to refer again to the cry, *oa*, makes it probable that Aeschylus used the same demonstrative pronoun in the strophe. See Broadhead, *Persae*, 62. The repetition enlivens Aeschylus's style.

the chorus members. The expression "my heart [is] clothed in black" suggests fear, but it may also point to black robes such as are appropriate to
the laments that are mentioned here for the first of many times and that
are later directly enacted by the chorus in their songs and in the finale with
Xerxes. The word *melagkhitōn* ("clothed in black") appears in an emphatic position, at the caesura of the first line of a strophe in which the
meter has changed from ionics to lekythia, the more agitated trochaic meter.[48] With anxiety expressed rhythmically in the agitated meters, visually
perhaps in the dark robes of the chorus, and verbally in the hints of ill and
the expression of the religious message, Aeschylus ends the first section of
the play (1–139), which in terms of the relationship of mood and theme to
the whole is comparable to the jo section of *Sanemori*. It features neither
a direct expression of intense emotion, visual, or kinetic interest, nor verbal explicitness.

After the end of the lyric parodos and at the beginning of the second
section of the play (140–248), Aeschylus makes an explicit statement in
transitional recitative anapaestic meters about the function of the chorus
and its motivation for entering. The chorus of elders says:

Come, Persians, sitting down
At this ancient place,
Let us take wise and deep counsel,
For the need has come for it.
How in fact does Xerxes, the king
And son of Darius, fare? (140–145)[49]

Here, in accordance with the meaning of their words, the elders presumably move around the orkhēstra for the first time and are on the verge of
sitting down when the arrival of the queen interrupts this action.[50] Near

[48] The oblique reference to the elders' costume is analogous to Aeschylus's mention
that the attacks of the Furies are "dressed in black clothes" (*melaneimōn; Eumenides*
370). In the prologue (52), the audience learns that the Furies are black. They are the
visual manifestation of fear suggested by the words in *Libation Bearers* 410–414. In
Suppliants 785, Aeschylus uses the word *kelainokhrōs*, "black-skinned," to describe the
word "heart." It is an appropriate epithet for the maidens who have come from Egypt.
Presumably the chorus of suppliant maidens wears black masks. At *Libation Bearers* 11,
Aeschylus refers explicitly to the black robes of the chorus, whose first song in this play
is a lament.

[49] S. Srebrny, *Critica et exegetica in Aeschylum* (Turin, 1950), 14–20, places a stop
after line 143 so that the chorus may sit down, take counsel, and then ask their questions. I agree that there is a pause as the chorus moves to a new location; however, I do
not think it necessary for the elders to sit down and deliberate on how Xerxes is faring
and whether the Persians or the Greeks have been victorious. Instead, in the course of
speaking lines 140–149, they move to a new location and are interrupted by the arrival
of the queen.

[50] See Broadhead, *Persae*, xliv–xlvi. Taplin, *Stagecraft*, 454, says that the elders are to

the beginning of nō, waki characteristically move around the stage during the michiyuki ("travel song") and come to a standstill in the tsukizerifu ("arrival speech"). Waki usually are explicit and say that they will go someplace, sing a song listing the places through which they have passed, and then say that they have arrived. The waki's words and movements function in part to draw the audience's attention to the location of the play, which in many nō is significant. By analogy we can conjecture that in the *Persians*, if the council chamber is the location to which Aeschylus refers, then he is following the lead of Phrynichus and making a gesture in recognition of his debt to that playwright.[51]

---

be thought of as inside the chamber rather than outside and that this arrangement avoids the necessity of using a skēnē ("stage building") to represent the outside of the chamber. In today's performances of nō it is customary to place a prop representing the appropriate structure on the stage when the story requires that a character be inside a structure, such as a cave, palace, or shrine. In *Matsukaze*, for example, a priest asks for lodging in a hut belonging to two maidens, but, since the dramatic action is never placed inside, a hut is not represented on stage. (*Matsukaze* has been translated by Royall Tyler in Keene, *20 Plays*, 17–34.) This practice suggests one possible solution for the problem of staging the *Persians*. It seems to me that the acting arena would become very cluttered if a separate structure representing a council chamber were used along with a chariot, which we later learn from the queen's words attends her first entrance. In addition, whether one sets up a prop or uses a skēnē to represent the council chamber, for the sake of consistency one would then have to represent a palace and a tomb to be used by the queen and by Darius respectively in their entrances and exits. The simpler and undoubtedly correct alternative is to say that Aeschylus represented a chariot, a prop directly connected with the moral lesson of the play, in the first half, and a tomb in the second half. There was probably no skēnē at all. Nor do I think that the scene required the presence of steps, as A. M. Dale did in "Seen and Unseen on the Greek Stage: A Study in Scenic Conventions," *Collected Papers* (Cambridge, 1969), 119.

[51] In the nanori of *Sanemori*, the kyōgen identifies the location, the waki's function, and the reason for his presence in a manner comparable to the chorus's identification of the location, the reason for its presence, and the arrival of the queen in the *Persians*. Usually in nō the travel song appears after the nanori, as I pointed out in the preceding chapter. In the nanori of *Atsumori*, for example, the priest says that he is going to Ichinotani, a famous battleground, to pray for Atsumori's soul. As he walks slowly across the stage, he sings the michiyuki and mentions the places he passes through: Yamazaki, Lake Koya, Ikuta River, and finally Suma Beach. In the tsukizerifu, he adds that he has traveled so fast that he is already at Ichinotani in the province of Tsu. The kind of formulaic entrances one finds for the waki in nō appears near the beginning of Euripides' works especially: the *Hecabe*, "I, Polydorus, the son of Hecabe, have come . . . leaving the gates"; the *Bacchae*, "I, Dionysus, the son of Zeus, have come to this land"; the *Andromache*, "I have reached the hearth"; and the *Trojan Women*, "I have come after leaving the Aegean depths of the sea." In Aeschylus's works, at the beginning of the *Libation Bearers*, Orestes says, "I have come to this land and return . . . at this mound of a grave" (3), and in the *Persians*, the queen says, "I have come, leaving . . . my home and . . . bedroom," (159–160). It sounds as if Aeschylus anticipates what becomes a formula. The choral introduction in the parodos of the *Suppliants* is even closer than that of the *Persians* to the beginning of *Atsumori*. There the chorus of maidens, the main character, says that it has come from the Nile delta and fled from a holy precinct to Argos, which is the setting of the play, and tells the audience why. Aeschylus delays

The chorus of elders next takes notice of the queen's entrance along the parodos, the passageway leading from "backstage" into the orkhēstra, and says that she, "a light like the eyes of the gods" (150), is approaching. (To the extent that they expressly acknowledge the presence of an actor, the chorus's words in this transitional section are much like those of waki near the beginning of maeba and nochiba.) Continuing in the trochaic meter, which though spoken is not as prosaic as the iambic trimeters and thus is closer to recitative, the chorus addresses the queen:[52]

> Hail, most exalted mistress of deep-girdled Persians,
> Old mother of Xerxes and wife of Darius,
> Who were both the bedmate of the Persians' god and
>   mother of a god. . . . (155–157)

In the maeba of *Sanemori*, there is no explicit preparation for the shite as there is in the nochiba; however, Zeami provides subtle verbal preparation for the old man's appearance with the waki's mention of one person in the "garden"[53] and with a feature of the performance—as the shite enters, he says that he hears the flute playing in the heavens; the flutist on stage has just played his instrument.[54] In the *Persians*, a connection between word and performance may be present in the chorus's use of the word "deep-girdled."[55] The adjective, which is commonly used to describe women or goddesses, would not be any more noticeable than the shite's reference to

---

focusing on the location of the play by setting it into the perspective of a distant place until later in the *Agamemnon*, in the beacon speech, and until the speech at the end of the messenger scene in the *Persians*, where the messenger enumerates the places through which the army passed on the way home from Greece to Persia. And yet, in the anapaestic passage of the *Persians*, Aeschylus also focuses on the specific location of the dramatic action within the city of Persia.

[52] The address is different, but serves a function similar to that of a *yobikake* ("voiced announcement") or special music preceding or accompanying the entrance of the shite in nō performances today.

[53] The preparation for the queen's arrival is subtly achieved with the last word of the lyric parodos, *monozux* ("singly yoked," 139), that is, a widow, as the queen is. According to Petrounias, *Funktion und Thematik der Bilder*, 9–10, the queen, an individual, represents the whole.

[54] We do not know whether there was special entrance or exit music in tragedy; however, several passages are tantalizing in this regard. For example, the playing of the "flute" is mentioned in the beginning stanzas of two odes (435 and 705) in Euripides' *Electra*, each of which is preceded by actors' exits. There is no evidence that the words of the chorus refer to a "flute" accompanying the exits rather than the song itself; however, the practice in nō suggests the possibility. But even in nō the mention of an instrument does not necessarily entail the playing of the instrument on stage. In the kuse of *Kiyotsune*, for example, the mention of the warrior blowing his flute need not be accompanied by the sound of a flute.

[55] According to F. R. Earp, however, the adjective is merely an ornamental epithet (*The Style of Aeschylus* [Cambridge, 1948], 61).

flutes playing in the heavens, except that the chorus begins its address to the queen with this word and the queen may appear dressed in a deep-girdled robe. We know from what she says later (607–609) that she arrives here with a chariot and is dressed in royal attire, signs of the Persian wealth she refers to, but the chorus says nothing explicit about this.[56] However, the introductory word, like the reference to black clothes in the lyric parodos, may attract attention to the costume, which later assumes significance, rather as the shite's words "waves of old age" subtly foreshadow the importance that old age and the old man's mask assume later in *Sanemori*.

The chorus's address to the queen, though it identifies her explicitly, does not include a report of the Persian defeat. Yet in it verbal hints of trouble become more apparent than in the lyric parodos; the chorus says:

> . . . Unless their [the Persians'] fortune of old has now forsaken the
> army. (158)

The queen in her address to the elders reinforces their foreboding with her words:

> Anxiety rends me as well in my heart. (161)

She repeats the verb *amussō* ("rends"), used by the chorus in line 116, but as Aeschylus moves from the objective to the subjective, he changes the verb from the passive to the active voice and uses the first-person pronoun, "me." Similarly in *Sanemori*, the shite, although he does not acknowledge the presence of the waki, repeats the priest's words *nori no niwa* ("the garden of the Law") and speaks of his *own* approach into the "garden," rather than that of the people reciting prayers.

The queen, recognizing the elders' function as the trusted ones (171–172),[57] seeks counsel from them over her fear that the good fortune that Darius brought to the Persians may be overthrown by great wealth. The elders had been disturbed because the Persians took to sea against god's will; here, in the second section of the play, concern is expressed once again, but now from the point of view of an individual. The queen knows that Darius, her husband and the father of Xerxes, acted in accordance with the gods (164), but now there is fear that the Persian well-being that he had assured will be lost (163–164). That fear is expressed more vividly than before in the next part of this second section—in the queen's *rhēsis*,

---

[56] On this scene, see W. G. Thalmann, "Xerxes' Rags: Some Problems in Aeschylus' *Persians*," *AJP* 101 (1980): 268.

[57] For a discussion of a prevalent theme in the *Persians*, the elders' function as counselors, see Holtsmark, "Ring Composition," *passim*. This function of the chorus makes an analogy between it and waki priests of nō particularly attractive.

a speech given in iambic trimeters, the first such speech to appear in the play and a type of verse especially appropriate to a narration that is set off from the preceding dialogue, which is spoken in the freer trochaic tetrameters.[58] The metrical change is comparable to the alternation between music and speech in the second dan of *Sanemori*. The shite recites at the beginning and the end of the second dan, but in the middle he speaks, when, facing the audience, he gives his old age as one reason and then hints at other reasons why he cannot approach the people in the garden. In the queen's narrative, which is framed by trochaics at beginning and end, she describes a dream, one of many she had seen since her son went to Greece, and an omen. Both of these, like Sanemori's reasons, foreshadow what we are only later to learn explicitly.

The queen says that in the dream she saw two women, one dressed in Persian, the other in Dorian clothes, both far more comely than women of her day and both of one race, who had been allotted Asia and Greece respectively to dwell in. (This reference to the women's clothing appears at first glance to be little more than a verbal flourish. However, it prepares for the later and more meaningful references she makes to clothing in the dream.) The queen goes on to say that when dissension arose between the women,

> . . . My child, on learning of it,
> Tried to restrain and calm them, and he yokes the two
> To a chariot and places straps beneath their necks.
> And the one exalted in this equipment
> And held her mouth well-disciplined in the reins,
> But the other balked and tears the harness of the chariot
> With her hands and without the bit drags it
> By force and breaks the yoke down the middle.
> My child falls and his father Darius stands nearby
> Pitying him. And as Xerxes sees him
> He tears the robes about his body. (189–199)

The straightforward narration, presented with little subordination in the syntax and enlivened by Aeschylus's use of present-tense verbs within the past-tense narration, provides a more explicit indication that Xerxes will be defeated than anything the chorus or the queen has mentioned before.[59] The speech also illustrates on the human level, albeit in a vision and

---

[58] On the alternation of meters in the *Persians* and the function of the iambic trimeter for narrative, see Michelini, *Tradition and Dramatic Form*; on this scene, see pp. 99–126.

[59] On the syntax, see W.A.A. van Otterlo, *Beschouwingen over het archaïsche Element in den Stijl van Aeschylus* (Utrecht, 1937), 46. Fraenkel, *Aeschylus Agamemnon*,

without placing blame on Xerxes, the overthrow of prosperity introduced in the preceding speech, and it transfers the image of the yoke, which was used in the lyric parodos to describe the crossing of the Hellespont by the Persian army, to a vivid depiction of Europe and Asia as two sisters, yoked to a chariot.

The narration also achieves a new level of personal expression. Although in the speeches preceding the narration the queen's only mention of her son, Xerxes, is in the circumlocution, "I think that the eye of a house is the presence of its lord" (169), in her dream-narrative she not only names him (199), but also refers to him as "my child" three times (177, 189, and 197), thus building toward the final appearance of Xerxes. The dream also helps to draw attention to the characters' costumes and accoutrements, not with the apparently irrelevant but in fact preparatory description of the difference between the Greek woman and the Persian one, but with an allusion to a chariot on which the queen arrives,[60] and certainly with the reference to Xerxes tearing the robes about his body, since at the end of the *Persians* Xerxes appears dressed in rags, which are set into contrast with the royal attire of Darius in the penultimate scene.

The dream serves as an important vehicle of meaning in the tragedy as a whole: because it is a dream, it suggests, as Kitto pointed out,[61] that there is something in the nature of things that is at work in the event and belongs to a different frame of reference than everyday reality—that is, it helps to raise the level of the play's significance. This point is well taken in a comparison of tragedy with nō, which is often a dramatization of the world of dreams. In the nō *Hajitomi*, for example, the main character, Yūgao, is called *yume no sugata* ("figure in a dream"), *yume ni kitarite* ("coming in a dream"), and *yumebito* ("dream person"). She tells a *yogatari*, a story about her life in the world of the living.

There is, of course, an important difference between the queen's narration of her dream and the narration by the ghost of Sanemori of his final battle: in one, a living person relates the content of a vision; in the other, a "vision" relates a real event. Yet to the extent that the *Persians* features both a dream and the ghost of Darius, it is closer than any other extant Greek tragedy to those nō which feature a spirit in the second half. In nō,

---

3: 650, says that in line 1383 of the *Agamemnon*, the many present-tense verbs in Clytemnestra's speech may "serve to enliven the recital." He suggests further that in the queen's speech, in *Persians* 181, she begins with past-tense verbs and uses present tenses when she "reaches the most exciting part of the dream."

[60] If, as P. Groeneboom, *Aeschylus' Persae* (Amsterdam, 1966), 106, says about lines 163–164, "de *olbos* wordt blijkbaar op een wagen gedacht," the queen's first speech may also subtly refer to the representation of a chariot before the eyes of the audience.

[61] H.D.F. Kitto, *Poiesis: Structure and Thought* (Berkeley, 1966), 86.

especially in the woman nō, there is a tendency to present life as but a dream. In *Matsukaze*, for example, the "dream" figures, Matsukaze and her sister Murasame, report what happened in the past; the "real" life comes into contact with the world of spirits when Matsukaze dons the fine silk robe, mentioned in her narrative, as a memento of a time that still haunts her. The subject of the dream and its narrator are the same person. The queen's chariot provides a connection between the dream and something concrete mentioned in it, but it is not her own chariot that she has seen. It is the torn robes of Xerxes, who is alive, that ultimately provide proof of the validity of the dream. Since they are his rags and he does not narrate the dream, the focus of the contributing parts is less sharp in the tragedy than in the nō.

A structural function of the dream report in the *Persians* is to delay, but also to prepare for, a report of the actual event by the messenger and a performance "event," Xerxes' appearance and lament. In the continuation of her narrative speech (201–210), the queen tells what happened when she approached the altar to make an offering. This report too prepares for an aspect of the performance. The queen later makes offerings to Darius and the nether gods. She says that she saw an eagle flee and a hawk tear at the eagle's head with its claws. The eagle simply cowered. The queen remarks that she was dumbstruck with fear at the sight of the mightier bird overwhelmed by the weaker and adds that it is a fearful thing for her to have seen, and for the elders to hear. The account of the omen, like that of the dream, both of which presage rather than verify the truth, focuses on Xerxes, her son, the focus of the play as a whole, whom the queen mentions at the end (211), but does not blame.

As the waki's initial mention of services forecasts his call for services on behalf of Sanemori later, so this report of the aborted ritual prepares for the successful ritual that the chorus recommends. In fact, taking their cue from the queen's mention of her son, the elders, again in the less formal and more melodic trochaic tetrameters in the last part of this second section, address the queen as mother (215), rather than as queen as they did earlier, and enjoin her to ask the gods to avert fulfillment of the ill omens and to send good for her, her child, the city, and all who are dear (217–219). They recommend action: that the queen pour libations to the earth and the dead so that her husband, whom she has seen in the dream, may send from the dead blessings for her and her son and keep hidden in obscurity what is the opposite of these, namely evil (219–223). This is advice that the chorus gives "prophecying by its own wit" (224), and that the queen says she will carry out when she goes to the palace (228–229). In the parodos, the chorus has said that its spirit (*thumos*) is a "prophet of evil" (*kakomantis*, 10); now it uses the word *thumomantis* ("prophecying by one's own wit," 224), as a nominative predicate of the understood pronoun "I," the subject of the verb "advise." The chorus, speaking in the first-person singular, is recognized both before and after the narration as a group of advisors who can help the queen. At this point in the play the chorus has become more like a waki priest than a chorus of nō. However, in its dialogue with the queen, it answers, she asks the questions; in *Sane-mori*, the shite answers, the waki asks the questions. There is not, as I said, a one-for-one correlation between the actors' roles in nō and tragedy, because the chorus serves the function of both an actor and a chorus.

Mondō, "spoken dialogues," the most prosaic and confrontational in style among the shōdan of nō, occur usually in the third dan of the maeba, after the waki and the shite have met. In *Sanemori*, the mondō begins with a short speech by the waki and a longer one, which includes melodic sections, by the shite; it then proceeds to a dialogue, stichomythic in form. In the *Persians*, the stichomythic passage (230–248) shared by the queen and the chorus on the subject of Athens appears at a position in the play that concludes the second section (140–248). Like a mondō, it is used to elicit information. In *Sanemori*, the priest wants to learn Sanemori's name; in *Yorimasa*, information about the place to which he has come. In the *Persians*, the information is different: the queen asks about a place, Athens, and learns, for example, that it is far away, that its men fight with spears and shields, that its wealth is based on silver, and that the people are not slaves to any man (232–242). The content of the stichomythy is factual information, to be sure,[62] but it also points explicitly to the cause of Persian defeat, yet to be announced: Athens. The revelation of what Athens means—the queen's perception that the land that destroyed Darius's great and noble army is something dreadful to ponder for the parents of those who went to Greece on the expedition (245)—is based on knowledge of the Greek military, economic, and political systems rather than on premonitions appearing in a dream at night[63] and provides a human, rather than divine, explanation for the defeat.

Within the structure of the tragedy as a whole, this stichomythy may be contrasted to the later stichomythy between the queen and Darius (715–738). In the earlier dialogue there is no tone of familiarity such as one finds in the stichomythies of Sophocles' later works. One can account for the lack of emotional interest here by arguing that the *Persians* is an early tragedy,[64] archaic in style, as the use of the trochaic meter in the stichomythy suggests. This partially, but not fully, explains the difference. The

---

[62] See Bernd Seidensticker, "Die Stichomythie," in *Die Bauformen der griechischen Tragödie*, ed. Walter Jens (Munich, 1971), 192.

[63] On this section, see Kitto, *Poiesis*, 87.

[64] See Seidensticker, "Die Stichomythie," 186.

later stichomythic exchange between the queen and Darius reveals keen personal interest on the part of the husband and wife as they discuss the army and their son. The subject matter and the characters involved account for this difference, which simultaneously serves Aeschylus's purposes well. If, as I am arguing in the light of nō, Aeschylus constructed the play so that he would create an increasingly sharper focus on Xerxes, that purpose is abetted by placing the dialogue between the chorus and the queen about a far-off city and its people earlier than a dialogue between husband and wife about the expedition of the Persians and their son.

The differences in subject matter and in the relationship between the characters of the two stichomythies reflect Aeschylus's consistent movement, interrupted only by Darius's predictions of the future and religious moralizing, toward a focus on Xerxes' tragedy and an increase in the emotional intensity of the performance. In *Sanemori*, the movement between the earlier and the later exchanges shared by the waki and the shite is marked with a greater amount of melody—there is only one line of prose—and fluidity of style in the latter as compared to the former. We do not know what the musical accompaniment to the *Persians* was like, as we do for nō performances today.[65] However, we can discern an increase in emotional intensity, revealed in the words and meters throughout Aeschylus's text, which corresponds, I suggest, to the movement in the direction of melody in nō at the end of most dan. The trochaic meters of the earlier stichomythy (230–248) serve the function, unusual in tragedy, of concluding one section and providing a transition to another, here the messenger scene. Since there is probably a musical accompaniment to them, they are better suited than iambic trimeters to replace the song one might expect at this juncture of the play.[66] The trochaic meters of the later stichomythy, like the earlier stichomythy, are presumably accompanied by music, but are used after the epirrhēma as a transition and introduction rather than a conclusion to the larger segment of the Darius scene that concludes with a full-scale choral song. In the first half of the *Persians*, Aeschylus concludes the second section with trochaics; in the second half, he ends all four sec-

---

[65] On the subject of nō music written in a Western language, see Akira Tamba, *La structure musicale du Nô: Théâtre traditionnel japonais* (Paris, 1974). See also William P. Malm, *Six Hidden Views of Japanese Music* (Berkeley, 1986), in which the author compares the nō *Sumidagawa* and Benjamin Britten's *Curlew River* (151–197). By analyzing the metrical structuring of the odes, William C. Scott, in *Musical Design in Aeschylean Theater*, has been able to shed light on the musical side of Aeschylean tragedy and to add appreciably to our understanding of the elements of which a performance is comprised.

[66] See Michelini, *Tradition and Dramatic Form*, 104. The meter functions here in a manner comparable to those parts of dialogue in nō which are labeled in the texts *kakaru*, that is, are melodic, like sashi, but are used specifically to mark a change from speech to song, as at the end of the second dan of *Sanemori*.

tions with song. This progression toward more music is not unlike that which we find in nō.

The next and third section of the tragedy (249–289) begins with the appearance of a messenger, who in a short iambic trimeter speech addresses the land and reveals that the army has not only left Persia, but has been destroyed. (His speech, 249–255, begins by revealing that the prosperity of the land has been destroyed and the flower of the Persians is gone and fallen, but ends with the whole truth, that the entire army has been destroyed.) The audience finally hears what it has known to be true from firsthand experience, or at least from Phrynichus's tragedy—the Persians have been defeated. This moment in the play is as important to the development of the "plot" as the revelation of Sanemori's name and his use of the first-person pronoun are to the content of the nō. The audiences know beforehand, but within the structure of both plays are again informed of the important content of a "contemporary" event.

The news precipitates an exchange between the messenger and the chorus, an epirrhēma (256–289), in which the chorus sings in syncopated iambs suited to lament[67] and uses onomatopoeic words, such as *otototoi* (268 and 274), that sound like part of a lament. In the conclusion to the third and final dan of the foreshortened maeba of *Sanemori*, the kakeai, shared by the waki who sings and the shite who speaks, reveals the tragic condition of the warrior. Even after two hundred years, he still has not been saved; he is lost in darkness and unable to distinguish between dreams and reality. In the ageuta that follows, the chorus maintains the same mood on behalf of the warrior. In the epirrhēma of the *Persians*, the elders call for the Persians to weep (256–259), say that their lives have been too long (263–265), add that the weapons left Asia for Greece in vain (268–271), cry out for the dead (274–277), enjoin another shout of pain for the destruction of the army (280–283), and conclude by saying that Athens is hateful to her enemies and has left in vain many Persian women without sons or husbands (286–289). In these exchanges, both the nō and the tragedy reach an emotional and rhythmic peak after an important revelation.

The epirrhēma and the kakeai of the tragedy and the nō respectively are also similar in the degree to which the actors, among whose number I here include the chorus of the *Persians*, for the first time speak and sing in a close verbal response with one another. In neither exchange do they continually acknowledge each other's presence; however, the messenger and the chorus keep echoing each other's words, and the waki and shite con-

---

[67] See Broadhead, *Persae*, 288 n. 2.

tinue each other's thoughts.[68] For example, when the messenger says that "contrary to his expectations" (*aelptōs*), he looks upon the day of return (261), the elders do not say, "Oh, yes, I see that you have returned," but reflect on their own life, how long it appears on "*hearing* of the *unexpected* calamity" (*akouein . . . aelpton*, 263–265). In his next speech the messenger addresses the Persians, but what he says has nothing to do with the subject of the elders' preceding song; instead he picks up on the word *akouein* ("hear"), and says that what he reports is not based on what he "heard" (*kluōn*, a synonym for *akouein*) from others (266). Similarly, after the messenger mentions that the shores of Salamis are full of "corpses" (*nekrōn*, 272–273), the elders address him in the second person, but, substituting a synonym for the word "corpses," cry out that he means the dead "bodies" (*sōmata*) are tossed about on the sea (275–276). They add to his account something he has not said. In the second half of the epirrhēma, the elders show signs of acknowledging the messenger's meaning. For example, the messenger says that the entire army was destroyed (279); the chorus echoes the word "army" (*stratou*, 283), which it says was destroyed. At the end of the epirrhēma, when the messenger says, "Alas, how I mourn on recalling Athens" (285), the chorus reacts with the words, "Athens, hateful to her enemies. I clearly can recall . . ." (286–287). Their recollection is different from his memory of firsthand experiences; and yet they respond to him more directly than they did at the beginning of the epirrhēma.[69]

After the epirrhēma, the rhythmic culmination to the important news of Persian defeat, the fourth section of the play (290–597), begins with the virtual entrance of the queen, who has not participated in the exchange between the chorus and the messenger, back into the dramatic "action." As if taking her cue from the last words of the chorus in the epirrhēma, ". . . [Athens] made many of the Persian women bereft of sons and husbands in vain" (288–289), the queen, the only female character in the play, a widow and a woman without her son, says, "I have been silent for a long time, struck in my misery by the evils . . ." (290–291). It is after this point and her return to the dialogue that the messenger scene, with its narrative

---

[68] Joachim Keller, *Struktur und dramatische Funktion des Botenberichtes bei Aischylos und Sophokles* (Tübingen, 1959), 6, who also thinks that the chorus and the messenger do not acknowledge each other, gives examples of the verbal connections between their speeches.

[69] On the formal structure and content of this type of exchange in Aeschylus's works, see Hansjürgen Popp, "Das Amoibaion," in *Die Bauformen der griechischen Tragödie*, ed. Walter Jens (Munich, 1971), 239–242. See also Taplin, *Stagecraft*, 85–87, who observes that this type of exchange occurs only occasionally in the works of Sophocles and Euripides.

speeches set off from the dramatic dialogue, assumes a form closer than that of the preceding scene to the normal messenger scene. However, as with other features of the *Persians*, this messenger scene also diverges from later tragic norms.[70] Usually messengers who report a tragic event, such as a murder, contemporary with the dramatic time do not arrive until three-quarters of the way through a tragedy; in the *Persians*, the messenger, like the kyōgen of *Sanemori*, appears earlier in the play and reports an event not contemporaneous with the dramatic time. Another function of these scenes is to prepare for the arrival of a main character—in the *Agamemnon*, for example, for the arrival of Agamemnon and Cassandra—and for a painful act—their murder at the hands of Clytemnestra. The messenger scene of the *Persians* is a variant of this type, because the appearance of Darius intervenes between the messenger scene and the arrival of Xerxes, the main character. (In the *Agamemnon*, the Cassandra scene intervenes between the arrival of the king Agamemnon and the murderous act, but not between the messenger scene and the king's arrival.) In addition, although it does prepare for painful action, the final lament, the messenger of the *Persians* does not prepare for a destructive or painful act or event per se.[71]

As I pointed out in Chapter One, in these respects the messenger scene is similar to the kyōgen scene of *Sanemori*: a character without a name or a clear identity delivers in prose (iambic trimeters used by the messenger are the meter closest to prose in tragedies) a long account of an event in which the main character of the play has been directly involved and prepares for the appearance of that character and the performance of a ritual. The major difference is that without the long and vivid account of the events delivered by an eyewitness, the messenger of the *Persians*, the audience would not know how Aeschylus envisioned the Persians' defeat on sea and land and how Aeschylus used, even altered, history for the sake of the drama, whereas even without the speech of the kyōgen, who is not an eyewitness, the audience learns from the shite's account at the end of *Sanemori* all the relevant details of the battle at Shinowara. Like the kyōgen interlude, the messenger scene is an entertaining section of the play in which the audience learns details related to the major character and the tragic event. (The kyōgen scene of *Sanemori* is also important in filling in details about the appearance of the ghost of Sanemori for the priest.) How-

[70] On this messenger scene and others, and for a bibliography on the subject, see Taplin, *Stagecraft*, 80–85.

[71] There is variety among kyōgen scenes as well. For example, in some late nō there are kyōgen who, unlike the kyōgen of *Sanemori*, do not report tales at all, but are effective in moving the "plot" forward. See, for example, *Momijigari*, translated in *Japanese Noh Drama*, NGS (Tokyo, 1959), 2: 141–156.

ever, whereas the kyōgen scenes are not considered a part of the jo-ha-kyū, the messenger's speeches assume a level of importance within the structure of the *Persians* comparable to the narration of the katari by the shite: it is in these narrations that the audience is introduced to an aspect of the tragic event that bears upon the character's moral qualities. In the former, one learns for the first time that Xerxes acted without sufficient knowledge and that the defeat was his punishment by the gods; in the latter, that by dyeing his hair and beard the warrior Sanemori brought undying fame to the Northern province.

In the major section of the messenger scene of the *Persians*, the queen begins by asking the messenger who is not dead and for whom of the leaders they should mourn (296–297). The audience straightaway learns that Xerxes is alive (299), and, from a long catalogue that duplicates some of the names from the list of leaders in the parodos, they also learn who has died. Aeschylus adds to this second list specific details that are missing from the earlier list. For example, he does not merely give names and epithets, but in the case of Matallus says, "He dipped his thick and woolly beard in a blood-red dye that changed the color" (315–316), an expression perhaps inspired by a passage from Homer (*Iliad* 4.141–147). In addition, Aeschylus emphasizes the goodness and valor, the wretchedness and misfortune of the men.[72]

The messenger answers the queen's next question about numbers with the specific figures on both sides—the Greeks had three hundred plus ten, the Persians one thousand—which, whether strictly accurate or not, make clear that the Athenians did not have a military advantage.[73] This messenger's response leads momentarily to his first use of the first person in the epic-style narrative sections,[74] not so that he includes himself as part of the action, but so that he remarks with an awareness of the listener, "We do

[72] The twofold repetition of an important verbal element, a list of names, in the *Persians* is not duplicated in kind in nō. Instead, we find that Zeami repeats all or parts of the same poem two or more times within the same play in order to bring its relevance more and more to the fore. See, for example, *Izutsu*, translated in NGS 1: 91–105, and *Obasute*, translated as *The Deserted Crone* by Stanleigh H. Jones, Jr., in Keene, 20 *Plays*, 115–128. The relevant parts are quoted in Chapter Four.

[73] Similarly Zeami, who also presents verbally in epic-style narrative, battles in which a potentially stronger army loses to one lacking numbers, includes concrete figures in the kyōgen speech of *Sanemori* and says that there were more than one hundred thousand cavalry with the Heike, as opposed to fifty thousand on the Genji side. These numbers appear in the Sanari text of the kyōgen scene, *Yōkyoku taikan* 3: 1253. In the katari of *Yorimasa*, Zeami also specifies the number of men in the army. The shite says that Tadatsuna and three hundred men of the Heike made their way across the river at Uji.

[74] For a virtually exhaustive list of Homericisms in the *Persians*, see Alexander Sideras, *Aeschylus Homericus: Untersuchungen zu den Homerismen der aischyleischen Sprache*, Hypomnemata 31 (Göttingen, 1971). On messenger speeches specifically, see Lamberto di Gregorio, *Le scene d'annuncio nella tragedia greca* (Milan, 1967).

not seem to you in this way to have been outdone in the battle, do we?" (344). Aeschylus otherwise reserves the uses of the first person for the end of the scene and the last speech, which is a speech of a different sort. (In lines 329, 330, and 430 the messenger uses the first-person endings on verbs in sentences that are part, not of the narrative account, but of the messenger's comments on that account.)

In *Sanemori*, the kyōgen comments on the moral example of the warrior and the need for prayers on his behalf; the priest agrees, as do priests in other kyōgen scenes, that prayers are in order. The messenger in the *Persians* makes several references to the role played in the battle by the gods (the queen comments explicitly on the divine role), hints at Xerxes' responsibility for the outcome, and recommends a lament. In the first of his references to gods, the messenger says that some spirit destroyed the army by weighing down the scales with an unequal fortune (345–346). In his use of the scale image the messenger is referring to Zeus, for in the *Iliad* it is Zeus who holds the scales; however, Aeschylus keeps the specific name in reserve, as he did earlier in the play. When the queen next asks who initiated the encounter, the messenger answers that an avenger or an evil spirit, appearing from somewhere, began the disaster as a whole (353–354), but he does not say that Zeus or Delusion (Atē) was responsible. And again, when the messenger concludes his indirect quotation of words spoken by the Greek man, a human agent, who deceived Xerxes into thinking the Greeks would not stay and risk their lives, Aeschylus does not identify the god, nor for that matter the Greek, by name. But he does say, in a sentence containing the first present-tense verb in what is a speech about the past, that because Xerxes did not recognize the treachery of the Greek man or the envy of the gods, he warned all the naval leaders (363) that they should expect the Greeks to flee. The messenger adds that Xerxes did not understand what the gods had in store for him (373), then drops all reference to divine involvement until very near the climax of the verbally absorbing report of the battle of Salamis, at lines 454–455. There he says that god gave the glory of the naval encounter to the Greeks.

In the messenger scene Aeschylus begins to suggest the responsibility that Xerxes bears, but he waits until later to articulate it fully.[75] Similarly, Zeami avoids mention in the kyōgen scene or the katari of Sanemori's cause of attachment, his desire to kill Lord Kiso and the intervention of Tezuka, revelation of which is delayed until the end of the nō. It is not the function of the messenger or the kyōgen scene (or for that matter of the katari) to provide the full religious message of the play. The function of these scenes is to entertain, inform, and prepare.

[75] The full significance of the messenger's report is not revealed until the Darius scene. See, for example, Conacher, "Aeschylus' *Persae*," 160–161.

In the continuation of the messenger scene, Aeschylus increases the dramatic interest with a vivid narration of the encounter of the Greeks and the Persians at Salamis, which entertains the audience at a length not duplicated elsewhere in the tragedy and in a form similar to the explicit account, unaccompanied by music, that is presented by the shite in the katari within the nochiba of *Sanemori*. After the messenger describes the alert maintained by the Persians against Greek flight and the fear that came over the Persians when, on the arrival of day, they realized that the Greeks were not fleeing, but rushing into battle, he adds:

> And the trumpet kindled everything with its sound;
> Straightaway with a measured plying of the oar's dash
> They struck the deep, which roared at the one command. (395–397)

The messenger goes on to say that there was a roar of voices in response to the Greek battle cry and a Greek ship began the charges. At first the Persian army held its own, he adds, but when the many Persian ships were piled up in the narrows, unable to help each other, the Greek ships, aware of their chance, hemmed them in and battered them. The sea became invisible, filled as it was with wreckage of ships and slaughter of men (401–420). The description of the battle concludes:

> With broken pieces of oars and fragments from the wreckage
> They were striking, hacking them,
> As if [they were] tunnies or a catch of fish.
> And wailing, along with shrieks, took over the expanse
>   of the sea. (424–427)

The queen responds, "Oh, what a great sea of disasters has broken upon the Persians and the entire race of barbarians" (433–434).

In the messenger's next speech, which serves ostensibly as an answer to the queen's inquiry about how "the vigorous, brave, and noble" Persians died (441–444), Aeschylus's preparation for the appearance of Xerxes, dressed in rags, in the finale of the *Persians* becomes evident even more explicitly than in the queen's narration of her dream. The messenger first describes the slaughter of Persians at the island of Psyttaleia. In this speech, Aeschylus emphasizes for the audience a specific event, not as familiar to the Greeks as the battle of Salamis recounted in the previous speech, but one that, because it is the battle where the best of the Persians died, is of keen interest to the queen in the play.[76] Without mentioning Xerxes' name, the messenger says that the king, "ill-informed about the future" (454), sent the men to the island, but that god gave the glory in the battle of the

[76] See Michelini, *Tradition and Dramatic Form*, 112–113.

ships to the Greeks (454–455). The Persians, he continues, were smitten and hacked to pieces until they all died (463–464). It is at the end of the encounter, the importance of which Aeschylus exaggerates,[77] that Xerxes' name is mentioned for the first time in over one hundred lines, and it is mentioned in the context of what appears to be an alteration of historical "fact." The messenger reports that Xerxes, on seeing the depth of disasters from his position high on a hill, cried out with a groan, tore his robes, wailed shrilly, and with orders to the foot soldiers immediately sent them off in disorderly flight (465–470). None of this is in Herodotus's account.[78] According to Herodotus, after the battle of Salamis, although the defeat was difficult for him, Xerxes took precautions to conceal from the Greeks his intention to take flight by constructing a causeway across the water in the direction of Salamis (8.97).

Aeschylus's version prepares as Herodotus's would not for the presentation of Xerxes at the end of the play. When the messenger reports Xerxes' reaction to the defeat, a slight tinge of sympathy at most for its former enemy may be aroused in the Greek audience; however, it is more likely that, if the audience is going to feel any sympathy at all for its former enemy, this feeling occurs when the messenger's words are realized in performance at the finale of the play, when the king appears dressed in rags, unattended by his forces, and cries out in his own voice. The verbal preparation and the dramatic realization are similar to the effect Zeami creates in *Sanemori* with the katari and the rongi respectively: in the former, the shite, with a slight movement of his head, quotes, in melody, Higuchi's

[77] Herodotus, 8.76 and 95, says little more than that the Persians landed a large force on the island of Psyttaleia as a base from which they could operate, and that Aristides took some Athenian infantry there after the battle of Salamis and killed all of the Persian forces.

[78] Because Herodotus's *History* postdates Aeschylus's tragedy, it cannot have been a written source for the playwright; however, it does serve as a written source for us on the subject of the Persian Wars, in which the *Life* of Aeschylus leads us to believe he himself fought. On the subject of Aeschylus's treatment of the Persian Wars, see H.D.F. Kitto, *Greek Tragedy* (London, 1950), 39–42; Broadhead, *Persae*, xxxi–xxxii and Appendix VI; A.S.F. Gow, "Notes on the *Persae* of Aeschylus," *JHS* 48 (1928): 133–159; A. J. Podlecki, *The Political Background of Aeschylean Tragedy* (Ann Arbor, 1966), 8–26, who thinks that the tragedy vindicates Themistocles and his policies (Podlecki's view presents a possibility not unlike the suggestion that Zeami wrote *Sanemori* with the approval and to the benefit of the shogun Yoshimochi; see Kōsai, "Sakuhin kenkyū: Sanemori," in *Nōyōshinkō*, 67); N.G.L. Hammond, "The Battle of Salamis," *JHS* 76 (1956): 32–54; Lattimore, "Aeschylus on the Defeat of Xerxes," 82–93, who lists similarities and differences between Aeschylus's and Herodotus's accounts; and Conacher, "Aeschylus' *Persae*," 147–148, who lists liberties that he thinks Aeschylus took with history. Wilhelm Kierdorf, "Erlebnis und Darstellung der Perserkriege," *Hypomnemata* 16 (Göttingen, 1966), thinks that historical inaccuracies are few in the *Persians* (52) and that Aeschylus changed the historical facts only where the dramatic form demanded (57).

reaction to the identification of Sanemori's head—"Alas, how pitiful!"; in the latter, the shite, after falling to the ground, says, in the voice of Sanemori, "Alas, he was an old warrior." The contrast between the objective narrative and subjective expression of feeling in both works helps to build into the plays a progression that can elicit an emotional response from an audience.

After the third-person narrative, which contains the apparent alteration of history, the messenger's closing words, spoken in the second person and addressed to his listener—"Such a misfortune is at hand for you to mourn" (471)—bring the audience back to the present theatrical reality. In *Sanemori*, similarly, at the end of his narration, a story told to the audience as much as to the priest, the kyōgen turns to the waki and expresses surprise again over his question. Each of these conclusions brings the audience back to the dramatic time after a narrative section. Aeschylus also draws the audience's attention away from the messenger's narrations with the first acknowledgment by a dramatic character of the combined human and divine responsibility for the defeat. The queen reacts to the news:

> Oh, hateful spirit, how, I realize now, you cheated the Persians
> of their wits;
> My son found bitter the vengeance he planned
> For famed Athens, and the barbarians did not suffice
> Whom Marathon destroyed before.
> My son, thinking that he would exact punishment on them,
> Drew upon himself so great a multitude of woes. (472–477)

Xerxes' responsibility is suggested in a context blaming a god, but Aeschylus does not dwell on the subject or explicitly say that, if one exceeds mortal bounds, he suffers a penalty imposed by the gods. He saves that, like the name of the god responsible, for later. At this point in the performance, the queen's recognition, marked as it is by the particle *ara*, is sufficient.[79]

Aeschylus might have ended the spoken part of the messenger scene at this point; instead, he concludes with yet another messenger speech.[80] This final speech, which lists places along the way back from Greece to Persia, serves as a means to bring the "action" of the play to the dramatic setting.[81] It also vividly accounts for the destruction of many Persians—the messenger now includes himself in the action, and Aeschylus intersperses

[79] See J. D. Denniston, *The Greek Particles* (Oxford, 1954), 40–41.

[80] Some scholars think that parts of the speech are interpolated, or are a revised version used in a Sicilian performance, or are taken from Phrynichus's play. For a summary of these views, see Broadhead, *Persae*, lii–lv.

[81] This is the function of a michiyuki, a genre itself in Japanese literature. On this genre, see Jacqueline Pigeot, *Michiyuki-bun: Poétique de l'itinéraire dans la littérature du Japon ancien* (Paris, 1982).

present-tense verbs among past tenses—and provides another specific example of the way in which a god and nature joined forces in inflicting
punishment upon them. Here, as in the preceding messenger speech, it is
likely that Aeschylus embellishes the real circumstances.

In answer to the queen's question about the location of the ships that
escaped, the messenger says that the leaders of the ships took flight and
the remainder of the army in Boeotia was destroyed. He then lists the
places through which the army passed on its way from Salamis to the river
Strymon and reports the heavy losses en route. No mention is made of the
Hellespont or of Xerxes' expected arrival; Aeschylus's version is here different from that of Herodotus.[82] And Aeschylus adds to historical fact, as
we know it, the description of a miracle: a god brought winter before its
time and froze the river that the retreating army planned to cross. The
messenger says:

> . . . And on this night a god
> Raised up a storm out of season, and freezes
> The entire stream of the holy Strymon; anyone
> Who did not at all believe in the gods before
> At that time began to pray, bowing to earth and heaven.
> But when the army stopped its many entreaties to the gods,
> It crosses over the icebound path.
> And whoever of us started before the rays
> Of the god scattered, he is saved.
> What I mean is that the bright circle of the sun burning with its rays
> Warmed and pierced the middle of the path with its flames.
> The men were falling over one another, and that man was clearly
> Lucky who most quickly broke off the breath of life. (495–507)

This ahistorical account concludes with the discouraging news that only a
few men succeeded in returning to their own homeland, "so that the city
of the Persians can mourn with longing for the dearest youth of the land.
This is the truth; in speaking I leave out many of the evils which god cast
down upon the Persians" (511–513).

Earlier, at the end of the parodos, the chorus said that the whole land of
Asia, which had reared the men who left, "mourns with a longing" (*pothōi
stenetai*, 62), because there had been no word of the men; at the end of the
messenger's last speech, one learns that "mourning with longing" (*stenein
. . . pothousan*, 511–512) for the dear youth of the land can be carried out
only with full knowledge that the youth have died. The repeated words

---

[82] See Herodotus, 8.113–119. Herodotus offers two versions of Xerxes' return: the
first that he traveled across land to the Hellespont, the second that he left the army at
Eion on the Strymon River and crossed to Asia by ship.

gain an emotional intensity over their earlier appearance by virtue of the intervening account of the defeat and are soon translated into the performance of the first full lament by the chorus. In *Sanemori*, the waki's recommendation at the end of the kyōgen scene that there be an odori nembutsu, the possibility of which is only hinted at in the nanori, is similarly carried out after the kyōgen has told the people that special services will take place on behalf of Sanemori's ghost and has made a concluding remark to the waki. In these performances lies a major similarity between the structures of the *Persians* and *Sanemori*: in both the playwright has composed a section inspired by ritual for the beginning of the second half of the play. But in neither play is the extent to which the central character is responsible for his own tragedy fully revealed at this point. We know no more than that Sanemori's spirit is attached and that Xerxes made a mistake. Later the audience learns the specific details of the main characters' tragedies; however, the performance of rituals in both works intervenes first to fill out the spiritual or emotional dimension of what has been reported.

Before the queen exits, the chorus in the *Persians* reacts to the messenger's account by saying that a spirit that brings toil leapt too heavily upon the Persian race (515–516); the queen then expresses her realization that the dream has come true (518–519) and says that she wants to pray to the gods first and then bring offerings to the earth and the dead from within the house (522–524). These last words recall the chorus's earlier advice that she pour out libations to the gods and her promise to do so (229). The queen then enjoins the chorus to comfort her son and send him into the palace if he arrives before she returns (529–531). (The queen reaffirms that the elders are the trusted counsel and thus emphasizes their function, introduced in the first lines of the parodos and stated explicitly at the beginning of the first scene after the lyric parodos.) The words constitute an order considered by some as spurious or misplaced, because they are unfulfilled before the queen returns to the stage.[83] However, placed where they are, the words serve, as do lines 849–851, to hint that Xerxes, the focal point of the tragedy, will eventually appear. To an audience listening in the theater, the repetition is a useful reminder of what will occur. In the finale, in fulfillment of her request, the chorus will indeed address Xerxes (918) and accompany him off stage, presumably into the palace.

[83] Taplin, *Stagecraft*, 92–98, suggests that the "false preparation" might better fit if placed following line 851, after the exit of Darius. Wilamowitz, *Aischylos Interpretationen*, 46–67, thinks that Aeschylus gives the audience a hint that it should not expect the queen to meet Xerxes. R. D. Dawe, "Inconsistency of Plot and Character in Aeschylus," *Camb. Phil. Proc.* 189, n.s. 9 (1963): 27–31, treats both 529–531 and 849–851 as inconsistencies of plot, but inconsistencies that, because Xerxes is mentioned in these passages, bring to the play a kind of unity. See also Broadhead, *Persae*, 143.

With the queen's exit in the *Persians*, the chorus introduces and sings a lament, which, inasmuch as it is clearly a response to what the messenger has said, could be viewed as forming the finale, the kyū, both to the messenger section and to the end of the first half of the play as a whole. The song, a kind of hymn, begins with the first direct call to Zeus in the play (532).[84] Gods have been referred to previously, but now, at a verbal and musical peak, Zeus is called upon by name. In the same breath, the chorus draws the audience's attention to the theatrical present with the word *nun* ("now," 532) and adds that the city mourns, as the messenger suggested it might. The earlier anticipations of lamentation (62 and 134), we are now told, are fulfilled by the women of Persia on behalf of the army that the city has lost. The chorus, in the transitional anapaestic meter, says:

> Women in great number, with their soft hands
> Rending their veils,
> As they share in the grief, moisten the folds of their garments
> With tears so that they are drenched;
> And the Persian women with delicate expressions of weeping
> Out of longing to see their recently yoked husbands,
> Leaving the delicately wrought coverlets of their beds,
> A source of joy to rich youth,
> Mourn with insatiable weeping. (537–545)

Earlier there have been only longing and fears; now the lament of the women, described in greater detail, is real and on behalf of the dead.

The description of a lament then gradually evolves into a real—and explicitly signaled[85]—lament sung by the chorus:

> And I sing out, as is right, the very mournful
> Death of those who have gone. (546–547)[86]

---

[84] On the limited use of Zeus's name in the *Persians*, see R. P. Winnington-Ingram, "Zeus in the Persae," *JHS* 93 (1973): 211. In *Sanemori*, Amida Buddha's name is not delayed, as Zeus's name is not in the *Oresteia*. These plays postpone the revelation of other aspects of the religious message, namely, the need for Sanemori to admit the cause of his attachment and the specific form that Zeus's justice can take in the human court.

[85] Other songs that Aeschylus explicitly signals include the binding hymn, *Eumenides* 306, 331, and 344; lament, *Libation Bearers* 342–343; and paean, *Libation Bearers* 151. See further Walther Kranz, *Stasimon: Untersuchungen zu Form und Gehalt der griechischen Tragödie* (Berlin, 1933), 135.

[86] On lament in ancient Greece and the works of Aeschylus, see Vittorio Citti, *Il linguaggio religioso e liturgico nelle tragedie di Eschilo* (Bologna, 1962), who also provides material on the traditional and ritual characteristics of the *anaklēsis*, or "calling-up hymn," 41–42, which the chorus sings in lines 634–680; Rode, *Untersuchungen zur Form*, 63–72, mentions such elements from real laments as correspondence in the structure of lines, use of interjections, repetition of words, and rhyme, and also discusses the "anakletic" hymn (68); M. Alexiou, *The Ritual Lament in Greek Tradition* (Cambridge,

Although from one point of view the hymn is a musical conclusion to the messenger scene, it also serves to introduce the second half of the tragedy. (Similarly, both at the beginning of the nochiba and in reaction to the preceding kyōgen scene of *Sanemori*, the waki says, "Come now, let us pray," and he and the wakizure proceed to do precisely that with the enactment of the odori nembutsu.) The words of the chorus look both backward and forward. The elders simultaneously refer to themselves with the pronoun *egō* ("I") and use the word *oikhomenōn* ("those who have gone"), a word that represents Aeschylus's major alteration in Phrynichus's line alluded to at the beginning of the play. (This repetition is analogous to Zeami's repetition of sutras at the beginning of the nochiba from the beginning of his play.) The lament proper begins with a repetition of the word "now" (*nun*, 548), from line 532, and the straightforward statement, "the entire land of Asia, left empty, mourns" (*propasa men stenei / gai' Asis ekkenoumena*, 548–549).[87] In the lyric parodos (117–118), the chorus expressed fear lest the city, the great capital of Susa, empty of men (*kenandron*), hear the cry "O, for the Persian army!" Now the city is emptied of men and hears the cry *oa*, which is used four times within this lament (571, 574, 578, and 582). In the first strophe, the chorus continues with a threefold repetition of the name of Xerxes, the king whom, on the basis of the messenger's information, the elders now hold responsible for ill-advisedly leading the fleet across the sea. One line, "Xerxes led" (*Xerxēs men agagen*, 550), suffices to repeat what the chorus had said in the parodos; the next line, "Xerxes destroyed" (*Xerxēs d' apōlesen*, 551) suffices to summarize the messenger's report. And the lines, "Xerxes did everything imprudently / with his ships upon the sea" (*Xerxēs de pant' epespe dusphronōs / baridessi pontiais*, 552–553), point to the reason that the Persian forces were defeated. The anaphoric repetition of Xerxes' name heightens the intensity of the brief, but all too true, statement. At the end of the strophe (555–557), the chorus asks why Darius was not the ruler of Susa at the time of the expedition and suggests a contrast between father and son that was only hinted at before in the narration of the queen's dream, but that will, like Xerxes' downfall, be developed with steadily increasing explicitness in the end and be realized visually on stage.

In the antistrophe, Aeschylus emphasizes the tragic consequences of Xerxes' reliance on his navy, a mistake that was hinted at in the lyric pa-

---

1974); Kranz, *Stasimon*, 128–129; and R. Hölzle, "Zum Aufbau der lyrischen Partien des Aischylos" (Diss., Freiburg, 1934), 34–36.

[87] On metrical grounds, read *ekkenoumena* with the manuscripts rather than the suggested emendation of Hermann, *ekkekenōmena*, printed in Page's text. See Broadhead, *Persae*, Appendix II, p. 289 n. 2 and the bibliography cited there.

rodos; the chorus says that both the "infantry" and the "men on the sea" were led by "the linen-winged, dark-eyed ships" (559–560). The words "ships led" and "ships destroyed" in the next line echo both syntactically and verbally lines 550-551 of the strophe: "Xerxes led" and "Xerxes destroyed."[88] However, the ships that have replaced Xerxes' name as grammatical subject, although repeated as Xerxes' name was, become those of the Greeks rather than the Persians—a verbal substitution points to the cause of the tragedy. To this antistrophe, the chorus adds that the king himself barely escaped over the Thracian plains and stormy routes.

The lament proper, as Broadhead describes it, "begins with dactyls, descriptive of their [the Persians'] doom, and punctuated by exclamations of woe, and closes with iambics culminating in the long drawn-out wail of 575 ['prolong a bitter and long cry in wretched voice'], with its marked syncopation."[89] In other words, the repeated cries of woe taken from real laments are likely to create a greater emotional impact here than in any reference to lament earlier in the play. In the second strophe, the chorus calls for cries; in the antistrophe, it cries out for the men who are mangled by the eddying water and those torn by the gnawing of fish. (In line 424, the messenger has likened the men to fish; here Aeschylus describes the men as the victims of the fish.)

In this antistrophe, the reference to childless parents (580) only increases the tone of suffering for those whom "each house now bereft mourns" (579). In his consistent movement toward narrower focus and greater specificity, Aeschylus directs the subject of the song from the land that mourns (548–549) to each house that mourns. The ode concludes with two stanzas, couched in a meter—the dactylic—that will prove to dominate the final ode before Xerxes' arrival. In the strophe, the chorus says that the people of Asia will no longer be subject to the rule of the Persians, nor will they pay tribute nor prostrate themselves upon the earth, for, as it explains, the king's strength has been completely destroyed (584–590). In the antistrophe, the chorus adds that the people are now free to speak since the yoke of strength has been loosened, and that the island of Salamis holds that which once belonged to the Persians (591–597). The ode, which simultaneously concludes the first half and introduces the second half of the play, serves not only as an important element in building up the emotional intensity of the performance, but also as an apt transition between the presentations of a Xerxes with power and a Xerxes without power. In *Sanemori*, the ageuta and the first dan of the nochiba similarly mediate between the shite's appearances as an ordinary old man and as the ghost

---

[88] The echo has been noticed by others. See, for example, Dietmar Korzeniewski, "Studien zu den Persern des Aischylos," *Helikon* 7 (1967): 45.

[89] Broadhead, *Persae*, 290.

of Sanemori, and between the presentations of his need to be freed of attachment and the beginning of the process of his liberation.

The second half of the tragedy is fully underway when, after the chorus's lament, the queen appears, now dressed in plain clothes and without the chariot that accompanied her earlier entrance. (The shite's change of costume in two-part nō is the opposite—from the clothes of an ordinary person to those of a warrior or deity, for example.) The queen expresses her own fears and says that they are her reason for appearing without the chariot and former signs of luxury (607–609).[90] Aeschylus thus draws attention to the costume of the actor as explicitly as Zeami does at a similar juncture in Sanemori, when the waki mentions the appearance of the old man dressed in the attire of a warrior. Aeschylus adds to the effect of the queen's appearance by having her list the offerings that she has brought from the house for her child's father. As products of nature, these offerings stand in sharp contrast to the gold and luxury of the Persians mentioned earlier:

> White milk from a sacred cow, the sweet drink;
> The liquid of the flower worker, bright honey,
> Along with watery libations from a virgin spring;
> A neat drink, this delight from an old vine,
> Its mother in the fields;
> The fragrant fruit of the green olive
> That is ever verdant amidst its foliage;
> And wreaths of flowers, the offspring of the bounteous earth. (611–618)

These are the offerings, consonant with the queen's simplicity of dress, that she says she will pour out while the elders incant an anaklēsis, an "evocation" of the ghost of Darius, a ritual probably familiar to the Greek audience.[91] Acknowledging her request that it sing hymns and call up Darius (619–620), in an anapaestic introduction the chorus of elders begins to sing.

In terms of the play's structure, the queen's speech and the anaklēsis (598–680) could comprise the first section of the second half of the play, but are also analogous to the later parts in the nochiba of Sanemori, in which the shite begins to move about the stage more than he had in the maeba. In the issei of the second dan, as the shite and chorus explicitly

---

[90] See Taplin, Stagecraft, 100, on the importance of the visual dimension to the drama.
[91] In addition to the works mentioned in note 86 above, see S. Eitrem, "The Necromancy in the Persai of Aeschylus," Symbolae Osloenses 6 (1928): 1–16, and H. J. Rose, "Ghost Ritual in Aeschylus," HThR 43 (1950): 257–280. Seeck, Dramatische Strukturen der griechischen Tragödie, 19, calls the song a "Totenanrufung" as well as a "Geistererscheinung."

define the meanings of *namu* and *Amida*, the invocation referred to often before, the musical beat accompanying the recitative increases in intensity, and the shite moves about the stage and stamps his feet. In the ageuta of the next dan, the highly melodic choral song about the warrior's outfit, the shite's movements continue to increase in number and level of kinetic interest. (In the ageuta following the katari of the fourth dan, and again in the kuse of the fifth dan, the kinetic, musical, and visual interest similarly increase.) So too in the *Persians*, Aeschylus increases the queen's and the chorus's activity. Although there are several references to sacrifice in the first half of the play, the queen makes offerings to the gods below only in the second half. Although the chorus has referred to laments and sung a lament expressing its grief in the middle of the play, the chorus, being as it is an actor as well as a chorus, adds kinetic interest to its song only at the end of the queen's first scene in the second half of the tragedy, when it represents the gestures of hitting and scratching the earth. (The words of Darius's ghost, "the city mourns, the ground has been struck and is scratched" [683], suggest the possibility that the chorus of elders carries out these gestures.)

The excitement of the scene, attested to in lines of Aristophanes' *Frogs*,[92] is further brought out, according to Broadhead, "by the variety of appropriate meters, in particular the choriambic, the ionic and the dochmiac." Choriambs are used especially in passages expressing "fear or anxious foreboding . . . or the struggles of a divided soul"; ionics often convey "excitement, but are used in a greater variety of contexts"; dochmiacs "are associated with intense feelings of distress or suspense or despair which accompany the crisis of a tragic action."[93] It is also possible that the pitch of the music in the anaklēsis differs from that of other songs in the tragedy and from that of the anapaestic introduction, for the chorus, which has already explicitly announced its intention to sing a song (626), adds that it is sending forth sounds which are *panaiola*, "of changing pitch that extends over the entire gamut" (636), that is, sounds more excited than before.[94] The kinetic, visual, rhythmic, and musical appeals of the hymn are

---

[92] After Aeschylus, the dramatic character in the *Frogs*, mentions his patriotic purpose in putting on the *Persians*, the god Dionysus, another dramatic character, says that he "enjoyed" the scene "about the dead Darius" in which "the chorus clapped its hands like so and said *iauoi*" (*Frogs* 1028–1029). Although there is no specific reference to the clapping of hands or to the cry of sorrow *iauoi* in our text of the *Persians*, both could have been a part of the performance. At the very least, Aristophanes provides evidence that some part of the Darius scene was worthy of the audience's attention.

[93] Broadhead, *Persae*, 290–291.

[94] Ibid., 168, lists the parallels in Greek for this meaning of *panaiola*. Pitch variation, like rhythm and beat, is an important means by which songs are distinguished from one another in nō. For example, the sageuta is sung on a lower pitch than the ageuta, the first part of the kuse on a lower pitch than the second part.

appropriate preparation for the most striking action within the play up to this point, the appearance of the ghost of Darius.

Because the hymn accompanies the queen's offerings and contains important elements of a lament, and because Aeschylus has duly prepared for the performance of both rituals, the queen and the chorus are naturally connected with the function and enactment of these. And in line with Aeschylus's practice in many other parts of the play, the anaklēsis moves verbally from the more general to the more specific and prepares for the appearance of Darius. The elders introduce the hymn with a request that the chthonic gods, Earth and Hermes, and the king of the dead, send up "the soul" (630) from below into the light. Within the first strophe, they ask whether "the blessed and god-like king" (634) hears them; in the first antistrophe, they ask Earth and the other nether gods to allow "the illustrious spirit and Susa-born god of the Persians" (642–643) to come up from his dwelling place. It is not until the second strophe that the chorus refers to the "dear man" (648) by name: "the divine lord Darian" (651). Once the name of Darius is uttered, the elders praise their former king. In the second antistrophe they say that he never destroyed men with the disasters of war and was called "a god in counsel by the Persians" (655); they repeat that he was called "a god in counsel" (655) and explain that it was because he led the army well. In the third strophe, the elders address Darius with an oriental title, "Balēn, Balēn of old" (658),[95] and request that he show his tiara and sandals over the mound of the grave. Then they say:

Come, Father Darian who brought no harm. (664)

Thus in the final line of the strophe they address him with his family title rather than the exalted titles that have preceded.[96] After mentioning the Stygian gloom that hovers over them now that all the young men have been utterly destroyed, the chorus repeats the final line of the third strophe at the end of the antistrophe (671), and the hymn concludes with an epode in which the elders cry out *aiai aiai* (673); address their former king, "Oh, much wept for and deceased king" (674); and moan over the loss of ships, "Ships, no longer ships, no longer ships" (680).

During the course of the anakletic hymn that announces his entrance, the main actor playing the role of Darius comes into the audience's view, either by entering along the parodos or by rising out of a structure repre-

---

[95] The word seems to mean "king." See ibid., 170.

[96] Helen Moritz, "Refrain in Aeschylus: Literary Adaptation of Traditional Form," *CP* 74, no. 3 (July 1979): 190, suggests that the movement of the ode from formal address by royal title to the use of a title denoting family relationship "may reflect Persian practice." Whether that is the case or not, the progression from formal to personal modes of expression complements similar movements within the tragedy as a whole.

senting a tomb. Given the analogy with *Sanemori*, where the shite is said to disappear across the water of the lake at Shinowara when there is no lake represented on stage, one need not suppose that Aeschylus represented the tomb of Darius in his productions. The actor could enter along the parodos. On the other hand, a lake is difficult to represent and a tomb is not. Moreover, since the chorus says that Darius should come to the top of the "mound" (*okhthou*, 659–660), and since, when he is about to disappear, he says that he will return "down into the darkness below the earth" (*gēs hypo zophon katō*, 839), the latter alternative, his appearance above a "mound," seems attractive.[97] I do not presume to know what the structure looked like, but I would suggest that on the analogy of those nō in which a prop is used, it need not have been a solid mound or tomb and might have been a portable prop large enough for an actor to hide within or behind. If, near the end of the lament following the messenger's exit, a portable prop with the main actor hidden behind it had been unobtrusively brought to a position near the parodos at the edge of the orkhēstra farthest from the audience (or onto the stage when one was in use), during the anakletic hymn the actor playing the role of Darius could have presented himself to view from a crouched position by standing up and rising above the top of the structure. In nō performances today, if a prop is required in the nochiba only, a structure with the actor already hidden inside is brought out by stage assistants after the kyōgen interlude scene. The actor, hidden inside these *tsukurimono*, usually walks along unnoticed. When there is no longer a need for these props, they are removed by the attendants. A similar arrangement would suit the requirements of the *Persians* very well.[98]

With the appearance of Darius before the audience in the second and third sections of the second half of the play (681–702 and 703–906), the verbal contrast that Aeschylus sets up between Darius, the good king who caused no harm, and Xerxes, the evil king who brought disaster to the Persians, begins to assume validity. We can assume from what the chorus says in lines 660–662 that Darius appears dressed in saffron-dyed sandals and a tiara; Xerxes appears at the end of the play dressed in rags. Aeschy-

[97] The form and site of this structure has been debated by many. I agree to some extent with Pickard-Cambridge, *Theatre of Dionysus*, 35, who suggests that "on the far side of the orchestra from the audience, probably just outside the circle" was "an erection representing the grave of Darius, sufficiently high to conceal [inside or behind it] an actor who in due course rises up out of or above it." For a summary of different views, see Taplin's *Stagecraft*, 116–119.

[98] In today's performances, a tomb mound constructed out of wood, paper, and artificial leaves is used in *Sumidagawa*. The voice of the dead child coming out of the tomb can be heard by his mother; later the child's ghost himself appears from the tomb. The play has been translated in NGS, 1: 145–159.

lus sets up the contrast to Xerxes' disadvantage and reminds the audience of the costume's importance again when, at the end of the scene, Darius instructs the queen to fetch new adornments for her son whose clothes are tattered (833–836). The contrast between the queen's simple attire and Darius's regal clothes is also a visual sign of moral significance; it reminds the audience that the former prosperity of Persia has been lost under the leadership of Xerxes. The translation of word into performance is accomplished in a manner analogous, if not similar, to that in *Sanemori*. There, near the beginning of the nochiba and after the appearance of the shite dressed in white wig, bearded mask, brocade robe, and warrior's clothes, the shite refers to the white hair and beard of the old warrior, the waki refers to his brilliant outfit, and the chorus in the ageuta refers to the robe and outfit. The various elements of the shite's costume are then emphasized separately during the remainder of the nochiba. In the katari and the ageuta of the next dan, the dyeing and the washing of the hair and beard is the subject of the narration and song and of the shite's gestures; the robe is the subject of the kuse of the fifth dan and the focus of the shite's gesture—he waves his sleeve; and the armor is, of course, the part of the costume most appropriate to the battle scene, in which the words refer to the swords and the skirt of the warrior's armor.

In the *Persians*, what we have called the second section of the second half of the play (681–702) begins with an address by the ghost of Darius, who mentions the anakletic hymn and his difficulty in coming up from below. He asks the chorus what new evil has fallen upon the city (693). Instead of answering his question, the awe-struck chorus expresses adulation for the former king twice in a short epirrhematic exchange (694–696 and 700–702). It intones in a rhythm that lies between anapaestic recitative, used in transitional passages, and ionic meter. (This short section comprised of Darius's speech and the epirrhēma is structurally like the short section shared by the messenger and the chorus in the first half of the play.)

At the beginning of the next (third) section (703–906), Darius's request that the queen speak, her response, the stichomythy shared by the ghost and the queen, and the two speeches that follow are delivered in trochaic tetrameter, the more melodic recitative that was used at the beginning and end of the queen's first scene in the first half of the play. As in the earlier section, the meter changes to iambic trimeter; simultaneously Darius's function, like the queen's, changes from interlocutor to narrator. In other words, there is a doubling of the structure of the first half in the second, as there is in the maeba and nochiba of many nō. This kind of doubling is unique among extant tragedies written by Aeschylus.

The part of the Darius scene shared with the queen begins with a generalization about the many disasters that come to mortals on sea and on land if they live too long (706–708). The queen replies that Darius surpassed others in good fortune, was enviable as long as he looked upon the rays of the sun, and led a successful life among the Persians, like a god (709–711). Aeschylus thus exaggerates the prosperity of this former enemy of the Greeks for the purposes of the play. The queen says that she envies him now because he died before witnessing the ruin of Persian fortunes (712–714). In the stichomythic exchange, the queen lists the evils that have occurred under Xerxes' leadership: that the entire army was destroyed (716), that "impetuous Xerxes" emptied the entire plain of the continent (718), that both the infantry and the navy were involved in the foolish attempt (720), that the Hellespont was yoked to provide the army's passage (722), that some god helped him in his plan (724), that the naval force destroyed the foot soldiers (728), that the men are all lost and the city is empty (730 and 732), and that Xerxes alone reached the bridge (734 and 736). In answer to Darius's questions, the queen provides an outline of Xerxes' actions, most of which the audience has heard before. However, Aeschylus presents them again, in contrast to Darius's actions and also as preparation for the lessons that Aeschylus will draw from them in Darius's narrative speeches. This second section of the Darius scene shares with the end of the ha section of *Sanemori* (comprising the kuri, sashi, katari, ageuta, and kuse) the important function of making explicit the thematic, proverbial, and ethical content of the play. In both, words from other authors are borrowed or alluded to; the major character is set into historical, as well as literary and proverbial, perspective; that historical tradition is altered in a manner dictated by the needs of the structure; and the moral lesson that the main character exemplifies is spelled out at the end—Sanemori must tell his tale of repentance, the Persians must not take to the sea on another expedition.[99]

Darius tells the queen that Zeus (here mentioned by name by a single actor for the first time) "hurled down" upon his son "the fulfillment of the oracles,"[100] which Darius knew in time the gods would fulfill (740–741). He adds:

[99] Seeck, *Dramatische Strukturen der griechischen Tragödie*, 13, observes that, unlike the queen and the chorus who hear the news of Persian defeat from the messenger, Darius reacts on the basis of second-hand information from the chorus and the queen, and that, unlike Xerxes and the messenger, Darius was not involved in the event itself. His observations suggest to me that the degree to which Aeschylus distances Darius in the scene as compared to characters in other parts of the tragedy is analogous in some respects to the distancing created in the third part of the ha section of *Sanemori* by Zeami's use of the third-person narrative in the katari and of the chorus in the kuse scene, rather than Sanemori's own voice. The penultimate scenes of both the tragedy and the nō set off and enhance the dramatic effect of the final scenes, in which the main characters speak in their own voices.

[100] On the oracles, see Herodotus 8.96 and 9.43.

Whenever one speeds something along himself, god also helps. (742)

The remark raises an important point in the light of the earlier references by the messenger and the queen to the role played by a divinity in the defeat of the Persians. In those earlier statements, Aeschylus emphasized the role of the gods; in the Darius scene, Xerxes' own responsibility is presented more straightforwardly than before.

This progression is similar to Zeami's technique in *Sanemori*. In the first sashi and ageuta he says that Paradise, though far away, is in one's heart, and that people, both high and low, can take passage to that Country. This preliminary statement is analogous to the passage early in the *Persians* (94–114) in which the chorus asks what man can escape god's treachery and explains that there was a decree from god for the Persians to wage war on land, which they ignored by taking to the sea. At first, in both the nō and the tragedy, man's ability to attain or to avoid what comes from god is suggested in quite general terms. Later it is spelled out. The possibility that Sanemori may be saved is foreshadowed in the shite's first sashi: he says that if Buddha's name is recited one time, the glory of Amida shines upon the reciter; in his first long speech, he expresses joy that he can be reborn in heaven; in the nochiba, he again relates his joy over the prospect that he can reach Paradise. However, it is not until after the chorus contrasts the treasures on earth (the warrior's costume) and those in Paradise that the priest explicitly states how, beyond one invocation of the nembutsu, Sanemori can be saved: by relinquishing his attachment. The chorus repeats this advice in the kuri, and then elaborates upon it when, singing for the shite in the following sashi, it says that the warrior must recount his tale of repentance. A similar delay is built into the structure of the *Persians*: it is not until the Darius scene that one learns the full extent of Xerxes' responsibility. By virtue of the priest's presence, the religious services, and the quotation of and allusion to Buddhist texts, the nō is hieratic as the tragedy is not; however, the authority granted to Darius by Aeschylus to present the religious and ethical lessons compensates for part of this difference. (In addition, the religious dicta are expressed at an earlier point in the second half of the nō than in the tragedy.)

Darius continues to make Xerxes' responsibility for the defeat of the Persians explicit. He says,

Now it seems a fount of disasters has been found for all who are dear;
And my child, unaware [of the divine law], brought these [disasters]
    to pass, in his youthful boldness. (743–744)

Darius next states plainly what was suggested in the lyric parodos, namely that the Persians should not have taken to the sea and bridged the Hellespont. By this act, Darius continues,

[Xerxes] though a mortal, foolishly thought he could conquer
    all the gods,
Even Poseidon. (749–750)

In concluding that a sickness of the mind must have taken hold of his child
(750–751), Darius makes it clear that Xerxes is responsible for the disaster.[101]

The queen tries to excuse Xerxes from some of the responsibility with
the argument that he planned the expedition against Greece because he
was taunted by evil men who claimed that out of cowardice he stayed at
home and did not increase his inherited wealth (753–758). Darius knows
better and says that Xerxes' deed is "most serious, one always to be remembered and one such as has never before emptied the city and plain of
Susa since Zeus handed the authority to them for one man to rule all of
Asia" (759–764). He sets the deed into the perspective of the kings who
preceded him, mentioning only those who are pertinent to the case. Aeschylus, who suppresses here the historical Darius's intention to gain revenge on Athens for his defeat at Marathon,[102] chooses and presents what
best serves his dramatic purposes, rather than what is necessarily historical
fact. In the list, Darius mentions Medus, the first to be the leader of the
army, then Medus's son, who completed his father's work. Third, there
was Cyrus, a fortunate man who brought peace because "his wits controlled the rudder of his mind" (767–769)—the contrast with Xerxes is
telling—and whom the gods did not hate since he was wise. Fourth, the
son of Cyrus led the army, and Mardus ruled fifth, "a disgrace to his father
and the ancient throne" (774–775). Darius adds that the good Arta-
phrenes, with the help of his friends, killed Mardus, significantly drawing
attention to the punishment that befell the only negative example in the
list. Next after Mardus comes Darius himself, introduced succinctly with
kagō ("and I") and characterized as the one who "carried out many military campaigns with a great host, but did not bring so great disaster upon
the city" (779–781). The list concludes with the name of Xerxes, about
whom Darius says:

[101] Among the many who have discussed the relationship between divine and human
responsibility in the *Persians*, see Kitto, *Poiesis*; Conacher, "Aeschylus' *Persae*"; Albin
Lesky, *Die griechische Tragödie* (Stuttgart and Leipzig, 1938), 54–56; and "Decision
and Responsibility in the Tragedy of Aeschylus," *JHS* 86 (1966): 78–85; Hugh Lloyd-
Jones, *The Justice of Zeus* (Berkeley, 1971), 88–89; P. E. Easterling, "Presentation of
Character in Aeschylus," *GR* 20 (1973): 19; Ottfried Becker, "Das Bild des Weges und
verwandte Vorstellungen im frühgriechischen Denken," *Hermes*, Einzelschr. 4 (1937):
151–192; Winnington-Ingram, "Zeus in Persae"; Michael Gagarin, *Aeschylean Drama*
(Berkeley, 1976), 49–50; and Mark W. Edwards, "Agamemnon's Decision: Freedom
and Folly in Aeschylus," *California Studies in Classical Antiquity* 10 (1977): 19–20.
[102] See Herodotus 7.1.

But my son, while still young and senseless in his youth,
Does not remember my behests. (782–783)

(This remark contradicts the account of Herodotus, who suggests that Xerxes was following the example of his forbears.[103]) Darius appends to the list a remark that "all of us who held the throne could not have made manifest so many calamities" (785–786). Although the Darius scene is more prosaic, sententious, and argumentative than anything we find in the nō, the suppression of historical material in Darius's list is as effective as Zeami's suppression of epic material about Sanemori. Xerxes' name, with which Darius's list ends, serves as the focus of Darius's first long iambic trimeter narrative. During the kuse scene almost immediately preceding the finale of *Sanemori*, Zeami sets Sanemori's request for a brocade robe into historical, proverbial, and poetic perspective; Sanemori's name serves as the focus of the kuse.

The second long speech, including the short dialogue shared by Darius and the chorus, similarly focuses on Xerxes. In it, Darius predicts the disaster at Plataea. The messenger has given the impression that all the surviving Persian forces left Greece, but here the chorus, to its surprise, learns differently (798–799).[104] And it is at this point in the tragedy that Aeschylus accumulates allusions to and borrows from other sources of traditional wisdom as explicitly as Zeami does in the kuse. On the authority of oracles, Darius informs the chorus that for the troops that his son, persuaded by empty hopes, left behind there awaits the suffering "of the greatest of evils in requital for hubris and godless thoughts" (807–808). The expression is proverbial, part of the Greek literary tradition and religious thought; to avoid overbearing thoughts sounds like a variation on the famous admonition of the Delphic oracle, "nothing to excess."[105] It is also connected traditionally with a diseased mind such as Darius has attributed to Xerxes. Solon, for example, says:

For satiety [of insolence] gives birth to hubris, whenever much
        prosperity attends
Men whose minds are not sound.[106]

---

[103] Ibid., 7.8. On this point, see Kierdorf, "Erlebnis und Darstellung," 61.

[104] One is reminded that in *Sanemori*, the kyōgen does not mention the red brocade robe (Itō Masayoshi's version of the kyōgen speech does refer to the robe), the Kantō dialect, the victim of Sanemori's sword, and, most importantly, the warrior's desire to kill Kiso specifically, the name on which Sanemori's tragic attachment depends. The effect of these omissions is to provide the audience with new information that enhances the impact of the play in the penultimate and ultimate dan.

[105] See also, *Agamemnon* 374–380 and Fraenkel's comment on line 377, *Aeschylus Agamemnon*, 2: 197.

[106] 6.3–4 West.

Darius amassed wealth, but used it rightly; Xerxes, who is not sound of mind, endangers that wealth with his hubristic acts and his godless thoughts. Since a lack of mental soundness can be said to come from the gods, the fault does not lie entirely with a human being. And yet a human being bears some responsibility.[107]

In nō, since wealth, like all aspects of this world, is considered ephemeral and insubstantial by comparison with the outlook implicit in the Greek tragedies, the main character is encouraged in two-part plays to rise above the mortal frame of reference and to free himself from all attachment to earthly things. On the other hand, in his tragedy, Aeschylus informs us that it is man's responsibility to maintain a proper balance, to avoid hubris and godless thoughts, including attempts to be like a god. In nō, not freeing oneself from attachment is tantamount to suffering the continued agony of a "hell"; in the tragedy, Zeus, the stern punisher of overbearing thoughts (827), forces mortals to pay, but that penalty is brought upon living persons, not the dead. And although that punishment can entail death, as it does for Agamemnon, there is nothing to suggest a Buddhist-like view of heaven and hell, as there is suggested in nō. The gods come to earth, like Athena, Apollo, and the Furies do in the *Eumenides*; Darius, though a ghost, speaks in terms of the world we live in. (When he says that wealth is of no value to the dead, 840–842, he advises the elders to enjoy it while they are alive.) The priest and the chorus of *Sanemori* contrast worldly treasures with those of Buddha's Lake and advise Sanemori not to leave any part of his soul behind in earthly attachment. The difference lies in the religious outlooks of the tragedy and the nō. However, to the extent that in the Darius scene Aeschylus introduces a character who belongs to a world of spirits, knows the will of god from oracles, and can speak about Zeus and his punishment with the authority of history and "literature" and religious sources, the play's structure is comparable to *Sanemori*. In the kuse, Zeami establishes the nobility of the warrior through the authority of the *Heike*, a proverb, a poem, and a Chinese model of virtue.

Aeschylus is very explicit in Darius's final speech about the play's moral lesson, and he expands upon what the ghost has already said. First Darius explains how the Persians were godless: they went to Greece and did not show reverence when they stripped the statues of the gods, burned the

[107] In the Japanese tradition, one also finds repeated warnings that wealth entails decay. (See the beginning of the *Heike*, 1.1, for example.) And to some of these is added the warning that pride must have its fall. (See *Atsumori*. The shite says, "When at the height of power, they are afflicted with humility"; the chorus adds, "When wealthy, they did not recognize their haughtiness." The reference is to the Heike defeated by the Genji.)

temples, and destroyed the altars and the shrines.[108] From this example, he draws the moral that because they acted wrongly they must suffer due payment (813–814).[109] He adds that there are sufferings to come, for much blood will be shed on the Plataean plain by the Dorian spear (814–817)—that is, land forces will suffer as greatly as the navy did. Darius continues with an explanation:

> Heaps of corpses will provide a voiceless sign to the eyes of mortals,
> Even unto the third-sown generation, that being mortal,
> One should not have overbearing thoughts. (818–820)

This latter remark, like others in the scene, is cast in the mold of Aeschylus's "literary" predecessors.[110]

With an implicit acknowledgment of his debt to Solon and other authoritative writers, Aeschylus sets the responsibility of Xerxes into sharp relief. Nor does Aeschylus stop with these warnings, any more than Zeami mentions only one source for the proverb about wearing a red brocade robe in *Sanemori*. He repeats them through the mouth of Darius, who says:

> For hubris bursting forth bears a crop
> Of disaster, whence it gathers a harvest fraught with tears. (821–822)

Near the beginning of the tragedy, the chorus had said that Delusion, the goddess Atē, draws men into her snares (98–99); here Darius says that hubris brings disaster, *atē*. In this way, Aeschylus makes Xerxes' responsibility explicit even before Darius mentions his name again.

Darius concludes his moralizing by urging that the Persians remember Athens and Greece and not lose their great prosperity out of excessive pride or a desire for more than what they have, "because," he adds, "Zeus, a severe chastener, is the punisher of overly proud thoughts" (824–828). In this speech, Darius addresses the Persian people at large, but since he does not use the name "Persians," the advice can apply to anyone, much as after the katari of *Sanemori* the remark about the nobility of Sanemori's example can apply to members of the audience as well. Of course, Aeschylus is not asking his Greek audience to remember themselves, but to be warned by what happened to the Persians during the height of their power. The speech is then directed to Xerxes specifically, whom Darius asks the

---

[108] The idea is also expressed at *Agamemnon* 338–340.

[109] The thought that those who act wrongly must pay is found in many places, but the most telling is at *Libation Bearers* 313–314, where it is called a "tale thrice-aged."

[110] See Solon; in particular, 13.72–76 West: "For those of us who have the greatest means / Try to get twice as much. Who could satisfy all? / Clearly the immortals have given profit to mortals, / But out of it disaster appears. Whenever Zeus / Sends disaster as punishment, it afflicts now one man and now another." See also 4.34–35 West.

139

elders to instruct to cease injuring the gods with overbearing boldness (829–831). The ghost tells the queen to fetch new clothes as a replacement for their son's torn robes and to comfort him (832–838), and he advises the elders to enjoy themselves while they can since wealth is of no benefit to the dead (840–842).

The spoken part of the Darius section concludes with the chorus's avowal of pain at the news of the many present and future happenings, and the queen's statement that what stings her most is the dishonor that is "wrapped about" her son's body (846–847). With her words Aeschylus creates a verbal interaction between the "dishonor" and the robes, and emphasizes both the defeat and the visual marker of that defeat, namely the rags in which Xerxes is soon to appear. The queen says that she will go into the house to fetch clothing in preparation for meeting Xerxes (849–850). She does exit, but does not return, for the stage must be cleared of all actors and the audience focused on Xerxes alone, as in nō it would be focused on the shite.[111] In fact, her words help to place the attention on Xerxes, who presumably does not meet the queen until after he exits at the end of the play, *exō tou dramatos*.

Before the entrance of Xerxes, the Darius section ends with a choral song that emphasizes the contrast between Darius and Xerxes already established in the anakletic hymn and the Darius section. Since the ghost of Darius and the queen have made their exits, the choral ode does not function in precisely the same way as do songs at the end of dan in nō, which, as I have mentioned repeatedly, are intended to serve as conclusions to dan before the exit of an actor or before the beginning of the next dan. In the *Persians*, the latter function is served, for it is clear that the content of the ode is closely connected to the Darius scene. (At the same time, the meters of this primarily dactylic ode, which is more stately than the preceding hymns and songs, presumably set it into contrast with the meters featured in the final scene, where the emotional impact of the song is great.[112]) The

---

[111] For a survey of the different views of the finale, including the possibility that the queen enters again or that Xerxes changes costume in the final scene from rags to robes, as they surely do not, see Taplin, *Stagecraft*, 120–122. More recently, there is Sylwester Dworacki, "Atossa's Absence in the Final Scene of the Persae of Aeschylus," in *Arktouros: Hellenic Studies Presented to Bernard M.W. Knox on the Occasion of His Sixty-fifth Birthday*, ed. G. W. Bowersock, W. Burkert, and M.C.J. Putnam (Berlin and New York, 1979), 101–108. Similarly, at the end of the nō *Shunkan*, Shunkan's companions in exile promise him that he too will be freed. But he is not. For a translation, see note 26 in Chapter 1.

[112] The chorus does not acknowledge its meeting with Darius in so many words or connect its song explicitly to the preceding Darius scene. Nor does the ode function primarily either as part of or as a full lament, which, as I have argued, is a musical feature of importance to the dramatic build-up of the performance of the *Persians*. And yet, as Seeck, *Dramatische Strukturen der griechischen Tragödie*, 20–21, points out and graph-ically represents with a chart, the ode participates in both the primary and the secondary

elders first praise their king for the great and good life they enjoyed under his government, for "when the aged king ruled the land he was equal to his responsibility, brought no disasters, was invincible, and was equal to a god" (853–856).[113] In addition, they say that his armies were worthy of their reputation,[114] and the men returned from war to happy homes without misery and suffering (857–863). To this introduction is appended, by means of a relative pronoun, the many places of which Darius gained control without crossing the river Halys or even leaving home, as Xerxes had done. The places listed are ostensibly those over which Darius held control when his empire was intact; however, since at the time of the production of the *Persians*, these places were under Greek hegemony, the list implicitly reinforces the warning to the Athenians that those who are prosperous can fall. The list includes the name Salamis, referring not to the site of the battle in which the Athenians were victorious over Xerxes and his forces, to be sure, but rather to a place in Cyprus that was colonized by that Salamis (895). And yet the name itself is emotionally charged within the context of the play. The song ends immediately before Xerxes' entrance with the words:

> Now without doubt we suffer these changes brought by god,
> Defeated terribly in war by the blows of the sea. (905–906)

The word "now" helps to bring the audience back to the theater and the arrival of Xerxes,[115] as at the end of the kuse immediately preceding the finale of *Sanemori* the word *ima*, which also means "now," brings the audience back from the time of Shubaijin and Sanemori's request to wear brocade to the theatrical present.

With the arrival of Xerxes dressed in rags and without a chariot or attendants, the religious and ethical lesson of the play is brought out in full force in the final section of the play (908–1077). Xerxes speaks straightaway and says:

---

levels that he has designated as operative within the structure of the play. The ode looks both backward and forward. Although I would say that the ode serves to delay and to set off the finale, I would not say, as A. F. Garvie does ("Aeschylus' Simple Plots," 71), that Aeschylus is surprising the audience or frustrating its expectations.

[113] On the translation of the words *pantarkēs* ("equal to his responsibility") and *amakhos* ("invincible"), see Broadhead, *Persae*, 214.

[114] There is a crux after this point in the text, in which "system of laws, steadfast as towers" (Headlam) is a less attractive reading than "attacked fortresses that were solid towers" (Page). The latter sets Darius's exploits into sharp contrast with Xerxes'; the son attacked ships on sea, the father attacked fortresses on land. See Broadhead, *Persae*, 215–216.

[115] On this point, see Duchemin, "Du lyrisme à la tragédie," 137.

Woe!
Poor me, I who have hit upon this
Cruel lot that gave no warning at all,
With what raw intent a god came upon
The race of Persians. What is to become of poor me?
[I ask this] for the strength of my limbs is weakened
As I look upon this group of old citizens;
Zeus, would that, along with the men
Who are gone,
The portion of death had enveloped me. (908–917)

Here the "I" resounds loudly in an anapaestic introduction to the kommos. Aeschylus singles out the person toward whom the verbal development of the play has led through his use of the first-person pronoun three times and the first-person ending of a verb once in this short introduction. He continues to use the pronoun in emphatic positions at the beginning of the first strophe (931) and the end of the answering antistrophe (943). The mention of Zeus by name, limited before to one use by the chorus and three by Darius, is another verbal marker of the importance of this speech. In addition, Xerxes calls attention to himself with a cry of woe, similar to the piteous expression of Sanemori—"Alas, he was an old warrior!" Added to these verbal markers is Aeschylus's use of the verb *oikhomenōn* ("[the men] who have gone"), repeated from his allusions to Phrynichus's work. The combined effect of the words, the unannounced entrance of the main character, the expression of emotion, and the sight of Xerxes' costume make the anapaestic introduction as striking as the beginning of the rongi in *Sanemori*.

Xerxes' first speech informs the audience that a god has come down upon the Persian race, that he is completely fallen and miserable, and that he wishes Zeus had allowed him to die with the others. To be sure, Xerxes does not assume responsibility for his actions in this first speech. It is only after the elders say that a god cut off the men, that the land mourns for the youths whom Xerxes killed and with whom he filled Hades, that many men in great numbers died, and that the land of Asia is fallen to her knees (918–930), that Xerxes admits his responsibility.

At the beginning of the second part of the finale (931–1001), at the point where the meter changes from the anapaests of recitative to more lyric anapaests, Xerxes says:[116]

[Look at me,] this one, alas, lamentable,
Miserable, to my race and fatherland,
I became an evil, yes, I recognize it now. (931–933)

---

[116] On the meters of the kommos, see Broadhead, *Persae*, 316–317.

In this single sentence one finds the deictic pronoun *hode* ("this one"), with which word the actor playing the part of Xerxes may point to himself; the unusual form of the first-person pronoun *egōn* ("I") in an emphatic position near the beginning;[117] the particle of recognition *ara*, used earlier by the queen when she first recognized that the Persians were defeated and that a god was responsible (472); and a directness of expression that marks Xerxes' acknowledgment that he has become an evil (he uses the first-person pronoun and verb ending). The neuter gender *kakon* ("evil"), used instead of the masculine gender *kakos*, suggests that Xerxes recognizes himself as the cause of trouble for other people.

Responding to Xerxes' words and sharing the strophe with him, the chorus reacts with a promise that it will greet his return with the cry of a Mariandynian mourner,[118] fraught with tears (935–940). Xerxes asks the elders to send forth a cry, "for," he adds, "this spirit has turned against me" (941–943). These lines suggest that while Xerxes has just admitted his responsibility for the evils, he also sees the hand of god in the defeat. Surely this is the religious meaning of the tragedy: human and divine responsibility go hand-in-hand. In *Sanemori*, one learns that Amida Buddha will save any person no matter who he is, but if a person helps himself, then "god" speeds along the end. This lesson, in reverse, is what Darius has presented in his speech (742) and what Xerxes exemplifies. The young and impetuous king made a mistake and thus god, some spirit, "helped" him to bring punishment upon himself and upon the Persians. That punishment is seen in the king's costume; heard in his words; verified by the chorus's statements and a list of the dead, some of whom were mentioned in two earlier lists of leaders; and felt in Xerxes' emotional reactions.

The chorus, in the continuation of the kommos, says that it will sing out its grief fraught with many tears over the sorrows at sea (944–947). In the next strophe Xerxes emphasizes the role of Ares, the god of war, in the battle of ships (951–952); the chorus cries out and asks where the others are. In four successive stanzas the chorus lists leaders about whom it asks the whereabouts, whom it says Xerxes left behind, or whom it says it longs for, but the list, with little identification of the place from which the leaders came and no extended description of the men or identification of their arms, is a mere skeleton compared to the Homeric type of catalogues that have preceded.[119] That the men are truly dead one can sense from the lack of adornment in the list itself. Xerxes' responses to the men's names emphasize the losses variously. First Xerxes reacts with an avowal of personal responsibility:

---

[117] See ibid., 227.
[118] The Mariandyni from Bithynia were known for their laments. See ibid., 228.
[119] On the skeletal form of this list, see Holtsmark, "Ring Composition," 20.

> I left them dead,
> Fallen from a Tyrian ship,
> On the shores of Salamis. (962–965)

Referring once again to the sea battle, he says:

> Oh, oh, me!
> Having seen . . .
> Hateful Athens, they all are gasping miserably
> With one stroke of the oar on the coast. (974–977)

Next he expresses his own feelings by saying to the chorus:

> You bring to mind my longing
> For the brave comrades
> By speaking of hateful evils [not to be forgotten], not to be forgotten;
> It cries out, cries out, for the luckless ones, the heart within [my]
>   limbs. (987–991)

This last outburst repeats a similar idea from lines 10–11 and 116, in which the chorus felt disquieted and its heart was torn with fear. But whereas the chorus was concerned about the men who left Persia and whose names were listed between the two expressions of concern, Xerxes' disquiet is for men, again listed, who are dead.

At the end of the list and at the beginning of the most emotionally intense part of the kommos, the last part of the final section of the play (1002–1077), marked again by a shift in rhythm from the lyric anapaests to iambs with frequent syncopation, Xerxes' response is a short one-line statement:

> For they have gone, indeed, the leaders of the army. (1002)

The chorus repeats the first word in the next line:

> They have gone, ah, inglorious. (1003)

The skeletal list of names is erased by the verb *bebasi* ("they have gone"), which represents Aeschylus's first use of Phrynichus's verb in place of *oi-khomai*, the verb used elsewhere in his allusions to Phrynichus's line. Xerxes and the chorus make it clear that the men are truly gone at the beginning of the lament proper, a ritual familiar to the audience and strikingly adapted to the play. This is the lament for which Aeschylus has prepared and which his dramatic characters, the elders and the king Xerxes, the defeated in war, are naturally suited to perform.

The chorus and Xerxes blend their identities more completely than they did in the preceding epirrhēmata, and more in the manner of a kakeai and rongi than one finds in other sections of the tragedy. The use of this format means that the main actor is featured in the scene without the distraction of a chorus acting as a separate character. The antiphonal lament[120] features a shift in the meter, single-line exchanges between Xerxes and the chorus, four three-line conclusions to stanzas by the chorus, many short lines and phrases, many repetitions of sounds and words,[121] and an increasing number of cries of woe.[122]

In the continuation of the exodos, as the chorus and king repeat each other's words again and again, both the king and the chorus cry out in woe—*iē, iē, iō, iō* and *iō, iō* (1004–1005). The chorus adds that "the gods have caused an unexpected disaster, manifest such as Atē looks" (1006–1008). The word *Atē*, meaning the goddess Delusion, as in the parodos where the religious dictum that Delusion draws men into her nets was first mentioned, is repeated in the plural as a common noun in line 1037, where the chorus refers to the disasters at sea as *ataisi pontiaisin*. And added to these, in a striking compound found only in the work of Aeschylus, is the use of the word *megalate*, "one great in *atē*" (1016), that is, great in disaster, which refers to both the perpetrator and sufferer of the defeat, Xerxes.[123]

The kommos, in addition to serving as the conclusion to themes introduced earlier in the tragedy, such as the disaster at sea, the responsibility of Xerxes and the gods in the disaster, Atē, and the loss of so many leaders, heightens the emotional pitch and also the kinetic and visual aspects of the play. To begin with, the kommos is the most emotionally intense lament performed during the course of the tragedy. In the parodos the chorus has mentioned tears and the rending of robes (115–125); in the wake of the messenger's report of defeat the chorus has sung a short lament (256–

---

[120] For a comparison of this lament with that at the end of the *Seven against Thebes*, see Popp, "Das Amoibaion," 237–239, and for examples in other tragedies, see Broadhead, *Persae*, 310–313.

[121] Zeami's repetition in the rongi of *Sanemori* is noticeable. There is not only alliteration, but also the shite's repetition *meguri megurite* ("keeps coming around and around"); the repetition of *kumu* ("fight"); the fourfold repetition of Tezuka's name; the repetition *oshi* ("push") and *ochi* ("fall"), and so forth.

[122] Zeami does not include in the text of the rongi emotional interjections such as those which punctuate almost every line at the end of the *Persians*. However, the drummers' cries, *yo, ha, iya*, as the rhythm in the kyū section accelerates and becomes more insistent, can be heard clearly.

[123] The meaning of the compound is ambiguous. See Broadhead, *Persae*, 238, for the problems connected with this compound and the preference of scholars for the meaning "sufferer." Richard E. Doyle, S.J., "The Objective Concept of *ATĒ* in Aeschylean Tragedy," *Traditio* 28 (1972): 1–28, comparing Aeschylus's use of *atē* to that of his predecessors, finds that more than half of the uses by Aeschylus are in the objective sense "ruin," as opposed to "folly." It seems that we can posit both meanings here where both are apposite.

289); and in the song following the messenger's exit (548–597) and parts of the anaklēsis it has lamented. But nowhere are the costume and choreography connected with a lament as striking as in the finale.

Aeschylus brings out verbally the visual aspects, as Zeami does in the rongi. Xerxes asks the chorus whether it sees what is left of his robe:

Do you see this, the remainder of my outfit [or entourage]? (1018)

Within the immediate context, the word *stolē* at the end of the line refers to the entourage, the men who went to Greece with Xerxes (see 1014); the audience can see that they are not with Xerxes. The word also refers to his meager outfit, which Xerxes emphatically, and presumably with a gesture, points to—an empty quiver(1020–1023) and torn robes (1030).[124] These, like the absence of a palanquin and entourage of men (1000–1001), are visible proof of the defeat and of his error.[125] Xerxes' lack of escort, already made clear by the lists of the dead and by the chorus's remark in line 1001 that the men are not following him, is further acknowledged when Xerxes says that he is "naked of escorts" (1036).

The kinetic dimension is added to the visual in the final part of this section (1038–1077), where the syncopated iambs change to the even more intensely excited and emotional iambs in catalexis and resolution. Here the chorus and the king sing, the former in response to the latter, and explicitly refer to elements of a lament, which they then perform. First there are calls for and replies of shouts and cries (1040–1045). Then Xerxes says:

Ply, ply and mourn for my sake. (1046)

Presumably he asks the chorus to move its arms like the wings of birds or the oars of boats, a motion well suited to the synchronized movements of a lament.[126] The movements are further specified by a mention of wounding blows mingling so as to blacken the person (1052–1053), beating of the breast (1054), tearing of hair (1056), clenching of nails (1057), rending of robes (1060), plucking out of hair (1062), and moistening the eyes with tears (1065). Xerxes and the chorus make gestures and move about vig-

[124] The word *stolē* means both "outfit" and "entourage." In line 192, the word refers to clothing. Scholars tend to choose one meaning or the other, but see Raffaele di Virgilio, *Il vero volto dei Persiani di Eschilo*, Bibliotheca Athena 13 (Rome, 1973), 66.

[125] On this last scene and the presentation of hopelessness in Xerxes' fate because he appears in rags, see Thalmann, "Xerxes' Rags," 260–282. On the close connection between costume and a character's situation in the *Oresteia*, see C. W. Macleod, "Clothing in the Oresteia," *Maia*, n.s. 3, no. 27 (1975): 201–203.

[126] On *eressein* ("ply"), see D. van Nes, *Die maritime Bildersprache des Aischylos* (Groningen, 1963), 116-117, and Lillian B. Lawler, "The Dance of the Ancient Mariners," *TAPA* 75 (1944): 31.

146

orously until, at the end, with "ill-sounding cries of grief" (1077), they leave the orkhēstra of the theater.

The dazzling finale, as emotionally explicit as tragedy can be, integrates the religious and moral lesson with which it begins into the rhythmically most insistent, the verbally most poignant, the visually most important, and the kinetically most vigorous part of the play. In *Sanemori*, a tale of repentance and invocations emerge in the kyū section; in the tragedy, emerge a call to Zeus and a full-scale lament. In the nō, Sanemori is a natural subject for the tale of repentance; in the tragedy, although Xerxes, like Sanemori, is not a character connected historically with the arts of song and dance, Aeschylus makes him a natural subject for the performance of the lament. In *Sanemori*, one is convinced that Sanemori will be saved; in the *Persians*, one knows that Xerxes has been punished by the gods. In both plays there is a sense of completion because, in the construction of their works, Aeschylus and Zeami have kept the performance in mind in such a way that the audiences can derive a lesson from the case of the main character upon whom the structure and the performance are ultimately focused.[127]

Although he probably did not have in mind emotions of the sort we find in the *Persians*, Zeami is reported to have said that a play is successful if the actor at the end has brought about a change in the emotions of his audience.[128] And his point is well taken for Aeschylus's tragedy, in which the playwright/actor, through his construction and performance of the play, has made the audience feel not only a sense of satisfaction over the punishment of its former enemy, but also a realization that in retrospect the enemy serves as an example of what can happen to anyone, even to oneself, if one commits an error against divine will. If the Athenian audience felt nothing but self-satisfaction and a sense of self-righteousness over the dramatization of Xerxes' defeat, it is difficult to explain how it tolerated Aeschylus's presentation of Darius as a good and wise leader. It seems more likely that through the construction of this play, in which Aeschylus universalized the cases of Darius and Xerxes, he elicited emotions from the audience that rose above individual cases, that is, such emotions as can be elicited on behalf of "heroes" from legend and epic. Otherwise it is difficult to explain why in 472 B.C., eight years after the battle of Salamis, Aeschylus won first prize with this tragedy.

[127] On Aeschylus's ability to captivate the spectator, see Croiset, *Eschyle*, 8, and Deichgräber, *Die Perser*, 189. Kranz, *Stasimon*, appreciated well the effect of combining word, thought, rhythm, gesture, dance, song, and instrumental music in tragedy.

[128] *Sarugaku dangi*, in ZZ, 270, and Rimer, 187.

THREE

The Style of Nō

From the discussion of structure in the two preceding chapters, it should be apparent that, although the finales of both Aeschylus's *Persians* and Zeami's *Sanemori* feature vigorous movements and gestures, excited rhythms and music, the effective use of "literary" sources, religious formulas, emotional intensity, and the most important presentation of the main character, the finale of the *Persians* lacks some of the interest that an audience can derive from that of *Sanemori*, namely, an engrossing account of the tragic event enacted by the main character. The messenger's narrative account of the battles of Salamis and Psyttaleia in the middle of the tragedy preempts this aspect of the climax in the *Persians*. In addition, Zeami gains a sharper focus with his use of language. As I pointed out, when the shite says in the rongi that the deep-rooted attachment of warrior hell has again come around, and mentions in the same breath the name of Kiso, the cause of his attachment—Sanemori wanted to fight with him and not a lesser opponent—the syllable *ki* serves both as a word meaning "come" and as the first syllable of Kiso's name. In the kommos of the *Persians*, when Aeschylus mentions the goddess Atē by name (1007), refers to the disasters at sea (*atai*, 1037), and calls Xerxes "great in disaster" (*megalate*, 1016, that is, both the cause and the victim of disaster), a number of meanings converge; however, they do so less economically and with less focus than in the nō because Aeschylus uses three separate words, whereas Zeami uses but one syllable. This economy of expression in Zeami's style, manifest in his language elsewhere, accounts for one difference in the style of the two playwrights. And yet Aeschylus's style more often bears resemblances to that of Zeami than do Sophocles' or Euripides'. It is to the discussion of style, both the similarities and the differences between the styles of Zeami and Aeschylus, that this chapter and the next are devoted.

Both Zeami and Aeschylus, as might be expected, drew on and were influenced by traditional and contemporary "literature" and rituals.[1] Because much of this material was public, such as the legends handed down by word of mouth, other theater, history, prayers, religious rituals, and the orally recited and sung, even performed, poetry, it was familiar to many members of the audiences. Among nō and tragedy, *Sanemori* and the *Persians* were particularly accessible to their audiences since these plays involved the enactment of "real" events—it was noised abroad in Japan that the ghost of Sanemori had appeared to the priest,[2] and much of the Athenian audience had experienced the Persian Wars firsthand. If Zeami followed his own advice concerning the use of the written classics, we can infer that his literary allusions and borrowings did not pass by the ken of the audience either.[3] His son indicates that Zeami suggested the use only of suitable materials and of familiar phrases from the classics, inasmuch as an audience would not understand phrases that were too obscure.[4] In Aeschylus's case, we must conjecture that, since he drew on a heavily oral and performance-oriented "literary" tradition, his allusions and borrowings were also easily recognizable.

If our evidence from the extant Greek texts is representative of the literature as Aeschylus knew it (and I work on that assumption here), then we can confidently say that in his plays he made allusions. Sometimes Aeschylus, like Zeami, borrowed significantly from other poetry; however, he did not quote directly as Zeami did and, given the more sophisticated written literary tradition at Zeami's disposal, was likely to do.[5] Another difference in their use of pre-existing materials lies in the extent to which they made their debt explicit: Zeami on occasion went so far as to specify by name the author of a work to which he alluded or which he quoted;[6] Aes-

---

[1] In the Japanese case, this literature certainly included many prose writings.

[2] It was not uncommon in kyōgen, but it was rare in nō, for a commercial theatrical troupe to put on a topical nō. See Kōsai, "Sakuhin kenkyū: Sanemori," 6.

[3] In the Japanese poetic tradition, a distinction is made between direct borrowing and *honkadori*, "allusive variation." The latter is defined by Robert H. Brower and Earl Miner, *Japanese Court Poetry* (London, 1962), 506, as the "echoing of the words, sometimes only the situation or conception, of a well-known earlier poem in such a way that recognizable elements are incorporated into a new meaning, but one in which the meaning of the earlier poem also enters, in a manner distinguished from mere borrowing and use of similar materials and expression." Other distinctions are made as well; for example, *honzetsu* is also allusion, but one that involves allusions to prose. For the most part, these distinctions will not be taken into account in this comparative study.

[4] In the *Sarugaku dangi*, in ZZ, 192, and Rimer, 221.

[5] Brower and Miner, in *Japanese Court Poetry, passim*, provide an account of the level of sophistication attained in the court poetry, which lay before and influenced Zeami.

[6] For example, Zeami refers to Murasaki Shikibu, author of the novel *The Tale of Genji*, in the nō *Yūgao*, and to Yukihira Chūnagon, the poet, in the nō *Matsukaze*.

chylus was less specific and never more explicit than to make a statement like, "As the proverb goes," or, "As they say."[7]

The special characteristics of medieval Japanese and ancient Greek as languages explain in turn some of the similarities and differences in Zeami's and Aeschylus's handling of literary allusions in their dramatic texts. Both imbedded these allusions in the very fabric of the plays by means not only of transitional phrases, but also of single words. Zeami could integrate these allusions with an economy and subtlety of expression that was more difficult to achieve in the Greek. Because the Japanese language is written using a syllabary, because only the verbs and the adjectives are inflected, and because there are an extraordinary number of homonyms, Zeami could use a single syllable, a unit of sound bearing two meanings and two grammatical functions simultaneously, as a pivot between the borrowed and his own written word. Because the ancient Greek language is alphabetic and highly inflected, Aeschylus was forced to use letters and syllables at the ends of most words as indicators of their grammatical function. Both classical Japanese and classical Greek could express, through inflection of verbs, a variety of tenses, aspects, and moods, and through inflection in the Greek and by means of particles in the Japanese, various grammatical functions of nouns. (Adjectives were inflected like verbs in the Japanese, like nouns in the Greek.) However, the Japanese did not and do not express number, gender, or person except by separate words and, in the case of number, a few isolated suffixes, whereas these categories are unavoidably specified by the inflection of the Greek language. Unlike Greek, moreover, Japanese does not have definite articles. These differences allow for a greater degree of ambiguity in the use of the Japanese language. Yet, compared to Latin, for example, the ancient Greek language exhibits a "naturalness" of syntax, an "elasticity and multiplicity" of vocabulary, and "grammatical liberties in the use of case and tense"[8] of a sort that allows Aeschylus to write in a style that can be compared to Zeami's.

Zeami's written style, as I have mentioned, is often more economical than that of Aeschylus; however, both playwrights, inasmuch as they write poetry, share the ability to multiply levels of meaning in their plays by means of words rather than the formal syntax of prose. In addition, they both occasionally connect one "scene" to another, one passage to another, one line to another, or one word to another verbally, that is, with an atten-

---

[7] In *Agamemnon* 264, Aeschylus invokes a traditional maxim with the words, "As the proverb goes"; in *Eumenides* 4, he refers to a written or oral version of the earliest succession to the oracular seat at Delphi by saying, "As it is told."

[8] William Bedell Stanford, *Greek Metaphor: Studies in Theory and Practice* (New York and London, 1936), 106.

tion to words *qua* words, rather than to the explicit thought that a combination of the words syntactically grouped together expresses. The resulting progression often involves words used at least as much for their various associations of meaning and their etymological or phonic potential within the environment of other words as for their syntactic and logical relationship to these words. To be sure, Aeschylus's style displays a higher incidence of the explicitly logical rather than what I call purely verbal progressions than does Zeami's. Yet given the attention that both playwrights pay to the special power of words and phrases, not only in the texts of their works, but also within the context of the performance, and given the relative lack of abstract nouns in classical Japanese and Aeschylean Greek, which makes the styles of both playwrights verbally concrete, their styles are comparable.

Before turning to an examination of Zeami's style in *Sanemori*, I shall begin by identifying some important features of Japanese literary style. In part, these features can be learned from Zeami himself. For example, in the first section of the *Sandō*, he advises that in the composition of nō an understanding of what kind of character is involved is essential to the process of choosing words appropriate to the character from the beginning of the play on, and that literary material should be appropriate to the nature of the work and express emotional qualities.[9] He also specifies on occasion where within a nō one should place literary allusions or quotations. (This type of statement makes it eminently clear that Zeami intended his audience to be able to hear and understand the words. Performances in his day must have differed from those today, for in present-day performances the words are sometimes difficult to understand when the actors chant in muffled tones and because some members of the audience do not know the classical Japanese language and its literature.) In another treatise, the *Sarugaku dangi*, his son transmits Zeami's advice about specific plays and about the effect of words, poetic allusions, and literary borrowings within them. For example, he says (sec. 15) that in the play *Furu* when the waki, a priest, begins the spoken exchange with the shite, a woman who is washing cloth, it is necessary, if the original order of the story is to be strictly followed, that the actor chant the history of the sacred sword of Furu (the god named Furu Myōjin).[10] However, he adds, to chant instead the lines,

Hatsu mi yuki *furu* no takahashi
First deep snow *falls* [on]

[9] In ZZ, 135, and Rimer, 150. Examples used by Zeami to characterize the "emotional quality" of a play are auspiciousness, grace (*yūgen*), love, "complaint," and "despair." I have translated the last two of these qualities according to Hare, *Zeami's Style*, 54.
[10] In ZZ, 288, and Rimer, 217.

Furu no Takahashi
[High Bridge of Furu],

gives the audience a sense of *enken*. Enken, though not technically a rhetorical term, is a stylistic device whereby an author creates a geographical perspective, for example, by naming places (Zeami even recommends using legends of famous places as a basis for nō in order to achieve this effect). Place names, in turn, often enrich a text because the author capitalizes on the literal meanings of the names or on associations that the names derive from their use in poetry. Of the chanted line above, we are told in the *Sarugaku dangi* that, in the phrase *hatsu mi yuki furu*, "the first deep snow falls," the word *furu* creates an effect "so appropriate to nō." What is meant, in part, is that by means of the single pivot word *furu*, the line shifts the context from the expected narration about the history of the sword of the god Furu Myōjin to a geographical perspective appropriate to the act of washing cloth. ("Pivot word" is a verbal device often called *kakekotoba*, which Brower and Miner define as "a rhetorical scheme of word play in which a series of sounds is so employed as to mean two or more things at once by different parsings."[11]) The word *furu* is part of the place name, Furu no Takahashi ("High Bridge of Furu"); it is also the verb of the introductory phrase, *hatsu mi yuki furu*, inasmuch as it means "fall," as in falling snow. The introductory phrase, in turn, is a preface, a verbal device called *joshi*, or simply *jo*, which is a phrase of unspecified length, often a conventional poetic phrase, that adds verbal texture to the passage in which it occurs. As in the example from *Furu*, joshi prepares for and anticipates "the basic 'statement' of the poem" to which it is related with a connotative or metaphorical affinity, often by means of wordplay.[12] The pivot, *furu*, is particularly significant in the quoted line because the word is also the title of the play and the name of the relevant deity; it is prominent because Zeami introduces it with joshi and because it is connected to the performance of the shite on stage, who is washing cloth.

Since *Furu* is not being performed in the repertory of nō today, one cannot appreciate the chanted line within its full context; however, in the often-performed nō *Matsukaze*, for example, one can appreciate not only poetic allusions and borrowings, but also the use of enken, kakekotoba, and other verbal devices, such as *engo* ("word association").[13] In fact,

---

[11] Brower and Miner, *Japanese Court Poetry*, 507 (see 13).

[12] See ibid., 14. I use the term *joshi* rather than *jo* so as to avoid confusion with the *jo* of jo-ha-kyū.

[13] Brower and Miner define engo as a "relation of disparate elements in a poem by the use of a word that has or creates an 'association' with a preceding word or situation, often bringing out an additional dimension of meaning and giving two expressions a secondary richness" (*Japanese Court Poetry*, 504). On Zeami's use of verbal devices, see Hare, *Zeami's Style*, 118–122. For a list of verbal devices used in nō, see, for example, Sanari, *Yōkyoku taikan*, 1: 73–76.

since an example of wordplay in the rongi of *Matsukaze* is specifically mentioned in the *Sarugaku dangi* (sec. 12),[14] it seems an appropriate passage whereby to illustrate the degree to which Japanese poetic style can be verbal in orientation, focused on words *qua* words, rather than formally logical and explicit in its progressions from one word, line, or stanza to another—and how, because this is drama, some words are connected to the action on stage. To be sure, some, if not all, of the stylistic features to be discussed here resemble features found in poetry elsewhere; however, it is important that only a minimal number of Western terms be applied in this introduction to Zeami's style so that something that approaches a Japanese outlook emerge as clearly as possible.

THE RONGI OF *MATSUKAZE* AND THE BEACON SPEECH OF THE *AGAMEMNON*

The rongi occurs in an early scene of *Matsukaze* during which Matsukaze, the shite, and her sister Murasame, the tsure, are engaged in the labor of scooping salt water from the sea, and with it the reflection of the moon, into pails at Suma, a seashore lined with pine trees.[15] In the exchange between the shite and the chorus, Zeami creates a distancing effect, enken, through the names of places famous for salt kilns where brine is boiled down to obtain salt and for the scenic beauty of beaches and pine trees, which thus pertain to the action of the two sisters and to the setting of the play. (The term enken is here applied to what is technically called a *monozukushi*, that is, a list of things; here it is a list of places where salt kilns are located.) The chorus introduces the rongi with a short song, a sageuta, immediately preceding the exchange:

Matsushima!	Matsushima ya.
At Ojima the women	Ojima no ama no
Take delight in	Tsuki ni dani
Scooping the reflection	Kage o kumu koso
Of the moon,	Kokoro are,

[14] In *ZZ*, 284, and Rimer, 209. This passage from the *Sarugaku dangi* will be discussed in Chapter Four. *Matsukaze* was revised by Zeami from a nō by his father Kan'ami entitled *Matsukaze murasame*, which was based on an earlier nō by Kiami entitled *Shiokumi*. The passage treated below, the rongi, is in turn said to derive from an original work called *Tōei*. See *YKS*, 57 and 429 n. 26. Thus the rongi should not be thought of as Zeami's composition alone; however, in my text I use his name as the author's for the sake of convenience.

[15] The Japanese and Greek of passages discussed in detail in this and the next chapter are printed in Appendices 3 and 4. First the entire text of *Sanemori* (except for the kyōgen section) and passages from other nō, beginning with the *rongi* of *Matsukaze*, are printed in Appendix 3. The Greek passages that are analyzed in this chapter and the next appear in Appendix 4 in the order in which they are treated. The Greek or Japanese versions of passages discussed more than once are not repeated in the Appendices.

Delight in scooping	Kage o kumu koso
The reflection.	Kokoro are.[16]

These lines, one of several verbal bases for Matsukaze's gesture of scooping, begin with two place names: Matsushima, a bay filled with pineclad islands, and Ojima, one of the islands in that bay. Both of these names, because they appear in what is a formal poetic introduction, joshi,[17] are prominent. The places named introduce the geographical perspective; they are far away from Suma, the setting of the play. In addition, because the literal meaning of Matsushima is "Pine Tree Islands," it is verbally associated with Suma, a pineclad beach, and, because the women at Ojima are carrying out the same labor as the two sisters on stage in the nō, the small island is thematically connected to the dramatic action.

After the short song, the nō continues with the rongi, the sung exchange, in which the chorus and Matsukaze, by mentioning names of places, move verbally from the distant Matsushima mentioned in the song back to the beach at Suma. The chorus begins:

They carry brine *far away*	Hakobu wa *tōki*
In *Michinoku*.	*Michinoku* no
Ah, that name! *Chika* no	Sono na ya *Chika* no
Shiogama.	*Shiogama*.

With the word *tōki* ("far away"), Zeami underscores the distancing effect and enhances it with his choice of the place name Michinoku, which literally means "Back Road." This area, the northern part of Japan's main island of Honshū, is the location of Matsushima, mentioned in the preceding song, and is thus distant from Suma. The self-conscious reference to the name in the phrase *sono na ya*, "Ah, that name," helps to point out the pun on *Chika no Shiogama*, a place located on the southwest shore of Matsushima Bay. The first part of the name, *Chika*, meaning "near," emphasizes the proximity of the place to Matsushima, while setting up a contrast with *tōki* ("far away").[18] The second part of the name, literally meaning "salt kiln," helps to associate this place and the action mentioned as occurring in Michinoku with the immediate context and action of the nō.

The rongi continues with the shite's words:

The lowly *makers of salt*	Shizu ga *shioki* o
Take firewood	Hakobishi wa

---

[16] The text is that of YKS, 60–61. However, I have printed *Ojima*, the Kanze reading, rather than *Oshima*, as YKS does. All translations are mine unless otherwise indicated.
[17] YKS, 60 n. 16.
[18] See Koyama Hiroshi, Satō Kikuo, and Satō Ken'ichirō, eds., *Yōkyokushū*, vol. 1, *Nihon koten bungaku zenshū*, vol. 33 (Tokyo, 1973), 367 n. 10, hereafter Koyama.

To the bay of Akogi	Akogi ga ura ni
When the tide is receding.	Hiku shio.

Akogi, a place several hundred miles nearer to Suma than Matsushima is, brings the geographical perspective within closer range of the setting of the nō. The lines are connected to what precedes not only by means of this spatial progression but also by the repetition of *shio* in *shioki* ("firewood," literally "saltwood"), and *shio* ("salt," as in salt water), which echoes the first syllable of Shiogama from above.[19] In the faraway place, Michinoku, mentioned in the first stanza of the rongi, women collect brine as Matsukaze and her sister do; at the bay of Akogi, the action is slightly different— the saltmakers carry wood. However, in the latter case, the repetition of the word *shio* brings Akogi and Suma together, as does the mention of the lowliness of the people and the ebbing tide, two themes introduced in the preceding scene of the nō. In this passage, there is no pun on the name Akogi; instead, the place enhances the song because it is made famous in poetry treating the subject of wood used in salt kilns.[20]

The chorus continues the rongi:

In the waters of that [place] Ise	Sono Ise no umi no
Lies *Futami* no Ura	*Futami* no Ura.
Oh, that [we] could *twice*	*Futatabi* yo ni mo
See [our] lives again!	Ideba ya.

Here the geographical setting remains the same as in the preceding stanza since Futami no Ura, a bay in which twin rocks lie off the pineclad shore, is located in the province of Ise, near Akogi. Zeami uses the place name Futami no Ura, "Bay of Two Glances," so that, through the repetition of the syllables *futa*, meaning "twice," he can prepare for the last two lines,[21] in which the chorus expresses a wish for the sisters that they might see (i.e., live) life a second time. Both the repetition of the syllables and the resultant pun are examples of how Zeami moves verbally rather than "logically" from one line to another.

The shite continues the rongi without overt reference to the thought expressed at the end of the preceding stanza:

Pine trees stand in a grove	Matsu no muradachi
On a hazy day	Kasumu hi ni

[19] *YKS*, 60 n. 19, calls this *ren'in*, that is, the repetition of sounds. The commentary also points to the alliteration between *shio* and *shizu*, the first word of the stanza.
[20] See Koyama, 367 n. 13.
[21] This is an example of a joshi in which one word echoes another in the line following; *YKS*, 61 n. 21.

When the tide recedes *far* beyond   Shioji ya *tōku*
Narumigata.   *Naru*migata.

This stanza moves geographically from Akogi to Narumigata, another bay, which, though in a different area, is approximately the same distance from Suma. Although the location shifts here and the subject of saltmaking is dropped, the words "pine trees stand in a grove," derived from a poem set at Futami no Ura,[22] provide a poetic link between stanzas. At the end, the shite names Narumigata, which is connected to the preceding line by means of the first two syllables, *naru*. In isolation these mean "is" and serve as a copulative verb to the preceding line, which literally means, "When the tide is far in the distance." Thus the syllables, which also serve as the first two of the place name Narumigata, are an example of a kake-kotoba,[23] the pivoting verbal device that was seen earlier in the lines from *Furu* and that so often contributes to the compactness characteristic of Japanese poetic style.

The chorus then continues with a self-conscious reference to the preceding stanza:

That is *Naru*migata.   *Sore* wa *Naru*migata.
Here is *Naruo*   *Koko* wa *Naruo* no
In the shadow of the pines   Matsukage ni
The moon is concealed from   Tsuki koso saware
Ashinoya.   Ashinoya.

This stanza moves geographically closer to Suma than the preceding, from "that" place, Narumigata, to the one "here," Naruo. Contrast and repetition of syllables between Narumigata and Naruo[24] within the stanza and the repetition of Narumigata from the preceding stanza help to effect the shift. The mention of the pine trees is well suited both to Naruo, a place associated with pine trees in poetry,[25] and to the play. The mention of the moon, in turn, recalls the chorus's introductory song and the words, "scooping the reflection of the moon." The stanza ends with the name *Ashinoya*, which refers to a place closer to Suma than Naruo and which literally means "thatched hut." It is possible that here Zeami verbally echoes part of the word *shioya* ("saltmaker's hut"), mentioned by a priest in the first scene of the play. (Zeami's recommendation in a section of the *Sarugaku dangi* [sec. 12] on the subject of chant that the shite emphasize the words "fishergirls' hut," *ama no ie*, in *Matsukaze* might suggest that

[22] A poem by Ōnakatomi Sukehiro in *Kinyōshū*. See ibid., 61 n. 22.
[23] Ibid., 61 n. 23.
[24] See ibid., 61 n. 24.
[25] See Koyama, 368 n. 18.

not only the musical effect, but also the content of the line is important.[26] This phrase appears in the first passage in which the shite, soon after his entrance, mentions the hut.) By drawing attention to the hut through repetition, intonation, and a pun, Zeami prepares for the next scene, in which the priest requests from the two sisters a night's lodging in their dwelling, a saltmaker's hut.[27] The sisters at first refuse because the hut is so modest, but after references to the hut and their lowly condition, they finally consent. The word *Ashinoya* serves a preparatory function.

The remainder of the rongi focuses on the action, location, and atmosphere of the dramatic and thematic context that preceded it. The shite says:

At Nada—bailing *salt water*	Nada no—*shiokumu*
For [our] livelihood.	Uki mi zo to
But, oh, that to anyone should be announced	Hito ni ya taremo
[Our] lowly plight [literally, *boxwood comb*].[28]	*Tsuge* no *kushi*.

The stanza is connected with what precedes geographically, since Ashinoya is located in Nada, a place near Suma, and verbally, since the sisters' condition is lowly, like a thatched hut. Because Zeami alludes to a poem here, he also maintains the literary dimension evident throughout the rongi. The stanza is drawn from a poem in which the relevant lines read as follows:[29]

At Ashinoya	Ashinoya no
In Nada, from boiling salt water	Nada no shioyaki
[I] have come without even inserting	Tsuge no kushi mo
A boxwood comb [in my hair].	Sasade kinikeri.

The words *Ashinoya*, *Nada*, *shio-*, *tsuge*, and *kushi* are repeated from the poem in the nō. Ashinoya, a place located in Nada, provides the verbal connection between the preceding stanza in which it appears and this stanza. *Shio-* ("salt water") is a repetition of several words within the rongi and the substance of the sisters' labor. *Tsuge* ("boxwood") and *kushi* ("comb"), words well integrated into the context of the poem, the mood

---

[26] YKS, 61 n. 24, understands it in this way.

[27] Before the shite and tsure enter the stage, the waki says he will spend the night in the "saltmaker's hut" (*shioya*). After the rongi, the *shioya* is referred to four times in the exchange between the priest and the sisters.

[28] The translation "lowly plight" is that of *Japanese Noh Drama*, NGS 3: 44.

[29] The poem comes from the *Ise monogatari* (The Tales of Ise), no. 87. See YKS, 61 n. 25.

of which they help to evoke in the nō, are intrusive within the context of the rongi. However, they are used to connect the line in which they appear to both the preceding and the following lines. *Tsuge* means both "box-wood" and "announce," and thus serves as both a description of the comb and as a verb in the expression, "Oh, that to anyone should be announced our lowly plight."[30] *Kushi*, which means "comb," a decorative piece inserted in the hair, prepares for the next line of the rongi, which begins with the word *sashi*,[31] meaning both "insert," as a comb, and "rise," as the tide.

The word *sashi* introduces the conclusion to the rongi shared by the chorus and the shite:

CHORUS: From the *rising* tide	*Sashi* kuru shio o
[We] draw salt water.	Kumi wakete
Look! The moon is	Mireba tsuki koso
In [my] pail.	Oke ni are.
SHITE: In *mine* as well, the moon	*Kore* ni mo tsuki no
Has been caught.	Iritaru ya.

The rongi returns, with a reference to the pails of the two sisters with which it began and to which the author draws attention with the word *kore* ("this," translated "mine"), to the location of Suma and, with the gesture of the tsure's placing the pail onto a cart (a prop visibly prominent on stage), to the dramatic action. The setting, the action, the object of that action (*shio*, "salt water"), and the word "moon," associated with the tide, all form part of the frame within which is created the effect called enken. The rongi ends after the shite and the chorus make further references to the moon, its reflection, the rising tide, and hauling brine.

Without considering fully the religious, emotional, and thematic significance of the rongi, I have pointed to the author's use of such features of Japanese poetic style as enken, kakekotoba (a kind of paronomasia), *ren'in* (alliteration), anaphora, repetition of words, engo (words associated in meaning), words contrasted in meaning, and joshi (preface), as well as more or less explicit allusions to other poetry. In addition, I have pointed to a feature of style not mentioned in the Japanese commentaries, that is, a kind of preparation in the word *Ashinoya*. What these features of style have in common is the preeminence they give to words *qua* words over the thought and the formal syntax of the lines. This does not mean that the playwright is unaware of the significance of the words to the rongi and the play as a whole; indeed, he multiplies the levels of meaning in both. For example, the mention of pine trees and famous places associated with

---

[30] See Koyama, 368 n. 22.
[31] *YKS*, 61 n. 27, says that *kushi* introduces *sashi*.

them helps to prepare for other passages in the nō that focus on a single pine tree at Suma. Among these passages is the finale, where before the exit of Matsukaze, whose name literally means "Wind in the Pines," the playwright has her circle around the prop on stage, which represents a pine tree, while the chorus is singing:

All that remains is the wind   Matsukaze bakari ya nokoruran.
         in the pines.

The name of the character Matsukaze and the setting of the play, which the audience can see represented by the tree, become fused. The repeated references to pine trees within the rongi help to prepare the audience for this finale and for the added dimension of meaning in it and the other passages of the nō in which a pine tree figures prominently.

Within the rongi, individual words as much as conventional syntax are the means by which Zeami moves from one line or one stanza to the next, even when there may not be an expressed connection between them. For example, between the first and the second stanzas, "salt" and "tide" connect the action of the firewood carriers with those who carry brine in Michinoku. The continued repetition of *shio* in turn prepares for the development within the rongi from the receding tide, called *shioji* and mentioned before the exchange, to the rising tide, mentioned at the end. The shift in the tide, connected with the new position of the moon in the pails at the end of the exchange and with the suggestion that the sisters' plight is a sad one, marks a rise in the emotional pitch of the play. This effect is achieved, as in much poetry, through verbal techniques and allusion, rather than explicitly. In addition, since *Matsukaze* is performed, the poetry is brought alive visually by the actors on stage, their gestures, and the props, which, being few in number, help in turn to emphasize the words.

The example from *Matsukaze*, not unique in form among nō, serves as a measure of the degree to which Zeami could place emphasis on words rather than syntax and illustrates the degree of economy in style that could be achieved. There is no passage quite like it among the works of Aeschylus; and yet an examination of the beacon speech in the *Agamemnon*—a passage chosen for comparison against the background of the rongi because it too involves a geographical perspective and a list of places[32] but is not unique in Aeschylus's plays—provides a preliminary example of the way in which an understanding of Japanese poetic style can enhance our appreciation of Aeschylus's style. The sum of my examples, not this one passage, will reveal the extent to which it is appropriate to speak of simi-

[32] The scholia to Aristophanes' *Frogs* 928a suggest that Aeschylus wrote often about mountains, rivers, etc.

larities and differences between the styles of tragedy and nō. But because the beacon speech is indeed a speech, where one would not expect the poetic mode to dominate over the prosaic, it provides a good test of this comparison of style.

In the first dialogue shared by the chorus and Clytemnestra, Aeschylus reveals his interest in the use of words *qua* words and thus employs features of style that bear a resemblance to those I noted in the rongi of *Matsukaze*: alliteration, anaphora, intrusion, introductory words or phrases, pivot words, paronomasia, word association, and allusions. For example, in the beacon speech Aeschylus applies the name Makistos, literally meaning "highest" or "farthest" (289),[33] to a mountain in the phrase *Makistou skopais* ("to the lookouts of Makistos"). In conjunction with the word *hekas* ("far away," 292), and supported by the compound adjective *tēlepompon* ("sent from afar," 300), Aeschylus's pun on Makistos underscores the length of the beacon's journey in a manner analogous to the way in which Zeami's pun on the word *Michinoku* ("Back Road"), used in conjunction with *tōki* ("far away"), underscores the distance from Suma in *Matsukaze*. Near the end of the speech, Aeschylus, like Zeami, returns verbally to the theatrical setting of the play. Clytemnestra says "To this . . . roof" (*Es tode . . . stegos*, 310). The repetition of the word "lookouts" in line 309, where the noun is modified by the adjective *astugeitonas* ("neighboring on our city"), emphasizes Aeschylus's return to the setting of the play. (The repetition of the name Ida in line 311 from lines 281 and 283 provides verbal support for the repetition of the word *skopas*.) The deictic *tode* ("this") draws the audience's attention to the palace roof, which, like the pails[34] in *Matsukaze*, is visually prominent; it is the backdrop to the dramatic action that Aeschylus explicitly introduces in the prologue. We can only conjecture that at line 310 the queen Clytemnestra points to the palace roof—in other words, like the shite and tsure in the nō, she makes a gesture.

Within the beacon speech, which both provides evidence that the Greeks have defeated the Trojans and creates a distancing effect, Aeschylus draws further on the meanings of place names. The reference in line 285 of the *Agamemnon* to the place *Athōion aipos*, meaning "the ridge that causes no harm," may help to emphasize Zeus's name within the triad of the gods, Hephaestus, Hermes, and Zeus, who are mentioned significantly in the first five lines of the speech. In the phrase *triton / Athōion aipos Zēnos*

---

[33] A. W. Verrall, *The "Agamemnon" of Aeschylus* (London and New York, 1889), 32, says the "mountain by its name would seem to have been 'the highest.' " *Makistos*, that is, *mēkistos*, may mean "greatest" or "tallest," but it may also mean "farthest," a meaning found in Xenophon and Apollonius of Rhodes.

[34] Compare the use of *kore* ("this").

("third / the Athos ridge of Zeus"), *Athōion aipos*, positioned between *triton* and *Zēnos*, functions somewhat, though not entirely, like a kake-kotoba. At first, the ridge, modified by the adjective "third," is mentioned as the place to which the beacon light passed third on its way from Troy to Argos. The ridge is then followed by the name of Zeus, the god connected with it.[35] With the word *Zēnos*, Aeschylus does not pass on to a different and grammatically unconnected expression, as Zeami does with the double function of *naru* in the rongi of *Matsukaze*. However, because the word *athōion* means "unharmed or harmless," almost synonymous with *sōtēr*, it may serve two semantic functions: it both names a ridge and evokes the well-known epithet of Zeus, *sōtēr*, "the savior."[36] Within the trilogy, of which the *Agamemnon* is the first play, and at a major climax after the trial scene in the third play, the *Eumenides*, Orestes thanks Athena, Apollo, and finally *tritos sōtēr*, the one who ordains all things (759–760), by whom he means Zeus.[37]

The verbal anticipation of a specific later scene in the *Oresteia* by the proper name in the beacon speech may or may not have been intended by Aeschylus. In fact, an audience would not be expected to remember that Aeschylus had referred to Zeus as third or as savior from one passage to another.[38] It is more probable that Aeschylus, like Zeami with his reference to pine trees in the rongi, begins to establish the role of Zeus as savior at the beginning of the *Agamemnon*, in a passage in which he exhibits a close attention to words *qua* words. Some of the examples of his verbal techniques, like *Athōion aipos*, are more prominent and significant than others. Aeschylus's mention of a "goat-trodden mountain" (*oros aigiplangkton*, 303), which prepares for the word *pōgōna* ("beard," as in a goat's beard, 306),[39] in the phrase "great beard of the flame" is not significant to the meaning of the play. (The alliteration of the "p" sound within the passage helps to signal the verbal technique.) The use of words associated in meaning here is analogous to the stylistic feature engo in the Jap-

[35] See Fraenkel, *Aeschylus Agamemnon* 2: 154. For further discussion of the passage and the speech, see J. H. Quincey's "The Beacon-Sites in the *Agamemnon*," *JHS* 83 (1963): 118-132.

[36] See Quincey, "The Beacon-Sites," 118 and George Thomson, *The Oresteia of Aeschylus* (Amsterdam, 1966), 2: 29. Fraenkel, *Aeschylus Agamemnon*, 154, thinks Beazley's suggestion that there is an allusion to *tritos (sōtēr) Zeus* ("Zeus, the savior, the third") is worth considering.

[37] In *Libation Bearers* 244–245, after Electra recognizes that her brother Orestes has returned, she names Zeus *tritos* ("the third"). She does not call him *sōtēr*.

[38] For the same reason, the words *Arachnaion aipos* ("Spidery Ridge," 309), are not necessarily a verbal anticipation of the later scene in the *Agamemnon* in which the chorus exclaims that the king lies dead in the web of a spider (1492 and 1516). See Verrall's suggestion, "*Agamemnon*," xxxviii.

[39] See Thomson, *Oresteia*, 30.

anese. However, Aeschylus makes no more of the pun later than Zeami does of his pun on *tsuge*, meaning "boxwood," in the phrase *tsuge no kushi* ("boxwood comb").

There are other signs within the scene, of which the beacon speech is a part, that point to Aeschylus's interest in words *qua* words. For example, at the beginning of the scene, Aeschylus puns on a word; repeats syllables to suggest the pun; signals that there is a pun by repeating other words that draw the audience's attention to words in the passage; and uses a proverb for emphasis. The chorus opens the dialogue preceding the beacon speech by saying to the queen (261–262):

> [If] in hopes of a favorable report   Euaggeloisin elpisin thuēpoleis,
>   you offer sacrifices,
> I would be *glad* to hear. . . .   Kluoim' an *euphrōn.* . . .

Clytemnestra responds with the allusion to a proverb (264–265):

> With favorable report, just as the   Euaggelos men, hōsper hē
>   proverb goes,   paroimia
> May dawn be born from her   Heōs genoito mētros *euphronēs*
>   *kindly* mother *night.*   para.

Within this context of an allusion to a proverb,[40] Aeschylus repeats the word *euaggelos* ("with favorable report") and the syllables *euphron* in order to underscore the pun on the latter.[41] In the chorus's request, *euphrōn* means "glad" or "with kindly intent"; in the response, *euphronēs* means "night" and, because of the preceding use, also "kindly." In line 271, Aeschylus uses the words *eu . . . phronountos . . . sou* ("you being kindly") as reinforcement of the earlier use of the word; in line 279, he turns to the meaning "night" again: *tēs nūn tekousēs phōs tod' euphronēs* ("the night now that gives birth to this light"). The word's shift in meaning at line 265 is aided by the repetition of other key words from the chorus's request in Clytemnestra's response: *pepusmenē* ("learning," 261) recurs in *peusēi* ("you will learn," 266), *elpisin* ("hopes") in *elpidos* ("hope," 266), and *kluoimi* ("I would hear") in *kluein* ("to hear," 266).[42] The twofold use of

---

[40] This is not properly a "literary" allusion and hence is different from the poetic allusions Zeami makes. However, even though the proverb cannot be definitively identified—it may be represented in Hesiod's *Theogony,* 124—there is reason to assume that Aeschylus, when he writes "as the proverb goes" (264), is drawing attention to words borrowed from an oral or written source outside the tragedy and familiar to the audience.

[41] Fraenkel, *Aeschylus Agamemnon,* 149, does not think a pun is intended. However, see Verrall, "*Agamemnon,*" 30, and his notes on lines 276–278.

[42] Similarly, in the *Suppliants* 249–273, where Aeschylus sets up another geographical perspective, he emphasizes words meaning "earth" and "land": *gē, khthōn,* and *aia.* Of these three words associated in meaning, Aeschylus puns on the first, with the help of

the word *euphrōn* is somewhat like a combination of Zeami's use of *naru-* in *Narumigata* and *Naruo* (that is, a word with two different meanings), and *futa-* in *Futami no Ura* and *futatabi* (that is, syllables repeated in two different contexts and with two different uses in the former, one of which applies to the latter).

In addition, Aeschylus's use of *euphrōn* and Zeami's references to pine trees and Matsukaze's name are comparable. Just as the latter, appearing frequently in the nō *Matsukaze*, provide verbal preparation for the fusion of word and dramatic character at the end of the nō, so the repetition of words based on the syllables *euphron*—in the first scene of the *Agamemnon*—and the references to the Furies and use of the word *euphrōn* throughout the trilogy may provide verbal preparation for the *Eumenides*. (There are also many significant uses of the syllable *eu*, meaning "good.") There the Furies, who are daughters of Night, change into "Kindly Ones," *Euphrones* (992). Stated another way, the word *euphrones*, sounding like the word meaning "night," is visually translated into the daughters of Night, who become *euphrones* in the other sense of the word. (In *Agamemnon* 265 the appearance of the word *mētros*, "mother," before *euphronēs* helps.) Although the meaning of *Matsukaze* is more concrete than that of *Euphrones*, there is in the tragedy, as in the nō, a visual manifestation in a character of what was introduced as a word.[43]

A further examination of the verbal texture of the beacon speech in the light of nō suggests that Aeschylus's emphasis on the name of Mount Ida— he repeats it twice within the speech—might invite special attention. In line 281, the queen says:

Sending the bright light out of Ida.   Idēs lampron ekpempōn selas.

In line 283, she continues:

---

the second, in King Pelasgus's self-introduction: "For I am Pelasgos, the son of the earth-born [*gēgenous*] Palaikhthonos [*Palaikhthonos*, literally, 'ancient earth'], and leader of this land [*tēsde gēs*]." This introduction is followed by the repetition of words meaning "land" within the speech and by another pun on Apollo's name *Paian* ("Healer"). The pun is suggested by the reference to the Paeonian people, *Paionōn* (257), before Aeschylus introduces in the speech the names of Apollo and his son Apis, the healer of the land. In another list passage, in the prologue of the *Eumenides* Aeschylus emphasizes the connection between the names of Phoibos and Phoibē (8) by means of the repetition of words.

[43] In some nō, characters are named after flowers or insects, as in *Yūgao* and *Kochō* respectively, and are transformed into the spirits of these. In tragedy, on the other hand, characters whose names are significant in their literal meanings are named after actions or states; for example, Apollo is Cassandra's "destroyer" in the *Agamemnon*; Polyneices is the cause of "much strife" in the *Seven against Thebes*; and Pentheus is "grief" in the *Bacchae*.

Ida [sent it] to the Hermaion rock	Idē men pros Hermaion lepas
Of Lemnos.	Lēmnou.

And in line 311, she adds:

This light not unsired by the fire	Phaos tod' ouk apappon Idaiou
of Ida.	puros.

In the first appearance of the name, Aeschylus identifies the geographical source of the beacon; in the second, he personifies that place; and in the third, he emphasizes it for the audience in several ways: with the deictic *tode* ("this"); with the double negative ("not unsired"); with personification again; and with the repetition of the word *puros* in the same position, at the end of the line, as it appears in three other places in the speech (282, 299, and 304).

In the first use of the word *puros* (282), which occurs between the first two references to Ida in the phrase *aggarou puros* ("courier fire"), the word *aggarou*, in proximity to the name of the god Hephaestus, suggests the *aggarēion*, the Persian "pony express," and a variation of the *lampadēphoria* ("torch race") held in honor of Hephaestus.[44] The torch race resembles the relay of beacon lights described in the speech, as Aeschylus suggests with the word *lampadēphorōn* ("torchbearers"), appearing immediately after the third mention of Ida. The relationship in meaning of *aggarou* and *lampadēphorōn*, not unlike engo "word association" in nō, is marked by the repetition of both *puros* and Ida's name. It is introduced with another related word—when the chorus asks Clytemnestra what messenger could arrive so quickly, she answers not with the identification of a messenger as a person, but with the name Hephaestus, both metonymy for fire and the god of the torch race festival. (The festival is something to which Aeschylus alludes—not a poem, to be sure, but part of what was presumably common knowledge with the audience.)

Toward the end of the rongi in *Matsukaze*, Zeami repeats the phrase "bailing salt water" (*shio kumu* and *shio o kumi*), once within the context of the allusion to the Ashinoya poem and once after. With the second use of the phrase, Zeami introduces an expression of surprise that the moon is in the pails of both sisters. Because, in the song immediately preceding the rongi, Zeami uses the verb *kumu* with the word *kage* in the phrase *kage o kumu* ("bailing [translated, 'scooping'] the reflection [of the moon]") and mentions the moon at Naruo, he prepares the audience for mention of the moon's appearance in the pails. This, in turn, is signalled by repetition of

44 See Herodotus 8.98. Fraenkel, *Aeschylus Agamemnon*, 153, and Verrall, "Agamemnon," 31, comment on this.

the word *tsuki* ("moon"), the deictic *kore*, and the actors' gestures. Aeschylus's preparation for the word "torchbearers" with the repetition of the name Ida and the word *puros* ("fire") at the end of the line is similar. There is also the possibility that a torchlight may have been represented on stage, as it surely was at the end of the *Eumenides*, and that the actor playing the role of the queen may have pointed to it as a way of translating the word into a concrete and visible thing.

During the beacon speech there is very little, if any, action on stage. Instead, Aeschylus sometimes enlivens the description of the beacon relay with personification and brings action in with words. For example, the queen says in lines 282–283 not that a person relayed the beacon fire, but that "beacon sent beacon here *from the courier fire [aggarou puros]*."[45] In addition, Aeschylus anchors the activity of the beacon relay in the beacon itself: he mentions the beacon repeatedly and even describes the material out of which the fire was kindled. Thus, in line 288, he calls the torch a pine torch (*peukē*) and in 295 says it was kindled from a heap of silvery heath brush (*graias ereikēs*), a phrase that is unnecessary and almost intrusive, but that makes the fire concrete. Given Aeschylus's mention of the kindling wood and the final use of Mount Ida's name, and given the methods applied to an analysis of style in nō, it is possible (although I make the suggestion with caution) that Ida, like Shiogama, not only serves as the name of a place, but also may suggest another meaning in its final use. In line 311, the word, because of the emphasis on places preceding it, refers to the mountain, but when taken with *puros* ("fire") suggests the meaning "firewood." (*Ida* literally means "firewood," a meaning found in Herodotus.) It is this type of suggestion, inspired by methods used in the analysis of Japanese poetry, that can illuminate features of the tragedian's style that have either been noted and then ignored or have remained unremarked. However, whether this approach to Aeschylus's style is justified will depend on the strength or weakness of the comparative analyses presented below.

In *Matsukaze*, Zeami refers to places and alludes to poetry in a manner characteristic of writers of nō and of Japanese poetry and creates a poetic mood particularly appropriate to the setting of the play and the plight of the two sisters; in the tragedy, Aeschylus refers to places to produce a geographical perspective such as one can find elsewhere in his works and in the works of other Greek poets, and alludes to a proverb and a festival, but does not create the same kind of poetic atmosphere as that found in

---

[45] While personification is not unknown in nō, place names are not personified, as they are in the Greek. What does occur, as it does in the Greek as well, is that the words are made concrete in dramatic characters' actions on stage. There is, as in the example of Matsukaze, a very real "personification."

Matsukaze. Aeschylus's purpose is in part to express the queen's exultation and to make a transition from Troy to Argos in preparation for the arrival of the herald and Agamemnon on stage. These differences obtain. However, in spite of the differences between the nō and the tragedy, we can conclude at this point that at the very least, to be appreciated fully, both passages demand from the listener a close attention to words *qua* words. (We know that the rongi provides the shite and the chorus with the opportunity to display their singing skills. It is not unreasonable to suppose that the beacon speech provides the actor who plays the role of Clytemnestra an opportunity to display his speaking skills.)

Stated in general terms, the stylistic features shared by Aeschylus and Zeami and illustrated in part by the analysis of the passages above are as follows: both pun on words and place names; both repeat words and sounds to emphasize, for example, the concreteness of important elements; both prepare verbally for later lines and scenes within their dramas; both use words that are intrusive in terms of the main tenor of a passage, but not on another level of its meaning; both employ pivot words or pivot syllables; and further, as in much poetry, both draw on the associative value of words so that they speak simultaneously on more than one level of significance; both make transitions from one word or line to another by means of individual words, as well as syntax; both allude to other works; and both bring out prominent words in performance, in props, gestures, or the actors' appearance. An analysis of other passages here and in the next chapter will show that these similarities extend beyond isolated examples.

AN ANALYSIS OF STYLE AND LITERARY BORROWINGS IN *SANEMORI*

It is my purpose in the remainder of this chapter, by means of a thorough examination of style in *Sanemori*, to identify and explain those features which have been formally recognized as verbal techniques in the Japanese literary and critical tradition, to present parallels for these in the *Agamemnon*, to supplement the Japanese figures of speech with a few stylistic features that have been applied to Aeschylus's work, to comment on some differences between Aeschylus's and Zeami's styles through analyses of specific passages, and finally, to bridge the gap and isolate the essential similarities between their styles, in part through the use of the terms "tenor," "vehicle," and "verbal interaction."[46] The word "vehicle" pre-

---

[46] I am clearly indebted to M. S. Silk (*Interaction in Poetic Imagery with Special Reference to Early Greek Poetry* [Cambridge, 1974], 9–13 and elsewhere), who used I. A. Richards's concepts of "tenor" and "vehicle" as terms that apply to individual words

cludes the need to distinguish a word either as a kind of trope or as a part of the "literal meaning" when it actually can be both of these; the word "tenor" provides us with an alternative to phrases traditionally used to designate that which is not an image, such as "literal meaning," "subject at issue," "context," and so forth.

The advantages of using these terms in parts of my analysis are, first, that they can be used to focus on words rather than ideas, and second, that they do not require us to set the subject at issue in a passage in opposition to the idea that is brought in from the outside. Some literary approaches to analogy or comparison set up the *illustrans* and *illustrandum* as clearly demarcated alternatives. It is not the case that nō and tragedy lack such alternatives; when they appear I use the appropriate terms: imagery, metaphor, and simile. And yet, tenor and vehicle are more convenient terms to use than literal context and metaphor, for example, in those many passages in which an idea is brought into a context from outside that context and not only is a trope in the specific line or phrase in which it appears but also functions simultaneously as a word associated in meaning with the subject at issue.

This is not a stylistic study that follows a particular school of modern literary criticism. The theoretical basis is derived instead from what Zeami has said explicitly or implicitly in his own treatises about the style of nō and from an analysis of that style in his plays. The purpose of this part of the comparison is to provide a detailed explication of style in Zeami's nō and to set forth some of the similarities and some of the differences between it and Aeschylus's style so that each may illuminate the other and thus sharpen our perception of both. The conclusions that will be drawn are that both nō and large portions of Aeschylean tragedy are as much performed poetry as they are drama, and that the audience was meant to appreciate the verbal techniques of the playwright and the significance not

---

and introduced the phrase "verbal interaction." Silk demonstrates how the tenor and the vehicle are interrelated by means of verbal interaction within individual passages, that is, by means of one or more than one word or syllable that semantically, phonetically, or grammatically belongs to both the tenor and the vehicle. (The phrase "verbal interaction" serves well as a definition of the function of both kakekotoba and engo.) Silk's is a *terminological* analysis, Richards's a *logical* analysis.

My use of these terms does not mean that I fully embrace the methodology of Richards or Silk. I use the terms only when they are helpful in pinning down essential similarities between the style of nō and Aeschylean tragedy (Silk's analysis of Greek tragedy is limited to the works of Aeschylus) and often in ways that differ from Silk's. For example, I think that verbal interaction is often effected in tragedy through polysemous words, those with two or more denotations or connotations, rather than what Silk calls "neutral" terms, those which assume more than one meaning on the basis of the context in which they appear.

only of ideas but of individual words within the plays. To be sure, the styles of *Sanemori* and the *Persians* cannot be fully appreciated from the texts alone, for the performance is important. And yet, these are not drama in an ordinary sense of the word. To my mind these are very much poetic texts, texts that are brought alive for a theater audience by the addition of visual and kinetic elements.

The following examination of stylistic features in *Sanemori*, including literary allusions and borrowings, in context and in order of appearance, is arranged in such a way that the significance of each to the meaning of the play is made apparent. Inasmuch as *Sanemori* is a short play, I include a detailed examination of all but the kyōgen section. In addition, I discuss parallels from the *Oresteia*, from the *Agamemnon* in particular, in order to show how it is that the style of tragedy can be compared effectively with that of nō. However, although I here identify and discuss allusions and borrowings in *Sanemori*, both literary and other, I reserve a discussion of this part of the comparison, along with an analysis of some further stylistic features, for the next chapter.

Near the beginning of the nanori, the first speech in *Sanemori*, Zeami uses a pivot word and pun in order to identify the waki as the itinerant priest named Taami:[47]

Yugyō	in the manner of	Yugyō no nagare ni,
Journeying		
Priest[48] Taami.		Taami Shōnin.

In this passage, the word *Yugyō* functions both as the name of the waki priest's ancestor, Yugyō Shōnin, better known as Ippen Shōnin, and also in its literal sense as a word meaning "journeying."[49] The next three words, *no nagare ni*, the equivalent of a preposition grammatically governing the word *Yugyō*, can be translated as "in the manner of"; literally, they mean "in the flow of." The passage suggests that Amida Buddha's Law passed on to Yugyō[50] and points to the relationship between the waki, Taami Shōnin, the thirteenth head priest at a temple called Yugyōji, and Yugyō Shōnin, the first head priest at that temple and founder of the Ji sect of Amida Buddhism; thus the passage refers to Taami Shōnin's credentials

[47] Unlike the translations of Chapter One, those in this chapter, again based on the text of Yokomichi and Omote, are often set up with the original word order in mind so that verbal interaction can be more easily explicated in the light of the Japanese version of the text.

[48] *Shōnin* ("Saint" or "Reverence") is a title that I have translated as "priest." See Renondeau, *Le bouddhisme*, 130–142, on nō featuring Ippen and his disciples. In particular, Renondeau points to similarities in the religious tenor of *Seiganji* and *Sanemori*.

[49] See *YKS*, 266 n. 2.

[50] See ibid., 266 n. 3.

as an itinerant priest. Zeami imparts all this information in but a few words.

The priest's hieratic function, and specifically his role as a disciple of Ippen, are introduced by the pun and made further evident in the "literary" borrowings of the waki's first recitative, a sashi, and the first song of the nō, an ageuta, which the waki shares with the wakizure. The waki priest begins the sashi with a recitation quoted from two sutras, the *Amidakyō* and the *Kammuryōjukyō*:[51]

Although Paradise is a place millions of miles away,	Sore saihō wa jūmannokudo
A long way for one to be reborn,	Tōku umaruru michi nagara
Here in one's heart is Amida's country.	Koko mo koshin no mida no kuni.

Lines from sutras appropriately introduce a play that dramatizes, through the example of Sanemori, how one can find salvation, though it be far away, within oneself. Zeami's subsequent quotation of the historical Ippen's poem, also familiar to audiences of nō,[52] strengthens the connection between Ippen and the priest, and thus adds authority to the priest's words. This is not unlike Aeschylus's use in the *Agamemnon* of the elders' "quotation" of a prophecy by Calchas after his first use of the proverb *pathei mathos*, "learning comes through suffering."[53] The elders' knowledge and use of Calchas's words help to reconfirm their authority pronounced at *Agamemnon* 104–106.[54]

In the first ageuta of the nō, the waki sings:

Just one person even if alone	Hitori nao
Let him pursue Buddha's holy name,	Hotoke no mina o tazune min,
Let him pursue Buddha's holy name,	Hotoke no mina o tazune min,
When each one leaves	Ono ono kaeru
The garden of the Law.	Nori no niwa.

[51] On the wording of the sutras, see ibid., 441 n. 107, for the *Amidakyō* (*Amitabha-sūtra*), and 441 n. 105, for the *Kammuryōjukyō* (*Amidāyurdhyāna-sūtra*).

[52] This poem also appears in the nō *Seiganji* and *Hotoke no hara*. On the history of the poem, see YKS, 446 n. 144, and Itō, *Yōkyokushū*, 108 n. 1. The latter commentator says that Ippen changed the version of the poem as it appeared in a work called *Hōmonhyakushū*. The subject of the different versions of the works that Zeami quoted or to which he alluded is important, but it is outside the scope of this comparative study.

[53] On the history of this proverb, newly employed by Aeschylus, see H. Dörrie, "Leid und Erfahrung, die Wort-und Sinn-Verbindung *pathein-mathein* im griechischen Denken," *Akad. der Wiss. und der Lit. in Mainz, geist.-und soz.-wiss. Klasse*, nr. 5 (1956).

[54] I do not, however, subscribe to the view of Rory B. Egan ("The Calchas Quotation and the Hymn to Zeus," *Eranos* 77 [1979]: 1–9) that the Zeus hymn is part of the quotation.

The poem conforms closely to the original, which reads as follows:

One person alone,	Hitori tada
Buddha's honorable name	Hotoke no mina ya
He will ponder,	Tadoruran
[When] everyone leaves,	Ono ono kaeru
Person[s] in the garden of the Law.	Nori no niwabito.

Zeami's slight alteration at the end of the poem—from *nori no niwabito* ("person in the garden of the Law," that is, Amida Buddha's Law) to *nori no niwa* ("garden of the Law")—facilitates the adaptation of the poem to the verbal context of the first two sections of the nō.[55] In the preceding sashi, the waki has said that the people are reciting Amida's prayer in the "garden," that is, at Shinowara, the setting of the play, called *nori no niwa*; in the shite's first speech that follows, he says that he will not enter the "garden" of the Law, *nori no niwa*, because he is too old and passion clouds his eyes. By repeating *nori no niwa*, a significant phrase within the play because the "garden" of Shinowara becomes verbally fused with that of Amida Buddha, Zeami helps the audience to link the sutras first to Ippen's words and then to the specific dramatic context. Although the shite does not enter the "garden" upon first encountering Ippen's disciple, he himself suggests, in accordance with the sutras and with Ippen, that one can be saved by invocation of Amida's name and that Paradise is not far away. With the repetition of *nori no niwa* at the conclusion to the second dan of the nō, Zeami connects the central character with the religious message.

In an analogous manner, Aeschylus concludes the lyric parodos of the *Agamemnon*, the introduction to the trilogy as a whole, with a fourth reference to Calchas and with a repetition of the essential point and words of the proverbial dictum *pathei mathos*.[56] In *Agamemnon* 250–251, the chorus sings:

Justice inclines the scales so that those who have suffered learn.	Dika de tois men pathoū- sin mathein epirrepei.

[55] Since we do not have all of Aeschylus's sources to the extent that we have Zeami's, we cannot always measure the degree of accuracy with which Aeschylus alluded to other authors' works. Of the Calchas prophecy, for example, we do not even know whether it was Aeschylus's own creation or was taken from one of the works in the epic cycle. But it is clear that in his handling of the prophecy, Aeschylus intended to create the effect of a quotation, at least in terms of the dramatic context.

[56] On the direction that the proverbial saying takes in the *Agamemnon*, see Lebeck, *Oresteia*, 26–29.

Aeschylus adjusts the dictum stated earlier to the exigencies of the trilogy as a whole, which on one level presents the development of justice from revenge to trial by jury, and further specifies that Justice is the agent of learning through suffering. The particular act entailing suffering that is described between the first and the second appearance of the dictum, Agamemnon's sacrifice of his daughter Iphigenia (184–247), explains one meaning of Calchas's prophecy. Thus, as Zeami elaborates upon both sutras and upon Ippen's words and applies these to the specific case of his main character, so Aeschylus applies the dictum to a character.[57] To be sure, it is not Agamemnon who actually "learns" but his son Orestes, who appears in the second and third plays,[58] whereas Sanemori does pursue Buddha's name; however, in the nō and the tragedy alike the audience is put into the position of learning from allusions to or quotations of familiar material and from an application of these to a dramatic character.

In *Sanemori*, before the shite appears on stage and in the continuation of the waki's and wakizure's song, Zeami expands upon the meaning of the sutras and Ippen's words by adding that both those who believe and those who do not can be saved, and that the passage to Amida's realm is an easy one. It is in this song that Zeami introduces the first instance of sustained verbal interaction in the nō.

Both hearts that believe and those	Shiru mo shiranu mo
That do not are *drawn*	Kokoro *hiku*
By His Vow. Through his *net*	Chikai no *ami* no
Will anyone *pass*? No.	*Moru*bekiya.
Both people who believe	Shiru hito mo,
And people who do not—	Shiranu hito o mo
He will help them *take passage*	*Watasabaya*
And go to that Country	Kano kuni e yuku
Aboard the *boat* of the Law	Nori no *fune*
[And be saved] that *floats* easily	*Ukamu* mo yasuki
Along the way, as it is said.[59]	Michi tokaya.

The words *ami* ("net"), *moru* ("pass"), *watasabaya* ("take passage"), *fune* ("boat"), and *ukamu* ("float") are vehicle words that pertain in meaning to water. They are brought into and move in and out of the tenor of the passage (that is, the priest's teaching, the subject at issue) by means of

[57] See Fraenkel, *Aeschylus Agamemnon*, 113.

[58] *Contra* Peter M. Smith, *On the Hymn to Zeus in Aeschylus' Agamemnon*, American Classical Studies 5 (Ann Arbor, 1980): 23 and 66 n. 68, Orestes does learn; see *Eumenides* 276.

[59] The words *ukamu mo yasuki* imply in religious language "to be saved." The word *tokaya* ("it is said") suggests a parable or saying. It is like the Aeschylean phrases that refer to what others say.

verbal interaction. For example, the word *hiku*, meaning "draw," grammatically is the verb of which the words preceding it, "both hearts that believe and those that do not," part of the tenor, are the direct objects. In this first line Zeami says that the people in the garden are drawn to the sermons. In addition, *hiku* is semantically connected with a vehicle word, "nets," in the following phrase, *chikai no ami* ("His Vow's net"), and, by means of engo,[60] serves as the focus of interaction between the tenor and vehicle. The lines thus suggest that both those who believe and those who do not can be saved, for they are drawn into Amida Buddha's net.

The expansion in the fifth and sixth lines, an almost verbatim repetition of the first two lines, facilitates the preparation in the word "net" for the reference to the vehicle, a passage by boat to "that Country," that is, Paradise. Verbal interaction is fully exploited here—*watasabaya* ("provide passage") is associated in meaning with the vehicle words *fune* ("boat") and *ukamu* ("float") in the following lines.[61] This verbal interaction is strengthened by the proximity of the two words *fune* and *nori*; the latter means not only "law," as in *nori no niwa* ("garden of the Law"), but also "board," in the sense "to board a boat."[62] In the next line, *ukamu* ("float"), another vehicle word naturally connected with boats, is juxtaposed with *yasuki michi*, literally meaning "the easy way." In the light of the meaning "be saved" for *ukamu no yasuki*, the phrase *yasuki michi* assumes the meaning "the easy way," the Way of several Buddhist sects and of part of the Ji sect. Unlike "the difficult way" (*jiriki*), which requires hard work and discipline to attain salvation, the easy way promises that Amida Buddha will be prompted to save a person by a single sincere invocation.

Aeschylus's use of words associated in meaning with birds, an important image in the trilogy,[63] within an account of the Greek expedition to Troy and its consequences is analogous to the interaction of the tenor and of the vehicle words associated in meaning with water in the passage from the nō. In *Agamemnon* 48–59, the elders say:

Loudly *crying out* "Ares" from their hearts,	Megal' ek thumou *klazontes* Arē,
Like *vultures* who, with exceeding	Tropon *aigupiōn* hoit' ekpatiois

---

[60] See YKS, 266 n. 15. Itō, *Yōkyokushū*, 108 n. 3, recognizes *chikai no ami* and *nori no fune* as "metaphors" (*hiyu*).

[61] Koyama, 184 n. 17, notes this association in meaning.

[62] See Sieffert, *La tradition secrète*, 353 n. 6.

[63] Among others, Petrounias, *Funktion und Thematik der Bilder*, 129–140, discusses the relationship of this image to others in the trilogy.

Grief for their children, high over the bed	Algesi paidōn hupatoi lekheōn
Eddy about,	Strophodinountai
Plying with the oars of their *wings*	*Pterugōn* eretmoisin eressomenoi,
Having lost their labor of guarding the bed,	Demniotērē
A labor for their *nestlings*,	Ponon *ortalikhōn* olesantes·
From high above, someone, Apollo	Hupatos d' aiōn ētis Apollōn
Or Pan or Zeus, hearing the *bird-lamenting*	Ē Pan ē Zeus *oiōnothroon*
Grief, shrill sounding, of these denizens,	Goon oxuboan tōnde metoikōn
Sends one who brings punishment later	Husteropoinon
A Fury against the transgressors.	Pempei parabasin Erinun.

In this passage, the vehicle functioning as image words (*aigupiōn*, "vultures"; *pterugōn*, "wings"; *ortalikhōn*, "nestlings"; and *oiōnothroon*, "bird-lamenting") are connected to the tenor in a way similar to that found in the passage from the nō. The word *klazontes* ("crying out") syntactically belongs with the words preceding—specifically, it modifies the Greek leaders Menelaus and Agamemnon—and with the word *Arē* ("Ares"), its direct object, which immediately follows; thus the lines inform the audience that the twin kings set out on an expedition and cried out, "War!" In addition, because bird cries are among the sounds that *klazō* commonly denotes, the verb functions aptly in a description of vultures. By means of the simile, Aeschylus says that the two sons of Atreus cry out like birds that have lost their young. (He does not specify whom they have lost, whether Helen or Iphigenia, for he means both.)

The vehicle and tenor interact further in the line "eddy about, plying with the oars of their wings" (51–52). The words *paidōn* ("children") and *lekheōn* ("beds") in the preceding line are used to denote "nestlings" and "nest" respectively; however, they are, according to normal usage, more appropriate to the human realm.[64] This semantic conflation is analogous to Zeami's use of the words *ami* ("net") and *fune* ("boat") which are appropriate to the human realm but refer also to Amida Buddha's "Vow" (*chikai*) and "Law" (*nori*) respectively. The word *pterugōn* ("wings") is clearly a vehicle word, yet it is governed syntactically by *eretmoisin*

---

[64] *Goos* ("lament") is another word that is more appropriate to human beings than to birds.

("oars"), a word that belongs to the human realm and suggests the ships that the Atreidae had launched against Troy ten years earlier. Tenor and vehicle converge in the word *eressomenoi* ("plying"), a word meaning both "fly," as suggested by the words "wings" and "high over . . . eddy about," and "row," as suggested by the word "oars" immediately preceding.[65] (Similar is Zeami's use of *nori* to signify both "to board [a boat]" and "law.") The verbal interaction is strengthened by the juxtaposition of *pterugōn* ("wings") and *eretmoisin* ("oars").[66]

Verbal interaction in both the nō and the tragedy serves to introduce significant interrelationships among different subjects that are treated in each. In the former, the words associated in meaning with water are part of the sacred language of Buddhism (and thus are not metaphorical), and at the same time they function as the vehicle within the ageuta, being brought in from outside the tenor. Thus they prepare for the use that Zeami later makes of words pertaining to water in order to bring the main character and the setting of the play into the purview of Buddha's Vow, Law, and Paradise. We learn that in Paradise, Amida Buddha sits in the midst of a Lake; that at Shinowara, the site of the sermons, there existed an actual pond in which the head of Sanemori was washed by his enemy; that the pond in the nō is verbally suggested as the place into and out of which the actor is said to disappear and reappear; and that the "water" in Sanemori's heart must be purified in order for him to attain salvation. Zeami's use of words associated in meaning with water interrelates the divine, the physical, and the "psychological" contexts.

Although Aeschylus does not quote a scripture in the *Agamemnon*, as Zeami does in the nō, Aeschylus introduces an image probably derived from religious language in a context that helps interrelate god and man. At the end of the important passage, in which the elders state that Zeus guides men along the path of understanding through suffering, they add, "the grace of the gods sitting upon the reverenced deck [of the ship] surely involves violence" (*daimonōn de pou kharis biaios / selma semnon hēmenōn*, 182–183). The expression "sitting upon the deck," inspired by the name of Zeus, *hupsizugos* ("on the highest deck") and familiar to the audience,[67] is intrusive, used instead of the expected "enthroned." However,

---

[65] See Lebeck, *Oresteia*, 170–171 n. 19, on the interweaving of simile and context in this passage and the relevance of the image to a later passage in the trilogy, *Eumenides* 250–251.

[66] For a discussion of this passage, see Silk, *Interaction*, 146–147, and Rosenmeyer, *Art of Aeschylus*, 125–127. The latter's observation that in Aeschylus one finds not a total replacement of tenor by vehicle, but "liaison" or "partial replacement" (128), is an apt characterization of the passage in *Sanemori* as well. In both there is a simultaneity of meanings.

[67] See Fraenkel, *Aeschylus Agamemnon*, 110. The epithet occurs in the *Iliad*. Aeschylus replaces it with *selma semnon hēmenōn*, in which *selma* ("deck") is synonymous with *zugos* (see *Agamemnon* 1618).

it is associated in meaning with ships, the actual ships of the Greeks mentioned earlier, and prepares for a return to that subject: in lines 184–185, Agamemnon is called "the leader of the Greek ships." The ships are also, like water in *Sanemori*, appropriate to a physical aspect of the play. Later in the *Agamemnon* (1011–1012), the house of Atreus, the setting of the play, is compared to a ship.[68]

In the continuation of *Sanemori*, Zeami effects a smooth verbal transition from the religious dicta of the first dan to the second. The shite says:

The sound of the flutes is heard in the distance above a lone cloud	Sei ga haruka ni kikoyu koun no ue
A holy multitude comes before the setting sun to receive [me].	Shōjuraikōsu rakujitsu no mae.
Ah, on this holy day as well a purple cloud hovers above.	Ara tōto ya kyō mo mata shiun no tatte sōrō zo ya.
The sound of the bell and of voices reciting the nembutsu are heard.	Kane no oto nembutsu no koe no kikoe sōro.
Ah, well, it is now time to listen to the sermons.	Sate wa chōmon mo ima naru beshi.
But, even if he were not trying to hurry, waves of old age would make the going difficult,	Sanaki dani, tachii kurushiki oi no nami no,
And he cannot approach those in the garden of the Law.	Yori mo tsukazu wa nori no niwa ni.

First Zeami quotes a Japanese version of a Chinese poem, which states that Bodhisattvas come to save one.[69] This is a religious dictum in itself and thus part of the tenor that preceded in the waki's speeches. By repeating a word from that poem, "cloud" (i.e., *-un* in *shiun*), in the third line, Zeami

[68] Parallel to the application of the ship to three spheres is Aeschylus's use of words pertaining to the wind. In line 105, *katapneiei* ("blows down") refers to the breath of divine inspiration; in lines 147 (*antipnoous*) and 192 (*pnoai*), the winds are literally real—they cause the delay of the Greek fleet at Aulis; and in 187 (*sumpneōn*) and 219 (*pneōn*), the "blowing" refers to Agamemnon's psychological state, an expression of his will. With the appearance of the Furies in the *Eumenides*, the blasts become "real" for the audience; see line 137. For other applications of this image in the *Oresteia*, see William C. Scott, "Wind Imagery in the *Oresteia*," *TAPA* 97 (1966): 459–471.

[69] The poem is by Jakushō, an eleventh-century Chinese monk. See above, Chapter One, note 63. Bodhisattvas are those who, on the verge of becoming Buddhas, decide to relinquish their own salvation so that they may save others.

helps the audience connect the words of the shite and of the poem.[70] Zeami next has the shite repeat words spoken by the waki and the wakizure, among them *nori no niwa*.[71] Finally, Zeami includes in the shite's speech words associated in meaning with water. In the phrase *oi no nami no yori* ("waves of old age approach"), the word *nami* ("waves") is a vehicle word, consistent with the vehicle in the waki's recitative.[72] Although the word *yori* means "approach" within the sentence as a whole—the shite says that he wants to approach and join those in the garden—when used in conjunction with *nami*, it connotes waves washing upon a shore and thus underscores the image in the shite's phrase.[73]

In the third dan, the priest and the old man engage in a dialogue in which the priest speaks straightforwardly, but the old man's language contains literary allusions and verbal techniques that enhance the meaning of his words. (In the first section of the *Agamemnon*, the chorus, functioning like the waki, questions the queen in straightforward language; the verbal double-entendre appears in the queen's responses.) When the priest asks the old man for his name, in one of many such requests, the old man claims that if he were someone worthy of a name he would divulge it, but he is a mere "country person from far away" (*amasagaru hinabito*). The word *amasagaru* ("far away") functions like a "pillow word" (makurakotoba), which is a conventional epithet or attribute of a word.[74] The pillow word brings out the importance of the word following, in this case *hinabito*. The phrase as a whole means that the old man, because he lives in the country, resides far from the capital city. At the same time, *amasagaru*, because it literally means "away from heaven," adds to the surface meaning the idea that the old man has not been saved. This latter meaning is suggested by the religious environment in which the word is used, and it is prepared for by the shite's quotation of a line from a sutra at the end of the second dan.[75]

---

[70] This repetition is analogous to the way in which, in the lyric parodos, Aeschylus connects Agamemnon to the *pathei mathos* dictum by use of the word *prōtopēmōn* ("the beginning of misery" 223), a word semantically related to *pathos*.

[71] The Hōshō textual variant *chōji no niwa* ("garden of the congregation") diminishes the effect of this repetition.

[72] *YKS*, 267 n. 23, says that *nami* is a connecting word between *oi* ("old") and *yori* ("approach").

[73] In *Agamemnon* 187–192, Aeschylus draws the audience's attention to the literal sense of the vehicle word *sumpneōn* ("blowing with") by referring five lines later to the real winds (*pnoai*, 192) that caused the delay of the fleet at Aulis.

[74] According to Brower and Miner, a pillow word "usually occupies a short, 5-syllable line and modifies a word, usually the first, in the next line. Some pillow words are unclear in meaning; those whose meanings are known function rhetorically to raise the tone and to some degree also function as imagery" (*Japanese Court Poetry*, 508). See *YKS*, 267 n. 31.

[75] Such "activation" of the meaning of a word as a result of the semantic environment

Literary borrowings and allusions within the shite's speech appear in the form of two proverbial sayings derived from two sutras, a poem,[76] and individual words also derived from sutras. The shite compares his feeling on meeting the priest both with that of a blind turtle which discovers a floating log in the sea and passes his head through the hole in it and with that of one who sees an udonge flower bloom, an experience that can occur only once every three thousand years. This joy is further described in a poem quoted almost verbatim from the original:

The happiness of one in his old age is exceedingly great.	Oi no saiwai mi ni koe.
Tears of joy on his sleeves are abundant.	Yorokobi no nanda tamoto ni amaru.

The only significant change Zeami makes in the poem in order to adapt it to the dramatic context is to replace the original word *nozomi* ("desire") with the word *mi* ("person"). The first line of the original poem reads as follows:

The happiness of one in his old age exceeds his desires.	Oi no saiwai *nozomi* ni koe.

In the line immediately following the quotation, Zeami repeats the word *mi*:

Even as he is, can he be Reborn in the land of peace and happiness?	Sareba kono *mi* nagara, Anrakukoku ni umaruru ka to—
This thought causes incomparable joy.	Muhi no kangi o nasu tokoro ni.

The shite says that his joy is great over the thought that, even though he is the *mi* ("person") that he is, he may be reborn in Paradise (that is, be reborn without passing through another life here on earth). The words "reborn" (*umaruru*) and "Paradise" (*anrakukoku*) are derived from sutras, the former from the *Amidakyō* quoted earlier by the waki.[77] The use

---

in which it appears is strikingly apparent in the parodos of the *Agamemnon*. There the words *antidikos* ("legal opponent," 41) and *arōgē* ("legal support," 47) affect the interpretation of *metoikoi* ("denizens," 57), a word that also means "alien residents," that is, those given a certain legal status in Athens. The latter meaning becomes relevant in the *Eumenides* when the Furies are given this status (1011).

[76] The sutras are the *Hokekyō* and the *Nehankyō*; see *YKS*, 446 n. 145. The poem is in the preface to the *Shin'yōshū*, another collection of poems.

[77] The second is found in the *Muryōju*. See *YKS*, 268 n. 39.

of *mi* and "reborn" aids in drawing the audience's attention to Zeami's adaptation of the borrowed material to the nō.

At this point there occurs the only instance in the nō of verbal confrontation and the use of persuasion between two characters on stage. (Such "confrontation" is the norm in mondō.) Zeami's repetition of words meaning "name," both the nouns (*na*) and the verbs (*nanori*)—he uses them thirteen times within the dan—emphasizes verbally the dramatic intensity of the scene. If we compare the stichomythic passages in Aeschylus's plays with this mondō of *Sanemori*, we find that they are similar in several respects. Bernd Seidensticker has identified three characteristic features of Aeschylus's stichomythic style: speeches are interlocked by means of (1) conjunctions and particles, (2) grammatical ellipse and continuation of constructions, and (3) *Stichworttechnik*, "repetition of the same word."[78] The first of these characteristics appears in the mondō: the priest begins with the words *geni geni* ("indeed"), acknowledges the old man's words, and asks his name; the old man begins his reply with *sate wa*, "[but] then," and next asks whether he cannot avoid giving his name. The words used to introduce each speech have an adversative function like certain combinations of particles in the Greek. For example, in *Agamemnon* 931–942, a scene of major confrontation between Agamemnon and Clytemnestra, the single-lined speeches are interlocked by means of particles such as *ge mentoi* (938) and *de* (939). This feature of prose style is one means by which the element of confrontation is marked within the passage in the nō. The second type of interlocking appears at the end of the mondō in the kakeai, where the waki and shite complete each other's thoughts. The fluidity of style that results is not characteristic of prosaic dialogue.

The third type of interlocking is the most nearly similar in the two playwrights' works, namely, the repetition of the same word to create connections between the speeches of two characters. In the *Libation Bearers* 168–180, for example, Aeschylus repeats words meaning "hair"; in *Suppliants* 293–322, he repeats the word meaning "cow" even more often. In each scene, one character, Electra and King Pelagus respectively, like the priest in the nō, is engaged in learning the identity of the other, Orestes and the suppliant women. And in each scene, the repeated word is important to the action: a lock of hair is the first concrete (i.e., nonverbal) means by which Electra recognizes her brother;[79] a cow is the form in which Io,

---

[78] Seidensticker, "Die Stichomythie," 185–191. (I have changed the order of the characteristics from that found in Seidensticker's work.)

[79] The repetition of words meaning hair, unlike the repetition of "name" in *Sanemori*, does not entail precisely the same word in each instance. However, the repetition is emphasized by Aeschylus's use of bird imagery both within the stichomythy and in the subsequent speech in which Orestes reveals his identity. In line 174, Electra remarks that the lock of hair that she has noticed is *homopteros* ("like-feathered"). Later (228), Orestes says that Electra, on seeing the lock of hair and the footprints, *anepterōthēs* ("took

through whom the maidens trace their lineage back to Argos, was approached by Zeus. (This is the lineage that the maidens use to convince the king that they are Argives like him, and therefore deserve his protection.) Repetition of a significant word in each of the Greek examples serves, like the repetition in *Sanemori*, to emphasize the prominence of that to which the word refers within the play as a whole. The revelation of Sanemori's name is the first step towards the warrior's salvation, since the priest can help the old man if he knows his identity; the revelation of the person to whom the lock of hair belongs brings Orestes and Electra together so that they can carry out a plot to kill their mother; and the revelation of the maidens' connection to Io, the woman transformed into a cow, leads to their protection at the hands of the king of Argos. And yet, in both the nō and the tragedies, Zeami and Aeschylus place emphasis on words *qua* words in order to communicate to their respective audiences the importance of a particular subject. The specific effect is different, but the stylistic procedure is similar.

In the mondō, on the basis of an analogy that the old man draws between himself and a cherry tree in a poem, the priest infers that his interlocutor is Sanemori, the warrior to whom the old man has just referred as if talking about a past event unconnected with himself. The poem, written by the warrior Yorimasa, also an old warrior, reads as follows:

A tree not seen among the many Miyamagi no sono kozue to wa
  other treetops on a   mie zarishi,
  mountain,
When in bloom, betrays itself as Sakura wa hana ni arawaretaru.[80]
  a cherry tree.

It is at this point that, for the first and only time in the play, the old man uses the pronoun *ware*, meaning "I":[81]

---

wing"). The reinforcement of the image continues in Orestes' prayer that Zeus "look upon the orphaned offspring of an eagle father" (247); and in Orestes' references to his sister and himself as "the nestlings of their father" (256) and as the children of the "eagle" (258). By these means Aeschylus connects the passage to the lyric parodos of the *Agamemnon*, analyzed above. On this point see Lebeck, *Oresteia*, 13–14, and Jørgen Meyer, "Recognizing What When and Why? The Recognition Scene in Aeschylus' Choephori," in *Arktouros: Hellenic Studies Presented to Bernard M.W. Knox* (Berlin, 1979), 115–121, esp. 120.

[80] The poem is found in the *Heike*, bk. 1, ch. 15, and the *Shikashū*, a collection of poems. On the occasion of the emperor's poetry contest, Yorimasa distinguished himself by writing this poem. In the original, the final word is *arawarenikeri*, the perfective form of the verb. The word *mie* ("seen") within the first line is a repetition of the same word from the waki's speech immediately preceding: "Then is it seen by people even now?" (*Sate wa ima mo hito ni mie sor ō ka*).

[81] *Watakushi*, also meaning "I," is used later, not as a pronoun, but rather in an expression meaning "not selfish."

I am the ghost of Sanemori.   Ware Sanemori ga yūrei naru ga.

This turning point in the development of the play emerges both from the repetition of words, which serves to engage the audience's attention, and from the quotation of a poem, and is marked by the use of a word not found elsewhere in the work; at the same time, Zeami moves out of the mode of treating words *qua* words to the logical mode. The inference that the waki makes is similar to that found in the *Libation Bearers*, where Electra infers that her brother has returned. As summarized by Aristotle (*Poetics* 1455a5–6), her reasoning runs: "Someone like me has come, but no one is like me except Orestes; therefore, he has come." In *Sanemori* the priest says that he thought he heard the story (of Sanemori) told about someone else, but it proves to have been about the old man; therefore, he infers, that the old man is the ghost of Sanemori. His identity is revealed through inference based on the "device" of a poem and on the old man's explicit comparison between himself and the old cherry tree; in the *Libation Bearers*, it is revealed through an inference and confirmed by a device not mentioned by Aristotle, a concrete object.[82] In neither scene is there what Aristotle would call the best kind of "recognition," one that entails the revelation of identity arising out of the events themselves.[83] In fact, that kind of revelation scene does not appear in any of Zeami's nō or Aeschylus's tragedies, as it does in the work of Euripides.

In the kakeai, "sung exchange," which is the emotional peak within the dan, the lines shared by the waki and the shite, unlike those in the mondō, blend into one long sentence in which transitions are made by means of word association (engo) and other verbal devices. The kakeai reads as follows:

WAKI: In sinful attachment to this   Nao shushin no enbu no yo ni
          transient world

SHITE: More than two hundred   Nihyaku yosai no hodo wa
          years have elapsed   furedomo

WAKI: But still he cannot be saved,   *Ukami* mo yarade Shinowara no
          floating on Shinowara's

SHITE: *Pond, in vain, waves wash*   *Ike* no *adanami yoru* to naku
          against the shore at night

WAKI: And by day without   Hiru tomo wakade kokoro no
          distinction in the darkness of   yami no
          the soul

---

[82] In the nō *Kiyotsune*, for example, the wife of the warrior Kiyotsune recognizes the truth—that her husband has drowned himself—when his retainer hands her a lock of his hair. In *Semimaru*, Sakagami goes to her brother's place of exile and recognizes him from the sound of his voice.

[83] See *Poetics* 1455a16–20, which may be a later addition to the work. See also 1452a29–1452b8, which is an integral part of it.

SHITE: Whether in a state of dreams Yume to mo naku
WAKI: Or in a state of wakefulness Utsutsu to mo naki
SHITE: He is obsessed with this Omoi o nomi.
  thought.

Within this passage, in which it is again explicitly stated that the old man has not been saved, Zeami is able to fuse the setting of the play and the warrior's spirit by his use of words associated in meaning with water. In the waki's second line, *ukami* ("float"), a vehicle word used earlier in the description of a passage to Amida's Country and salvation, and a word that here also connotes one's existence "floating" in this world, is associated in meaning with *ike* ("pond"), here the pond at Shinowara, and with *adanami* ("vain [that is, impermanent] waves"), here a reference both to the waves of the pond and to the impermanence of one's existence in this world.[84] The two levels of meaning in one word converge in the word *yoru*, meaning both "night," associated in meaning with the word "darkness" in the next line (i.e., the darkness of the soul), and "wash against the shore," in association with the immediately preceding "waves." The shite's expression of vain existence in this world of illusion formally ends with the word *nomi* ("only"), but is grammatically dependent on the first syllable of the first word, *Shinowara*, in the poetic line that follows—the syllable *shi* serves as the conclusion to the expression "I am obsessed with this thought."[85] The syllable *shi*, serving as the first in the place name Shinowara, the setting of the play, connects Zeami's references both to the pond and to the warrior's condition in the kakeai with what follows.

Zeami's artistry is revealed in part by his simultaneous treatment of two levels of significance in the kakeai, the artistry of Aeschylus in part by his treatment of the second stasimon in the *Agamemnon*, in an analogous manner. In *Agamemnon* 699–716, after introducing the subject of Helen and, through a pun on her name, the destruction she brought to Troy, the chorus says that Wrath sent a *kēdos* rightly named to Troy. *Kēdos*, meaning both "a connection by marriage" and "grief," is used, like *yoru*, with two denotations within the stanza.[86] The former meaning is suggested by the chorus's subsequent references to *to numphotimon melos* ("a song in honor of the bride") and *humenaion hos tot' eperrepe gambroisin aeidein* ("a wedding song which at that time it fell to the lot of the bridegroom's relatives to sing"). But in line 709, Aeschylus pivots to the meaning "grief" with the phrase *metamanthanousa d'humnon*. In this phrase, the syllables

---

[84] See *YKS*, 268 n. 12, on this example of engo.

[85] See ibid., 268 n. 14.

[86] The two denotations regarding death and marriage associated with the word *kēdos* are facilitated in part by Aeschylus's various and skillful uses of *telos* and related words. See Lebeck, *Oresteia*, 68–73. Fraenkel (*Aeschylus Agamemnon*, 334) quotes scholia giving the two significances of the word.

meta- at the beginning mark the shift; they mean both "afterward" and "instead"—that is, the city of Troy "learns afterward, and instead, another song." *Humnon* ("song") is the neutral word on which the stanza as a whole pivots: in the preceding sentence *humenaion* means a wedding song; in this next sentence the song changes to one *poluthrēnon*, "full of lament." The chorus adds that the city of Priam, Troy, now calls Paris, the husband of Helen, "evil-wedded," in realization of the shift in the type of song it sings. Simultaneously a shift has taken place in the meaning of *kēdos*.

In this passage, *kēdos* is polysemous and *humnon* is neutral, both assuming particular meanings on the basis of the verbal environment in which they appear. In this respect they are like *yoru* and *ukami* respectively. Another analogy to Zeami's use of *yoru* might be found in Aeschylus's use of *meleon* (716), which means "vain" or "miserable," as it is usually interpreted in the phrase, "having endured miserable bloodshed." (The phrase refers to the city of Priam.) But the word, because it sounds like *melos* ("song," see 706), may also be treated as if it were an adjective meaning "of song." The phrase then means first "bloodshed about which they lament in song," and pivots to the meaning "miserable bloodshed."

The stanza of the ode ends with the phrase "miserable bloodshed"; however, the chorus continues at the beginning of the next stanza with the words, "and it reared in its home a lion's whelp deprived of milk." This connection is not as verbally economical as Zeami's use of the syllable *shi-*, a link between the kakeai and the following line that includes a quotation from a poem; however, there is a pivoting between the two stanzas by which Aeschylus connects the preceding to a story drawn from tradition in the latter. The story is formally introduced by the word *houtōs*, meaning "thus," but since the word is delayed the preceding stanza flows smoothly into the beginning of the story.[87] (The particle *de*, "and," is not adversative, but rather helps to make the transition.) The story begins as if Troy were said to have reared a lion's whelp. However, after the word *houtōs*, the grammatical subject of the verb *ethrepsen* ("reared") is expressed and one learns that in the animal fable on which Aeschylus has drawn to illustrate his point, it was a man who reared the animal. Although less economical, Aeschylus's continuation of thought from one stanza to the next with the fable is analogous to Zeami's method of continuing the thought of the kakeai in the ageuta and connecting the tenor of the former with material borrowed from a poem in the shite's line beginning with the word *Shinowara*.[88]

[87] Fraenkel (*Aeschylus Agamemnon*, 339) is surprised that the word *houtōs*, also meaning "once upon a time," is delayed until so late in the sentence.

[88] I do not of course mean to suggest that the paraphrase of a fable and the borrowing of words explicitly from a poem are the same technique.

As the nō continues, the shite says:

At Shinowara	Shinowara no
Very much like hoarfrost on the grass is the old man.	Kusaba no shimo no okina sabi.

The words *okina sabi* are the beginning of a poem of which a version is found in *The Tales of Ise*.[89] There the poem expresses a man's reaction to the emperor's request that he handle a falcon on an outing—the person considers himself too old to undertake the task, yet in view of the insult to the emperor if he does not, he attaches the following poem as an apology to the sleeve of his hunting costume:

With the appearance of the old man	Okina sabi
Let no one find fault.	Hito na togame so.
The hunting robe	Karigoromo
Is only for today.	Kyō bakari to zo
[Only for today] is the heron's cry.	Tazu mo naku naru.

In the nō after the words *okina sabi*, the chorus continues:

With him, let no one find fault	Hito na togame so
Temporarily	Karisome ni
Revealed. . . .	Araware. . . .

Zeami diverts the direction of the original poem, quoted up to and including the syllables *kari-*, so as to adapt it to the case of Sanemori. He changes *karigoromo* ("hunting robe," literally meaning "temporary robe") to *karisome ni araware* ("temporarily revealed"), words well suited to a context in which the shite, dressed in a plain outfit, appears on stage temporarily. The phrase on one level means that the warrior still exists in the temporary world and has not been saved; in terms of the performance, that the shite has appeared on stage only temporarily—in fact, he disappears from the stage at the end of the song.

Whether the word *-goromo* ("robe") in the original poem might later come to the audience's mind when the shite reappears on stage dressed in the robes of a warrior is doubtful. However, the mention of "hoarfrost on the grass" in the first line introducing the poem is likely to point to the appearance of the shite as an old man wearing a mask and wig of an old man, because it is a common metaphor for old age. In nondramatic poetry,

---

[89] *Ise monogatari*, no. 114, by Ariwara no Yukihira. On this poem, see Sieffert, *La tradition secrète*, 354 n. 20; and on Zeami's alteration of it, see Itō, *Yōkyokushū*, 111 n. 10.

the phrase *kusaba no shimo no* would be joshi, introductory to the poem that follows. In the nō, the phrase is more than an excuse for introducing the next lines, inasmuch as old age assumes great significance in this play about a warrior who dyed his hair and beard black so that, disguised as a young man, he might die fighting bravely in battle. The transition between the introductory words and the poem is accomplished by the syllables *oki*, which function simultaneously as the beginning of the first word of the poem, *okina* ("old man"), and as the end of the phrase *shimo no oki* ("deposit hoarfrost"). *Oki* serves as the verb of which "hoarfrost" is the object.[90]

After quoting the beginning of the poem from *The Tales of Ise*, the chorus continues to sing on behalf of the old man and, elaborating on the expression "do not find fault," says that Sanemori has come and asks that one not let his name leak out, for rumors will cause him shame. In the preceding mondō the warrior has privately revealed his identity only after the priest has sent the other people away; here the chorus expresses the shame he still feels over that name and his request for indulgence. The chorus then remarks that the old man has left the priest's presence and concludes the maeba with the words, "At the edge of Shinowara's pond the form of the ghost disappears." These words point to the action represented on stage by the shite's exit as straightforwardly as Agamemnon's words, "Stepping on the purple I enter the chambers of the house" (957), describe his exit (that is, his entrance into the palace).

After the kyōgen section,[91] Zeami verbally connects the nochiba, the second half of the nō, to the kyōgen's words, to those of the chorus at the end of the maeba, and to those of the waki at the beginning of the nō. The waki, who has spoken with the kyōgen character, begins the nochiba with a call for special prayers, *rinji no odori nembutsu*, on behalf of the ghost, prayers connected with Ippen's form of Amida Buddhism and specifically referred to by the kyōgen in his last speech. Then, with the wakizure, the waki sings an ageuta, which begins with words repeated from the end of the maeba:

At the edge of	Shinowara no
Shinowara's pond.	Ike no hotori no.

These words refer to the dramatic setting and the spot at which the old man is said to have disappeared; in the continuation of the song, they are connected with the water of Buddha's Law in reminiscence of the first song

[90] See YKS, 269 n. 16.

[91] As mentioned above, the kyōgen section is written in prose and more colloquial language than the other sections of the nō, and therefore does not need to be treated under a discussion of poetic style.

of the maeba. There, before the shite has appeared and has mentioned the sound of the bell and of the voices of prayer in the Garden of the Law, words associated in meaning with water have been employed in a passage promising that everyone will be caught in the net of the Vow and take passage on the boat of the Law. Here, at the beginning of the nochiba, the waki says that the services are taking place specifically on behalf of Sane-mori's ghost, connecting the people's invocation, prayers, and voices with water in his words:

Over the *water* of the Law	Nori no *mizu*
Deep is the invocation,	*Fukaku* zo tanomu
In recitation of prayers	Shōmyōno
Clear the voices *cross*.	Koe *sumi wataru*.
Hold a memorial service	Tomurai no
From the first to the last	Shoya yori goya ni
Watch of night.	Itaru made.

The water of Buddha's Law is the vehicle connected with the tenor, the pond mentioned in the preceding recitation, by the word *fukaku* ("deep"), which because it also means "sincere" is associated with the invocation as well. The word *sumi* ("clear")[92] describes both the voices of the invokers and the water over which the voices "cross" (*wataru*). (Both *mizu* and *wataru* have appeared in the first song of the maeba.) The three spheres of signification—Buddha's Lake in Paradise, Shinowara's "garden," and the people's participation in a religious service—are connected through verbal interaction. These spheres, in turn, verbally converge in what follows—a borrowing from a poem by Ippen appearing at the same juncture in the nochiba as did the quotation of another of his poems in the maeba. The words in the nō are:

The heart also, Westward,	Kokoro mo nishi e
Goes with the moon	Yuki tsuki no
Light	Hikari to tomo ni
Cloudless.[93]	Kumorinaki.

The poem by Ippen reads as follows:[94]

Cloudless are	Kumorinaki
The heavens from the start	Sora wa moto yori
Because the place is not far away	Hedateneba

[92] *Fukaku* and *sumi* are associated in meaning with *mizu* ("water"). This is an example of engo. *YKS*, 269 n. 20.

[93] A prose rendering of the lines would read: "The heart also goes West with the moon's light, unhidden by the clouds."

[94] For the wording, see *YKS*, 269 n. 23.

The heart to the West Moves, as does the light of the moon.	Kokoro zo nishi ni Fukuru tsuki kage.

The two poems are different, yet the main idea and the important words are repeated: *kokoro* ("heart"), *nishi* ("West"), *tsuki* ("moon"), and *kumorinaki* ("cloudless"). Ippen's poem lends authority to the priest's words and to the description of the services taking place near the pond at Shinowara where the water and the voices are clear. In the nō, the moon, a symbol of enlightenment, is explicitly called "clear" (i.e., "cloudless"), as the heavens are in the original poem. By association with both, the heart, because it moves with the moon to Paradise in the West, must also be clear and free from the impurities that bar a person from being saved. The case in point is, of course, Sanemori, to whom Zeami turns after the waki and wakizure add that the bell rings throughout the night and after the waki invokes Amida Buddha in prayer. These lines echo the shite's statement in the maeba that he heard the sound of the bell and the voices of prayer and invoked Amida Buddha. The verbal repetition prepares for his appearance.

In one example of verbal echoing between the beginning and the middle of a tragedy, in the *Agamemnon*, Aeschylus repeats words and develops themes from the lyric parodos in the ode following the messenger episode, a juncture comparable to the first dan of the nochiba, after the kyōgen section. In Calchas's prophecy (140–155), the chorus sings that Artemis was kindly toward the cubs of ravenous "lions" (*leontōn*), a delight to the tender offspring "who love the breast" (*philomastois*). At the end of the same prophecy, Calchas expresses the hope that Artemis will not "cause" (*teuxēi*) the Greeks a delay and "speed along another sacrifice [*thusian*], one that is unlawful and inedible [*adaiton*]." "For," he adds, "a 'Wrath that does not forget' [*mnamōn Mēnis*] waits." Given his use of *thusian*, ("sacrifice"), it seems that Calchas is referring to the sacrifice of Iphigenia.[95] The case is specified differently, however, after the messenger scene.

In lines 699–716, the chorus says that "Wrath that accomplishes its will" (*telessiphrōn Mēnis*) drove sorrow to Troy, changing the wedding song in honor of Helen and Paris to a hymn of much lament. The chorus then (717–736) relates the tale about a man who reared a tender "lion's" (*leontos*) whelp that was not given milk, but "which loved the breast" (*philomaston*). In Calchas's prophecy, the *Mēnis* ("Wrath") was one that remembered; here it brings fulfillment in the form of destruction to Troy.[96]

[95] On this point, see Fraenkel, *Aeschylus Agamemnon*, 91. On this passage and the bibliography connected with it, see William D. Furley, "Motivation in the Parodos of Aeschylus' *Agamemnon*" *CP* 81, no. 2 (April 1986): 109–121.

[96] See Fraenkel's comments, *Aeschylus Agamemnon*, 334, on lines 700 and 701.

In the tale, Aeschylus repeats the words "lion" and "breast-loving" from Calchas's prophecy;[97] however, whereas the earlier passage seemed to forebode the sacrifice of Iphigenia, the latter applies to the tragedy at Troy, foretold at the beginning of Calchas's prophecy. Like the lion's whelp that grew from a young thing that was "delightful to the old" to one that "showed forth its parents' character" and then "caused" (*eteuxen*) havoc, "a 'meal' [*dait'*] with the disastrous slaughter of many sheep," so with time Helen and Paris brought destruction upon Troy. (Helen, the subject of the next stanza, [737–749], is especially singled out for illustration by the tale.[98]) In these lines, with the help of the verb *teukhō* ("cause"), used in the past tense here (731) rather than in the future tense as it was in the prophecy, and the repetition of *dait'* ("meal," 731) from *adaiton* ("inedible"), Aeschylus expresses one fulfillment of the prophecy.

In the continuation of *Sanemori*, Zeami explicitly translates the statement made in the maeba that a person can reach heaven with one invocation of Amida Buddha into the shite's request for an invocation. At the end of his first recitation of the nochiba, the shite says:

Inochi wa *muryō*jūbutsu to no o tanomoshiya
       infinite
Life is   Buddha, invoke him.
      Amida

This request involves a pivot word, a kakekotoba[99]—*inochi wa muryō* means "life eternal"; *muryōjūbutsu* means "Amida Buddha," the name one should invoke. The name of Amida Buddha is then emphasized in the issei, the exchange that follows, by Zeami's explicit definition of what each part of the name means literally. The shite begins by saying, "Every time [*nennen*] a person repeats the name of Amida Buddha"; the chorus continues, "Then, every time [*nennen*] he is saved." With a stamp of the foot the shite adds, *Namu to ippa* ("As for *namu*"); the chorus explains the meaning of *namu*—"That is, to submit one's destiny to Buddha." With a stamp of the other foot the shite says, *Amida to ippa* ("As for *Amida*"); the chorus explains the meaning of Amida—"By virtue of righteous acts." Like his etymological and etiological explanations elsewhere, Zeami's definition of Amida Buddha's name, the name one invokes as the means to salvation, specifies concretely and explicitly an important ingredient of the play. The best illustration of this practice in Aeschylus's work is that pas-

[97] On the repetition of *philomaston*, see Fraenkel, *Aeschylus Agamemnon*, 84.

[98] That Helen is not the only one to whom the tale applies, see Bernard M. W. Knox, "The Lion in the House," *CP* 47 (January 1952): 17–25. See also Rosenmeyer, *Art of Aeschylus*, 123–124.

[99] See *YKS*, 269 n. 26. The same commentary (270 n. 2) mentions that the shite's recitation is inspired by the *Ōjōyōshū* (Compendium on Rebirth into Paradise).

sage of the *Eumenides* in which Athena founds the court of the Areopagus in which Orestes will be acquitted and in which she, a god, will serve as the judge (681–706), and in so doing explicates the literal meaning of the name "hill of Ares."

In *Sanemori*, in addition to the etymological definition of Amida Buddha's name, the "dramatic action" of the nochiba, that is, the meeting of the priest and the ghost of the warrior, also makes more explicit what was suggested in the maeba. The priest first acknowledges the presence of the old man. He says,

Amazing!	*Fushigi* ya na
On the surface of the *pond*	Shiramiaitaru *ike* no omo ni
growing white from the	
light of dawn,	
The one faintly *floating* into view	Kasuka ni *ukami* yoru mono o
Is the *old man* he [I] just saw,	Mireba aritsuru *okina* naru ga
But he is dressed in armor. It is	Katchū o tai suru. *Fushigi* sa yo.
amazing.	

The words *ike*, *ukami*, and *okina*, repeated from the maeba, where they referred to the setting (i.e., the pond at Shinowara); the boat floating to Paradise (and one being saved); and the old man, have been translated into the appearance of the *old man* (the shite dressed in armor) *"floating"* into view over the surface of the *pond* (that is, gliding across the stage). Immediately before the old man revealed his identity to the priest in the maeba, he quoted Yorimasa's poem about a cherry tree. The priest reacted to the revelation by saying *fushigi ya*, "It is amazing!" Here the priest repeats his expression of amazement: *fushigi ya na* and *fushigi sa yo* in the context of the shite's quotation of the first lines of two poems written by Yorimasa.

The shite's response to the waki begins with the following lines:

[Like] a fossil tree	Umoregi no
That no one knows,	Hito shirenu mi to
Submerged.	Shizumedomo.

The original poem by Yorimasa from which the first line is drawn reads as follows:[100]

Like a fossil tree	Umoregi no
That has borne not a blossom	Hana saku koto mo
Sad has been my life	Nakarishini

[100] The poem appears in the *Heike*, bk. 4, ch. 12, and also at the end of the nō *Yorimasa*. The first line of the poem is used in other nō as well, for example, *Sotoba Komachi*.

Sadder still to end my days	Mi no naru hate zo
Leaving no fruit behind me.[101]	Kanashikarikeru.

The poem refers to Yorimasa's old age and the loss of his sons. In the battle at Uji, the wounded Yorimasa decided to commit suicide; however, the enemy approached and his sons, coming to his defense, were killed in battle. Yorimasa, no longer wanting to live, requested from one Watanabe that his head be cut off, a request to which the latter agreed if Yorimasa would first kill himself. Thereupon, Yorimasa prayed to Amida Buddha ten times, composed the poem, and thrust the point of the sword into his side. Zeami quotes only the first line of this poem, as much as is appropriate to the specific case of Sanemori, who, like Yorimasa, fought his last battle at an old age and thought that he would be forgotten by posterity.

In the second line of the shite's response, "that no one knows," Zeami uses the first line of another poem by Yorimasa. The original reads as follows:

One whom no one knows—	Hito shirenu
The Imperial palace	Ōuchiyama no
Keeper	Yamamori wa
From behind the shade trees	Kogakurete nomi
Gazes at the moon.	Tsuki o miru kana.

This poem, which appears in another chapter of the *Heike*,[102] was written by Yorimasa to the Imperial court in the hope that he might receive a promotion in rank that would allow him to look upon the "moon" (that is, the emperor) from within rather than from without the palace. (He was promoted on this occasion.) Once again, Zeami quotes only that part of the poem which applies to the case of Sanemori, the part regarding his anonymity. In the next line of the nō, Zeami's own composition, the word *shizumedomo* ("submerged"), associated in meaning with the words *ukami* ("float") and *ike* ("pond") in the waki's preceding speech, lyrically expresses the depths of Sanemori's tragic condition.[103] The word provides a link between the fates of Yorimasa and Sanemori, both of whom wanted to avoid "submersion," that is, anonymity.

Although Zeami's use of three poems written by Yorimasa need provide no more than poetic enhancement to the contexts in which they appear, I suggest that they help to associate the fates of the two old warriors from the *Heike* and to enhance the reputation of Sanemori. Yorimasa was distinguished for his poetry as Sanemori was not; Yorimasa had a higher rank

---

[101] The translation is that of Kitagawa and Tsuchida in *The Tale of the Heike* (Tokyo, 1977), 1: 271.
[102] The poem is quoted in the *Heike*, bk. 4, ch. 14.
[103] This is another example of engo. See *YKS*, 270 n. 6.

than Sanemori; Yorimasa is featured in the *Heike* as a great warrior fighter more often than is Sanemori.[104] However, in writing a nō about each of the old warriors, Zeami diminishes the differences. Yorimasa and his forces were defeated and he committed suicide at the battle of Uji—in the nō *Yorimasa* the ghost of the warrior wants to be saved; Sanemori, fighting on the other side when it was defeated, died at the battle of Shinowara— in the nō *Sanemori* he too as a ghost wants to be saved. I would suggest further that, given Zeami's inclusion of Yorimasa's poems in the nō *Yorimasa* and his addition to and embellishment of the epic version of Yorimasa's death there with the etiology of a specific spot at Uji, the Fanshaped Turf, by which the warrior could be remembered, Zeami may prepare, through the references to Yorimasa's poems in *Sanemori*, for the original lyric line that he adds to and with which he embellishes the *Heike* account at the end of the nō on behalf of the warrior Sanemori. In this way, Sanemori is remembered not only for bravery, but for poetry as well, both that which Zeami has borrowed from elsewhere and that which he has composed on behalf of one not known as an artist himself.

Aeschylus's allusion in *Agamemnon* 48–49, where Menelaus and Agamemnon are compared in a simile to vultures (*aigupiōn*) crying out (*klazontes*) "Ares," to two epic passages that contain a simile comparing humans to vultures (*Iliad* 16.428–429 and *Odyssey* 16.216–218), functions in part like Zeami's use of Yorimasa's poems: both playwrights, like other authors, heighten the mood of the contexts in which the borrowed material appears. Aeschylus's simile comparing Menelaus and Agamemnon, who go off to a war in which both Greeks and Trojans suffered alike (see 66–67), to vultures recalls Homer's simile in the *Iliad* comparing the Trojan warrior Sarpedon and the Greek warrior Patroclus, when they go after each other on the battlefield crying aloud (*keklēgontes*), to vultures (*aigupioi*) going after each other and crying (*klazonte*) loudly. This "literary" echo heightens the foreboding of the passage in the *Agamemnon*. Because Aeschylus says in the continuation of the simile that the vultures have lost their young, he also alludes to Homer's comparison of the shrill crying (*klaion*) of Odysseus and his son Telemachus, when after many years they are reunited, to the crying of vultures (*aigupioi*) whose nestlings have been stolen by farmers. This echo heightens the personal tragedy of Agamemnon, whose situation is the antithesis to that of Odysseus: Agamemnon kills his daughter, is killed by his wife, and does not live to see his son; Odysseus returns to the faithful Penelope and, in the passage alluded to, is reunited with Telemachus. There are many obvious differences between

---

[104] In bk. 4, ch. 14 of the *Heike*, Yorimasa is awarded a fine robe for killing the monster Nue. However, we also learn from the epic account that Yorimasa had foolishly attempted nō raise a rebellion against the Heike.

Zeami's and Aeschylus's approaches to literary allusion, both of which I have simplified for the sake of this study. The examples under discussion point to one specific difference. The figure Yorimasa, through whom Zeami sets Sanemori's fate into perspective, is both the subject and the author of the poems quoted. Here, as in other examples, the author of the poetry to which Zeami alludes is linked to the subject of the nō. This type of linkage seems not to occur in Greek tragedy; unless, that is, Aeschylus was alluding in the simile, as he may have been, to Archilochus's poem frr. 172–181 (West), which expresses that poet's personal feelings toward Lycambes by means of the fable of the fox and the eagle.[105]

Zeami does not dwell on a connection between Yorimasa and Sanemori. Instead, he continues with words from another poem and by a different author:[106]

| From the pond [i.e., depths] of the heart | Kokoro no ike no |
| *To express* is difficult. . . . | *Iigataki.* . . . |

(These words are syntactically connected with words that are not in the poem: "The innumerable agonies of the warrior hell in which [I] float.") The original version of the poem reads as follows:

At Oyamada	Oyamada no
For transplanting rice the water	Nawashiro mizu wa
Is plentiful [which]	Taenu tomo
The pond in the heart	Kokoro no ike no
Emits.	Ii wa hanataji.

The original poem states that the supply of water for transplanting rice at Oyamada is plentiful (literally, "endless"), even as the release of water from the heart, that is, the feeling of love, is plentiful. Although the subject of love is irrelevant to the nō, the quoted words add a poetic resonance. In addition, with the use of but two syllables from the poem, *ii*, Zeami is able both to prepare for the warrior's confession and to suggest the difficulty

---

[105] On the possibility of an Archilochean influence here, see M. L. West, "The Parodos of the *Agamemnon*," *CQ*, 29, no. 1 (1979): 1–6, and R. Janko, "Aeschylus' *Oresteia* and Archilochus," *CQ* 30, no. 2 (1980): 291–293. The verbal similarities between Aeschylus's and Archilochus's images are not close as they are between Aeschylus's and Homer's similes. The parallels are in content: Menelaus has lost his wife Helen to the Trojan Paris, Archilochus has lost his fiancée to his father-in-law Lycambes. On the complexities of epic allusion in this passage in particular, see P. E. Easterling, "Notes on Tragedy and Epic," *Papers Given at a Colloquium on Greek Drama in Honour of R. P. Winnington-Ingram*, The Society for the Promotion of Hellenic Studies. Suppl. Paper 15 (1987): 52–62.

[106] A poem in the imperial anthology of poetry, the *Gosenshū*. See YKS, 270 n. 7 and Itō, *Yōkyokushū*, 113 n. 16.

Sanemori has in expressing himself. Up to and including the syllables *ii*, which mean "express" or "release," the poem suggests that there is a release from the depths (literally, "pond") of the warrior's heart, like the release of water from a water pipe in a rice field. However, in combination with the suffix *-gataki*, meaning "difficult," the two syllables mean "tell" and the compound word, *iigataki*, means "difficult to tell."

At this point in the nochiba, the kakeai, and at a juncture comparable to the end of the third dan of the maeba, the waki and shite sing as one person. Here, by means of both intricate and extensive verbal interaction, the appearance of the dramatic character on stage, wearing an old man's mask with white hair and beard, a brocade robe, and a warrior's costume, is associated with the moon and a bright night.

WAKI: I see a form, the *traces* of snow,	Miru ya sugata mo *nokori* no *yuki* no
SHITE: White hair and beard of the old warrior, but	Binpige shiroki rōmusha naredomo.
WAKI: Brilliant is the appearance	Sono idetachi wa hanayaka naru
SHITE: Of his outfit, *bright*	Yosooi koto ni *kumorinaki*
WAKI: Is the moon's radiance	Tsuki no hikari
SHITE: In the burning lantern's light	Tomoshibi no kage
CHORUS: Not dark	Kurakaranu
Is the night's *mantle*	Yoru no *nishiki* no
A *brocade* robe.	Hitatare ni.

In the waki's first line, the word *nokori* ("traces," literally meaning "remainder"), is a pivot word between the tenor word *sugata* ("form")—the form of the warrior's ghost remains—and the vehicle word *yuki* ("snow")—there are traces of snow.[107] "Snow," in turn, is a natural introduction for the words "hair and beard of the old warrior," which, like snow, are "white" (*shiroki*). In the shite's second line, the word *kumorinaki*, meaning "clear" and "bright" (literally, "cloudless"), which was used earlier in connection with the glory of Buddha's light, the moon, the heart, the voices, and the bell, serves as a significant verbal link between the person and the moon.[108] Although it reinforces the word *hanayaka* ("brilliant"), used to describe the outfit worn by Sanemori, in its literal sense *kumorinaki* is more suitable as a description of the moon's light, which is both the vehicle (that is, the moon stands for enlightenment) and the tenor (that is, the night is bright and moonlit). The verbal connection Zeami makes between the brightness of the moon's radiance and that of a

---

[107] See Koyama, 192 n. 9.
[108] See YKS, 270 n. 10.

burning lantern helps to lessen the distinctions between enlightenment and the human realm.[109] Further, *nishiki* ("mantle") is a pivot word between "night," with which it functions as a vehicle word, and the warrior's robe made out of "brocade," the literal meaning of *nishiki*, with which it functions as part of the tenor.[110] The verbal interaction is connected visually to the performance on stage, inasmuch as the shite wears the bearded mask and wig of an old man and a bright brocade robe.

The degree of complexity in the verbal interaction of the kakeai finds a parallel in Aeschylus's *Agamemnon*, lines 1178–83. There Cassandra, speaking in "prosaic" iambic trimeters, says:

And no longer will the *prophecy* from behind veils	Kai mēn ho *khrēsmos* ouket' ek kalummatōn
Look out like a newly-wedded bride, but	Estai dedorkōs neogamou numphēs dikēn,
Clear toward the rising of the sun	*Lampros* d'eoiken hēliou pros antolas
Blowing it will arrive, so that like a wave	Pneōn ephēxein, hōste kumatos dikēn
It will surge toward the rays much greater than this suffering.	Kluzein pros augas toude pēmatos polu/meizon.

Khrēsmos ("prophecy"), the tenor and the subject at issue, which serves as the grammatical subject of the entire passage,[111] is identified with the vehicles: the wind, an unveiled bride, and a wave surging toward the sun. The word *lampros*, meaning "bright" and "clear," serves as a link between the different parts of the passage in a manner analogous to the words meaning "bright" in the passage from *Sanemori*. (In this particular example, Aeschylus's style is more economical than Zeami's in the kakeai: the latter accumulates a number of words meaning "bright"; Aeschylus uses only one word.) Describing the prophecy, *lampros* connotes "unambiguous"; describing the face of the unveiled bride, "bright-complexioned"; describing the wind, "keen"; describing a wave's surge, "clear." The word is also suited to a description of the sun mentioned in the passage, since it can mean "bright." The various levels of both the tenor (Cassandra and her prophecy) and the vehicle (an unveiled bride, blowing wind, and sun) are connected by means of one word. In addition, the passage, like the

[109] See ibid., 270 n. 11.

[110] On the verbal interaction of the passage, see Koyama, 192 n. 12.

[111] I discuss the passage also in "Breaking Down the Barriers between Text and Audience in Noh and Aeschylean Drama," in *Ancient and Modern: Essays in Honor of Gerald F. Else*, ed. John H. D'Arms and John W. Eadie (Ann Arbor, 1977), 24–25.

kakeai, may refer to aspects of the dramatic character: both the delivery of Cassandra's words, which are more clearly articulated than the excited lyric meters in which she has spoken before this speech, and her appearance, the bright complexion of the mask. If the actor playing the role of Cassandra lifts a veil and reveals the bright complexion of his mask, then the vehicle interacts with this kinetic element of performance as well.

In the continuation of the nō, Zeami connects the tenor of the kakeai with the tenor of the play, namely, the religious message, in the ageuta that follows. The chorus sings:

He wears green armor	Moegi nioi no yoroi kite
And swords with sheaths decorated in *gold*.	*Koganezukuri no tachikatana.*
But, I ask, under the present conditions	Ima no mi nite wa, soretote mo
What kind of *treasures* are these?	Nani ka *takara* no,
In the Lake of *Treasures*, there is a lotus	Ike no hachisu no
Calyx, this should be the real *treasure*.	Utena koso *takara* narubekere.
Indeed, there is no doubt	Geniya utagawanu
The teaching of the Law *does not tarnish*.	Nori no oshie wa, *kuchi mo senu.*
If the *golden* words you respect,	*Kogane* no kotoba *omoku*seba,
Why should you not be there?	Nado ka wa itarazaru beki.

In this song, the chorus, speaking for the priest, moralizes on the subject of worldly treasures. The first use of the word *takara* ("treasure") refers to the armor and the swords of the warrior; the second use refers to the "lotus calyx" in Buddha's Lake, which the chorus adds is the real treasure.[112] In neither reference is there an image. Through the repetition of a word, Zeami connects the character's worldly treasures with those of Buddha, only to devalue the importance of the former.[113] The chorus then adds that the teaching of the Law *kuchi mo senu*, "does not tarnish," as we infer gold does. This inference is justified by the next words, *kogane no* ("golden"), in the sentence, "If the golden words you respect, why should you not be there [that is, reach Paradise, in which Buddha's Lake is located]." The relationship between gold and Buddha's teachings is shown by the repetition of the word *kogane* ("gold") and supported by the asso-

---

[112] On the repetition, see *YKS*, 271 n. 15.

[113] This theme appears frequently in the religious works, the Amida sutra and *Jōgyō-wasan*. Itō, *Yōkyokushū*, 114 n. 3.

ciation of meanings between *kuchi mo senu* and *omokuseba*. The latter word means "if you respect," but its first three syllables alone mean "heavy," as metal. Thus *omokuseba*, through verbal interaction, connects the gold with the golden words,[114] and the character's worldly treasures, the immediate tenor, previously connected with nature, with Buddha's "heavenly" treasures, the religious tenor of the play. Zeami maintains the relationship between these spheres throughout the kakeai and the ageuta.

Similarly, in lines 434–444 of the *Agamemnon*, Aeschylus interrelates one tenor with another through a type of verbal interaction that is comparable to that of the ageuta analyzed above. The chorus sings:

. . . Instead of men	. . . Anti de phōtōn
Armor and [*urns* with] *ashes* [dust] to each one's home arrive.	*Teukhē* kai *spodos* eis hekastou domous aphikneitai.
The gold-*changer* Ares, *changer* of bodies	Ho khrus*amoibos* d'Arēs sōmatōn
And holder of the scales in the battle of the spear	Kai talantoukhos en makhēi doros
Sends from Troy	*Purōthen* ex Iliou
To the dear ones the *burnt* and *heavy*	Philoisi pempei *baru*
Dust that brings hateful tears, with *ashes* in exchange for men filling the *jars* easily-stowed.[115]	*Psēgma dusdakruton* antēnoros *spodou* gemizōn *lebētas* euthetous.

The word *teukhē*, meaning both "urns" (the idea is resumed later with the word *lebētas*, "jars," 444) and "armor," and the word *spodos*, meaning both "dust" and "ashes" (the word is repeated and the idea supported later by the use of *psēgma*, meaning "dust," 442), begin, like the word *takara* ("treasure") in *Sanemori*, the process by which two tenors are interrelated. The sentence suggests that both armor and ashes of the men who died at Troy, as well as urns filled with dust (that is, gold dust), the loot from war, were returned to the home of each man. In the continuation of the choral song, the relationship between these two meanings is supported by Aeschylus's use of the suffix *-amoibos* as a pivot between Ares as *khrusamoibos* ("exchanger of gold") and as *-amoibos* . . . *sōmatōn*

---

[114] See *YKS*, 271 n. 17.
[115] This translation is greatly influenced by that of Fraenkel, *Aeschylus Agamemnon*, 1: 117–118. In the last line, I print Auratus's *euthetous*, an adjective with *lebētas*, in place of the manuscript reading *euthetou*.

("changer of bodies").[116] The words *purōthen* and *baru psēgma* ("burnt" and "heavy dust") also suggest two meanings, namely, "heavy ashes of men cremated,"[117] a meaning reinforced by the word *dusdakruton* ("that brings hateful tears" and also "burnt, heavy gold dust"). Aeschylus says that the ashes of many men who died at Troy were sent to Greece, but simultaneously suggests that gold dust was sent to Greece, a preparation for his later warning against the dangers of excessive wealth and the punishment that comes from the gods.

In *Sanemori*, Zeami turns immediately from the ageuta to the warrior's statement in the kuri that if one invokes Amida Buddha once, one's innumerable sins will pass away, and then to the chorus's observation, derived from the *Kammuryōju* sutra, that a heart blessed with its own virtue desires Paradise.[118] The chorus adds a request that the warrior not leave his heart behind in attachment. In other words, the playwright establishes explicitly the religious point introduced earlier by means of verbal interaction.

In the sashi that follows, the shite acknowledges that he has received the teachings difficult to encounter.[119] The teachings then take effect in the following section. There the chorus, speaking for the warrior, says that he will tell his tale:

The tale of shame and repentance—	Zangisange no monogatari—
Still he [I] cannot forget the past	Nao mo mukashi o wasurekanete
And recollects how at Shinowara	*Shinobu ni* nitaru Shinowara no
He [I] died like dew on the grassy plain.	Kusa no kage no no tsuyu to kieshi
He [I] will endure to tell his tale.	Arisama katari mosubeshi.

Within these lines is embedded the phrase *shinobu ni*, which is not directly translated above with a single equivalent phrase in English. It means not only "recollect," but also "endure" and "a kind of ferngrass."[120] My English version attempts to bring out these meanings by rendering *wasurekanete* as "forget," followed by "recollects"; *kusa no kage no no* as "grassy plain"; and *mosubeshi* as "endure to tell." Emphasized by alliteration with

<hr>

[116] See Fraenkel, *Aeschylus Agamemnon*, 2: 229.
[117] See ibid., 2: 230.
[118] According to YKS, 271 n. 21, there are three hearts: *ekōhotsuganshin*, one blessed with its own virtue; *shisetsushin*, one blessed with sincerity; and *jinshin*, one blessed with depth of feeling. Of these, the last two are capable of being suspicious and attached to this world.
[119] His words, found in other nō as well, are derived from a *rokudō kōshiki*, a Buddhist service. See YKS, 431 n. 39.
[120] See ibid., 271 n. 25.

Shinowara in the same line, the single phrase *shinobu ni*[121] points through its three different denotations to the physical setting of Shinowara on the grassy plain of which the warrior died; to his recollection of the past that is the cause of his suffering; and to his new resolve to tell the tale that can bring him release from that suffering. It is to the tale of the warrior's last battle, "a tale of repentance" (*zangisange no monogatari*), that Zeami next turns.

Before discussing the narrative account of Sanemori's death in battle, I offer by way of partial analogy to Zeami's use of *shinobu* a passage from the *Agamemnon* in which Aeschylus takes advantage, not of two connotations, but of two different denotations each of two words. In lines 134–136 of the *Agamemnon*, the chorus, reporting Calchas's prophecy, says:

In pity Artemis the holy one is angry	Oiktōi gar epiphthonos Artemis hagna
At the flying hounds of the father,	Ptanoisin kusi patros
Eating the young and all before birth in the wretched cowering animal.	Autotokon pro lokhou mogeran ptaka thuomenoisin.

Since there is no pronoun or article expressed with the word *patros* ("father"), it can refer either to Artemis's father, Zeus, or to Iphigenia's father, Agamemnon. The sentence can be understood to mean that Artemis holds Zeus, who is suggested by the words "flying hounds," responsible for the destruction of Troy, which is metaphorically suggested by the pregnant animal. However, since the word *thuomenoisin*, translated "eating," literally means "sacrificing," an action inappropriate to the agents of gods (men sacrifice to the gods, not gods to men), and since the father is not specified, the meaning of the sentence shifts with this last word to Agamemnon's sacrifice of his daughter. The polysemous words *autotokon*, meaning both "young and all" and "his own child," and *pro lokhou*, meaning both "before birth" and "before the military host," support either of these interpretations.[122] On the second of these interpretations the lines would be translated as follows:

In pity Artemis the holy one is angry
At the flying hounds [that is, the attendants] of the father,
Sacrificing his own child, the shivering poor creature, before the host.

[121] See ibid., 271 n. 26.
[122] Fraenkel, *Aeschylus Agamemnon*, 2: 82: "We cannot say whether Aeschylus found the word in earlier poetry in the sense of 'giving birth' or gave it the new meaning himself . . . , which in view of the obvious etymology and the connection with *lokhios, lokheusthai, lokheia* would be easy enough."

In this passage Aeschylus refers simultaneously to two different events with an economy of style reminiscent not only of the sashi in the nochiba of *Sanemori*, but also of many other passages in this and other nō. It should not be surprising to the reader that the Aeschylean passage, like that of Cassandra's speech analyzed above, appears in the context of prophecy, the style of which is consistently ambiguous (that is, polysemous), both within tragedy and without. The voices of the elders, inspired by god, and of Cassandra, a prophetess, raise the level of discourse from the prosaic and down-to-earth to a loftier spiritual level.

Although the style of nō is more fluid and less discursive than that of Aeschylus, similarities in the structures of *Sanemori* and the *Persians* and in the language of *Sanemori* and the *Agamemnon* certainly justify the conclusion that Aeschylus's style, like Zeami's, is directed toward performance and emphasizes words *qua* words, and that the outlook of both playwrights is religious. In the remainder of *Sanemori*, where Zeami focuses on the story of the warrior's death in the battle of Shinowara and its attendant circumstances and closely follows the narrative account of the *Heike* (bk. 7, ch. 8), the playwright's style is quite different from the approach to Homer taken by Aeschylus or the other tragedians. I offer below a brief discussion of these concluding passages so that the reader unfamiliar with the conventions of shura nō may see how closely Zeami adheres to the original, as we know it, and where and why he diverges from it. Zeami's use of the epic material is in the spirit, if not the form, of Aeschylus's alteration of history in the *Persians* in terms of his own milieu. In addition, further lyric sections appear in the final section of *Sanemori* that bear directly on this comparison.

In the narration itself, the katari, verbal interest lies not in poetic techniques such as I have been discussing, but rather in Zeami's adaptation of the "epic" story to the nō.[123] As I said in Chapter One, for the sake of creating a jo-ha-kyū development, Zeami chooses to present material from the *Heike* about the identification of Sanemori's head *before* narrating the actual battle scene, which is postponed until the end of the nō. In addition, within the section represented by the katari, Zeami makes some alterations in the "epic" version.[124] For example, when the shite tells how Mitsumori brought the head of his opponent to his commanding officer, Lord Kiso, he says that Mitsumori remarked first that his opponent seemed like a great leader but had no forces behind him, and second that he seemed like

---

[123] A translation of the katari set next to a translation of the relevant section of the *Heike* appears in Appendix 2, along with a similar set of translations for the kuse and the rongi.

[124] On the alterations Zeami made in the katari, kuse, and the rongi, see Hoff and Hoff, "Staging Epic," and Kobayashi, "Heike monogatari," 683–714.

an ordinary warrior but wore a brocade robe. The order of the two remarks is reversed from that in the *Heike* account so that the brocade robe,
which is important in the following kuse, appears second, in a position of
emphasis.

In the continuation of the katari, Zeami follows the narrative order of
the *Heike*: the shite adds to Mitsumori's statement that his adversary re-
fused to divulge his name and that he spoke in a Kantō dialect; he then
reports Lord Kiso's reaction—a preliminary identification of Sanemori's
head, but an expression of surprise that the hair and beard are not gray—
and his summoning of Higuchi, a former friend of Sanemori; next he presents Higuchi's reaction, his tears and a verbal outburst of pity at the sight
of Sanemori's head, which he then identifies. The katari ends with the
shite's narration of Higuchi's account of what Sanemori had said in the
past, namely that if he went into battle at an old age he would color his
hair and beard black and die fighting like a young man. Although the narration follows the *Heike* closely, Zeami abbreviates the account: he omits
Lord Kiso's remark that, when he was only a young boy, he had seen Sanemori, and Kiso's interruption of Higuchi with a question about the color
of the hair. Most significantly, whereas the *Heike* account concludes with
an observation that the head of the warrior was washed and the hair and
beard became white, the katari ends with the words, "Scarcely had he spoken when holding the head." The words describe an action taken in response to Higuchi's request that the warriors have the head washed and
see for themselves whether the hair was dyed, and they are accompanied
by the movements of the shite who mimes the action—an action mentioned but not described in the *Heike*. The *Heike* version of the identification of the head ends with the words, ". . . though his soul had departed
from his body. How sad it is that his corpse mingled with the dust of that
northern province." Zeami saves this idea for the end of the nō, where it
is suitably appended to an account of Sanemori's death in battle, the action
reported at the beginning of the *Heike* chapter about Sanemori.

The shite's movements on stage continue to represent those of Higuchi;
however, Zeami embellishes the *Heike* account with his own words and a
verbal device. The chorus sings:

He leaves the lord's presence	Onmae o tatte atari naru
And faces the shore of the pond	Kono ikenami no kishi ni
	nozomite
In whose green waters he sees	*Mizu* no midori mo kageutsuru
reflected	
The leaves of willow branches	Yanagi no ito no eda tarete.
hanging above.	

The shift from a description of Higuchi's movements towards the pond to a description of the setting pivots on the syllable *mi*, homophonic with *mi*, meaning "see," in the word *mizu*, "water."[125] Higuchi goes to the *water* and *sees* the green color of the willow branches reflected in it.

The reference to a willow tree, green in color like the armor worn by Sanemori, introduces a poem to which Zeami alludes in the following lines:[126]

The weather is clearing,	Ki harete wa
The hair of the young willows	Kaze shinryu no
Is combed by the wind.	Kami o kezuri,
The ice is melted,	Kōri kiete wa
The beard of the old moss	Nami kiutai no
Is washed by the waves.	Hige o araite.

The words "hair," "comb," "beard," and "wash," which are metaphorical in the poem written by Miyako no Yoshika, are germane to the tenor of the nō.[127] "Hair" and "beard" point to the hair and beard of Sanemori being washed by Higuchi and to the miming action of the shite. Moreover, while the first words in the poem, "the weather is clearing," are not metaphorical in their original context, they assume a metaphorical function in the nō, suggesting that Sanemori's mind is clearing and that he will lose his attachment to the world. By alluding to a poem after the narrative of the katari, Zeami creates a lyric moment in the nō.

After the quotation of the poem and a reference to the nobility of Sanemori, Zeami returns to the *Heike*, not in a narrative form, like the katari, which approximates the delivery of a bard, but in a choral song, the kuse, in the midst of which the shite delivers one line.[128] Although Zeami follows the *Heike* account fairly closely, Zeami does not mention Sanemori's cowardly flight as the reason he wanted to fight in battle, wearing a brocade robe. In addition, he again embellishes the *Heike* account by adding the poem: "Maple leaves, while brushing them aside, he returns home wearing brocade and the people see him."[129] The robe, introduced in the first half of the kuse in a saying from the classics and in Sanemori's request that

[125] *YKS*, 272 n. 4, states that *mi* supports, rather than serves as a pivot.

[126] The poem is found in the *Wakan rōeishū*, an anthology of poetry. See *YKS*, 272 n. 5. The version of the poem given in the text is taken from *YKS*.

[127] *YKS*, 272 n. 5, states that "comb the hair" and "wash the beard" are examples of *jo*, introductory words.

[128] See Appendix 2 for a translation of both the kuse and the *Heike* version.

[129] The poem is from the *Gosenshū*, an imperial anthology of poetry. See *YKS*, 272 n. 16. The section of the *Heike* covering Sanemori's death in battle does not contain poetry, as many other chapters do. According to Itō, *Yōkyokushū*, 116 n. 6, this poem has the tone of a *honmon* ("authoritative expression").

Lord Munemori permit him to wear one, is mentioned in the poem itself. The poem, in turn, is "in the spirit of the original saying," that is, a proverb associated in both the *Heike* and the nō with the paradigm of the Chinese Shubaijin (Chu Mai-ch'en),[130] who waved the sleeves of his brocade robe in the battle of Kaikei.

The layering and depth of literary allusion here reach a degree of complexity not previously encountered in the play. Zeami, who earlier has had the shite speak for his epic counterpart only through the words of another Heike character, here allows him to speak about himself in the narrative voice. He thus creates a new relationship between the two Sanemoris, the Sanemori of the nō and the Sanemori of the *Heike*. To these he adds the poem and the proverb. These all combine to associate Sanemori's name with that of Shubaijin in a connection that is made visible on stage by means of a gesture: the shite twirls the sleeve of his costume tightly over his arm as the chorus tells how Shubaijin waved his sleeves.

Zeami concludes the kuse with a verbal transition from the past to the dramatic present. In the last lines of the kuse, the chorus sings:

Visible to all	Kakurenakarishi
The celebrated warrior	Yumitori no
His name *has lasted* through	Na wa matsudai ni
generations.	
Without ceasing till *dawn*	Ariyake no
Throughout the moonlit night	Tsuki no yosugara
He will relate his tale of	Sange monogatari mōsan.
repentance.	

The first two syllables of the word *ariyake*, meaning "dawn," serve as a kakekotoba between the three lines on the subject of the celebrated warrior that precede and the three on the subject of the warrior ghost's tale of repentance that follow. The syllables *ari*, which mean "is" (and are translated "has lasted"), function as the verb ("is" links "visible" and "warrior's name" in the first three lines) and as the first two syllables of the word *ariyake* in the last three lines.[131] The words *matsudai ni* also serve a linking function: with what precedes, they mean "through generations"; with what follows, "without ceasing."[132] Zeami says both that the warrior's name will last *forever* and that he will *continue* to relate his tale of

---

[130] The proverb is a *honmon* ("authoritative expression"), here from the Chinese history *Kanjo*, ch. 64. Itō, *Yōkyokushū*, 116 n. 7. On Chu Mai-ch'en, see above, Chapter One, note 108.

[131] See *YKS*, 273 n. 20.

[132] See ibid., 273 n. 19.

repentance. The latter of these two statements is emphasized in the beginning of the rongi with the words,

Indeed, the tale of repentance. . . .   Geniya sange no monogatari. . . .

The focus of the nō at this point is the tale of repentance that the chorus,
speaking for the priest, asks that the warrior relate so that he can cleanse
the water in his heart and leave no impurities behind. In the rongi, the shite
tells the tale, which is an account of his death in battle, drawn again from
the *Heike*.[133]

The shite begins his "confession" with words that contain what I consider to be one of the most important kakekotoba within the nō:

The deep-rooted attachment of	Sono mōshū no
Warrior hell	Shura no michi
Going around and around	Meguri megurite
Again to this place	Mata koko ni
Has come—Kiso. . . .	Kiso to. . . .

The words *mata* ("again") and *koko ni* ("to this place") direct the shite's
words to the warrior's cause of attachment, namely that Sanemori could
not fight and kill Lord Kiso because Tezuka, a less distinguished warrior,
intervened. The occasion of this resentment, as I have already mentioned,
is expressed in the syllable *ki*: in itself it means "has come," but simultaneously it serves as the first syllable of Kiso's name.[134] Thus Zeami uses a
verbal device to bring the "plot" of the play, the process by which the
warrior's salvation is attained, to a climax. Here, it is not a speech, nor a
line, nor a phrase, nor even a word, but a single syllable that functions as
the link between the warrior's acknowledgment of his attachment and the
cause of it.[135] Although the tale is drawn from the *Heike*, it is significant

[133] See Appendix 2 for a translation of both the rongi and the *Heike* version.
[134] See *YKS*, 273 n. 23.
[135] To understand better how the syllable functions as a pivot here, one might look at
the example of the *Suppliants*, line 322. There, when the king Pelasgus asks the maidens
to tell him the name of their father's brother, hating that very name, they at first respond
with an interjection, *ai* ("alas"), and then fill out the hated name, *Aiguptos*. The one
syllable *ai* might very well serve the double function of being an interjection of woe and
the first part of the name that is the cause of the woe, inasmuch as Aeschylus seems to
prepare for the apparent pun on this name with puns on two other names in the immediately preceding lines: in lines 313–315 he puns on Epaphus's name, meaning "laying
upon of hands," which echoes from two lines earlier syllables in the noun *ephaptōr* ("the
one who lays hands upon," that is, Zeus, the father of Epaphus); in lines 320–321 he
may be punning on the name Danaus, which because it is etymologically associated with
da-, meaning "learn," picks up the adjective "all-wise" (*pansophou*) in the preceding
line. With the reading of the manuscript *to pansophon onoma* ("the all-wise name"),
Aeschylus could have emphasized a pun on Danaus's name. We cannot say that Aeschylus intended the pun on Aegyptus; however, the presence of these other two puns, as

that Sanemori's desire to fight Lord Kiso is not mentioned there, that the dramatic character Sanemori is at this point in the nō speaking in his own person as he has not done in either the katari or kuse, and that the actor stamps his foot on the floor of the stage both before and after he expresses the word *Kiso* so as to draw attention to it.

Although Zeami follows the account in the *Heike* closely, he does not include the dialogue between Kiso's retainer, Tezuka, and Sanemori, the content of which might serve to emphasize Sanemori's bravery—he stays and fights when other men flee. Instead, Zeami chooses in the rongi not to have the shite speak in the voice of another character as he has done in the katari and the kuse. In this fast-moving section, the finale, Sanemori speaks in his own voice and uses words drawn from his own Kantō dialect: *gunjōzu yo* ("Ah, you want to grapple," that is, "with Japan's number one warrior"), and *sutetengeri* ("threw away," that is, the head of his victim).[136] In addition, Zeami adds a line in which the warrior expresses his personal feelings: he says, "Alas, he was an old warrior!" Finally, he adds poetic lines to the *Heike* account: "An old tree, beaten by the wind, whose strength is broken." Although these words are poetic, they seem not to have been borrowed as other poems about trees have been, the poems about the cherry tree, the fossil tree, the willow tree, and the maple leaves.[137] Here Zeami has *composed* a poetic line about an old tree to heighten verbally the most exciting moment in his account of the battle scene. The effect is to increase our pity and sympathy for the warrior. Thus Zeami bequeaths to the future *his* version of the warrior's tale, which enhances the warrior's prowess on the battlefield, and *his* poetry, which the chorus sings in celebration of the warrior. The memorable words all combine to make the name of Sanemori "last through generations."

At the end of the rongi, the chorus concludes the nō by calling for prayers on Sanemori's behalf:

He became one with the earth at Shinowara.	Shinowara no tsuchi to natte,
His form and shadow leave no traces.	Kage mo katachi mo naki ato no,
His form and shadow— Namuamidabu.	Kage mo katachi mo *n*amuamidabu.

---

well as the appropriate intonation and gestures by the chorus, would attract the audience to it.

[136] See note 110 of Chapter One.

[137] On the other hand, Itō, *Yōkyokushū*, 117 n. 19, asks whether the poetic lines might not have been inspired by a poem in the *Wakan rōeishū*.

| Offer memorial prayers on his behalf. | Tomuraite tabitamae, |
| Offer memorial prayers on behalf of his ghost [literally, his traces]. | Ato tomuraite tabitamae. |

In the third line, most of which is a repetition of the second line, the syllable *na* in the nembutsu (i.e., the invocation of Amida Buddha) serves as a kakekotoba, pivoting between the invocation and what precedes.[138] By itself *na* serves as a negative that alliterates with *naki* ("not"), the word suggesting that the ghost's attachment to the world is ended; but it is also the first syllable of *namu*, a part of the nembutsu that Zeami defined etymologically near the beginning of the maeba. By means of this verbal device, which appears almost at the end of the nō, Zeami creates a significant connection between the disappearance of the form and shadow of Sanemori's ghost and the nembutsu, the sacred words prescribed throughout the play as a means of reaching salvation.

Zeami does not explicitly say that Sanemori is saved, as, for example, he says Atsumori is in the nō named after him.[139] However, given the warrior's religious conviction, the admission of the cause of his resentment and attachment to this world, the poetic words Zeami composed for him and the alterations he made in the *Heike* version of Sanemori's story, and the use of verbal devices, there is both substantive and stylistic support for belief on the audience's part that Sanemori is saved. Zeami develops the nō gradually but consistently, from divulgence of the warrior's name, through his admission that he needs to be saved, to his recollection of the past (most specifically, of his cause for attachment), and he does so with a careful attention to style that reinforces the overall structure by verbal means and lends it a literary resonance.

[138] See *YKS*, 273 n. 38.
[139] See Kobayashi, "Heike monogatari," 683.

FOUR

The Style of Aeschylean Tragedy

The third chapter has characterized the style of nō and, in preparation for this final chapter, has pointed to Aeschylean passages, especially from the *Agamemnon*, that are analogous to that style. The purpose of the present chapter is to demonstrate not only that Aeschylus's works, like Zeami's, must be thought of as the product of a talented artist who composed his tragedies with the theater audience in mind, but also, and more specifically, to examine how Aeschylus attracted attention to the words of his plays so that the audience in the theater could be made to appreciate them, and how and to what purpose they function as words *qua* words. Furthermore, I will show with the example of the *Persians* that, in spite of the absence of a written literary tradition in Aeschylus's day analogous to that which was available to Zeami, Aeschylus not only used the language and the style of the "literature" he knew, but also, by availing himself of the audience's knowledge of it, like Zeami, made allusions to and borrowed from it in order to add authority to and increase the interest and emotional impact of the tragedy.

There are clear advantages to the use of the comparative method here, as there were in the discussion of structure. I have already mentioned that writings by Aeschylus on his own style do not exist, as they do for Zeami. One can infer that Zeami thought an audience could be made to appreciate words *qua* words and literary allusions, since in his treatises he gives practical advice to actors about which words or syllables to emphasize and how to intone or sing them, and he specifically discusses the subject of borrowing from other literature. Although we cannot reconstruct performers' methods of delivery in tragedy, and although much of the poetry that preceded Aeschylus's day and might have influenced his style is missing or fragmentary, some of Zeami's advice is relevant to a discussion of the tragedian's style. Furthermore, what literature has survived from before or during Aeschylus's day does not bring with it an explicitly formulated poetics, such as we have from Zeami. In fact, much of the subsequent critical tradition, because it developed when rhetorical norms different from those which influenced Aeschylus were in fashion, has tended to hinder rather than to promote an understanding of his work.[1]

The ancient criticism is not all wrong. In fact a good part of it seems to have been influenced by Aristophanes' portrait of Aeschylus in the *Frogs*, a comedy dating from the end of the fifth century B.C., a time when Aeschylus's plays were enjoying a revival in the theater. Aristophanes' observations are surely correct when he suggests that there is a lack of action in Aeschylus's plays and often a delay in the presentation of the main character's first speech, that there is a moral and ethical purpose to his plays, that there is little everyday language and characterization on the one hand and sophistic reasoning on the other, and that Aeschylus knew and admired the works of the great Greek poets. At the same time Aristophanes strongly suggests, and many later critics concur, that Aeschylus's style suffered from an excessive weightiness of diction, a diction that included long compound words, verbal padding that did not add meaning, and an unnecessary repetitiveness of language. Thus, although criticisms expressed by the dramatic characters in his comedy help us identify certain features of Aeschylus's tragedies, Aristophanes' assessment is exaggerated for the sake of comic effect and does not provide us with a serious discussion of Aeschylean style.[2] Unfortunately, Aristophanes has left posterity with the impression that Aeschylus's style was obscure, an impression that to a perceptive critic has shown itself again and again to be an unfair evaluation. Although the remark attributed to Sophocles that even if Aeschylus did what he needed to, he did not do so with understanding, is probably apocryphal,[3] it is one of many ancient testimonia that suggest Aeschylus was not a skilled artist. However, an analysis of Aeschylus's style informs us otherwise, especially when we note that where the critics of the past have found fault with his style, it is often comparable to that of Zeami, who was not only a genius, but also a consummate artist. The alternative to this conclusion is that the "Sophoclean" remark is correct and that Aeschylus

---

[1] William Bedell Stanford has summed up the view of later critics, in *Aeschylus in His Style* (Dublin, 1942), 1–14. See also Americo de Propris, *Eschilo nella critica dei Greci, Studio filologico ed estetico* (Turin, 1941); and Mary R. Lefkowitz, *The Lives of the Greek Poets* (Baltimore, 1981), 67–74.

[2] Although the end of the *Frogs* vindicates Aeschylus's claims to be a good tragedian, it would seem that, in the hopes of evoking laughter, Aristophanes composed jokes at Aeschylus's expense because he believed that at least some members of the audience in his own day did not like the tragic style of the old-fashioned tragedian Aeschylus.

[3] See Athenaeus, *Deipnosophists* 1.22a.

stands alone as a great playwright who was successful in the theater but lacked method. This is patently absurd.

Any analysis of Aeschylus's style must begin and end with his texts, and in that analysis we need to be certain that the ancient critics do not prejudice our views. One way to break out of the mold set so long ago and preserved by those scholars who have been influenced either explicitly or implicitly by the critics of antiquity is to look at a different tradition, a tradition that, precisely because it *is* different and yet shares obvious similarities with Aeschylean tragedy, can suggest a fresh approach to the texts of Aeschylus. The advantages of comparing the style of Aeschylus's tragedies with that of nō include not only those stated above, but also the fact that nō texts are short and verbally economical. This means that to those familiar with the conventions and the language of nō and the poetry that influenced it, the plays reveal better than most traditional theaters not only the skeletons of their structure, but also the characteristic features of their style. We also know that it is legitimate to look for these stylistic features in nō since Zeami, a man concerned with success in the theater, acknowledges his use of them in his own treatises.

Aeschylus's style, like Zeami's, cannot be described in a single way—it can be simple and direct, elaborate and repetitive, colloquial and prosaic, lyrical and poetic.[4] As shown in the preceding chapter, Zeami's style can be at times highly poetic, characterized by syntactical overlapping of sentences and verbal interaction, and at other times conversational or prosaic; yet this variety does not obscure Zeami's method. Nor is it the variety of style that has obstructed a clear view of Aeschylus's method, but his verbosity. However, if one looks closely at Aeschylus's use of language in the light of the economical style of Zeami's nō, whose brevity makes special verbal effects and repetition especially prominent, the verbosity and repetitiveness that might seem blemishes in a silent reading of the text can be seen to function as a means of attracting an audience's attention to particular words in the course of performance. This repetition—as well as puns, word association, and verbal interaction, which are also marks of Zeami's style—is in turn a feature of Aeschylus's style that points to the crucial role of individual words and sounds as conveyors of meaning.

Given Zeami's use of special verbal techniques and his references to some of these in his treatises, I assume that the individual word stood out clearly in the nō performances of his day and created effects intended to be apparent to members of the audience. To be sure, in his treatises Zeami advises that a performance should conceal art, rather than display it. Yet it is clear from what he says that method and art are fully employed. For

---

[4] See the views of Thomas G. Rosenmeyer, *The Art of Aeschylus*, 106–108.

example, in the *Sarugaku dangi* sec. 12, on the subject of chant and the use of the voice, Motoyoshi transmits his father's recommendations to actors about the delivery of specific lines in specific plays, such as which part of a line or which word or syllable should be intoned in a certain pitch, volume, and so forth. Within this discussion, as in others, there are clear indications of the importance Zeami places on words *qua* words. For example, he says explicitly that the actor should pause in the delivery of a specific line from *Matsukaze* in order to emphasize the effect of the word-play on the specific word *mitsu*. (The word means "rising," but it also sounds like the number three.) In this line, which is quoted in the *Sarugaku dangi*, the word *mitsu* fills out the series: "The moon is one, her reflection two, three/rising tide . . ." (*Tsuki wa hitotsu, kage wa futatsu, mitsu shio no*).[5] Although Zeami's advice about this line is as succinct as it is about lines from other nō, if we examine the rongi of *Matsukaze* in which the word *mitsu* appears, we can see from the context that he emphasizes this pun and helps the audience recognize it by his choice of words. First, the words *shio* ("salt water"), as in a tide, and *tsuki* ("moon") are repeated frequently in clusters within the rongi and therefore given special status. Second, another closely related pun in the same passage helps to underscore the play on *mitsu*. The word *yoru*, immediately following *mitsu shio no*, means both "roll in" (like the tide) and "night." In addition, the first syllable *yo* sounds like the number four (*yotsu*). (The English translation "the tide *rolls forth*" brings out two of the three meanings of *yoru*.) If we were to reconsider the word *yoru* in this passage, from one point of view it would seem overworked and a source of obscurity. And yet this feature of style is not unusual in nō, as was made clear in Chapter Three, nor is the meaning obscure to those who understand the conventions of Japanese poetic diction and listen to the actors and the chorus. If we were to reconsider the repetition of *shio* or of *tsuki*, it might seem excessive. The repetition of *tsuki* within the context of the puns on *mitsu* and *yoru* is as follows:

CHORUS: . . . I scoop up salt water, but look,	. . . Shio o kumiwakete
The *moon* (i.e., reflection) is in my pail.	Mireba *tsuki* koso oke ni are.
SHITE: The *moon* is in here too.	Kore nimo *tsuki* no iritaru ya.
CHORUS: How happy I am,	Ureshi ya
The *moon* is in here as well.	Kore mo *tsuki* ari.

[5] In ZZ, 284, and Rimer, 209. The line appears at the end of the rongi that is translated above, p. 158. The Japanese version appears in Appendix 3.

SHITE: The *moon* is one, her	*Tsuki* wa hitotsu, kage wa
reflection two,	futatsu,
Three, the rising tide rolls forth	Mitsu shio no
At night we take the *moon* aboard	Yoru no kuruma ni *tsuki* o
the cart.	nosete.

This repetition of *tsuki* is neither lacking in purpose nor excessive, but, I submit, because the word appears repeated in a cluster, it is a measure of the extent to which the playwright, like a nondramatic poet, attracts the attention of the audience to his use of words *qua* words.

In the light of Zeami's examples, I am convinced for two reasons that verbal techniques of Aeschylus's style also could be appreciated by the Greek audience. First, the Greeks were familiar with the performed poetry and drama that came before Aeschylus's work, and thus accustomed to absorbing poetic diction by ear, as the Japanese were in Zeami's day. Second, the actors and the chorus could emphasize important words through their mode of delivery. Since we cannot reconstruct the delivery practiced in the Greek theater, the specific instructions that Zeami gives about music, breathing, and so forth cannot be used effectively in this comparison. But his advice helps to point out how important it is for the scholar of Greek tragedy not to forget that an actor can make the difference between an audience's hearing or not hearing a particular word, and further, that Aeschylus was not only a playwright but also the main actor in his own productions and the trainer of the other actors and of the chorus. Thus Aeschylus, like Zeami, could take active measures to ensure that performances in his day, at least, were not only visually, kinetically, and musically effective, but verbally effective as well.

In many passages Aeschylus's use of words has struck readers as mere embellishment and bulk; his verbal techniques, such as puns, have been ignored, glossed over as mere wordplay, or, like repetitions, studied as if they belonged to a text intended for a silent reading rather than a performance; and his fluidity of style has appeared to verge on impressionism or obscurity.[6] However, Zeami's style, which is neither faulty nor inartistic when considered within the context of his own milieu, offers parallels. Remembering that an actor, who in the leading role is the playwright himself, can emphasize particular words, the reader is asked to consider these "faulty features" of Aeschylus's style in the context of theatrical performance. Each can serve as a means by which Aeschylus attracts the audience's attention to words *qua* words and thus underscores his meaning. The first of these features, embellishment, repetition, or bulk, gives emphasis to words by sheer quantity. At first glance this technique would appear

---

[6] See Stanford, *Aeschylus in His Style*, 139.

to be less in evidence in Zeami's nō than in tragedy because the nō are shorter. And yet there is repetition and embellishment, the latter of which is found, for example, in long compound words, a few makurakotoba, and joshi. The second stylistic feature, paronomasia (punning), places emphasis on a single word. It is possible for an audience to appreciate a pun if the word is properly delivered by the actor or chorus and is prepared for by the words that precede. Zeami speaks specifically about puns, especially those connected with the names of characters important in particular nō and with the names of places, such as the settings of nō. He says that these should not be repeated (in kind) within a play and that each should be properly anticipated with appropriate phrases so that the audience does not miss the significant verbal device. (From Zeami's example, these phrases seem to involve repetition.[7]) The third characteristic of Aeschylus's style is the syntactical and semantic overlapping of sentences, clauses, and phrases, which, as demonstrated in the preceding chapter, is a normal feature of nō style and need not obscure the meaning of a particular passage to a Japanese audience.

In sum, by means of these stylistic features written into the poetry of the texts and brought out by the intonation and timing of the actors and chorus, the playwright can emphasize word over logical syntax, facilitate aural comprehension, and add verbal interest to the performance. In addition, the fusion of tenor and vehicle through verbal interaction, which often emerges as the function of this style, is in turn the means by which the playwrights create significance on more than one level simultaneously. The combined analysis of how the style of a text (and the actor) aids the audience in paying attention to words, about which we can learn from Zeami, and of how the style conveys meaning, about which we can learn from the work of philologists and critics, is informative to an appreciation of both Greek tragedy and nō.

The first of these three features of style, the use of repetition, a kind of embellishment, is the means by which Aeschylus and Zeami most obviously draw attention to words *qua* words.[8] The repetitions may involve identical or semantically related words, synonyms, syllables, and parallel sentence structures. For example, audiences are bound to take notice of long lists adorned by epithets or descriptive phrases, that is, the repetition of words drawn from the same semantic category. Lists can serve by means of words rather than explanations to create a certain atmosphere, to emphasize a person, place, or thing, or to set a subject of the play into per-

---

[7] *Sarugaku dangi*, in ZZ, 290, and Rimer, 220–221.

[8] I subsume the stylistic characteristic embellishment under Plutarch's infamous word used to describe Aeschylus's style, *onkos*, which means bulk and weight. See A. F. Garvie, *Aeschylus' Supplices: Play and Trilogy* (Cambridge, 1969), 57.

spective. These lists appear frequently in both nō and tragedy. In the *Persians*, for example, the list of the queen's offerings to the dead (611–618) draws attention to their natural simplicity and so sets them into contrast with the Persian wealth.[9]

Near the beginning of the nō *Kayoi Komachi*, another woman play, written by Kan'ami and revised by Zeami, fruits and nuts that the poetess Ono no Komachi, the shite, has brought to a priest, the waki, are listed and embellished with descriptive phrases in a manner analogous to the queen's list of offerings in the *Persians*.

WAKI: Tell me what fruits you have brought me today.
TSURE: What are all these fruits and nuts
   I have gathered here?
   Windfall acorns,
   The easy prey of storms
   That see them rolling
   Like carriage wheels I used to know.
CHORUS: And what fruits have I to evoke
   The houses of the poets?
TSURE: Persimmons from the hedge,
   To recall Hitomaro;
   Chestnuts from the hillside,
   A memento of Akahito;
CHORUS: Plums from the window
TSURE: And peaches from the garden;
   Pears from Ōnoura
   Where cherry-flax grows,
   Named for the cherry blossoms;
   Boughs of burning-oak
   And twigs of fragrant beech,
   Kindlings of the broad-leaved oak;
   Oranges both large and small,
   The mandarin and the cumquat,
   And for sweet, sad remembrance
   Of long-ago loves,
   A flowering spray of orange blossom.

[9] See the translation of the passage above, p. 129. Consider as well the list of places along the beacon path in the *Agamemnon*, and the list of places along the Persians' return home from Greece, the list of kings who preceded Darius, and the list of islands that Darius had once controlled, in the *Persians*. In nō there are, for example, the names of flutes in *Atsumori*, the list of places connected with saltkilns in the rongi of *Matsukaze*, and the lists of places found in michiyuki. In fact, in Japanese song and poetry there is a specific genre called monozukushi ("lists of things") that found its way into some nō, as I mentioned in Chapter Three.

The explicit references to two famous poets, Hitomaro and Akahito, and the quotation of part of a poem, *sakura-asa no Ōnoura . . . nashi* ("Pears from Ōnoura / Where cherry-flax grows"), which includes the poetic word *Ōnoura* found especially in waka, create an atmosphere appropriate to the main figure of this nō, a poetess.[10] In the queen's list of offerings in the *Persians* the poetic resonance is only implicit; Aeschylus adapts the Homeric *euōdes elaion* ("fragrant olive-oil," *Odyssey* 2.339), for example, in his phrase *elaias karpos euōdes* ("fragrant fruit of the olive-tree"), but does so without overt reference to Homer. We need not dwell upon this difference, attributable to the fact that the written poetic tradition in which Zeami worked was more highly codified than that of Aeschylus's day, for in the *Persians* Aeschylus does evoke the style and the atmosphere of Homeric epic almost as directly with the three lists of leaders as Zeami evokes a poetic mood in *Kayoi Komachi*. The first and second of these lists, because they not only contain many Homeric words but also closely resemble Homeric catalogues in form, are especially effective in bringing Homer's work before the mind of the audience.[11] Appearing as they do, at the beginning, near the middle, and at the end of the *Persians*, the lists are certainly as prominent as Zeami's single list in *Kayoi Komachi*. Like it, they help to create a poetic (in the case of the *Persians*, specifically epic) atmosphere, which, as I shall discuss below, is significant to an appreciation of the play.

Lists are the most obvious means by which Aeschylus and Zeami attract the audience's attention to semantically related words, used in a way that is as important as the logic of the passages in which they occur. Just as prominently Aeschylus, like Zeami, repeats the same or semantically associated phrases, words, and syllables within a passage, section, or play as a whole in order to heighten its significance.[12] Of course there is repetition in any kind of literature, and certainly in that intended for oral presentation, because repeated words do assist in attracting the attention of an audience, especially when an actor emphasizes them in his performance. Comedy (for example, kyōgen and satyr plays) employs repetition, often

[10] The section of *Kayoi Komachi* quoted above is taken from the translation of Eileen Kato in Keene, *20 Plays*, 55–56. The poem from which Kan'ami quotes several words was written by Minamoto no Toshiyori and appears in the *Shinkokinshū*, Zatsujō (book 16). See *YKS*, 77 n. 28.

[11] Deichgräber, in *Die Perser*, 167 n. 2, says, "Der Archetypus solcher Schilderungen ist immer der Schiffskatalog der Ilias."

[12] This kind of repetition differs from the repeated use of the same words and interjections in a passage, as, for example, in the laments of the *Persians* and the repetition of the nembutsu in *Sanemori*, which the playwrights use to underscore the ritual or emotional atmosphere of a performance. On cult elements and repetition in tragedy, see Kranz, *Stasimon*, 127–134. In nō, an important part of this atmosphere is created by the cries of the drummers.

for the purpose of leading up to a joke. The stylistic function is similar to that found in nō and Greek tragedy; however, the difference is that in the latter, the repetition and various verbal techniques, including puns, can be used to raise the language, as in nondramatic poetry, to a higher level of significance.

One out of many examples of the most obvious type of repetition in Aeschylean tragedy, that involving the same word, appears in the follow-ing passage from the *Suppliants* (40–49), where it connects form and con-tent, and prepares for a pun on a proper name. (Repetitions in the mondō of nō and in stichomythic passages of Aeschylean tragedy have already been mentioned in the preceding chapter.) In this long, run-on sentence, an invocation in form, the ancestor of the suppliant maidens, Epaphus, is the content that bears on issues of the play, the maidens' lineage from this offspring of a cow and their hope of protection. The connection of parts (i.e., the invocation and its content) and the significant pun on the name Epaphus ("Laying Upon [of hands]") are achieved here by an extraordi-nary number of repetitions of the same syllables, *epi* and the truncated form *ep'*, meaning "upon." (The word *epibēnai*, "come upon," at line 39, introduces the series of repeated syllables.)

Now calling *upon* Zeus's calf,	Nun d'*epi*keklomena
The avenger from over the sea,	Dion portin, huperpontion
the offspring of the	timaor' inin g'
flower-browsing cow	anthonomousas progonou
progenitor from the	boos ex *epi*pnoias
blowing *upon* [her]	
By Zeus; the *ep*onymous laying	Zēnos· *eph*apsin *epō*numian d'
upon [of hands] was	*ep*ekraineto morsimos
fulfilled *upon* [her] by	aiōn
fated time	
In a blessed birth, and she bore	Eulokhōs, *E*paphon d'egennasen·
*E*paphus;	
Whom calling *upon* by name....	Hon t'*epi*lexamena....

With the repetition of the two syllables *epi*, an audience is assisted in hear-ing the name Epaphus, which begins with the prefix *ep'*, and which is es-sential to the maidens' claim; the pun on his name is emphasized by Aes-chylus's use of the synonym *ephapsin*, meaning "laying upon of hands," within the same passage. In the last sentence of this song the word *epilex-amena* ("calling upon") returns to the subject of the invocation, intro-duced in line 40, which is a calling upon by name.

In nō, repetition of the same word will occur in those passages which prepare for puns on proper names, as it seems from his examples Zeami recommended, and also in those passages in which some significant motif, theme, idea, or word is being emphasized. The repetition of the same syllable need not be as concentrated in any one passage as it is in the Aeschylean passage above, inasmuch as in the shorter nō Zeami can achieve a similar effect more economically. And yet, the following passage in the important kuse section of the nō *Eguchi*, influenced by Chinese paratactic style, serves not only as one of many examples of repetition (the rongi of *Matsukaze* is another), but also as one that is particularly comparable to the example found in the *Suppliants*.[13]

The *red* color of the spring morning	Kōka no haru no ashita
The *red* brocade of the mountain	Kōkinshū no yama
. . . .	. . . .
The *yellow* leaves of the autumn evening	Kōyō no aki no yūbe
The *yellow*-dappled forest.	Kōkoketsu no hayashi.

The syllables *kō* ("red") and their homonym *kō* ("yellow"), as well as the repetition in syntactical pattern, connect the image words ("red brocade" and "yellow-dappled," dappled as in tie-dyed fabrics) and the tenor (the two seasons, times of day, and locations) within and between each pair of lines. The two pairs of lines are further connected to each other by the parallelism of the expressions following them (the blossoms of spring are carried away by the wind and the leaves of autumn fade away with the morning frost), and by the reference a few lines later to the *red* bedroom of the women, *kōkei*, from which lovers are said to drift apart, again marked by the two syllables *kō*.[14] With the help of the repeated *kō* and the parallel constructions, neither of which, given their proximity, one is likely to miss, the audience is told that no plants or trees or human beings can escape from their sad fate.[15]

A passage in the last stasimon of the *Libation Bearers* (935–971) is analogous to the one from *Eguchi*, inasmuch as its repetition of a syllable for sound and its syntactic parallelism not only attract the attention of the

[13] The authorship of *Eguchi* is uncertain; however, whether Zeami wrote the play or not, it was known to him. *Eguchi* is translated in NGS, 1: 107–124, and Chifumi Shimazaki's *The Noh*, vol. 3, *Woman Noh*, book 2 (Tokyo, 1977), 12–37. My translation is influenced by the latter.

[14] In the Japanese language, what we designate as a long syllable is actually two syllables.

[15] Because the texture and color of a forest and a mountain are described in terms of fabrics, which belong to the human sphere, the meaning of the lines supports the connection made by means of repetition and syntactical parallelism between the vehicle and tenor. Because the shite wears a colorful red costume, the meaning of these lines interacts with an element of the performance.

audience but also heighten the significance of the passage. After Orestes' murder of his mother, the chorus sings:

The daughter of Zeus—we call her Justice.	Dios kora—Dikan de nin Prosagoreuomen.

Aeschylus minimizes the effect of the break in the syntax here through the repetition of the syllable *di*, which points to a pun on the name of Justice.[16] The repetition in this line is signalled for the audience by the repetition of the same syllable *di* in the same position of the corresponding line of the preceding strophe—that is, by syntactic parallelism. In line 938, Aeschylus writes that Vengeance "has come" (*emole*) upon the sons of Priam and that there "has come" (*emole*) to the house of Agamemnon:

A twofold lion, a twofold Ares.	Diplous leōn, diplous Arēs.[17]

Aeschylus emphasizes the repetition of the syllable *di* with a repetition of the syntactical pattern, adjective–noun, adjective–noun. The effect is to suggest, without making explicit, an important analogy between the penalties brought against Troy and Agamemnon and those brought against Aegisthus and Clytemnestra. The content of the passages from *Eguchi* and from the *Libation Bearers* is different, but just as significant to the moral of the work. Stylistically the passages are analogous: in both, with the help of the proper intonation by a chorus, the playwrights lead their audiences to a comparison with the repetition of syllables and of syntax, but do not do so explicitly.

In the following passages of Aeschylus's and Zeami's works, which again are not unique examples, the connection between sentences is achieved primarily by means of a different kind of repetition, grammatical or syntactic parallelism, the rhythm of which is then enhanced for the audience by repetition of words and sounds. In the *Suppliants* (226–228), Danaus, the father of the maidens, asks:

How could a bird, eating a bird, be holy?	Ornithos ornis pōs an hagneuoi phagōn;
How could one marrying one unwilling from the hand of one unwilling	Pōs d' an gamōn akousan akontos para
Be holy?	Hagnos genoit' an;

[16] See Walter G. Headlam, *On Editing Aeschylus: A Criticism* (London, 1891), 153.
[17] The verb *emole* is the first word of both the strophe and the antistrophe and is repeated in the strophe; the word *poina* ("vengeance") is repeated in the same position of the second line of each.

The repetition of *pōs* ("how"), of the root *hagn-* ("holy"), of the particle *an*, of the optative mood of the verb, of the genitive cases of *ornithos* ("bird") and *akontos* ("unwilling"), of the nominative cases of *ornis* and *gamōn* ("marrying"), fuses the image of the first line, the birds, with the content of the second, the maidens and their male cousins.[18]

In *Sanemori*, at the beginning of the ageuta preceding the kuse, Zeami similarly connects tenor and vehicle with grammatically parallel sentences:

The weather is clearing, the wind in the young-willows combs the hair,	Ki harete wa kaze shinryu no kami o kezuri,
The ice is melting, the waves in the old-moss wash the beard.	Kōri kiete wa nami kiutai no hige o araite.

Each line begins with a noun followed by the continuative form of the verb and the particle *wa* marking the subject. Two nouns follow and describe the agent and natural location, after which the particle *no* connects the nouns to another noun, which, as the particle *o* indicates, is the object of the final word, a verb. Zeami fuses the season of spring and the activity of the wind and the waves with the tenor, the hair and beard of Sanemori, through verbal interaction, and connects the tenor with the willow and moss through the Chinese-influenced syntactic parallelism. The fusion and the style are enhanced for the listening audience by the alliterative *ki, ka, ke, ko*. The verbal effect is very much like the repetition of a line of music in which the words are different from the line being repeated, but the melody the same. In this passage of *Sanemori*, the musical notations are different, the syntax the same.

In the selected examples above, we discover that repetition of the same words, of semantically related words, and of grammatical structures that create verbal interconnections is not, as some critics of Aeschylus suppose, "too irregular, too pervasive, to suggest any purposefulness at all."[19] An

---

[18] On the mingling of the literal and the metaphorical here, see T. G. Tucker, *The "Supplices" of Aeschylus* (London, 1889), 52. On Aeschylus's use of paratactic constructions, balanced sentences, and repetitions in other passages, see, for example, Holger Friis Johansen, "Some Features of Sentence-Structure in Aeschylus' Suppliants," *Class. et Med.* 15 (1954): 1–59.

[19] Rosenmeyer, *The Art of Aeschylus*, 107. Of course, some repetition is not significant, such as one of Rosenmeyer's examples: the word "great" is repeated four times in twelve lines at *Agamemnon* 355–366. We must discriminate between the important and unimportant, and between words that actors and chorus might have emphasized and those they did not. The examples from nō provide clues to the identification of the latter types of repetition. On repetition as a stylistic feature in Aeschylus's works, see, among others, van Otterlo, *Beschouwingen over het archaïsche Element*, 50–51. On the weight of meaning that repeated words *qua* words can accrue, see, among others, Harry C. Avery, "Dramatic Devices in Aeschylus' *Persians*," *AJP* 85, no. 2 (April 1964): 173–184.

examination of these and many other examples of repetition reveals that both Aeschylus and Zeami use it to signal for their audiences specific words in passages where they fuse vehicle and tenor or emphasize a certain point. We would not call this kind of repetition mere verbal baggage or simplicity of style. Similarly, although critics find fault with Aeschylus's accumulation of epithets and the addition of compounds that seem to be superfluous to the sequence of thought in a passage,[20] we discover that a related kind of "bulk" or "embellishment" occurs in nō and Japanese poetry with the use of joshi ("introductory words") and makurakotoba ("pillow words"), which is recognized in the Japanese critical tradition as a means of attracting the audience's attention to other words. For example, the phrase "very much like hoarfrost on the grass" in the ageuta of *Sanemori* is joshi and introduces the beginning of a poem: "the old man" (*okina sabi*). The word *amasagaru*, meaning both "far away" and "away from heaven," is a makurakotoba that modifies and emphasizes *hinabito*, "country person." Comparable to the latter example from nō is the use of such seemingly superfluous adjectives as *bathuzōnōn* ("deep-girdled," 155) and *melagkhitōn* ("clothed in black," 116) in the *Persians*.[21]

To these types of "embellishment" I would add the use of long compounds, such as *shōjuraikōsu rakujitsu no mae* ("holy-multitude-coming-welcoming before the setting sun") in the first sashi of *Sanemori*, or *koganezukuri no tachikatana* ("gold-ornamented long-blade-sword") in the second ageuta of the nochiba in *Sanemori*. These may appear to add verbal weight only, but one can see from the second of these, for example, that the compounds serve a purpose. Zeami's mention of gold, emphasized by the long compound, allows him to associate the warrior's outfit with the golden words of Buddha. The compound word, as well as other words in the same passage associated in meaning with metal, prepares for the repetition of the word "gold" and helps the audience make this connection on a verbal, rather than a logical, level.[22]

Agamemnon 57 is one of many passages in which Aeschylus seems to add mere embellishment to his style with the use of "superfluous" adjec-

[20] On the subject of Aeschylean "bulk," see Rosenmeyer, *The Art of Aeschylus*, 105–106. On the piling up of words in Aeschylus's works, see, among others, Casmirus Felix Kumaniecki, *De elocutionis Aeschyleae natura* (Cracow, 1935), 34–35, and Earp, *The Style of Aeschylus*, 100; Homer's use of epithets provides a clear precedent. In Japanese literature, the *Manyōshū*, the earliest poetry anthology, is one source for the epithets found in nō. Although only indirectly related to this discussion, I mention the stylistic analysis of parts of the *Manyōshū* by Ian Hideo Levy in *Hitomaro and the Birth of Japanese Lyricism* (Princeton, 1984) because he briefly compares Hitomaro's poetry in the anthology with the Homeric epic.

[21] See my discussions of these passages in Chapter Three, pp. 109–110 and 105–106, respectively.

[22] A translation and discussion of the passage appears on pp. 194–195 of Chapter Three.

tives. One could argue that Aeschylus might have said simply "the cry of birds" rather than *oiōnothroon goon* ("bird-lamenting sound of grief"), inasmuch as the syllables *throon* ("lamenting") repeat the idea suggested by *goon* ("sound of grief").[23] However, this is not mere bulk; the syllables emphasize and elucidate the word *goon*, which belongs to the human realm but is used of birds, an important image in the tragedy.[24] Without openly explaining himself, Aeschylus fuses the realms of human beings and birds by means of the adjective and noun. The word that follows helps: *oxuboan* ("shrill-crying"), related in meaning to the preceding words, is appropriate to both men and birds. All of this prepares, in turn, for the phrase *tōnde metoikōn* ("of these metics"), which like *goon* is intrusive (that is, Aeschylus applies it to birds, but its semantic field pertains properly to the human realm). (The word "metic" assumes importance in the *Eumenides*, where the Furies, who are referred to in this same verse of the parodos, are granted a metic's status in Athens, 1011.) In this example, Aeschylus is more repetitive than Zeami, yet like him, by means of both repetition and "embellishing compounds," assists the audience in fusing two levels of significance.[25]

In addition to repetition and the use of compounds, which can be emphasized for the audience by the actor's mode of delivery, Aeschylus and Zeami use paronomasia, specifically punning on names. Because it appears conspicuously in their plays, this verbal device is a clear indication of the importance that the playwrights place on words *qua* words. The first features of style treated above serve primarily to emphasize the significance of a passage or other words in the same passage; puns are words that are themselves important and are therefore emphasized. Classical scholars have noticed that Aeschylus puns on names self-consciously in every one of his extant tragedies. I have included above one example (on Epaphus) from the *Suppliants* and one (on *Dikē*, "Justice") from the *Libation Bearers*. Punning is a verbal device of which Zeami himself acknowledges his use; he says explicitly in the *Sarugaku dangi* that it should not be repeated (in kind) within a nō, and he advises that the writer of a nō play should prepare the audience for it.[26] Among the examples already mentioned in the preceding chapters, there are the puns on the names of Matsukaze, Yugyō, and Furu. Another is the pun on the name of the poetess Ono no Komachi in *Kayoi Komachi*:

[23] The translation of this passage appears on page 173 of Chapter Three.

[24] Stanford, *Aeschylus in His Style*, 63, calls this pleonastic.

[25] See below the analysis of style in the *Persians* for further examples of so-called "verbal padding."

[26] In ZZ, 290, and Rimer, 220–221.

| I am embarrassed about my name. | Hazukashi ya ono ga na o. |
| I am called Ono. | Ono to wa iwaji. |

The syllables *ono* ("oneself," translated "my") prepare for the pun on the poetess's name, which is Ono. One may recall that in the nō *Furu*, Zeami prepared for a pun on the name of the god Furu with a poetic introduction, joshi.

In his works, Aeschylus, like Zeami, puns on names and often (although not always) does so only once for each name on which he puns in any given tragedy. In the *Agamemnon*, the chorus asks who named Helen so true to the mark before it puns on her name and calls her "hell to ships, hell to men, and hell to the citadel" (689–690); Cassandra repeats Apollo's name, which sounds like the verb meaning "destroy," six times before she puns on it (1073–1082); and in the *Seven against Thebes*, Eteocles puns quite explicitly on the names of warriors mentioned in the seven pairs of speeches that he shares with a messenger.[27] In the *Persians* as well, Aeschylus puns on the name of the Persians, as I point out below in the discussion of that play.

Another example of paronomasia in the *Persians* is found in the queen's long narrative speech, where we can observe how Aeschylus prepares for a pun on the name of Phoebus Apollo by means of the repetition of proximate words within a passage in the wider context of which other repetitions of words are not pervasive. When the queen says that after awaking from her dream she witnessed a frightening omen, she uses the word *anestēn* ("I got up," 201) and then echoes part of it with the word *prosestēn* ("I approached [the altar]," 203); the "hands" (*kheroin*, 201) with which the queen says she touched a lovely streaming fount are echoed by "hand" (*kheri*, 202) with which she makes a sacrifice. The queen says that as she prepared to make the sacrifice, she saw an eagle fleeing toward the altar of Phoebus and stood dumbstruck with fear. The repetition of the words in the passage, far from being superfluous, prepares for the pun on the word *phobōi* ("fear"), which appears immediately after the word *Phoibou* ("Phoebus," 206). The appearance of Apollo's name in Homer's *Odyssey* (15.526) next to the mention of a hawk (*kirkos*), the subject to which the queen next turns (207), may help to emphasize the pun.

Since tragedy and nō are performed in the theater, and the audience

[27] On Aeschylus's preparation for puns on proper names, see Fraenkel, *Aeschylus Agamemnon*, 2: 328. Fraenkel says of this preparation and of delaying the object, "The practice is not uncommon and seems to have been particularly favored in choral lyric." See also his comments on Cassandra's pun, 2: 492, and on the puns in the *Seven against Thebes*, 1: 331. For the *Seven*, see also H. D. Cameron's "Word Power in 'Seven Against Thebes'," *TAPA* 101 (1970): 95–118.

must be able to grasp the words and verbal techniques used by the playwrights, it is important that puns be not only vocally prominent, but also properly prepared for by other words. That the audience of nō can appreciate a pun is suggested by Zeami's reminder in the *Sarugaku dangi* that the playwright should properly introduce and anticipate significant verbal devices. That the Greek audience could appreciate these as well is suggested by the tradition of oral and performed poetry lying behind Aeschylus's works, in which punning on names is a recognized stylistic feature; by Aeschylus's careful preparation for such puns with verbal repetition and the use of compound adjectives; and by the stylistic parallels Aeschylus's work shares with nō.

In the preceding chapter I have shown that verbal interaction, including the repetition of words as well as the use of words associated in meaning (engo) and pivot words (kakekotoba), provides a means by which Aeschylus and Zeami move from one passage, line, sentence, clause, phrase, or word to another. This accounts for the third feature of style, syntactical and semantic overlapping, which, like the other two features, enriches the meaning of passages by means of words *qua* words as much as or more than by means of prosaic syntax and logic, and again points to the importance of individual words in nō and Aeschylean tragedy. Rosenmeyer's comment, apropos of the lyric sections of Aeschylus's works, that "the sentence tends to lead a shadow existence, with words and phrases taking over as the chief conveyors of poetic and dramatic impulses," aptly describes the "lyric" style of Zeami.[28] In the detailed analysis below of the strophe beginning at *Agamemnon* 1001, which follows on Agamemnon's exit into the palace, I identify those aspects of Aeschylus's style and handling of the language that have led to the semantic and syntactical overlapping. In addition, although I am fully aware that the effect is sometimes achieved differently in the Japanese and Greek languages, I compare the strophe with the kakeai in *Sanemori* in order to point out in what respects they are similar. The passage from the *Agamemnon* is one of a number of examples that illustrate how, when "syntax withdraws and with it the need for intellectual understanding of the progress of the thought,"[29] Aes-

---

[28] Rosenmeyer, *The Art of Aeschylus*, 98. One might compare with this what Brower and Miner say about Japanese poetry in *Japanese Court Poetry*, 468: "The private, traditional, and contextual implications that constitute the most immediate kinds of predication in Japanese poetry are conveyed primarily by means of diction and imagery, that is, by individual words and phrases." That is not to say that there is no syntax or rhetoric in Japanese poetry, as Brower and Miner point out, but that words are prominent in serving as conveyors of "thought."

[29] See Garvie (*Aeschylus' Supplices*, 64), who makes this statement about Aeschylean *onkos*. My test of the limits of the comparison, an examination in the last chapter of the rongi from *Matsukaze* and the beacon speech from the *Agamemnon*, made clear some of the ways in which the styles of nō and Aeschylean tragedy can differ.

chylus's language can signify simultaneously on more than one level at a time while its meaning remains clear.

In the passage from the *Agamemnon*, *words* with more than one connotation, *words* associated in meaning, intrusive *words*, and a repeated *word* are means by which Aeschylus fuses the vehicle and tenor. An almost total lack of articles, an unexpressed subject, asyndeton (lack of connection by conjunctions), and anacoluthon (the passing from one construction to another before the former is grammatically completed), all potential sources of obscurity to anyone expecting prose rather than poetry, are means by which Aeschylus creates a syntactical overlapping that helps to place emphasis on the words *qua* words. As Rosenmeyer observed, the result is that "the terms of comparison [the vehicle and the tenor] . . . lose their privileged status toward one another, and guide the eye of the imagination to the realization of a larger truth of which they are segmental manifestations."[30] Surely the same view applies to the style of Zeami's nō. The choral passage of the *Agamemnon* (1001–1017), important in the articulation of the lesson cautioning one against excess, progresses as much by words as by sentences, from the subjects of health, disease, and property, to an overloaded ship and an implied cautious sailor, back to property and the ship again, before concluding with the subject of disease (that is, hunger) allayed by Zeus's gifts from a bounteous harvest.[31]

Clearly the limit of much health	Mala †gar toi tas pollas hugieias†[32]
[Is] insatiable(?); disease, I'd say, [A] neighbor sharing one wall, encroaches.	Akoreston terma· nosos gar Geitōn homotoikhos ereidei.
〈 〉	〈 〉[33]
And human fate moving forward on [a] straight path	Kai potmos euthuporōn
Struck upon [an] unseen reef.	Andros epaisen aphanton herma.
And caution jettisoning in time	Kai to men pro khrēmatōn
A portion of [the] collected property	Ktēsiōn oknos balōn
With well-measured cast,	Sphendonas ap' eumetrou,

[30] Rosenmeyer, *The Art of Aeschylus*, 124.

[31] Brackets around words in the English translations of all the following passages in this chapter mark additions to the text. Note in particular the number of articles bracketed.

[32] No one has satisfactorily emended this corrupt line so that its meaning is intelligible. Among those who have obelized this passage, see Fraenkel, *Aeschylus Agamemnon*, 2: 452, and F. A. Paley, *The Tragedies of Aeschylus*, 2nd ed. (London, 1855), 371.

[33] In this strophe, the lacuna, which Page posits after line 1005 with Klausen, I place before line 1005.

[The] entire house did not sink	Ouk edu propas domos
Too laden with abundance	Plēsmonas gemōn agan,
Nor did [one] overwhelm [the] ship in [the] sea.	Oud' epontise skaphos.
Many [a] gift indeed from Zeus, bounteous and from yearly [harvests of the] furrows,	Polla toi dosis ek Dios amphila-phēs te kai ex alokōn epeteian,
Destroyed [the] disease of hunger.	Nēstin ōlesen noson.

Although the word *nosos* ("disease") in the second line belongs syntactically to a new clause that is signalled by *gar* ("for"),[34] *nosos* is connected outside the confines of the syntax, through semantic association, to *hugieias* ("health") in the first clause, and as the subject of the second clause is, in turn, associated syntactically with property holders by the words *geitōn* ("neighbor") and *homotoikhos* ("sharing [the] same wall"), each of which pertains more closely in meaning to the other than either does to "health" and "disease." The two vehicle words, disease and property holding, converge in the final word of the second clause, *ereidei* ("encroaches"), which, because it is appropriate to either meaning, grants the two vehicles equal importance. The precise meaning of the corrupt first line is not certain; however, an inference about the meaning of the sentence is easy to make, because from hearing the words we can associate the ideas of limit, health, insatiability, and disease, which as a neighbor encroaches on health, in an intelligible relationship one to the other. We can infer that Aeschylus warns how if one ignores due measure (*terma*, meaning "end" or "limit," and *akoreston*, meaning "insatiable," suggest this reading) and does not maintain good health, disease attacks.

In the next sentence, which continues without apparent logical connection to what precedes but is given equal value by Aeschylus's use of the conjunction "and," the participle *euthuporōn* ("moving on [a] straight path"), which describes the fate of man, suggests verbally rather than syntactically an analogy between human fate and a ship. One would expect Aeschylus to say that human fate strikes upon disaster, but he substitutes *herma* ("reef"), a vehicle word, for a word meaning disaster and belonging to the tenor. Within the context of the vehicle, a ship, Aeschylus repeats the lesson "nothing to excess," introduced in the first line, and adds to it explicit advice: he says, "Caution jettisoning in time a portion of [the]

---

[34] We do not know for certain whether the word *gar* is the correct reading in the first or the second clause. However, since *gar* or some other particle or conjunction in its place is expected in the second clause, the points made here about the sentence are not significantly affected by the corruptions in the text.

collected property with well-measured cast, [the] entire house did not sink too laden with abundance." Grammatically speaking, there is an anacoluthon in this sentence—the particle *men* ("on the one hand") is not answered with the expected particle *de* or *te*. Such balance in sentence structure is not absent in Aeschylean tragedy, or for that matter, in nō (the suffix -*domo*, "but," for example, creates a balanced relationship between clauses in nō), but the lack of balance here eases the verbal interaction between the ship and the house. In addition, the nominative participle, *balōn* ("jettisoning"), and the substantive, *oknos* ("caution"), lack a finite verb.[35] We have to infer that the phrase explains the reason why "the entire house did not sink." Pendent constructions lacking a verb or sudden shift in syntax, as we have seen in the preceding chapter, are common in nō. In the sentence ostensibly about a ship, the word *domos* ("house") is intrusive; and yet, because it is associated in meaning with the words *geitōn* and *homotoikhos* that precede (in nō we would say that they are engo), *domos* is not intrusive within the passage as a whole. It is important to Aeschylus's application of the moral lesson to various aspects of the play. Within the passage, by substituting *domos* for the intended subject, human fate, which is the tenor, and the ship, which is a vehicle, Aeschylus helps to bring a ship, appropriate to the case of the Greek expedition to Troy and thus one aspect of the play, and a house, appropriate to another—the setting of the play in which the series of tragic events takes place—within the purview of the warning against excess.[36]

The syntactical overlapping and the verbal interaction that mark the passage are abetted by the absence of an expressed subject in the next part of the main clause, where one assumes that a cautious sailor is the intended subject of the words *oud' epontise skaphos* ("did not overwhelm [the] ship in [the] sea"). (In fact, one also expects the object of the verb to be *domos*, "house.") After leaving the subject unexpressed, Aeschylus turns to a new idea, marked by the intensifier *toi*, and concludes with the final word *noson* ("disease"), repeated from the first sentence. At the beginning of the strophe Aeschylus seems to suggest that excess brings disease; in the middle he gives advice against excess. At the end Aeschylus says that Zeus destroys the disease of hunger with his bounteous gifts, thus concluding with an expression of the blessings that can come from observing due measure. He reaches this expression by means of an "almost imperceptible transition from one stage to the next,"[37] but one connected to the passage

---

[35] On the various interpretations of this passage, see Fraenkel, *Aeschylus Agamemnon*, 2: 455–456.

[36] On the interweaving of literal and "figurative" in Aeschylus's work, see Garvie, *Aeschylus' Supplices*, 68.

[37] See Fraenkel's note, *Aeschylus Agamemnon*, 2: 457, on line 1013.

as a whole and concrete because he repeats the word *nosos*, which the chorus would probably sing in a way that emphasizes it.

When we consider the passage from the *Agamemnon* quoted above, it is clear that its fluidity of style arises from possibilities inherent in the Greek language and from the tradition of Aeschylus's predecessors and contemporaries, such as Homer, Hesiod, and the lyric and choral poets, all of whom would have been familiar to the audience. This fluidity of style is especially enhanced by two means that are also available to Japanese writers. First, Aeschylus can easily shift from thing to person by means of personification, transforming disease into a neighbor and caution into a sailor that jettisons cargo. Since gender is not grammatically marked in the Japanese language, such a shift can be made easily and frequently in Japanese as well. Second, the scarcity of definite articles contributes to the fluidity of style in the *Agamemnon* passage. (In Homer's works, definite articles are used infrequently as such, but are often used as demonstrative pronouns. Even in the dialogue sections of tragedies, including the works written by Sophocles and Euripides, articles appear less frequently than in Greek prose.) In the Japanese language no articles, definite or indefinite, are used.

In the *Agamemnon*, lines 79–82, Aeschylus's use of only one article, as well as of a grammatically marked shift in gender, helps again to create a fluidity of style in a passage that, because it fuses man and his old age with the leaves of trees and a dream, is particularly amenable to a comparison with nō. That is, instead of using personification, Aeschylus reverses the process and compares people to things. (One could compare with this many passages in nō, like the cherry tree poem written by Yorimasa, in which inanimate things are easily referred to in the same breath as human beings because gender is not expressed.) The chorus sings:

That over-age, with leaves now Withering, along triple-footed paths	*To* th'hupergērōn phullados ēdē Katakarphomenēs tripodas men hodous
Makes [its] way, and not at all stronger than [a] child *[he]* Wanders, [a] dream appearing in daytime.	Steikhei, paidos d' ouden areiōn Onar hēmerophanton alainei.

The only article in the passage, *to*, is a neuter singular modifying *hupergērōn* ("over-age"). "Over-age" is compared with withering leaves, to which it is semantically related, and is said to walk on three legs, that is, with a cane; the ending *-ōn* of *areiōn* ("stronger"), a masculine singular adjective, is anticipated by the word *paidos* ("child"). (The connection between child and old age depends in part on the audience's familiarity with the riddle of the Sphinx, which is evoked with the word *tripodas*, "triple-footed."[38]) At the end of the passage, Aeschylus returns to the neuter gender with the word *onar* ("dream"). This passage is not an exception—Aeschylus elsewhere avoids the use of articles, alternates between genders, and also alternates between plural and singular number and between first and third person, even when the same referent is at issue.[39]

Another feature of Aeschylus's style observed in *Agamemnon* 1001–1017 is the lack of a subject at line 1014. Again, this is not an isolated instance. For example, in lines 724–726 of the *Persians*, an important ambiguity arises because the subject is not expressed. The exchange between the queen and Darius reads as follows:

QUEEN: Thus it is, and I think someone of [the] gods helped him in his plan.	Hōd' ekhei, gnōmēs de pou tis daimonōn xunēpsato.
DARIUS: Alas, some great god came so that he was not thinking right.	Pheu megas tis ēlthe daimōn hōste mē phronein kalōs.
QUEEN: Yes, since it is possible to see what kind of bad result he accomplished.	Hōs idein telos parestin oion ēnusen kakon.

In line 726, since it is not stated whether a god or Xerxes caused the bad result, Aeschylus allows for both and anticipates the conclusion that both god and man are responsible for the defeat of the Persians.[40] In line 251 of the *Agamemnon*, the absence of an expressed subject for the verb *prokhairetō* ("let one greet beforehand") allows Aeschylus to apply the words simultaneously to characters in the play, as well as to anyone.[41] (The conclusion to the nanori, a speech that the kyōgen may be directing to an imaginary audience at Shinowara or to anyone who listens, is similarly ambiguous, even though the kyōgen addresses it to "everyone.") In nō, the absence of an expressed subject is very common.

Another stylistic feature of the passage at *Agamemnon* 1001–1017 is the way in which one clause continues naturally into another. This kind of overlapping is not unique to this passage in Aeschylus's works (its presence in *Agamemnon* 716–717 was discussed in the preceding chapter).[42] The

---

[38] See ibid., 2: 50.

[39] See van Otterlo, *Beschouwingen over het archaïsche Element*, 109.

[40] On the ambiguity of this line, see Broadhead, *Persae*, 182.

[41] On some sources of ambiguity, see Kumaniecki, *De elocutionis Aeschyleae natura*, 56–58.

[42] See van Otterlo, *Beschouwingen over het archaïsche Element*, 114, for other examples of passages in which a thought is extended beyond the "normal" bounds of syntax. This "spilling over" can also be found in the temporary continuation between

continuation of the thought of one line in another is found frequently in nō, in kakeai, for example. We also find that it is not unusual in nō for a sentence or part of it to flow into parts of words, as in the case of kake-kotoba, and then to shift to another sentence. Or, to express the same idea another way, part of a word can serve one grammatical or semantic function in relation to what precedes and another in relation to what follows. (Consider the example of *Shinowara*, in which *shi-* serves as a verb for that which precedes and as the first syllable of the place name itself.) This degree of economy is more common in Aeschylean tragedy than one might expect. For example, in the *Persians*, at line 945, in referring to the sufferings sustained at sea by the Persian forces, the chorus uses the phrase *halitupa barē*. *Barē* means "sorrows," yet, falling as it does at the end of the line, and given that *baris* means "ship" (see *Persians* 1076), there is the possibility, since the word *halitupa* ("defeated at sea") precedes and since the chorus could emphasize it in performance, that the audience for a moment would think that the word "ship" is being uttered. It would not of course be surprised when the chorus completes the word and hears that it means "sorrow."[43] Grief is the subject of the next line; ships of the lines after.

By re-examining briefly one out of many passages from *Sanemori*, the kakeai that precedes the final ageuta of the maeba, in the light of the passage from the *Agamemnon* 1001–1017, some of the similarities and differences between the styles of the nō and the tragedy emerge even more clearly than from the examples presented in the preceding chapter. The passage reads as follows:

WAKI: In sinful attachment to [this] transient world

Nao shushin no enbu no yo ni

SHITE: More than two hundred years have elapsed

Nihyaku yosai no hodo wa furedomo

WAKI: But still he cannot be saved, *floa*ting at Shinowara's

Ukami mo yarade Shinowara no

SHITE: *Pond* in vain waves *wash* [*against the shore*] *at night*

Ike no adanami *yoru* to naku

---

strophe and antistrophe at *Suppliants* 62–63, 581–582; *Seven against Thebes* 749–750; and *Agamemnon* 237–238. The divisions between strophes and antistrophes are more marked in Euripides' works than they are in Aeschylus's. On this aspect of Aeschylus's style, see Kranz, *Stasimon*, 154, and Rosenmeyer, *The Art of Aeschylus*, 150–151.

[43] For the meaning "ships smitten by the waves," see H. W. Smyth, *Aeschylus* (Cambridge, Mass., 1963), 191.

WAKI: And by day without
distinction in darkness of
[the] soul

Hiru tomo wakade kokoro no
yami no

SHITE: Whether [in a state of]
dreams

Yume to mo naku

WAKI: Or [in a state of]
wakefulness

Utsutsu to mo naki

SHITE: [He is obsessed with] this
thought only.

Omoi o nomi.

(The first word of the ageuta that follows is *Shinowara*.)

In this kakeai, there are, of course, no articles and no inflections on nouns to mark case, number, or gender. Any definition of which substantive and which attribute belong together is indicated by particles that, especially in the case of *no*, often lack the precision seen in the Greek inflection.[44] The subject "he" is understood throughout the kakeai passage, but is not expressed. And further, when Zeami compares the spirit of the warrior (*ukami mo yarade Shinowara no*, "floating indeed at Shinowara") to the waves that float in vain (*ike no adanami yoru*, "[the] pond's waves in vain wash"), he does not do so explicitly—one has to draw the comparison out of the two associations of meaning in the word *ukami*, which are evoked by the word *adanami*. The first half of the word, *ada*, meaning "vain," is associated with the warrior's spirit only; the second half, *nami*, means "waves" and is associated with the image of water only. The word *ike* ("pond") refers to the location of the warrior's spirit and the waves. Zeami's method here is comparable to the verbal connection Aeschylus makes between disease and a property owner: the word *hugieias* ("health") is semantically related to the word *nosos* ("disease"); *geitōn* ("neighbor") and *homotoikhos* ("sharing one wall") to the property holder; and *ereidei* ("encroaches") to both. The playwrights shift from one context to another primarily with words, rather than with syntax. (There is a semantical marker in both: *gar* in the Greek, *-domo* in the Japanese.) In the Japanese passage up to and including the word *ike* ("pond"), one might think that Zeami is giving the location of the warrior's attachment and that the words pertain to the spirit; however, with but one part of a word *-nami* ("waves"), supported as it then is by *yoru* (which connotes "washing") as waves wash upon the shore, it is clear that the playwright has shifted to the subject of the waves. A major point of difference between the Greek and the Japanese examples is in the economy of the latter.

[44] The particle *no* can serve to mark the relationship of one substantive to another, but that relationship is in itself ambiguous. The Greek use of the genitive case is equally ambiguous; it can mark a subject or object relation, possession, and so forth.

Closer to the example of the kakeai in its economy of expression is Aeschylus's use of the word *aprosoistos* in line 91 of the *Persians*:

Or with strong defences to block   Ekhurois herkesin eirgein
   unconquerable wave[s] of   amakhon kuma thalassas·
   [the] sea;
Invincible, I'd say, are the Persian   *Aprosoistos* gar ho Persan stratos
   army and strong-willed   alkiphrōn te laos.
   people.

The adjective *aprosoistos* ("invincible") serves as a pivot between the vehicle—the waves—and the tenor—the army.[45] As a dual-ending adjective (that is, one that has only one ending for the masculine and feminine and another for the neuter gender, rather than three separate endings such as one finds on adjectives that are not compounds), *aprosoistos* in its context can refer to the sea, which is grammatically feminine, or to the army, which is masculine. Because the adjective is in the nominative case, it syntactically modifies *stratos* ("army") only. However, until the word *stratos* has been uttered, the audience is unaware that the sea will not be the grammatical subject of the new sentence. The adjective modifying the word *kuma* ("wave"), that is, *amakhon* ("unconquerable"), a synonym of *aprosoistos*, prepares for the momentary ambiguity and the semantic overlapping.

In line 1011 of the choral passage from the *Agamemnon*, the unexpected subject *domos* ("house") shifts one's attention away from human fate, the subject of the preceding sentence. The effect is analogous to but less economical than that of a pivot in nō—for example, of the word *yoru*, which marks a shift in subject from the waves "washing" to the warrior's thought "at night." Aeschylus replaces "ship" with the word *domos*, for unlike *yoru*, the Greek words for ship and house do not have two meanings. However, Aeschylus does use the word *ereidei* ("encroaches") to pertain both to disease and to a neighbor's property, and the word *euthuporōn* ("moving in [a] straight line") to pertain both to human fate and to a ship. In addition, the word *euthuporōn*, like *yoru*, prepares for other words: *herma* ("reef"), *edu* ("sank"), and *epontise skaphos* ("overwhelmed [the] ship in [the] sea"), which in combination are associated in meaning. *Yoru*, meaning "night," prepares for and is associated in meaning with the words *yami* ("darkness") and *yume* ("dreams"), which follow. The difference here between the Greek and the Japanese examples is that although the words *ereidei* and *euthuporōn*, like *yoru*, each pertain to two contexts,

[45] The word *aprosoistos* may mean "not to be approached," or "not to be withstood" (Smyth), or "irresistible" (Sidgwick). Any of these meanings can serve either the vehicle or the tenor. See Broadhead, *Persae*, 53.

each is one word that derives its meaning from the context, whereas *yoru* is one word with two denotations. This difference, as we have seen in other examples, is an important reason why Zeami could achieve semantic overlapping with greater ease than Aeschylus could.

And yet, one does not have to look far for examples of words with two denotations employed by Aeschylus to their full value. One of these occurs near the end of the *Persians* (991) in Xerxes' line: *boai boai [moi] meleōn entosthen ētor.* The word *meleōn* means both "luckless ones" and "limbs," and is the pivot word.[46] The full meaning of the sentence is: "It cries out, cries out *for [the] luckless ones*, the heart within my *limbs*." This example of a pivot is, like others, one for which Aeschylus prepares the audience in an earlier line. In line 931, where Xerxes first admits his error, the meaning of the word *aiaktos* ("lamentable") is emphasized by the next word, which is related in meaning to it: *meleos* ("miserable"), the word used with two meanings in line 991:

Here am I, alas, *lamentable*,   Hod' egōn oioi *aiaktos*,
Miserable. . . .   Meleos. . . .

The first two syllables of the word *aiaktos* echo syllables from the chorus's words (922-923):

The land *laments* her native   Ga d'*aiazei* tan eggaian
Youth.   Hēban.

The word *aiazei* ("lament") is emphasized by assonance with *eggaian* ("native") and reinforced by the cry of lament *aiai* (928) and the repeated word *ainōs* ("lamentably," 930). All prepare for the adjective *aiaktos*, which Xerxes applies to himself and which contains within it the cry of lament.

At the end of the Japanese passage from the kakeai and of the Greek passage from the *Agamemnon* respectively, Zeami and Aeschylus repeat a word from the beginning of each, *Shinowara* and *nosos* respectively, both of which can be emphasized in performance. In the meantime, each playwright has deepened the significance of the passage as a whole at a similar juncture within the structure of the play. The verbal interaction is more economically achieved in the nō than in the tragedy. This is a difference between them. Had Aeschylus followed the practice of Zeami, the ancient critics might have found him more obscure, more impressionistic, more uncontrolled than they did. Yet my point is that Zeami's passage, which is not as complex as some of the others examined in the last chapter, is controlled in Zeami's choice of words that fuse tenor and vehicle, concrete in

---

[46] Smyth understands "hapless ones," 193; Broadhead, "body," 235. See Broadhead, *Persae*, 235, on the two alternatives, for both of which there exist parallels.

that it is verbally tied to the setting of the play, and clear in meaning. In the light of the Japanese norm, there is at least some basis for saying that the same is true about Aeschylus's style.

Given the parallels in nō, enough has been said here to suggest that what Aeschylus wrote need not be obscure or lacking in method. If the chorus and actor deliver lines well, a single word is easier for an audience in a theater to absorb than complicated sentences with subordinate clauses. The choral passage from the *Agamemnon* analyzed above is not an isolated example of syntactical overlapping that can be explained away as the expression of a group of distraught elders who are not thinking straight due to fear for the king, who has just entered the palace. In fact, Clytemnestra's words preceding the ode (*Agamemnon* 966–974) display sustained verbal interaction, even though they are spoken in iambic trimeters, the meter used in dialogue and the closest in tragedy to prose, and by a woman who is controlling the situation, rather than fearful of the results.[47]

The verbal interaction within Clytemnestra's speech is equal in complexity to that of the choral passage and again fuses different levels of significance with words rather than syntax. The passage reads (966–974):

For if there is [a] root, foliage *arrives at [the] house*	Rhizēs gar ousēs phullas *hiket' es domous*
Covering [it] over in *shade* against *[the] dog star*;	*Skian* huperteinasa *seiriou kunos·*
And with your coming to [the] domestic hearth,	Kai sou molontos dōmatitin hestian,
Warmth coming in *winter* do you signify.	*Thalpos* men en *kheimōni* sēmaineis[48] molon.
And when Zeus makes wine from [the] bitter	Hotan de teukhēi Zeus ap' omphakos pikras
Grape, then straightaway there is *coolness* at home,	Oinon, tot' ēdē *psukhos* en domois pelei,
If [the] consummate lord moves about [the] house.	Andros teleiou dōm' epistrōphōmenou.

[47] It is interesting and perhaps relevant that in the *Sarugaku dangi* sec. 13, one learns that Zeami considered passages unaccompanied by music more difficult to deliver than those in melody. Spoken lines, which cannot be learned by rote, he advises, require that the actor enter fully into the character role and not be distracted from it. Zeami's son adds that his father was talented in this respect and gives as an example of his delivery of the two syllables *seme*, markers of inflection on the verb "name" in the line, "He would give his name." (In ZZ, 285–286, and Rimer, 212.) This line occurs in the mondō of *Sanemori*.

[48] The reading *sēmaineis* is that of the codices. See Fraenkel, *Aeschylus Agamemnon*, 2: 439.

Zeus, Zeus O Consummate [One], consummate my prayers.	Zeu Zeu teleie, tas emas eukhas telei·
May they be your concern, those things which you intend to consummate.	Meloi de toi soi tōnper an mellēis telein.

In the lines, "Foliage arrives at [the] house, / Covering [it] over in shade against [the] dog star [i.e., summer's heat]," the words *hiket' es domous* ("arrives at [the] house") introduce the idea of Agamemnon's return. (Because the actor exits as if to enter the palace, the words also signal an element of the performance.) Although foliage can be said to return in the summer, the words "arrives at [the] house," not commonly used of plants, are intrusive within these two lines. They are tenor words that Aeschylus applies to the vehicle. In the continuation of the passage he applies vehicle words to the tenor: Agamemnon's presence is said to signify *thalpos* ("warmth"), *en kheimōni* ("in winter," 969), and *psukhos* ("coolness") in summer (971). Since the warmth associatively hearkens back to the dog star (summer's heat) and the coolness to the shade,[49] the seasons of the year and Agamemnon's return continue to cohere. *Thalpos* is one of the words with which Aeschylus fuses man and nature through verbal interaction: warmth acquires more than one connotation—the word *thalpos* follows immediately on the word *hestian* ("hearth") and is thus locally taken to mean the fire's heat. But since reference to the summer's heat, *seiriou kunos* ("dog star"), precedes the mention of the hearth, we can retrospectively think of the sun. This thought in turn prepares us for Aeschylus's comparison of Agamemnon to coolness in the midst of shade. The passage converges in the name of Zeus, which is mentioned in line 970 within the context of a human activity and, by implication, a season of the year, the late summer when "he makes wine from [the] bitter grape." The repetition of Zeus's name and of the stem *-telei* ("consummate"), which is applied to Agamemnon and to Zeus, lessens the distinctions between god, man, and nature.[50]

The difference in the number of times the same words and synonymous words are repeated in Clytemnestra's passage from the *Agamemnon* and in the passage discussed immediately before from *Sanemori*, I submit, is due to the greater length of Aeschylus's work, which requires that he be more repetitive if the audience is to grasp the full significance of a special

[49] *Psūkhos* ("coolness" of night) appears in *Odyssey* 10.555; *thalpos* ("warmth," meaning "summer's heat") appears in *Agamemnon* 565.
[50] On this passage, see Rosenmeyer, *The Art of Aeschylus*, 121–122.

verbal effect.[51] However, as I have pointed out repeatedly, Zeami also frequently reuses the same word—consider the repetition of *shio* in the rongi from *Matsukaze*—and uses synonyms to create verbal interaction in a passage. For example, in the kakeai of the nochiba of *Sanemori* the waki and the shite sing:

WAKI: Brilliant is [the] appearance	Sono idetachi wa hanayaka naru
SHITE: Of [his] outfit, bright	Yosooi koto ni kumorinaki
WAKI: [Is the] moon's radiance	Tsuki no hikari
SHITE: In [the] burning lantern's light	Tomoshi bi no kage
CHORUS: Not dark	Kurakaranu
Is [the] night's mantle	Yoru no nishiki no
[A] brocade robe.	Hitatare ni.

After the first two lines of this passage, Zeami moves by verbal association and with asyndeton from a reference to the warrior's appearance, described as *hanayaka* ("flowery") and *kumorinaki* ("bright," literally "cloudless"), again with asyntaxis, to that of the moon and the fire's light. The passage converges in the first word of the choral song (ageuta), *kurakaranu* ("bright," literally "not dark"). This word describes *nishiki* ("the night's mantle"), with which word Zeami pivots back to the subject of the warrior's dress, *nishiki* ("the robe of brocade"). In the continuation of the ageuta, the chorus sings about the calyx of the lotus and Buddha's golden words, which, unlike the outfit and the swords of gold, it says, are the true treasures. The kakeai, like Clytemnestra's speech, progresses by means of words semantically related: "flowery," "cloudless," and "not dark" are all words that mean "bright" in one sense or another. The first refers to the appearance and the outfit, but prepares for the mention of the lotus calyx in the ageuta that follows. The second is used in a line about the outfit, but describes the moon's radiance and the light of the burning lantern. The third applies to the moonlit night, but also by means of the pivot word *nishiki* ("brocade") applies to the robe of the warrior.

In Clytemnestra's speech, Aeschylus connects the first and the second clause of the first sentence by means of the word *thalpos* ("warmth"), which is associated in meaning with the summer's heat as well as with the warmth from a hearth. The word *psukhos* ("coolness") connects the first sentence to the later sentences, in which there are references to winter and to coolness that can come in summer when Zeus makes wine. At the con-

---

[51] A. W. Verrall, not appreciating the importance of repetition in the theater, says about the passage as a whole, "Note here again the artificial manner in which the images, splendid as they are, are accumulated and repeated" ("*Agamemnon*," 114 on line 957).

clusion of the Greek passage there is no pivot word; Aeschylus repeats words based on the root *tel-*, which he uses to characterize both a human and a god and thus to bring these two together in a manner analogous to Zeami's fusion of the night and of the warrior's robe with but one use of the word *nishiki* in *Sanemori*. The verbal connection between the warrior's outfit and the seat of Amida in Paradise is made in the continuation of the ageuta, where Zeami draws a distinction between the treasures of earthly possessions and those of the lotus calyx in Paradise. Here by repeating words verbatim, he bridges the gap between the vehicle and the tenor, with the words "treasures" and "gold." The latter describes both the warrior's swords and the words of Buddha and is supported by Zeami's use of words associated in meaning with metal, that is, "does not tarnish" and "heavy," which is part of the word *omokuseba* ("if you respect").[52]

Repetition, paronomasia, and syntactical overlapping, all of which can contribute to verbal interaction, are three stylistic features on which I have concentrated up to this point in this chapter. Because these features are found in much poetry outside the theater, one could say that an understanding of poetic style is a means to understanding Aeschylus's and Zeami's styles, particularly how they emphasize important words and fuse vehicle and tenor in order to express the higher level of significance of their religiously and morally oriented plays. However, one may need to be reminded that important words in Aeschylus's and Zeami's texts can be emphasized not only by the intonation of the actor but also sometimes, because they attract attention to a certain element of performance, by that element of performance. In Clytemnestra's speech, for example, Aeschylus points to the entrance of Agamemnon into the palace, an actor's exit; in the kakeai of *Sanemori*, Zeami points to the costume of the shite. This kinetic or visual dimension is one that written poetry cannot achieve, that recited or sung poetry is not likely to achieve, that performed poetry, song, and dance can realize to a degree, but that theater alone can fully express. As I have mentioned, connections between word and performance are especially noticeable in the *Persians* and in most nō because these plays lack intellectual argumentation, elaborate stage effects, and such side issues and actions as might distract the attention of the audiences from the words. That is, these works are closer to performed poetry or song than many other dramatic plays are; yet these works are theater because they employ some props, more than one actor dressed in costume, masks, entrances and exits, movements and gestures carried out on an acting area, and a combination of song, poetic recitation, dialogue, and narration.

[52] *YKS*, 271 n. 15, states that the words pile up here. See the analysis of this passage on pages 194–195 of Chapter Three.

In the *Persians*, with the words "and I sing out as is right [the] death much-lamented of those who have gone (546–547)," the chorus informs the audience that it will sing a lament, and it does; in *Sanemori*, with the words "he will tell his tale" immediately preceding the katari, the chorus informs the audience that the warrior will give his narration, and he does. In these two passages, word is connected immediately and explicitly with performance in a way that a written work cannot duplicate, but that song and recitation by a chorus and a soloist outside drama can. Again, when Aeschylus writes "strike your breasts" (1054) in the final lament of the *Persians*, or Zeami writes "as he fell" in the rongi of *Sanemori*, the gestures and movements of the actors can be realized in performances of both poetry and of the theater. However, when the queen appears in all her royal splendor in the first half of the *Persians*, exits, and then returns later dressed in simpler attire and unattended by a chariot, and when the warrior appears in the guise of an ordinary person in the first half of *Sanemori*, exits, and then returns later dressed in warrior attire, we are in the world of drama and drama alone. The actors and the chorus not only dance and move, but also act within a theatrical environment set off from the world of the audience by the physical structure of the theater, by the masks, by the movements, including entrances and exits, and by the words of the text that is being enacted.

In many passages Aeschylus and Zeami use repetition, paronomasia, word association, and verbal pivots that are effective in shifting from one tenor or vehicle to another. Some of these are delivered simultaneously with or prepare for an aspect of performance, including references to masks and costumes and to entrances and exits. One example, Aeschylus's use of words meaning "light," "eye," and "sight," drawn from a number of passages in the *Persians* rather than from one passage alone, should suffice to show how Aeschylus artistically directs attention to words, which on their own can engage the audience and which at an important juncture point to a visual element of the performance. Aeschylus achieves these effects by creating verbal interaction, by choosing words associated in meaning, by repeating the same words, and by creating puns that he anticipates by verbal preparation. These techniques are similar to those found in nō; the major difference, as I have said, is that Aeschylus's work is longer and as a consequence he must prepare more fully than Zeami.

In the *Persians*, before the queen relates her dream, she expresses a two-fold concern (166–167):

One should not honor [a] mass of wealth without men	Mēte khrēmatōn anandrōn plēthos en timēi sebein

| And [a] *light* should not shine as strongly as possible without wealth. | Mēt' akhrēmatoisi lampein *phōs* hoson sthenos para. |

However, it is not with the wealth, but with a person that she is primarily concerned, as she makes clear with the use of three words, each of which has two meanings. First she uses the word *phōs* (167), which means both "light" and "salvation."[53] Then the queen says (168):

| [My] fear is over the eye. | Amphi d' omphalmōi phobos. |

Ophthalmos means both "eye" and "a loved or esteemed person." The queen then explains (169):

| [The] presence of a master, I think, is the eye of the house. | Omma gar domōn nomizō despotōn parousian. |

Omma here means both "eye" and "a precious person."[54] The Aeschylean audience would not be confused by the passages as a Greekless audience might; they would know that each of the three nouns has two connotations and that the nouns are all associated in meaning with each other. Aeschylus almost creates a riddle out of the queen's words, which she solves by mentioning her son specifically in the introduction to her dream at the beginning of her next speech. (The movement from general to specific, which I have emphasized in Chapter Two, is facilitated by Aeschylus's use of synonyms that are applied to progressively more specific referents and are noticeable because they are repeated in close proximity.)

Words associated in meaning with light continue to be important in the messenger speech at the climactic moment when the audience learns that Xerxes is alive. The messenger says (299):

| Xerxes himself lives and sees [the] light. | Xerxēs men autos zēi te kai phaos blepei. |

The Homeric phrase "sees the light" seems redundant after the word "lives"; however, it is important that Aeschylus emphasize Xerxes' survival, a point over which the queen has been especially concerned. In addition, the word *phaos* provides a link with the queen's response to the good news. She says (300–301):

---

[53] Compare line 261, where the words *nostimon . . . phaos* mean both "light of return" and "day of return."
[54] See Broadhead, *Persae*, 75.

| You spoke of [a] great *light* for [our] house | Emois men eipas dōmasin *phaos* mega |
| And [a] *bright day* after [a] black night. | Kai *leukon ēmar* nuktos ek melankhimou. |

The word *phaos*, in the course of being repeated, changes meaning from "light" in the messenger's news to "joy" in the queen's response. Aeschylus continues in her response by restating the point more vividly. The queen adds that the great "light" (that is, "joy") is a "bright day" appearing after a dark night. (Zeami probably would have created the same effect more economically, by using one word meaning both "light" and "joy" only once as a pivot between the messenger's and the queen's speeches.) Using synonyms, Aeschylus passes smoothly from the announcement of Xerxes' survival to the effect of that survival on the queen and the household after a dark night. The darkness of the night, semantically related to its antonym, light (antonyms, called *taigo*, can be found in nō also) may in turn call to mind the nights during which the queen experienced dreams after her son's departure (175). In addition, because the night is called *melankhimos*, literally meaning "dark and stormy," it anticipates the event which the messenger will report—the survival of the king during a storm in the dark of night (see lines 495–496), in which the other leaders died. "To see the daylight after a storm" is proverbial (see *Agamemnon* 900), but here the idea, imbedded in the meaning of a common compound adjective, properly anticipated by a series of words associated in meaning, is closely connected to the reality of the case—Xerxes' survival of a storm.[55]

The survival of the king in the *Persians*, and thus the meaning of the messenger's and the queen's words, is realized visually at the end of the play when Xerxes appears, when Aeschylus again uses words related in meaning with sight in an emphatic manner. One of the words appears in the chorus's observation that the retinue of Xerxes' leaders has not returned with him; the chorus asks about the leaders, whom it calls Xerxes' trusted "eye" (*ophthalmon*, 979), and says, "I marvel, I marvel [*etaphon etaphon*, 1000] that they are not following behind in a wheeled palanquin." The repetition of *etaphon* points to the lack of the retinue and of a chariot.[56] In addition, Aeschylus uses the verb meaning "see" three times within two lines (1017–1018) in order to emphasize the verbal interaction

[55] According to the historical account of Herodotus, Xerxes did not actually return with what was left over of the Persian forces. But Aeschylus is writing drama, not history. Nowhere does the playwright suggest that Xerxes traveled separately. See Broadhead, *Persae*, 184–185.

[56] Among others, Broadhead thinks that a palanquin or chariot was used in the final scene. For the correct view, namely that Xerxes lacks both a retinue and a chariot, see Taplin, *Stagecraft*, 121.

mentioned in Chapter Two (see p. 146), which in turn again points to the lack of both a retinue and the full regalia appropriate to a king.

Do you see here what is left of my entourage and apparel?	Horais to loipon tode tas emas stolas;
I see, I see.	Horō, horō.

When Xerxes asks the chorus of elders to look at the remainder of his outfit, he uses the word *stolē*, which means both "entourage" and "outfit." Within the immediate and preceding context the word refers to the men who went to Greece with Xerxes (see line 1014); in relation to what follows, it refers to his meager outfit, consisting of only torn robes and a quiver (see lines 1020 and 1030). Aeschylus's extended use of words associated in meaning with light and sight in the *Persians* shows that he prepares by means of repetition for the use of significant words and of verbal interaction; thus he enhances the meaning and enriches an aspect of the performance of the play, the entrance of Xerxes and the costume of the actor playing his role.

VERBAL TECHNIQUES IN THE *PERSIANS*

To treat exhaustively the examples of verbal techniques and verbal interaction in Aeschylean tragedy (or even in the *Persians*) and how they pertain to the comparison of style in nō and Aeschylean tragedy would extend this chapter beyond the limits of appropriate length. However, in order to provide the reader with a discussion of Aeschylean style that is comparable to the discussion of *Sanemori* in Chapter Three, and to demonstrate how repetition of words, verbal padding, and paronomasia function within the context of a tragedy as a whole, I will treat the style of the *Persians* in conjunction with only one theme, sea and water, and limit my analysis to important words and phrases associated in meaning with it. I have chosen this theme because it, like that of water in *Sanemori*, is used both as an image and as part of the literal meaning of many passages.[57] (It is, of course, coincidental that water is an image in both works.) One finds in the *Persians* that because some of the words associated in meaning with

[57] Some of those scholars who have discussed water as an image in the *Persians* include Michael Anderson, "The Imagery of *The Persians*," GR 19 (1972): 166–174; Alain Moreau, "L'attelage et le navire: la rencontre de deux thèmes dans l'œuvre d'Eschyle," *Revue de philologie de littérature et d'histoire anciennes* 53, fasc. 1 (1979): 98–115; Petrounias, *Funktion und Thematik der Bilder*; van Nes, *Die maritime Bildersprache des Aischylos*; Jacques Péron, "Réalité et au-delà dans les Perses d'Eschyle," *Bulletin de l'Association Guillaume Budé* 1 (1982): 30–39. Edinger ("Vocabulary and Imagery," 52–57) discusses the double armament, on land and by sea.

water are both vehicles and a part of the tenor, Aeschylus achieves verbal interaction by means of these words. In addition, through words semantically related with the sea and with water, Aeschylus helps the audience to perceive and appreciate the significance of his work. To be sure, Aeschylus is quite explicit about the moral of the play, namely, that Xerxes and the Persians should not have taken to the sea when it was fated by god for them to fight on land—this is made clear in the lyric parodos and in the Darius section—just as Zeami is explicit about the warrior's nobility and Amida's saving grace. Nevertheless, Aeschylus, like Zeami, artistically enhances the religious and moral lesson of the play through verbal interaction. Aeschylus identifies the sea not only as something about which Xerxes makes an error and as the location of that error—the tenor—but also uses words semantically related to the sea as an image—the vehicle.

It is the case that the religious atmosphere created in the *Persians* and in *Sanemori* is different. The hieratic character of the nō, in which the waki is a priest, and in which Zeami quotes and alludes to "written" scriptures and other religious works and presents dramatic versions of religious services, is not shared by the *Persians*. In the *Persians* the religious spokesman is the ghost of Darius, rather than a priest, and Aeschylus alludes to the authority of oracles and of religious and moral poetry, which most likely were not the codified scriptures of a religious sect. In addition, he presents dramatic versions of religious rituals, but not religious services. Thus, although the terms in which the tragedy's lessons are articulated are moral and religious, as they are in *Sanemori*, they are not, as in *Sanemori*, hieratic as well. However, this difference does not detract from our observation that there are important similarities between the means used by Aeschylus and Zeami to articulate the purposes of their respective works. The role played by the sea and water in the imagery and the moral and religious content of the *Persians* and of *Sanemori* is one example. The waters of Buddha's Lake and the pond at Shinowara, the setting of the play, are associated through verbal interaction. If the ghost of Sanemori purifies the water in the pond of his heart, we learn, he will be freed from his attachment to this world. Some of the words pertaining to water are instances of traditional religious imagery: for example, the water of the Law; the boat; the net of the Vow; and the Garden of the Law in which Buddha's Lake is located, which Zeami connects with the actual pond and garden at Shinowara through verbal interaction as well as by explicit statement. In the *Persians*, the water of the seas to which Aeschylus compares the Persians and their ills is the location and the physical cause of the destruction of the Persians as well as the moral cause of their destruction—their decision to take to the sea is the reason, Aeschylus tells us, why they have been punished by a god, who at one point is identified with the sea. In both the nō and the tragedy, the role played in human destiny by the divine is expressed both explicitly and through verbal interaction involving words related in meaning to a specific theme.

A difference between the use of these themes that is significant to this comparative study is that the water theme is slightly more complicated in the tragedy than in the nō. The moral is expressed in terms of both the sea and the land in the contrast that Aeschylus sets up in the lyric parodos. There we are told (94–114) that the god Delusion draws a man, like an animal, into her net, and he cannot escape; it was destined for the Persians to fight wars on land, but they learned to look to the sea and relied on "man-transporting devices." We learn later in the play that this is why they are punished. The contrast gives rise to verbal interaction between words pertaining to water and to land. In the nō, we are told that Amida saves everyone by drawing them, like fish, into his net and, in addition, that the ghost must purify the water in his heart from its attachment. There is no contrast connected with the image of water articulated in the nō. In the *Persians*, both the contrast between land and sea and a related contrast between Darius and Xerxes are of great importance in the characterization of Xerxes.[58] However, these types of contrasts are not a regular feature of two-part nō, to a large extent because deities or ghosts appear in them. The contrasts, or better, the tensions, dealt with in these strongly Buddhistic nō tend to be between this world and "that" world, between illusion and reality.[59] Aeschylus's presentation, without irony or rationalization, of a ghost who interacts among living human characters helps to explain why the *Persians* is more like two-part nō than any other extant Greek tragedy. And yet the *Persians* resembles other tragedies in that the contrasts that Aeschylus develops within the play on the verbal and the character level are an indication of tension that in other tragedies is presented in the form of character confrontation as well.[60]

In spite of this difference, which helps to explain the many differences that developed between tragedy and nō in their later histories, there remains the major similarity between the styles of Aeschylus and Zeami: the two playwrights prepare their audiences for important elements of performance, for prominent words and passages, and for the use of verbal inter-

---

[58] On the contrasts between Darius and Xerxes, see Péron, "Réalité et au-delà," 26–29; on the connection of Darius and Xerxes to land and sea, see ibid., 31–34.

[59] See LaFleur, *The Karma of Words*, 119.

[60] As I have mentioned before, confrontation is not entirely absent from nō. For example, often in the mondō, the shite and the waki will engage in some difference of opinion. In *Sanemori*, for example, the old man does not want to give his name. In *Kayoi Komachi*, there is an open altercation between the shite and the tsure. However, in comparison with Greek tragedy, there is a strong tendency for nō to be free of conflict, especially the kind of conflict that leads to a fatal or painful act.

action, which is effective in bringing different levels of significance together. (I shall limit my use of the terms vehicle and tenor to those passages in which I illustrate verbal interaction.) The following discussion is intended to provide the reader with examples of this style as it is connected with the theme of water in the *Persians* and to illustrate how much a performance of the tragedy gains in interest if we allow that the actors and chorus could direct the attention of the audience to individual words. The examples from nō, which are included in the discussion, are intended to serve as reminders to the reader of similarities and of some differences between the styles of Zeami and Aeschylus.

The verbal emphasis on water in the *Persians* assumes importance in the first stanza of the lyric parodos, where Aeschylus attracts the attention of the audience to the sea. (He has only hinted at the importance of the sea in the parodos with the mention of ships and the crossing of the Persian expedition to Greece.) The lyric parodos begins with the alliterative line (65) *peperaken men ho perseptolis ēdē* ("already it has made passage, the city-destroying [royal army]"). The compound word *perseptolis* is perhaps inspired by the Homeric word *ptoliporthos*, which also means "city-destroying"; however, Aeschylus reverses the two parts of the adjective and accommodates it to the play by emphasizing the part that is derived from the verb *perthō* ("destroy") and that sounds like the name of the Persians.[61] This alliterative line prepares for a pun later on the name of the Persian nation, who are, in a sense, a main character of the play. We can be fairly certain that Aeschylus attracted the audience's attention to this line, which leads to his emphasis on the word "sea," for there is external evidence to suggest that he did: the line was parodied by Eupolis, a comic writer of the fifth century B.C.[62]

In the next line and the continuation of the sentence Aeschylus mentions the goal of the royal army's passage: "to [the] opposite neighboring land." But he does not stop there; he continues the sentence with a specification of the location and the means of passage: "with [a] raft bound with ropes, having crossed [the] strait of Helle, [the] daughter of Athamas" (70). And as if that were not sufficient to make his point that the army crossed the Hellespont, in another participial phrase Aeschylus adds to the sentence in the next line that the army "cast [a] roadway made of many rivets, a yoke,

---

[61] See Garvie, *Aeschylus' Supplices*, 72, and H. N. Couch, "Three Puns on the Root of *perthō* in the Persae of Aeschylus," *AJP* 52 (1931): 270–273.

[62] See Heinrich Theodor Becker, *Aischylos in der griechischen Komödie* (Darmstadt, 1915), 14, and H. J. Rose, *A Commentary on the Surviving Plays of Aeschylus*, Verhandelingen der Koninklijke Nederlandse Akademie van Wetenschappen, afd. Letterkunde, n.s. 64, no. 2 (Amsterdam, 1958): 93, on line 65. The scholium in manuscript M writes, "*peperake(n) men ho perseptolis ēdē Marikas*." Marikas is a name used by Eupolis.

over [the] neck of [the] sea."[63] The stanza, the first strophe, and the sentence conclude with the word *pontou* ("sea"), the most important word and the verbal focus of the passage. The word "sea" sets up a contrast between sea and land mentioned in the following antistrophe, which in turn prepares the audience for the contrast between the land and the sea in the moral stated in the third strophe and antistrophe. There the devices employed to cross the water, mentioned twice in the first strophe, are emphasized as part of the reason that the elders are fearful for the Persians. The many epithets and repetitions of the same idea in the strophe are not mere embellishment, but rather, with the help of the alliteration and pun in the first line, a means to catch the audience's attention so that it hears the important word "sea" at the end of the strophe and absorbs the moral when it is stated.

The sea again appears prominently in the second antistrophe of the lyric parodos (89–91), where tenor (the Persian army) and vehicle (the waves of the sea) are fused through verbal interaction of the type we have seen in both Aeschylean tragedy and in nō.

No one is worthy enough to make [a] stand against [the] great *torrent* of men	Dokimos d' outis hupostas megalōi *rheumati* phōtōn
Or with strong defenses to block [the] unconquerable wave[s] of [the] sea;	Ekhurois herkesin eirgein amakhon kuma thalassas·
For *invincible* are the Persian army and strong-willed people.	*Aprosoistos* gar ho Persan stratos alkiphrōn te laos.

In this antistrophe there is a movement from literal statement, the tenor—"no one is worthy enough to make [a] stand against [the] great"—to the vehicle word, "torrent" (*rheumati*).[64] After the word *rheumati* Aeschylus shifts back to the tenor, the word *phōtōn* ("men") and the phrase *ekhurois herkesin eirgein amakhon* ("with strong defenses to block unconquerable"), and then returns again to the vehicle, the words *kuma thalassas*

[63] A "yoke" is mentioned in line 50 in the midst of a list of leaders who went to Greece. However, the reference is to a yoke of slavery cast over Hellas, not to the Hellespontine bridge. On the use of the yoke as an image, see B. Hughes Fowler, "Aeschylus' Imagery," *Class. et Med.* 28 (1967): 1–10.

[64] The word *megalōi* ("great") lessens the degree of abruptness between tenor and vehicle, since both an army, the tenor of the preceding strophes, and a torrent can be "great." In the Greek *megalōi*, grammatically in the same dative case as *rheumati* ("torrent"), modifies only that word; however, before the audience hears the word *rheumati*, it does not know that Aeschylus will shift to a vehicle word rather than use a word meaning "army."

("wave[s] of [the] sea"). The phrase "wave[s] of [the] sea" metaphorically represents the Persian army, as the listener understands from the next line, which after *aprosoistos* ("invincible"), a word that can apply to waves or men, returns to the tenor, the army. Because Aeschylus has mentioned before this line that the king's army "cast a yoke over [the] neck of [the] sea" (71), an audience would probably associate *kuma thalassas* with the tenor at first and only later with the vehicle. Aeschylus creates a verbal interaction between the two with the words *rheumati*[65] and *aprosoistos*. This verbal interaction in turn anticipates a later development in the play—water used metaphorically becomes actual when the Persian men are reported to have died at sea. In addition, this passage, characterized by fluidity of style, syntactical and semantic overlapping, and verbal interaction, helps to prepare for Aeschylus's pun on the name of the Persians, a major "character" in the tragedy. In the first and alliterative line of the lyric parodos and in the last line of this antistrophe, there appear the only two articles within the four stanzas. These immediately precede and thus draw attention in both cases to the same sound, *pers*, meaning "destroy" in the former (*ho perseptolis*) and "Persian" in the latter (*ho Persan*).[66]

It may be worth considering, by way of a digression, an example in nō of verbal interaction that depends in part for its effectiveness on the repetition of a word from the tenor of a preceding passage in the vehicle of a subsequent passage, similar to Aeschylus's use in the lyric parodos of a synonym for "sea" echoed from the tenor of the first strophe as a part of the vehicle. The passage is found in the nō *Yorimasa* where Zeami presents the confrontation of two armies rather than of two warriors as in *Sanemori*. In his description of the mustering of the Heike and the Genji troops at Uji River, Zeami says that both armies at the banks of the river raised a loud "clamor of battle" (*toki no koe*), and that this noise and the "cries of archers" (*yasakebi no oto*) mingled with[67] the roaring of the waves. The lines prepare for the choral passage in chūnori rhythm in which Zeami describes how the Heike plunged into a river:

Without the least hesitation	Sukoshi mo tamerawazu
Just as *flocks* of *flocking* birds	*Mure* iru *mura*tori no
With their *wings lined up*	*Tsubasa* o *naraburu*

[65] See Ole Smith, "Some Observations on the Structure of Imagery in Aeschylus," *Class. et Med.* 26 (1965): 26, who says that *rheuma* is not a proper image. Actually *rheuma* ("torrent") serves both the tenor and the vehicle and helps to set up an expectation on the part of the audience for the latter.

[66] See my discussion on page 265 below.

[67] *Tagueru* means "compared to," but see *YKS*, 263 n. 36, for the meaning "mingled with."

And *with [the] sound of fluttering wings, at least that's how we perceived it*, into [the] *white* waves	*Haoto* mo *kaku ya* to *shira*nami ni,
They plunged with [a] splash.	Zazzatto uchiirete.

Within the passage itself, Zeami shifts from the tenor to an analogy of men with birds by means of a repetition: *mure* and *mura-*, which mean "flock," "swarm," or "crowd." The second *mura*, combined with *-tori* ("birds"), introduces the vehicle that continues with the word *tsubasa* ("wings"). The word *naraburu* ("lined up," like birds or an army in formation) applies to both the tenor and the vehicle, as *aprosoistos* applies to both the tenor and the vehicle in the *Persians*. *Haoto* ("[the] sound of fluttering wings") is the vehicle, but by virtue of the preparation made for the word *oto* ("sound") from the earlier phrase "cries of archers" (*yasakebi no oto*), Zeami smoothly moves back to the tenor. The phrase *kaku ya to shira* ("at least, that's how we perceived it"), a reference to the Genji reaction, concludes with *shira-*, a pivot onto *nami* ("waves").[68] *Shira* is a homonym for "know," translated "perceive," and for "white," as in white waves. The passage ends with the splash of the men plunging into water, in a line marked by the onomatopoeic word *zazzatto*. In the lyric parodos of the *Persians*, the alliteration of the first line (65) provides aural interest.

In the mesode and the two stanzas following the antistrophe in the *Persians*, Aeschylus introduces the important moral and says that the Persians took to the sea when it was destined for them to fight wars by land (94–114). Instead of using verbal interaction, Aeschylus accumulates epithets and phrases to emphasize actions on both land and sea and thus to bring out the contrast between them. The chorus says (101–114):

For by will of [the] gods Fate made	Theothen gar kata Moir' ekratēsen
[Her] decree long ago, and ordered [the] Persians	To palaion, epeskēpse de Persais
To attend to wars *that destroy city walls*	Polemous *purgodaïktous*
And turmoils *of [the] cavalry,* and overthrows of cities;	Diepein *hippiokharmas* te klonous poleōn t' anastaseis·
But they learned, *when [the] broad-pathed sea*	Emathon d' *euruporoio thalassas*

68 See *YKS*, 264 n. 43.

Was growing white with foam from [the] *wind*,	*Poliainomenas pneumati labrōi*
To look to [the] precinct of [the] sea,	Esoran pontion alsos,
Trusting in [the] *fine-drawn* cables and *people-carrying* devices.	Pisunoi *leptotonois* peismasi *laoporois* te mēkhanais.

The italicized words are all superfluous in terms of the requirements of the thought being expressed in the sentence—namely, Fate ordered the Persians to engage in wars on land but they looked to the sea and trusted in cables and other devices. However, since it would be difficult for an audience to miss these words, it would seem that this "verbal baggage," by virtue of its sheer weight, serves as a means to establish the importance of the contrast between the land and the sea to the moral of the tragedy, and that the extended genitive absolute, "when [the] broad-pathed sea / was growing white with foam from [the] wind," serves, as joshi in nō, to introduce the sea with a flourish that is not superfluous, but important to the point—the yoking of the sea—which Aeschylus emphasizes with two more epithets.

Aeschylus then reinforces the moral[69] and makes it more vivid in the audience's mind by comparing, in one of his few uses of a simile, the Persian land forces, foot and horse, to a swarm of bees (130), which has made its way across the sea to another land. Aeschylus's comparison of the Persians to bees is still one more of many passages in which he creates verbal interaction. The passage (129–132) reads as follows:

For all [the] horsemen and men on foot	Pas gar hippēlatas kai pedostibēs leōs
Like[a] *swarm* of *bees* has left with [the] leader of [the] army,	*Smēnos* hōs ekleloipen *melissan* sun orkhamōi stratou,
And has crossed the double-yoked projectory of [the] sea	Ton amphizeukton exameipsas amphoteras halion
Which is shared by both lands.	Prōna koinon aias.

[69] One is reminded of the number of times and ways in *Sanemori* Zeami expresses the joy of the warrior in the shite's one extended speech in the third dan of the maeba, thus preparing for his renewed expression of joy in the nochiba. This example is somewhat analogous to the way in which, later in the *Persians*, Aeschylus has Darius draw a connection between the yoking of the Hellespont and Xerxes' folly. See lines 744–751, in particular. Aeschylus anticipates this connection with his repetition of the same idea in the lyric parodos.

The word *smēnos* ("swarm"), suited in meaning to a swarm of bees, but used metaphorically of any crowd, such as an army, provides a smooth transition from tenor to the vehicle word, *melissan* ("bees"). The word order in the Greek helps: *smēnos* ("swarm"), *hōs* ("like"), *ekleloipen* ("has left"), *melissan* ("of bees"). Aeschylus shifts with verbal economy out of the epic simile, the vehicle, by means of the word *orkhamōi* ("leader"), a tenor word, but an epicism.

In the *Persians*, the emphasis on the Persians' ill-advised bridging of the Hellespont prepares for the messenger section, in which the sea figures prominently—the audience hears that the Persians in great numbers died in battles at sea. In lines 88–89, the chorus compared the Persians to water and expressed confidence that the Persians could conquer water; in the messenger scene, water reappears as both tenor and vehicle, but this time as the source of disasters. The sea is mentioned repeatedly in this section. For example, the messenger concludes his longest speech and the vivid account of how ships rammed each other and waters were filled with corpses, hacked like fish by the enemy, as follows (426–432):

. . . And wailing along with Shrieks took over *[the] expanse of [the] sea* Until [the] eye of black night removed [it].[70] ʼ*[The] multitude of disasters*, not even if for ten days I should count, could I fill out for you. For mark this well, never in one day Has such [a] large number of men died.	. . . Oimōgē d' homou Kōkumasin kateikhe *pelagian hala,* Heōs kelainēs nuktos omm' apheileto. *Kakōn de plēthos,* oud' an ei dek' ēmata Stoikhēgoroiēn, ouk an ekplēsaimi soi. Eu gar tod' isthi, mēdam' hēmerai miai Plēthos tosoutarithmon anthrōpōn thanein.

The multitude of disasters and the sea, each a part of the tenor, converge verbally in the queen's reaction, where the sea, the tenor, becomes a vehicle again. Repeating the words *kakōn* ("disasters," also meaning "evils") and *pelagos* ("sea") from the messenger's speech, she says (433–434):

Oh, what [a] great sea of disasters has broken upon [The] Persians and [the] entire race of barbarians.	Aia, kakōn dē pelagos errōgen mega Persais te kai propanti barbarōn genei.

[70] This rendering is based on the reading of the manuscripts rather than that of the Oxford text, *kelainon nuktos omm'*, which means "black eye of night."

In the phrase "great sea of disasters has broken," and by means of the repetition of specific words from one speech to the other, Aeschylus begins to make artistically a connection on the verbal level between the sea and the disasters.

Aeschylus continues the metaphorical use of "water" in the next long messenger speech, which describes the slaughter at the island of Psyttaleia. The god, says the messenger, gave the glory in the battle of the ships to the Greeks and on the same day a victory on land; the Persians were smitten and hacked to pieces until they died. In the first sentence in which he mentions the king by name, he adds that Xerxes on seeing the "depth of disasters" (*kakōn . . . bathos*) cried out with a groan (465). The phrase "depth of disasters"[71] conveys the intensity of the catastrophe while suggesting, as in the English idiom, the "depths" of the sea. (In the messenger's final speech, water again figures prominently within the context of the miracle—a god froze the river out of season when what remained of the Persian forces made their way home across the land.[72])

Aeschylus reinforces for the audience the connection between the phrase "depth of disasters"—what Xerxes saw—and the sea, both by preparation with the queen's words at line 433, "sea of disasters" (a phrase that is part of the tenor as well as a vehicle), and with the messenger's next words related to the tenor—he reports that Xerxes held a seat with a view of the entire army, on a high hill near the "expanse of [the] sea" (*pelagias halos*, 467).[73] In lines 88–89, the Persians were compared to the water, here that great sea is the location and the cause of the disasters, unconquerable still, but overwhelming the Persians. By means of verbal interaction, the metaphorical sea becomes the literal sea; vehicle becomes the tenor.[74]

In the choral lament following the messenger section, Aeschylus prepares for the explicit presentation of the moral in the Darius scene by

[71] The phrase, which is not unrelated in meaning to the earlier phrases "multitude of disasters" and "sea of disasters," is repeated by the queen later, in her first speech addressed to the ghost of Darius. There she says that she envies him for having died before seeing the "depths of disasters [evils or woes]" (*kakōn . . . bathos*, 712). The connection drawn between old age and water in the short phrase "waves of old age" in *Sanemori*, although mentioned only once, is similarly effective in connecting two important themes of the play.

[72] On the role of both natural phenomena and divine retribution in the destruction of the Persians during their return, see Conacher, "Aeschylus' *Persae*," 158–159.

[73] Compare the use of the words "sea of disasters" in line 429.

[74] In *Sanemori*, Zeami suggests an analogy between the ponds at Shinowara and in Paradise, but this identity does not entail a reversal. In *Matsukaze*, there is a kind of reversal: *matsu*, meaning "pine tree," is part of Matsukaze's name; the pine tree on stage is one that she imagines is her lover; at the end of the nō, as I have mentioned, she becomes a wind in the pines. However, because the character becomes identified with the object of her own imaginings, one would hardly say that they are turned *against* her. The effect is very different from that of Aeschylus's presentation of water in the *Persians*.

drawing a contrast between Darius and Xerxes and by emphasizing the error of Xerxes' decision to take to the seas. In the first strophe of the lament, Aeschylus summarizes the important themes of the play in a few words. "Xerxes led" (550), says the chorus; one line suffices to recapitulate what it said in the parodos. Its next words, "Xerxes destroyed," suffice to capture the essence of the messenger's report. And finally, in "Xerxes did everything imprudently with [his] ships upon [the] sea," it points to two contributing factors in the Persian defeat, Xerxes and the sea. The anaphoric repetition of the name Xerxes in one verse after another heightens the intensity of the brief, but all too true, statements. At the end of the strophe (555–557), the chorus sets up a contrast between father and son only hinted at before in the queen's narration of her dream, and asks why Darius, lord of the bow and dear leader, remained unharmed.

Aeschylus emphasizes the tragedy of Xerxes' use of ships in the antistrophe by means of parallel constructions and repetition. The chorus sings, *linopteroi kuanōpides / naes men agagon popoi* ("linen-winged, dark-eyed/ships led, alas") and *naes d'apōlesan, totoi* ("ships destroyed, alas") (559–561). The two epithets describing the ships are Homeric, but they are not purely ornamental;[75] they serve, somewhat like makurakotoba, to focus attention, here on the ships as the cause of the Persian disaster. The words "ships led" and, in the next line, "ships destroyed" echo the syntax and words of lines 550–551 in the strophe: "Xerxes led" and "Xerxes destroyed." (The cries *popoi* and *totoi* are also repeated from lines 550–551 and help to emphasize the words for the audience.) However, the "ships" that have replaced Xerxes as the subject of the verbs, although mentioned three times, as Xerxes' name was, prove to be the Greeks' ships, rather than the Persians'. When the chorus says "ships led," in the light of the preceding strophe, one thinks that it refers to the Persian ships; however, when it says "ships destroyed," one knows from the messenger speech that it is referring to the Greek ships. Aeschylus economically shifts from one to the other by means of anaphora.[76]

In a prominent position, immediately after the choral song and at a juncture that marks the start of the second half of the tragedy, Aeschylus *begins* the queen's speech with a bit of traditional wisdom[77] that points out the significance of the present disasters for any and all human beings, including those in the audience (598–602):

[75] That is Earp's term, in *The Style of Aeschylus*, 62.

[76] Anaphora and repeated syntax occur in the issei of the nochiba of *Sanemori*, for example. There Zeami's use of *namu to ippa* and *Amida to ippa* emphasizes the nembutsu and gives the literal meaning of its parts.

[77] See, for example, *Odyssey* 18.132–133, where this idea appears without the use of an image, and Pindar's *Olympian* 2.33–34, with a water image.

Friends, whoever is experienced
   in *disasters*
Knows how for mortals,
   whenever [a] *wave*
Of disasters attacks, he is wont
   to fear everything,
But when a *god is favorable*, to
   have confidence
That *the same wind* of fortune
   will blow forever.

Philoi, *kakōn* men hostis
   empeiros kurei,
Epistatai brotoisin hōs, hotan
   kludōn
Kakōn epelthēi, panta deimainein
   philei,
Hotan d' ho *daimōn euroēi*,
   pepoithenai
Ton auton aien *anemon ouriein*
   tukhēs.

In this passage, the "wave of disasters/evils/woes," the vehicle (actually, only "wave" is a vehicle), as common as *kokoro no mizu* ("water in [the] heart") is in nō,[78] intrudes into the tenor, the disasters that humans have experienced. However, the audience knows by this point in the play that waves are also the tenor. Aeschylus points to this twofold meaning of the sea through continued verbal interaction in the queen's speech. The vehicle and the tenor converge in the word *epelthēi* ("attacks," 600), a word suited to both,[79] after which the passage returns to the tenor. With the word *euroēi* ("is favorable," literally, "flows freely," 601), which is a dead metaphor brought to life, the vehicle becomes prominent and words belonging to the tenor intrude on the vehicle. *Pepoithenai* ("to have confidence," 600) appears before the words *ton auton aien anemon ouriein* ("the same wind of fortune will blow forever," 602). The word *tukhēs* ("fortune") appears at the end of the passage.

In the anakletic hymn, for which the queen prepares in the continuation of her speech, it is noteworthy that Aeschylus mentions ships in the final line *only*, where he says that all the three-tiered ships (these are mentioned again at the end of the tragedy, 1075) have been destroyed, "ships that are not ships, not ships" (*naes anaes anaes*). The single syllable of the alpha-privative verbally annihilates the ships of the Persians[80] as economically as

[78] The phrase *kokoro no mizu* ("water in [the] heart") is used in the rongi and appears in a slightly altered form as *kokoro no ike* ("pond in [the] heart") in the kakeai of the nochiba of *Sanemori*.

[79] See Silk, *Interaction*, 21–23.

[80] Helen Moritz has suggested further that Aeschylus may also be drawing a contrast between father and son not only with words, but with the use of syllables. See "Refrain in Aeschylus," 187–213. For example, Moritz thinks that the letters *kak . . . a . . .* in *kakōn akos* ("cure for evils," 631), prepare for and play on those in *akake* in the address to Darius—*akake* ("not evil," 663 = 671). Darius is a cure for evils, is not evil, and is one who has not caused disasters or woe. I question whether an audience would absorb this pun, because there does not appear to be the type of verbal clue here that we find elsewhere in passages in which Aeschylus emphasizes a pun. And yet, an audience surely can hear the repeated use of the *a*-privative in *anaes* of line 680. Because *akake* is repeated in a repeated line at the end of two stanzas, the *a*-privative, which negates an

Zeami creates verbal interest in some of his expressions with but one syllable.[81] There is little doubt that the audience was meant to hear the effect of these words, for this is not an isolated example of negation by means of repetition and the *a*-privative in Aeschylus's work.[82]

Xerxes' responsibility is spelled out at greater length in the Darius scene than anywhere else in the play, and it is here that the religious and moral lessons of the tragedy are stated most explicitly. In his first speech to the queen, Darius sets the highly moral tone of the speeches that follow by observing that if one lives a long time, calamities strike both on sea and on land (706–707). In his next extended speech delivered in trochaic tetrameters, Darius identifies Xerxes as the cause of the disasters in terms of water, used as both vehicle and tenor. He says, "Now it seems [the] *fount of disasters (kakōn . . . pēgē)* has been found for all who are dear; and my child, without knowing it, accomplished these things, in [his] youthful boldness" (743).[83] This explicit criticism of Xerxes' actions arises verbally out of the various meanings of line 743. The word *pēgē*, meaning "abundance," points to the abundance of troubles caused by Xerxes. Since the word *pēgē* also means "source," in this sense it points directly to Xerxes, the grammatical subject of the next line. And finally, with *kakōn* as a subjective genitive, *pēgē* means "fountainhead,"[84] that is, only the beginning of troubles to come, and thus foreshadows the Persian defeat at Plataea, which Darius prophesies. In one expression Aeschylus refers to the source of the disasters, the abundance of troubles, and the beginning of new disasters.[85]

Although the reference to Poseidon near the end of Darius's speech is anticipated in part by the earlier references to Xerxes' mistake in crossing

---

epithet eminently appropriate as a description of Xerxes, that is, *kakos* ("evil"), and establishes the authority of Darius as a spokesman, may be noticed by an audience and prepare for the more striking use of the *a*-privative at the end of the hymn.

[81] In nō, the negation of one word by means of a suffix tends to create two alternatives, both of which are relevant, rather than one excluding the other. See, for example, in the first ageuta of *Sanemori*, *shiru mo shiranu mo* ("both those who believe and those who do not"). Neither alternative is excluded from Amida's Vow.

[82] Aeschylus uses this verbal device again in the plays of the *Oresteia*. See *Agamemnon* 1545—*akharin kharin*; *Libation Bearers* 44—*kharin akhariton*; and *Eumenides* 457—*apolin Iliou polin*.

[83] On the interconnection of *kakōn . . . pēgē* and "youthful boldness," see Jens Hansen, *Bildhafte Sprache des Aischylos: See und Schiffahrt in metaphorischer Verwendung* (Kiel, 1955), 22–25.

[84] See Broadhead, *Persae*, 187.

[85] Since the main character in two-part nō is a ghost, it is understandable that prediction of the character's future on earth would not figure in such plays. However, prophecy and oracles are not unknown in nō; for example, in *Kiyotsune*, the warrior's ghost, in speaking of the past, tells his wife that an oracle had declared that his side would lose the war.

the water, Poseidon's name is not mentioned before this. Within the speech itself, Aeschylus prepares the audience for the name of the god of the sea by repeated references to divinity. There is no pun on Poseidon's name, but the preparation for its appearance is as carefully executed as if there were. In this way Aeschylus makes clear that Xerxes' error was not simply a miscalculation but entailed a religious transgression. To begin with, Darius mentions Zeus (740), who, he says, brought upon his son the fulfillment of oracles (*thesphatōn*, literally meaning "that which is spoken by god"). (This mention of Zeus is only the second in the play and the first by someone other than the chorus.) Darius adds in the next two lines that he expected the gods (*theous*) to bring this about after some time (741), but when a person speeds an act along himself, god (*theos*) helps (742). Next, only one verse later, in a sentence that by virtue of the length of the subordinate clause alone emphasizes Xerxes' mistake, Darius says, "My son accomplished these things in youthful boldness and ignorance, because he hoped to restrain [the] flow of [the] sacred Hellespont, like [a] slave in chains, [the] Bosporus, [a] river of [the] god (*theou*), and he tried to alter [the] passageway and, by throwing on hammer-wrought fetters, made [a] path for his great army" (744–748). This lengthy verbal preparation converges on the next lines, in which Darius says, "He [Xerxes], though mortal, in thinking that he could conquer all [the] gods (*theōn*), even Poseidon (*Poseidōnos*), acted foolishly" (749–750). He adds, "Surely [a] sickness of [the] mind must have taken hold of him" (750–751). The audience is not likely to miss this kind of preparation for the name of the god who is closely connected, indeed identified, with the sea, and against whom Xerxes transgressed. Xerxes' moral and religious guilt is clearly established.

After Darius's long list of the kings of Persia, which includes himself, who, he says, had not "cast such ill upon [the] city" (781) as Xerxes had, Aeschylus borrows from the words of oracles and the wisdom of the poetic sage Solon. He thus adds authority to Darius's words. Aeschylus's artistic hand can also be seen in the verbal techniques by which he connects the water and the land to the lessons of the tragedy. Darius says that, persuaded by empty hopes, Xerxes left behind a select body from the army (803–804). He adds, "Where [the] Asopus river waters [the] plain with its streams, [the] source of friendly drink to [the] land of [the] Boeotians, there awaits [the] men to suffer [the] highest of evils (*kakōn hupsist'* . . . *pathein*) in requital for hubris and godless thoughts" (805–808). Darius sets up a contrast: what lies ahead for Xerxes' men is suffering, but the waters of the Asopus river are kindly to the native inhabitants. Darius's words are also proverbial and thus familiar to the audience—that mortals should avoid overbearing thoughts is a variation on the famous "nothing to excess" admonition of the Delphic oracle. The words are also reminiscent of Solon's lines on satiety, which "gives birth to hubris whenever much prosperity attends men whose minds are not sound."[86] In other words, Aeschylus gives to Darius's words the authority of tradition, both the religious authority of Delphi, the center of the Greek religious world, and the moral authority of Solon, the early political leader of Athens.[87]

After Darius explains how the Persians were godless in their actions in Greece, drawing on traditional morality again, he explains that they suffer their due penalty. (In *Libation Bearers* 313, "he who acts pays" is called a "tale thrice-aged.") Referring to water in lines 814–817 Darius says that there are sufferings to come and:

. . . The spring of evils is not yet dried up, But still gushes forth,	. . . Koudepō kakōn Krēnis apesbēk', all' et' ekpiduetai,[88]

"for very great bloodshed will be spilled on [the] Plataean plain by [the] Dorian spear," that is, the land forces will suffer as the navy did. (Darius's words *kakōn krēnis*, "spring of evils" [814–815], recall the words *kakōn . . . pēgē*, "fount of evils" [743]. The kindly drink from the waters of Asopus, a contrasting idea, intervenes at line 806.) What Darius means he explains in lines 818–820, namely that "heaps of corpses will provide [a] voiceless sign to [the] eyes of mortals unto [the] third-sown generation that [a] mortal should not have overbearing thoughts." Darius's words, associated with water—the waters of evil that gush forth—are closely connected with the moral of the play, that mortals should not have overbearing thoughts. The moral gains authority again because it is inspired by Solon.[89]

Darius continues with a warning against overbearing thoughts (821–822):

For hubris *bursting forth* bears [a] crop Of disaster, whence it *gathers* [a] harvest fraught with tears.[90]	Hubris gar *exanthous'* ekarpōse stakhun Atēs, hothen pagklauton *examai* theros.

[86] 6.3–4 West. A similar idea is repeated in Pindar's *Pythian* 3.59–60.
[87] On the subject of the relationship between Aeschylus's thought and that of Solon (and Hesiod), see Friedrich Solmsen's *Hesiod and Aeschylus* (Ithaca, N.Y., 1949).
[88] I read *krēnis apesbēk'* with Housman, and *all' et' ekpiduetai* with Schütz. For other alternatives, see A. J. Podlecki, "Three Passages in Persae," *Antichthon* 9 (1975): 1–3.
[89] See above, Chapter Two, note 110.
[90] The word order of the original is: "whence" (*hothen*); "fraught with tears" (*pagklauton*); "it gathers" (*examai*); "[a] harvest" (*theros*).

These two lines contain an image that pertains closely to water. In earlier passages, the audience has heard of the potential for water on land to create good crops and to quench thirst; however, the gushing water mentioned in line 815 leads only to a crop of corpses at Plataea, a sign "unto [the] third generation" (*tritosporōi gonei* [818]; *tritosporos* means literally "sown for [the] third time") that a mortal should not have overbearing thoughts. The adjective *tritosporōi*, associated in meaning with *stakhun* ("crop") and the other words pertaining to harvest in lines 821–822, serves to prepare the audience for them (a preparation analogous to the use of engo in many passages of nō).[91] Neither rich nor healthful, this crop is the crop of disaster (*atē*), first mentioned in the play as the goddess Atē, who draws men into her snares. Earlier she is the cause of disaster; later she is the *disaster* that grows from *hubris* and out of which is gathered a harvest *fraught with tears*. The mention of *atē* is noticeable in part because the ghost of Darius can emphasize it and in part because it appears within a passage marked by verbal interaction. *Atēs*, *hubris*, and *pagklauton*, words belonging to the tenor, interact with the words of the vehicle. This effect is skillfully achieved for the sake of a listening audience by the alliteration of verbs belonging properly to the vehicle, of which *hubris* is the grammatical subject: *exanthous'* ("bursting forth [like flowers]"), *ekarpōse* ("bear [as a crop]," gnomic aorist), and *examai* ("gathers [as a harvest]"). In addition, *Atē*, associated in meaning with *hubris*, serves as both subjective and objective genitive with the word *stakhun* ("crop")—she is the planter and the plant. The audience has been informed of Xerxes' hubris; it has heard repeatedly about tears. The two ideas converge here in a passage where *Atē* reappears and where the image of a harvest makes vivid Darius's moral.

Darius then repeats the moral again with words directed as much to the audience as to anyone "on stage" and asks that "one not despise the present fortune and out of yearning for other [fortunes] pour out [his] great prosperity" (824–826). He concludes with gnomic advice that Zeus will punish those who are too overbearing (*huperkompōn*) in thought and specifies that instructions be given to Xerxes to cease from injuring the gods with overbearing (*huperkompōi*) boldness (827–831). The audience cannot be unaware of the religious and moral lesson, which has been poetically connected with the land and sea and with Xerxes, and which emerges clearly from the repetition.[92]

[91] The image of a harvest in these lines is further integrated verbally into the speech by the repetition of the word *hubris* from line 808, where Darius warns of suffering that will fall upon the Persians at Plataea for their hubris and godless thoughts.

[92] The repetition of an important religious or ethical thought is frequently found in nō. For example, in *Yorimasa* Zeami repeats the Buddhist idea that life is weary, sad,

In the Darius scene, Aeschylus has prepared for the appearance of the defeated Xerxes, punished by the gods. In the following ode he prepares further, not only by setting the deeds of Darius into contrast with those of Xerxes, but also by listing the many places that Darius managed to control without crossing the river Halys or leaving home, as Xerxes had done. The list serves in part to extol Darius because many of the places referred to by name are islands (880–895) or appear in the context of the river Strymon (867) and the Hellespont (877), thus suggesting that the cause of Xerxes' disaster was the source of Darius's strength. The chorus's concluding remark, made immediately before Xerxes' appearance, states the case against Xerxes explicitly. There is nothing "metaphorical" in the language (905–906):

Now without doubt we suffer	Nun d' ouk amphilogōs
these changes brought by	theotrepta tad' au
god in war,	pheromen polemoisi,
Defeated terribly by blows at sea.	Dmathentes megalōs plagaisi
	pontiaisin.

Once again, as in 71, the word reserved for the emphatic final position is *pontiaisin* ("at sea"). There the repetition of phrases synonymous in meaning and all pointing to the method by which Xerxes crossed the water of the Hellespont leads up to the significant word, here a list of places, among which the islands of the sea are most numerous.

Within the kommos, Aeschylus again emphasizes ships, the shore, and the sea. However, in the anapaestic introduction to the kommos, he refers to and emphasizes the land first. Xerxes says that a god "reaped" the men, that "the land mourns for her native youth," that the "flower of [the] land" is dead, and that the "land of Asia is fallen on its knees" (920–930). Particularly effective is the manner in which Aeschylus, through assonance, echoes the cry of woe, *aiai*, within the word *eggaian*, "earth," and thus connects Xerxes' lamentable state with the earth (see page 229 above).[93]

In the next part of the kommos, after Xerxes has acknowledged that he became an evil to his people and his native land (932–933), he mentions

---

and ephemeral. He says that it is difficult to cross life, and life is hard to eke out; life is tiring; Yorimasa leaves but dew-laden grass behind; the warrior reveals himself to the transient earthly world; the world is evanescent; waves of illusory attachment roll upon the warrior; and life is weary.

[93] The effect is as striking as the repetition of the syllable *ya*, an interjection, repeated in the first syllable of the next word *Yashima*, the location of the nō entitled *Yashima*. Sanari Kentarō, in the first volume of *Yōkyoku taikan*, 74–75, gives this example of the technique of adjoining rhyme, called *setsuin*.

the disasters at sea. With each mention of the sea, interspersed between names of the leaders who have died, there is a mark of Aeschylus's stylistic artistry. First Xerxes mentions the sorrows involving ships beaten (945), in which line (as discussed above on page 226) *bar* serves as a pivot between the meanings "ship" and "sorrows." In lines 951–952, Ares' name appears for only the second time in the play—in line 85, he was wielding a bow on land, here he is on sea with warships.

Ares with embattled array of Ionian ships, inclining [his] strength to [the] other side,	Iaōn naupharktos Arēs heteralkēs
Reaping [the] dark sea and ill-fortuned shore.	Nukhian plaka kersamenos dusdaimona t' aktan.

In these lines there is verbal interaction between the vehicle word *kersamenos* ("reaping"), which grammatically modifies the word *Ares* and pertains to the image of crops, and the tenor, namely, the sea, which Ares is said to reap as if it were the land.[94] Xerxes next mentions those whom he "left perished from [the] Tyrian ship upon [the] shores of Salamis, dashed upon [the] hateful shore" (964–965). In this line Xerxes makes his first specific reference to Salamis. And finally he mentions the men who "with [a] stroke of the oar are all miserably gasping [like fish] on [the] dry land" (976–977).[95]

In the last section of the kommos, Aeschylus emphasizes the importance of the sea to the punishment of the Persians both explicitly and by means of the verbal technique, referred to at the end of Chapter Two. He first says that the "gods have brought an unexpected disaster, clear as [the] look of Atē" (1006–1007). In the answering antistrophe, as if to explain, he says that "they [the Persians] met [the] Ionian sailors in battle without good fortune" (1011–1012). As I have already pointed out, the mention of Atē, the goddess who first appears in the moral dictum of the lyric parodos where she is said to draw men into her net (on land), then occasions a repetition of her name in the compound adjective *megalate* ("great in

---

[94] Although there is no ambiguity about the Persian defeat mentioned in the line, the word *heteralkēs* allows the line to yield two possible interpretations: "The Persian fleet obtained a harvest of woe from the Ionians *by yielding victory to the foe* and having the dark surface of the sea and the ill-fortuned shore reaped close," and, "The embattled array of Ionian ships *turning the tide of battle* robbed the Persians of their men by ravaging the dark surface of the sea and the ill-fortuned shore" (see Broadhead, *Persae*, 229–230). The repetition of the word *naupharkton* ("with embattled array"), in line 1029 to describe the Ionians, not the Persians, supports the second interpretation.

[95] There is an implicit allusion to fish here; see Herodotus 9.120. In lines 424–426 the Persians are compared to fish. But if there is an image here, it is not striking; the gasping of the men is real enough.

atē," 1016), describing Xerxes,[96] and next in the words *ataisi pontiaisin* ("disasters at sea," 1037). The word *atē* is thus transformed from the singular goddess, Delusion, into the plural, the results of the goddess's and Xerxes' actions, which are directly connected with the sea by means of the adjective *pontiaisin* ("of [the] sea") modifying the plural noun.[97] None of these references to ships and the sea, including the final and emphatic mention of the ships near the end of the *Persians*—"destroyed by three-tiered ships" (1075–1076)—is metaphorical. (The land is also referred to in lines 1070 and 1074 without metaphorical connotations.) The "disasters confronted at sea" are the facts of the case recognized as fully by Xerxes and the chorus as they are realized in the language for the audience.

Aeschylus's references to disasters, evils, and woes (*kaka*), so inextricably linked with the sea (as both vehicle and tenor) and with the moral, converge in line 1041, where the evils are presented in their own terms without a mention of the sea or the land: *dosin* ["gift"] *kakan kakōn kakois*.[98] Although there is some ambiguity about the syntax and meaning of the line arising out of the use of the genitive (*kakōn*) and dative (*kakois*) cases, the lack of articles, and the threefold use of *kakon* with a different shade of meaning and a different referent in each, we can be certain that the chorus is saying that its cries of lament are a "sorry gift" (*dosin kakan*; that the "gift" is the cries and the lament, see 1040 and 1042). We can be almost certain that it says the sorry gift has arisen "from disasters" (*kakōn*), but must infer that it sings "for those who have caused the disaster" (*kakois*; specifically, the impious and hubristic Xerxes and his men). The performance of a lament, the disasters themselves, and the cause of disaster converge in this one line, after which Aeschylus turns to the subject of the line, the lament proper and the gestures appropriate to it. The connection between the words pointing to the moral and the performance of the lament is analogous to the connection Zeami makes between the cause of Sanemori's attachment, Kiso, and the shite's movement forward on stage as he says that the attachment of warrior hell "has come" again and begins his performance of the tale of repentance.

At the end of *Sanemori*, once the warrior is asked to purify his heart, Zeami does not use the image of water. The only image to appear is that

---

[96] The repetition of *peplēgmeth'* ("we have been struck") at lines 1008–1009 after the name Atē, and again at line 1015, *peplēgmai* ("I have been stricken") before the compound, helps to emphasize the words.

[97] In lines 652–653, the word *atais* ("disasters") is modified by the compound adjective *polemophthoroisin* ("war-destroying") which is an *hapax legomenon*, a word found nowhere else in ancient Greek literature. Aeschylus may have created a neologism in order to emphasize the word *atais*, which he then uses again with the same and not uncommon meaning, "disasters," at line 1037.

[98] See Broadhead, *Persae*, 240–241, on this passage.

of the tree, one repeated in several poetic lines of the nō that Zeami borrows, quotes, or alludes to, and repeated for the final time in the poetic line that Zeami adds to the *Heike* account of the warrior's death and that the chorus delivers as the shite mimes a fall. The final section of the kommos of the *Persians* involves no metaphorical language either, except perhaps in the repeated *eress' eresse* (1046). The two words are part of the first instruction Xerxes gives to the chorus before he tells the men to carry out such conventional gestures of lament as tearing their hair and beating their breasts. With these words, he asks them to "ply" their arms in lament, but also, given the preceding references to ships in the kommos, to ply them as if they were oars.[99] There are of course no sailors, ships, or oars on stage at the end of the play, any more than there is a tree at the end of *Sanemori*. Yet the verbal hint of a metaphor that is translated into performance adds to the pathos of a scene, in which the elders and Xerxes ply their arms in time to the rhythm of a lament and mime the rowing of a ship, an action that caused their woe. The combination of gestures and a repeated word contributes to the impact of the finale, much as the shite's mime of the fall of a tree and the fall of the warrior in *Sanemori* adds pathos to the end of the nō. Although Aeschylus is more repetitive than Zeami because the greater length of the tragedy demands that he continually set up in the audience an expectation of what is to follow, an understanding of the style of Zeami enhances an appreciation of the attention that Aeschylus pays to the individual words and his artistic method of drawing out their full value in one passage after another in the *Persians*, as well as in his other tragedies.

ALLUSIONS AND BORROWINGS IN THE *PERSIANS*

The *Persians* is in a number of respects a unique tragedy, one in which there is little plot or action to entertain the audience. Instead its appeal derives in part from Aeschylus's gradual intensification of the emotional, kinetic and visual aspects of the performance, in part from his skillful manipulation of the words, and in part from his use of Homer and other sources with which the audience was familiar.[100] An understanding of

[99] "Row" is the translation of Podlecki, *Aeschylus: The Persians*, 112. There is probably a metaphor here because Aeschylus has prepared for it with many references to ships and sailors. He uses the word to mean "row" at line 422 of the *Persians*. He uses it in the other sense elsewhere. (At *Agamemnon* 52 the word connotes the plying both of birds' wings and of oars.) At 1046, the gesture might have had an impact similar to the shite's twirl of his sleeve over his arm in *Sanemori*, where, however, the gesture occurs several times during the course of the play and the expression "wave the sleeve" only once. In the *Persians*, the gesture may have occurred only once; the word "row" several times.

[100] There are of course allusions and borrowings in the works of Sophocles and Euripides, which I have omitted from my discussion. What is said about these features of style

Zeami's technique of literary borrowing and allusion in nō can help one to determine what techniques Aeschylus might have used to incorporate Homeric allusions, for example, into his text; how he enhanced the immediate context in which an allusion or borrowing occurs; and what, if any, cumulative effect there is to these allusions. We know, for example, that in his nō Zeami alludes to and borrows from other works, which he recommended should be familiar to the audience. We also know that he sometimes features verbal interaction between the text of the nō and the poetry or prose on which he draws (for example, in *Sanemori*, the word *mie* is repeated from the waki's speech in the cherry tree poem written by Yorimasa) and between the contents of the different sources themselves (for example, in *Sanemori*, the proverb and the maple tree poem and passages from the *Heike* are combined in a particularly striking example of this interaction of literary sources within the kuse).[101] Moreover, I have suggested that in *Sanemori*, not only does Zeami create a lyric atmosphere at certain junctures by means of literary borrowing, but also at the end of the nō he adds to the account drawn from the *Heike* a lyric line about a tree. I presume that, because of its familiarity with the *Heike*, the audience can recognize Zeami's artistry here in adding the line and, because of the cumulative effect of Zeami's repeated use of poems featuring trees, can appreciate the various associations of meaning and moods that the line conveys.

With the example of a few passages in which Aeschylus could very well be alluding to Homer,[102] it is possible to demonstrate how the practice in

---

in the *Persians* can apply to them. However, given the more prosaic dialogue and the greater complexity of the later plays in other spheres, the allusions gain more prominence in the *Persians* than in these works. I also leave out of consideration the theoretical questions that have arisen around the subject of intertextuality. To raise these would, I think, obscure the effect that an understanding of Zeami's techniques can have on our appreciation of Aeschylus's works.

[101] In *Yorimasa*, Zeami's comparison between warriors and fish in nets illustrates well this kind of intertextuality. The shite says in the sashi of the nochiba, "At Takuroku, [the] blood becomes [a] river, crimson waves pour forth shields, white-flashing swords crush bones. Making life regrettable, Uji River's fish nets in waves—turbulently my heart longs for its earthly life." The lines prepare for a quotation of a poem from the *Heike*, written by a certain Nakatsuna, who observed the warriors in red armor tangled in the fish nets of Uji River: "The Ise warriors, / All in crimson-corded / Armor attired, / Within Uji's fish nets / Were caught." The poem in turn introduces a Chinese fable: "[CHORUS:] Over snail's horns / To dispute— / [SHITE:] How vain. . . ." The allusion is to a fable about two warlords who fought against each other, one from the right, one from the left horn of a snail (see *YKS*, 261 n. 25). The allusion, though slight, serves to draw a moral against the petty quarrels of men and armies and points to the folly of Yorimasa's ghost harboring thoughts about the real world in which such fighting takes place.

[102] The ancient evidence for Aeschylus's use of Homer is strong. For example, see Aristophanes' *Frogs* 1030–1036 and Athenaeus 8.347e. Many scholars of Aeschylus have observed his indebtedness to Homer; these include Alexander Sideras, *Aeschylus Homericus*, who has identified most of the Homeric parallels I mention below; Broad-

nō might pertain to that in the *Persians*, not because the two are alike, but because an understanding of nō can provide us with a fresh approach to the text of the Greek tragedy. As I have already said, one finds that when Aeschylus borrows from another source, he most often does not quote it closely. A comparison of Zeami's use of authoritative sources in the beginning of the maeba and nochiba and in the kuse scene of *Sanemori* with Aeschylus's allusions to Delphic maxims, to proverbs, to Solon, most probably to other poets, both lyric and choral, and to traditional wisdom in the Darius scene, provides ample proof of that difference. The difference between Aeschylus and Zeami is one of degree, measured in terms of an oral or performed tradition, rather than a highly codified written tradition that carried with it a poetics. And yet, Herington has convincingly argued not only that there was a highly sophisticated oral and performed tradition of "literature" both before and during Aeschylus's day, from which Aeschylus, like other playwrights, borrowed, and with which members of the audience were familiar, but also that the works from which these were derived were written down.[103] In other words, we seem justified in looking for allusions. We cannot always determine the level of accuracy of quotation in tragedy to the same extent that we can in nō, since so much of ancient Greek literature has been lost. Yet we do know from ancient evidence that Aeschylus altered a line taken from Phrynichus's play *The Phoenician Women*,[104] and we can show that important words have been retained from original sources, when the appropriate texts are extant.

---

head, *Persae*, who comments on the catalogue and mentions other parallels throughout his commentary; Johannes Seewald, *Untersuchungen zu Stil und Komposition der aischyleischen Tragödie* (Greifswald, 1936), 34–35, who acknowledges Aeschylus's debt to Homer in the catalogues, but says that Aeschylus has added new materials, even allusions to the prose writer Hecataeus (n. 30); J. A. Schuursma, *De poetica vocabulorum abusione apud Aeschylum* (Paris, 1932); Susan B. Franklin, "Traces of Epic Influence in the Tragedies of Aeschylus" (Diss., Bryn Mawr College, 1895); Matelda Gigli, "Dell' imitazione omerica di Eschilo," *Rivista Indo-Greco-Italica* 12 (1928): 43–59; Guilelmus Kahlenberg, "De paraphrasis Homericae apud tragicos poetas Graecos vestigiis quaestiones selectae" (Diss., Strasburg, 1903); Max Lechner, "De Aeschyli studio Homerico," *Jahresbericht von der königlichen Studienanstalt zu Erlangen in Mittelfranken* (1862): 3–28. My translations of Homer are based on *Homeri opera* (Iliad), ed. David B. Monro and Thomas W. Allen (Oxford, 1920); and *Homeri opera* (Odyssey), ed. Thomas W. Allen (Oxford, 1917).

[103] Herington, *Poetry into Drama*. On p. 41, he says, "Only the existence of written texts can account for its [archaic Greek song culture] astounding sophistication, refinement, and variety and also for the transmission and preservation of its songs in reasonably uncorrupt form." See also p. 79 for general remarks, p. 114 on Aeschylus's debt to his predecessors for metrical forms, and p. 128 for the many poems of the epic cycle on which the tragedians drew but which are no longer extant except in prose summaries. See also Charles Segal, *Interpreting Greek Tragedy: Myth, Poetry, Text* (Ithaca, N.Y. and London, 1986), 75–109.

[104] This information, and the original line itself, is given in the hypothesis to the *Persians*, ascribed to Glaucus, a grammarian of Rhegium, late fifth century B.C.(?).

Aeschylus's indebtedness to the *Iliad* is particularly prominent, inasmuch as he lists Persian leaders three times in a style modeled on Homeric catalogues and thus places the Homeric mode emphatically before the audience. Because these lists, unique in Greek tragedy, appear three times, they approximate Zeami's repetition of the same poem or parts of it in nō in that an audience cannot ignore them. In *Izutsu*, for example, in both the quantity and the quality of the literary debt that the playwright seems to acknowledge, Zeami's quotation of a poem or parts of it in three contexts is analogous to Aeschylus's use of the lists, which, of course, are not quoted, but represent a stylistic borrowing.[105] The quotation of half of the poem occurs first in *Izutsu* in the context of the waki identifying the site of the play as Ariwaradera, which, like Mt. Tatsuta mentioned in the poem, is near Nara.[106] In the first sashi he says:

When [the] wind blows,	Kaze fukeba
White waves at sea *rise high*—	Okitsu shiranami
*Tatsu*ta Mountain.	*Tatsu*tayama.

The poem itself contains a verbal technique: the word *shiranami* ("white waves") introduces the syllables *tatsu*, which both mean "rise high" and serve as the beginning of the name of the mountain.[107] However, in this instance, Zeami self-consciously acknowledges his quotation and adds that the poem must have been composed at Ariwaradera, the setting of the play. He does not insert it into the text of the sashi by means of verbal interaction.

In the sashi that precedes the kuse of *Izutsu*, the shite, a woman who recollects the past and the visits of her husband, the poet Narihira, to another woman, quotes the entire poem:

SHITE: When [the] wind blows,	Kaze fukeba
White waves at sea rise high—	Okitsu shiranami
Tatsuta Mountain.	Tatsutayama.
CHORUS: At night, are you, my lord,	Yowa ni ya kimi ga
Crossing [that mountain] alone?	Hitori yukuran.

In the context of this second quotation of the poem, Zeami informs the audience that the woman won her husband's love back and that the number of his visits over the mountains to see his lover decreased. The repetition of the syllables *nami*, meaning "waves" (from the word *shiranami*, "white waves," in the second line of the poem) in the word *obotsukanami*

---

[105] See Broadhead, *Persae*, 252.
[106] The poem is drawn from the *Ise monogatari* (The Tales of Ise), no. 23.
[107] *YKS*, 278 n. 8.

("waves of fear") in the line of text following the quotation helps to integrate with the context a poem by means of which the woman touched her husband's heart and prompted him to change his mind.

And again, before the shite makes his first exit, in the rongi Zeami repeats part of the poem at the moment when the woman identifies herself to the chorus. She says that she is the daughter of Ki no Aritsune, whose name is as elusive as:

. . . White waves—	. . . Shiranami no
Tatsuta Mountain—	Tatsutayama
At night. . . .	Yowa ni. . . .

Here the first word quoted from the poem, *shiranami* ("white waves"), contains within the first three syllables the meaning "unknown," which pertains to the woman. She says that she has come "unrecognized." She is a woman who has traversed the same path as her husband, that is, over Mt. Tatsuta. The repetition of *Tatsutayama* in the line following the allusion to the poem helps to integrate it with the context of the nō. Within the maeba of *Izutsu*, the quotation adds a poetic atmosphere appropriate to a husband and wife who exchanged poetry; moreover, the poem prepares for the nochiba, in which the woman recollects the past and the times she waited for her husband to return.

The lists of leaders in the *Persians*, unlike the poem in *Izutsu*, are not quotations, but like that poem, they help to create an atmosphere in which the main character, although a historical figure, is represented with an epic coloring. In fact, Homer's poems provide for the *Persians*, not the kind of specific source that the *Heike* provides for warrior nō, but the kind of source on which Zeami draws for his lyric allusions in order to add a lyric quality to the strongly "epic" play, *Sanemori*. The catalogue of leaders at the beginning of the *Persians* sets an epic tone that is especially prominent in the parodos and the lyric parodos and that Aeschylus maintains throughout the play by alluding to important scenes in Homer's works. These allusions, to material with which the audience was very familiar, in turn affect the meaning of each context in which they appear.[108]

The first allusion to Homer occurs before the first enumeration of the leaders. The chorus says (10–11):

[108] Many scholars have pointed out the problems involved in the identification of Homeric allusions; however, their concerns are often directed toward different goals than mine. For example, Garvie (*Aeschylus' Supplices*, 45–48), warns against trying to date the plays of Aeschylus on the basis of his allusions. That is not the issue here. I have chosen only those allusions which clearly echo significant words from the original works, as we know them.

| *Prophesying evil,* [the] *spirit within* is Greatly troubled. | *Kakomantis* agan orsolopeitai *Thumos esōthen.* |

Here Aeschylus appears to conflate allusions to two different Homeric passages, adapting them to his purposes with a change from the second to the third person and with an addition of his own words. In the *Iliad* (1.106), Agamemnon, the leader of the Greek forces, calls the army's prophet, Calchas, *manti kakōn* ("prophet of evil"), after he advises Agamemnon to relinquish his mistress Chryseis. Later in the same book (243), Achilles threatens Agamemnon because he has been ordered by the leader to hand over his mistress in recompense for the loss of Chryseis, and says:

| You will tear at [the] *spirit within.* | Su d'*endothi thumon* amuxeis.[109] |

To be sure, no prophet, mistress, or argument between leaders figures in the context of the play,[110] any more than Sanemori's case involves the loss of sons or expertise as a poet within the context in which Zeami alludes to poems written by Yorimasa, who did lose his sons. The nō contains a poetic resonance, where one situation is set off against the other. The beginning of the *Iliad* and the argument between Agamemnon and Achilles, in which the latter warns that the Greeks will die at the hands of Hector, similarly resonate beneath the surface of the chorus's words in the *Persians* and add foreboding of imminent disaster. (It helps that in the *Iliad*, the verb "tears at" is in the future tense; in the tragedy, the verb is in the present tense.) The contents of these lines in which Aeschylus appears to allude to Homer add an important emotional dimension to the play, for, as I pointed out in Chapter Two, the idea within them is repeated several times in the *Persians.*[111]

[109] *Kakomantis* is also found in the *Seven against Thebes* (722). Fraenkel (*Aeschylus Agamemnon* 2: 446) lists other places in Aeschylus's works where the phrase "the heart within" is used in expressions of emotion. Aeschylus, like Zeami, does not restrict phrases, whether borrowed from another source or not, to one passage or one work. Unless germane to this discussion, these repetitions will not be pointed out. For a partial list, see Garvie, *Aeschylus' Supplices,* 73.

[110] *Baüzei* (13) may hint at discontent with Xerxes' leadership. See Conacher, "Aeschylus' Persae," 149 n. 2. For the various interpretations of the passage, see Broadhead, *Persae,* 249–250.

[111] Broadhead (*Persae,* 251, note on line 16) thinks that because Aeschylus's language is "constantly redolent of epic," it does not necessarily follow that "a particular word or phrase was directly taken over from Homer or post-Homeric epic poets." He believes that Aeschylus probably owes more to the lyric poets than to Homer. I have no argument with the statement that the tragedian owes much to the lyric poets. However, when the original source of an allusion can be identified as that of a well-known work, such as the *Iliad* or the *Odyssey,* it is legitimate to assume that the resonance is dependent primarily

Further, in lines 74–80 of the lyric parodos, Aeschylus supports the mood of these allusions with the use of numerous Homeric epithets to describe Xerxes and the army—*thourios* ("impetuous"), commonly used by Homer to describe Ares, whose name appears in line 85 of the *Persians; poimanorion theion* ("awesome flock"; *poimanorion* recalls the epic phrase *poimena laōn*, "shepherd of [the] people," regularly used as a description of king Agamemnon in the *Iliad*); and *isotheos phōs* ("a man like a god," which recalls a phrase found several times in the epic poems, *isotheos phaos* [or *phoōs*], and in a similar position in the metrical line as in the lyric parodos).[112] These epithets, of which I mention only a few, also prepare the audience for another allusion to Homer. In the second strophe (83–85), the chorus says:

Looking [a] dark glance in [his] eyes, that of [a] murderous serpent,	Kuaneon d' ommasi leussōn phoniou dergma drakontos
With many [a] band of soldiers and many [a] sailor, and pursuing [a]	Polukheir kai polunautas Surion th' harma diōkōn
Syrian chariot, he leads forth bow-wielding Ares against men famous for [the] spear.	Epagei douriklutois andrasi toxodamnon Arē.

There are several words within this passage that are associated in meaning with sight: *kuaneon* ("dark," the antithesis of light), *ommasi* ("eyes"), *leussōn* ("looking"), and *dergma* ("look"). These, in turn, emphasize the metaphor *dergma drakontos* ("dark look of [a] serpent"), which is supported by the word appropriate in meaning to a serpent, *phoniou* ("murderous"), a word that is also appropriate in meaning to the warlike leader of the Persians.

The alliteration of the words *dergma drakontos* may well draw attention to the presence here of an allusion to *Iliad* 22.93–96, in which passage the Trojan warrior Hector, compared to a serpent, waits as Achilles approaches:

As [a] serpent from [the] mountain waits for [a] man at [a] hole,	Hōs de drakōn epi kheiēi oresteros andra menēisi,

---

on the audience's knowledge of that work rather than on the work of another poet who has made the same allusion.

[112] See Sideras, *Aeschylus Homericus*, 140. Kumaniecki, *De elocutionis Aeschyleae natura*, 6, points out that in the instance of *kraipnōi podi* at line 95, Aeschylus joins the epithet with the same noun that Homer does.

One who has fed on evil poisons
    and whom [a] terrible
    anger has entered,
And coiled about [the] hole he
    looks [a] fearful look,
So Hector. . . .

Bebrōkōs kaka pharmak', edu de
    te min kholos ainos,

Smerdaleon de dedorken
    helissomenos peri kheiēi·
Hōs Hektōr. . . .

The words *drakōn* and *dedorken* (*dergma* is from the same root), key words drawn from the Homeric simile, point to an analogy between the Trojan warrior, who loses in the duel with Achilles, and Xerxes, who will lose the war with the Greeks. The analogy that Zeami draws between Yorimasa and Sanemori with his use of the *umoregi* ("fossil tree") poem is similar in effect. There *umoregi*, a key word, is sufficient to evoke Yorimasa's poem in the context of *Sanemori*. The Homeric passage prepares for the emphasis that Aeschylus later places on the crucial words meaning "sight" and "light" within the tragedy, the poem of Yorimasa for the implicit comparison between Yorimasa and Sanemori.

In the second line of the strophe, Aeschylus shifts from the metaphor to the subject at hand with the epithets "many [a] band of soldiers" and "many [a] sailor," neither of which is specifically Homeric (although the prefix *polu-* is common in epic) or appropriate to a description of a serpent. These epithets, which Aeschylus may have created, serve instead to connect the image of the serpent, with which Xerxes is compared, to the words *Surion th' harma diōkōn* ("pursuing [a] Syrian chariot," 85), of which Xerxes is the understood grammatical subject. The connection is analogous to that accomplished by the phrase *mi to shizumedomo* ("body submerged"), which glosses words drawn from the two poems written by Yorimasa and alludes to one after the other, *umoregi* ("fossil tree") and *hito shirenu* ("person no one knows"). The phrase provides a transition between Yorimasa's poems and a love poem, part of which is quoted in what follows: *kokoro no ike no ii* ("release from the pond in the heart"). Similarly, the two epithets in the *Persians* beginning with the prefix *polu-* serve as a transition between two allusions; however, they gloss an earlier line (76), where the land forces and the sea forces are mentioned, rather than the line immediately preceding.

The words *Surion th' harma diōkōn* are Homeric (see *Iliad* 8.438–439, *harma kai hippous . . . diōke*) and may allude to a passage in which Zeus has sent an order to other gods to desist from aiding the Greeks in gaining victory over the Trojans. It is his wish to allow the Trojans to enjoy *temporary* gains on the battlefield. In addition, given the presence in the next line from the *Persians* of the word *Arē*, not found in the epic verses, the passage is likely to have been inspired by an oracle delivered at Delphi during the Persian Wars. The lines of the oracle, as they are recorded in Herodotus's *History* (7.140.2–3), read:

(But all is ruined), for fire and keen Ares	. . . Kata gar min ereipei
Bring you down as he speeds along in [literally, pursues] [a] Syrian chariot.	Pur te kai oxus Arēs, Suriēgenes harma diōkōn.[113]

Aeschylus's version is very close to the "original"; he "quotes" the four last words almost as closely as Zeami quotes the love poem. It would seem that the function of the allusion within the *Persians* is to foreshadow defeat for the Greeks as the original oracle had. However, because a second oracle was delivered to the Athenians, which suggested victory for the Greeks (see Herodotus 7.141.3–4), the content of Aeschylus's allusion to the first oracle, like that of the allusion to the Homeric passage and several references in the lyric parodos to Persian strength and invincibility (89–91), are soon discovered to be ill-founded. The tension created between the victory suggested in the Homeric and the oracular allusions and in the surface meaning of the text, and the eventual defeat of the Trojans in the Trojan War, of the Persians in the Persian Wars, and of the Persians in the battle of Salamis as presented in the *Persians*, is subtly articulated. It is only as much in evidence as the hint of alternatives Zeami incorporates into his text with the word *iigataki* ("release is difficult"). The tension lies in the antithetical meanings of the two parts of the compound word "release" (*ii-*, syllables drawn from the love poem) and "difficult to express" (*-gataki*). Zeami achieves tension by means of one word functioning as a pivot between a literary borrowing that suggests the warrior will be able to release from his heart the burden of his attachment with the narration of his tale, and the dramatic text that suggests this task will be difficult. Not surprisingly, given the many other examples of Aeschylus's relative prolixity, the audience of the tragedy must hear both the first and the second lines of the passage in full, which converge on the contrasting phrases, "men famous for [the] spear" (that is, the Greeks), and "bow-wielding Ares" (that is, the Persians), before the tension there becomes apparent.

In the next stanza, Aeschylus moves in the direction of suggesting that

---

[113] See Kranz, *Stasimon*, 93. J. Fontenrose, *The Delphic Oracle* (Berkeley, Los Angeles, and London, 1978), 128 n. 9, suggests that Aeschylus may have influenced Herodotus, whose *History* was written after the *Persians*. However, the oracle, appearing as it does in the *History* and in the *Persians*, is likely to have existed independently of both. Marcia Dunbar-Soule Dobson, in "Oracular Language: Its Style and Intent in the Delphic Oracles and in Aeschylus' *Oresteia*" (Diss., Harvard University, 1976), addresses the practice of shared traditional tags and phrases in oracles and epic and didactic poetry.

the Persians might be victorious when he compares them to the waves of
the sea (89–91):

No one is worthy enough to make [a] stand against [the] great torrent of men	Dokimos d' outis hupostas megalōi rheumati phōtōn
Or with strong defences to block [the] unconquerable wave[s] of [the] sea;	Ekhurois herkesin eirgein amakhon kuma thalassas·
For invincible are the Persian army and strong-willed people.	Aprosoistos gar ho Persan stratos alkiphrōn te laos.

In this passage, which contains no finite verb ("is" remains merely understood), Aeschylus juxtaposes what preceded not with an explicit borrowing, but with an allusion to another Homeric simile transformed into a
"metaphor." Thereby once again, as I have shown above, he creates interaction between tenor and vehicle. The possibility that Aeschylus is alluding
here to a passage from the *Iliad* (5.87–94) that extols the Greek warrior
Diomedes' strength in battle supports the surface meaning, namely that
the Persians are invincible.[114] Diomedes, scattering the Trojans, is compared to a swollen river that scatters dikes with its swift current and destroys beneath it the works of man. The Trojans, although great in number, cannot withstand the Greek leader. The comparison of the Persians to
Diomedes, implied by the allusion, is apt; they, like water with its torrent,
cannot be blocked. However, beneath the surface of this passage and on
the surface of passages that follow, the optimism of the elders is undercut.

Aeschylus turns next to the moral lesson of the play in the mesode of the
Persians (94–98):

What mortal man will flee [the] *deceitful treachery* of god?	*Dolomētin* d' *apatan* theou tis anēr thnatos aluxei;
Who is there who is *swift-footed* and can master [an] easy jump?	Tis ho *kraipnōi podi* pēdēmatos eupeteos anassōn;
For at first friendly *Delusion* by flattery leads	Philophrōn gar potisainousa to prōton paragei
[A] man into [her] nets,	Broton eis arkuas *Ata*,

---

[114] Other passages in the *Iliad* that may serve as the source of the maritime metaphor
are 2.208–210, 4.422–428, 14.393–395, 15.381–384 and 624–625. Van Nes (*Die maritime Bildersprache*, 30) points out that the Homeric simile of a river, since the Greeks
thought of the water of a river and of the sea as one, is suggested in our passage.

265

Whence it is not possible for [a]   Tothen ouk estin huper thnaton
mortal, even one who has   aluxanta phugein.
fled, to escape.

In *Sanemori*, the waki's words in the first ageuta present the image of a net
into which Amida draws all humans alike; in the *Persians*, the chorus says
that all men who are taken in by flattering Delusion are drawn into a hunting net. One image is positive, the other negative in tone, a difference attributable in part to the sources on which the playwrights draw. Zeami
shapes his religious moral out of quotations drawn from sutras and
Ippen's poem. Aeschylus continues to imbue the parodos with a Homeric
tone and Homeric authority, as can be seen in his use in this mesode of the
important words *dolomētin* ("deceitful"), *apatan* ("treachery"), *kraipnōi*
podi ("swift-footed"), *Ata* ("Delusion"), and the idea of the inability to
escape from god.[115]

Some of the words in the passage appear together in the section of the
Iliad in which Agamemnon tests the troops. At the beginning of his speech
(2.111), Agamemnon says:

Zeus, son of Cronus, bound me   Zeus me mega Kronidēs *atēi*
fast in dire *delusion*.   enedēse bareiēi.

And later in the same speech (114) he says:

Now he has devised [an] evil   Nun de kakēn *apatēn* bouleusato.
deception.

Agamemnon, receiving a dream from Zeus, who falsely promises him victory in order to help Achilles, lies to the troops and blames Zeus for the
Greeks' difficult position. The king says that he is bound in delusion and
has been deceived, when he thinks that he is not. But of course he actually
is. Later, in the context of a crisis that strikes the Greek forces and when
Agamemnon does in fact need help and knows it, Homer repeats the line
(9.21).[116] Since the Greeks suffer only temporary losses, the foreboding of
defeat for the Persians, who like the Trojans are ultimately defeated, resonates behind this and the other passages of the parodos that are of Homeric origin.

The moral lesson of the play is explicitly directed at the Persians in the

---

[115] For this idea, see *Odyssey* 16.447, *theothen d' ouk est' aleasthai* ("it is not possible
to escape from god"). *Dolomētis* is found a number of times in the *Odyssey*, but only
once in the *Iliad* (1.540) applied to Zeus.

[116] At *Iliad* 9.505–506, Phoenix tells Achilles that Atē is strong and even faster than
prayers. In 19.87–89, Agamemnon blames Zeus, Fate, and Erinys for placing savage
folly, *atē*, in his mind. At line 91, Atē, he says, is the daughter of Zeus who deludes
everyone and has bound fast others before him.

following strophe and antistrophe (101–114), again Homeric in tone but not indebted to a specific passage of Homer's works. The Homeric features include tmesis in *kata . . . ekratēsen* ("decreed"), the personification of *Moira* ("Fate"), the epithets *purgodaiktous* ("destroying city walls") and *hippiokharmas* ("horse and chariot"), the noun *klonous* ("turmoils"), the genitive ending of *euruporoio* ("broad-pathed"), and the construction *pisunoi* ("relying upon") with the dative case.[117] In these passages Aeschylus introduces to the play the reason for the Persian defeat (that is, Xerxes' error) and the punishment inflicted by the gods. Having alluded to Homer and having thereby hinted at Persian defeat, Aeschylus now openly states that the Persians countered the will of the gods.

Aeschylus next clearly articulates the antithesis between land and sea that occasions the chorus's most explicit expression of fear. It says in the next strophe (115):

About these things my heart clothed in black is gashed with fear.	Tauta mou melagkhitōn phrēn amussetai phobōi.

The sentence is directly connected to the preceding moral with the word *tauta* ("these things"), which refers to its content and involves two expressions drawn from Homer. The first of these is *melagkhitōn phrēn* ("heart clothed in black"), which resembles the Homeric phrase *phrenes amphimelainai* ("heart surrounded in black") used of Agamemnon immediately before he calls Calchas a prophet of evil in *Iliad* 1.103. (Of course, Aeschylus is only suggesting the Homeric passage, for he changes both the epithet and the emotion that it expresses—anger in Homer, fear in the *Persians*.) The second is the "gashing" of the heart, in which phrase Aeschylus uses the same verb, *amussō*, as Homer does in *Iliad* 1.243, the passage that inspired line 10 of the *Persians*. Thus in this Homeric allusion Aeschylus returns to his point of departure, and he does so in a passage that for the first time directs the audience's attention to an element of the performance, namely the costumes of the elders. It is highly likely that the Homeric reminiscence would be understood as such by the audience, inasmuch as it appears as well in the work of Bacchylides, Aeschylus's contemporary, and with similar intent. Within the context of a threat of war upon the city of Athens, Bacchylides writes (16.19):

Or what is it that tears your heart?	Ē ti toi kradian amussei;

[117] See pp. 243–244 above. Broadhead, *Persae*, 55, thinks that *moira* is the equivalent of portion or lot and is not personified. However, the Homeric goddess Fate seems appropriate within the Homerically inspired lyric parodos.

Pindar, another contemporary of Aeschylus, seems to allude to *Iliad* 1.103 with the words *melainan kradian estuphelixen* ("has struck hard [his] black heart," fr. 225). If these are not direct allusions, they at least suggest that such phrases were part of the poetic currency of the time.

Because the beginning of the *Iliad* resonates behind more than one passage in the parodos, it seems reasonable to assume that Aeschylus intended to keep the epic situation before the minds of the audience as a way of increasing the foreboding of disaster for the Persians. Indeed he continues to allude to the beginning of the *Iliad* (2.87–93) in comparing the Persians to bees in the next stanza (129–132). Only one word, "bees," is taken from the epic passage; however, the presence of the epic word *orkhamos* ("leader") and of one of Aeschylus's rare uses of a simile[118] is a signal for the audience that he is alluding to Homer's work, in which similes abound.

The allusions to Homer do not appear as frequently after the parodos as they do within it, yet they continue to provide an epic resonance at important junctures. Consider, for example, Aeschylus's Homeric way of saying that Xerxes is alive and "sees [the] light" (299), in preparation for a pun on the word "light" in the next line. The messenger's reference to a spirit "weighing down [the] scales with unequal fortune" (345–346), a veiled allusion to Zeus, who in Homer's work holds the scales, prepares for the use of Zeus's name later in the stasimon. The messenger's speeches are highly epic, not only in their use of grammatical and syntactical forms but also in their allusions to Homer. The most striking among these is the comparison of the Persian dead to fish (424–426), which may be drawn from *Odyssey* 22.383–387 or, more likely, from *Iliad* 21.22–26, where Homer compares the Trojans in their flight to fish fleeing in fright from a dolphin. (Later, when the Persians are implicitly compared to the victims of fish, 576–578, Aeschylus may have drawn on *Iliad* 21.126–127, where Achilles says that his defeated opponent Lycaon will find his fat nibbled upon by fish.) A series of Homeric allusions appears in the stasimon following the messenger's speech (532–547); for example, the words "in [a] dark cloud of grief you [Zeus] enveloped [the city]" (536) may call to mind similar expressions in passages of the *Iliad*, such as 17.591 (a cloud of sorrow closes over Hector when he hears that his trusted companion has been killed) and 18.22 (a cloud of sorrow closes over Achilles when he hears that his friend Patroclus has died). Later, when Aeschylus has Xerxes say in his first speech that he wishes the "portion of death" had "enveloped" him (917), his phraseology may have been inspired by a number of

---

[118] See Earp, *The Style of Aeschylus*, 96. Another simile that probably signals an allusion to Homer appears at *Agamemnon* 49.

Homeric passages, including *Iliad* 22.361, where Homer says that the "end in death enveloped" Hector.[119]

Zeami quotes the section of the *Heike* concerning Sanemori closely; Aeschylus merely alludes to the *Iliad*. There is certainly not a one-for-one ratio in how the two playwrights borrow from epic sources. However, as I have suggested above, the epic tone that Aeschylus adds to the *Persians* as a whole and within specific passages with his allusions to Homer is comparable to the lyric tone that Zeami creates in *Sanemori* with his quotation of, allusion to, and borrowing from other poetry. In nō, the borrowings, expected by an audience familiar with the practice of borrowing elsewhere, are skillfully integrated into the dramatic text by means of such verbal techniques as kakekotoba or repetition. These borrowings are used both to create an overall mood and a specific effect within the context of each borrowing, and as a means of character depiction in plays that are not realistic in their portrayal of character. Aeschylus's allusions to Homer are analogous in these respects. In addition, some borrowings seem to be repeated by Zeami for the cumulative effect of making the finale literarily striking. It is to this feature of style I now turn with a close examination of Aeschylus's use of the first line of Phrynichus's play, *The Phoenician Women*, a subject already discussed in Chapter Two in terms of its application to the structural development of the *Persians*.[120] Here it is discussed in terms of the effect that Aeschylus's repeated allusions to the Phrynichean line have on his use of specific words within the *Persians*.

It is with Aeschylus's use of Phrynichus's line that I conclude and with which I hope, on the basis of the parallels with Zeami's style, to convince the reader that the instincts of those classical scholars who have combed through the texts of Aeschylus in search of allusions and verbal techniques might in fact be correct. Careful attention to the text is not out of place in the theater of Zeami when he alludes to familiar material, and provides signals for the audience, in both the words of the text and the performance, of his use of an allusion and a verbal technique; it is not, as I have said

---

[119] This passage comes to mind because it is one in which Hector's mother and father and all the people around him in Troy react with intense grief at the sight of the warrior's head dragged in the dust by Achilles. Although Xerxes only wishes that he had died and has not, his use of the Homeric passage serves to intensify the emotions within Aeschylus's introduction to the most forthright lament in the tragedy.

[120] Aristophanes, in his comedy the *Frogs* (1299–1300), has Aeschylus say that he does not want to be seen culling the same meadows of the Muses as Phrynichus, thus implying that he did cull the same meadows of poetry. The statement in the hypothesis to the *Persians*, ascribed to Glaucus, that the first line of the *Persians* is drawn from Phrynichus's work, is likely to be true inasmuch as Aeschylus appears to have borrowed from Phrynichus elsewhere: *puros malera gnathos* ("ravenous jaw of fire," *Libation Bearers* 325) may echo *margois phlox edainuto gnathois* ("the flame feasts with its greedy jaws," Phrynichus fr. 5).

repeatedly, out of place in the theater of Aeschylus when he provides signals.

In the first line of the *Persians* Aeschylus borrows, but alters, the first line of Phrynichus's play.[121] He changes the metrical form, as Zeami would not, but he drops two words and accommodates another to his own needs, as Zeami might. The *Persians* begins with the following line sung in anapaestic rhythm by the chorus of elders:

These, of the Persians who left. . . .	Tade men Persōn tōn oikhomenōn. . . .

In Phrynichus's play, a eunuch speaks the following iambic trimeter line:

These are, of the Persians who left long ago.	Tad' esti Persōn tōn palai bebēkotōn.

Phrynichus's *bebēkotōn* ("left") and Aeschylus's *oikhomenōn* ("gone") have almost the same meaning; euphemistically both can mean "have been lost" or "have died." The latter connotation is especially obvious to an audience that knows from the history of the Persian Wars the manner in which many Persians died. In Phrynichus's play, since the eunuch announces the defeat immediately, the audience knows that the playwright means by his use of the word *bebēkotōn* to say that many Persian men have died.[122] However, in the *Persians* the chorus does not announce defeat and thus diverts attention away from the course of the Phrynichean play, which may have included a lamentation for the dead. Instead, the elders say in the second line of the *Persians* that the men went to Greece, not that they were defeated, and direct the emphasis of the sentence, the subject of the pronoun *tade* ("these") onto themselves and their function as guardians.

[121] Of the many who have commented on or discussed Aeschylus's debt to the play, written four years before the *Persians*, see Stanford, *Aeschylus in His Style*, 35–37; A. W. Verrall, "The Part of Phrynichus in the *Persae* of Aeschylus," *Cambr. Phil. Proc.* 79 (1908): 13–15, who goes so far as to say that other passages, 465–471 and 480–514, are indebted to Phrynichus; Gottfried Hermann, *De Aeschyli Persis dissertatio*, 87–104; Franz Stössl, "Die Phoenissen des Phrynichos und die Perser des Aischylos," *MH* 2 (1945): 148–165; F. Marx, "Der tragiker Phrynichus," *Rh. Mus.* 77 (1928): 337–360; O. Hiltbrunner, *Wiederholungs -und Motivtechnik bei Aischylos* (Bern, 1950), 49; J. B. Bury, "Two Literary Compliments," *CR* 19 (1905): 10–11; and Guido Paduano, *Sui Persiani di Eschilo problemi di focalizzazione drammatica, Filologia e Critica* 27 (Rome, 1978), 39, who suggests in his discussion of line 18 of the *Persians* that *leipō* ("leave") carries funeral connotations that would be appropriate to Phrynichus's play as we know it.

[122] Except for Phrynichus, Aeschylus's predecessors seem not to have used *bebēka* with the meaning "die." That meaning became common later. At *Libation Bearers* 636, Aeschylus uses *oikhomai* to mean "perished"; at *Suppliants* 738 and 786, "carried away [by fear]."

Aeschylus underscores the importance of the verb *oikhomai* by repeating it twice in the parodos[123] and thus frames the list of Persians who went to Greece. At lines 12–13 he writes:

For [the] full strength of   Pasa gar iskhus Asiatogenēs
    Asia's sons
Has gone.   Ōikhōken.

He begins the Homer-like catalogue of Persian leaders who did in fact leave by using synonyms that explain for the audience the intended meaning of *oikhomai: prolipontes eban* ("leaving they went"; here the verb, *eban*, an Homeric form of Phrynichus's word *bebēkotōn*, means "went," not "died") and the participle *prolipontes* ("leaving" [transitive]).[124] The pleonasm functions like a verbal gloss and for the sake of the audience points to the importance of the Phrynichean line and Aeschylus's alteration of it. Aeschylus again emphasizes the word with another of related meaning, *baden* ("at [a] walking pace"), which is further glossed by the word *pezoi* ("foot soldiers"). There is no question as to the meaning of *oikhomenōn* in Aeschylus's version of Phrynichus's line: it means "gone," not "died." After the catalogue and near the end of the parodos (59–60), Aeschylus repeats the gist of the first line:

Such is [the] flower of [the]   Toiond' anthos Persidos aias
    Persian land
Of men that has gone.   Oikhetai andrōn.

Near the beginning of the parodos the elders said that their hearts were troubled (10–11) because there had been no news about the men; at the end of the parodos they append to the "Phrynichean" line another expression of distress (61–64) and say that the entire land of Asia mourns for the men, as the parents and wives tremble and count the days that have passed (since the men left).

There are other references to the departure and passage of the Persian forces in the lyric parodos, but it is not until the queen delivers her narration in iambic trimeters, the meter of Phrynichus's line, that Aeschylus explicitly and in an emphatic position alludes to the line again. The queen says (178):

[123] R. P. Winnington-Ingram, "A Word in the *Persae*," *BICS* 20 (1973): 38, says of *oikhomenōn*, "The word has a life and potency of its own; and it could well be this power of the word as such that accounts, partly, for that repetitive verbal technique in Aeschylus which is so alien to our mental habits that some critics have been reluctant to acknowledge its importance."
[124] One finds in *Sanemori* that Zeami uses the synonyms *mida no kuni* ("Amida's land") and *saihō* ("Paradise") in the first two lines of the nō in order to emphasize an important idea at the outset.

[My child] left wishing to destroy	[Pais emos] Iaonōn gēn oikhetai
[the] land of [the] Ionians.	persai thelōn.

The verb *oikhomai*, used first of the Persian forces in general (1) and the entire strength of Asia (13), then of the flower of men (60), now applies specifically to the action of Xerxes, who raised the expedition. Aeschylus, in the process of repeating the line, gradually accommodates it to the requirements of the play and reaches the point where, in line 178, only the syllable *pers*, which means "destroy" but sounds like *Persōn* ("Persians"), remains from the original line in Phrynichus's play. Aeschylus's use of no more than the words *persai* ("destroy") and *oikhetai* ("has left") to evoke the audience's recollection of the first line of the play, and thus of Phrynichus's line, is not unlike the accepted practice in nō of evoking a poem with the quotation sometimes of only a word or two. Aeschylus's punning on the name of the Persians in this allusion is also not unlike Zeami's practice of devising a pun on the name of the main character of a nō in a line for which he has properly prepared. (See my discussion above of line 65 of the *Persians*.)

Zeami is more repetitive in *Obasute*, for example, where he quotes a poem in full and in part. However, at one point in the nō he refers to the poem with the use of only a single word, as Aeschylus has alluded to Phrynichus with one word in line 178.[125] The poem reads:

My heart	Waga kokoro
Aches beyond consolation	Nagusame—kanetsu
At Sarashina	Sarashina ya
Seeing [the] moon shine	Obasuteyama
On Mount Obasute.	Teru tsuki o mite.

At the beginning of the mondō, the waki, a traveler, questions the shite, an old woman, about the place where an old woman was left to die. The shite says that if he is asking about the remains of the woman who sang the poem, which she quotes in entirety, her remains are in the shade of a small tree. As the two continue to talk of her abiding attachment, the chorus, by reciting the first three lines of the poem, say that even now her heart aches. (In the kyōgen interlude scene, the villager mentions that an old woman appeared and recited the poem about Mount Obasute to him.) In the nochiba, when the ghost of the old woman, who was the woman abandoned on the mountains (that is, Obasute) dances, the chorus, singing for her, repeats the poem. It is at the end, when nothing from the poem except the word *Obasuteyama* appears, that the technique approximates Aeschylus's use of two words to evoke the line from Phrynichus's play. While the word

[125] The poem is drawn from the imperial collection, the *Kokinshū*, no. 878. The play is translated by Stanleigh H. Jones, Jr., in Keene, *20 Plays*, 115–128.

designates the place where the old woman was abandoned, the first part of the word designates the woman Obasute herself. The word is sufficient to evoke the poem as a whole, which during the course of the play has become focused on the central character. In the *Persians*, the line from Phrynichus is evoked by the verb that Aeschylus changes and by his use of the syllable *pers*, which is part of the name of the Persians. That important words in both plays are derived from another source, recognizable to the audience, brings to them the atmosphere of the original.

In the *Persians* the next allusion to Phrynichus's line appears at the important moment in the play when the queen *first* hears from the messenger that the Persians have been defeated. The messenger says (252):

| ... And the flower of [the] | ... To Persōn d' anthos oikhetai |
| Persians is gone and fallen. | peson. |

With an effective delay of the word *peson* ("fallen"), Aeschylus at last explicitly informs the audience what it knows to be true from firsthand experience, hearsay, and Phrynichus's play. The revelation appears in a line that repeats the verb *oikhomai* and the word "Persians" from the first line of the play, repeats the words "Persians," *anthos* ("flower"), and *oikhomai* from line 60 of the parodos, and repeats the iambic trimeter meter, the verb *oikhomai*, and the syllable *pers* from the queen's allusion to the line (178). However, Aeschylus makes an important addition to the earlier passages with the word *peson* ("fallen"), which serves as a gloss on *oikhomai* that differs from the glosses in the parodos. Here the gloss restores to the Phrynichean line its original meaning, which is emphasized in the words of the messenger—"for [the] whole army of barbarians has been destroyed" (255)[126]—and by the repeated references to the destruction of the forces in the epirrhematic exchange between the chorus and messenger that follows. The list of the leaders who have died (302–328) provides confirmation of the defeat. (The first list of leaders appeared in the parodos after Aeschylus's first use of the altered version of Phrynichus's line.)

The next allusion to the beginning of the *Persians*, and thus to Phrynichus's line, appears significantly in Xerxes' *first* speech of the tragedy, in a line inspired by Homer. Xerxes calls on Zeus and says he wishes that death had enveloped him (915–916):

| ... Along with the men | ... Met' andrōn |
| Who are gone. ... | Tōn oikhomenōn. ... |

This line appears within the anapaestic introduction to the final kommos, in which the names of the leaders are again repeated but with many fewer embellishing epithets than in the earlier versions of the lists.

---

[126] Aeschylus refers to the Persians and Asians as barbarians even though the expression is in the mouth of the messenger. This is normal in Greek.

The catalogue, the list of leaders, is connected again with the first line of the play in the first line (1002) of the most excited part of the kommos. After the list of names is completed, in this final allusion to the Phrynichean line, the chorus says that it marvels that the men are not following Xerxes. Xerxes says:

> For they have clearly gone, [the]   Bebasi gar toiper agretai stratou.
> leaders of [the] army.

The chorus responds with an echo of the first word (1003):

> They have gone, ah, inglorious.   Bebasin oi nōnumoi.

The skeletal list of names is erased by the repeated *bebasi* ("have gone"), in particular because this is Aeschylus's first use of the Phrynichean verb in the same tense, the same iambic meter (the iambic meter is accentuated by the change that takes place in the meter at this point in the kommos), and the same meaning as the original. The effect is particularly striking because the line is delivered by the character upon whom the finale, and the play as a whole, is focused. (Zeami would have appreciated Aeschylus's art here.) The Homeric word *nōnumoi* ("inglorious"), because it literally means "nameless," functions like a pun; with the word Aeschylus negates the names in the list of the men who are no longer even worthy of fame and are gone, dead. This is a point that Aeschylus emphasizes in the continuation of the exodos—Xerxes lacks an entourage (1000–1001) and Xerxes is left with little: a quiver, torn robes, and no attendants (1022, 1030, and 1036).

The play reaches a climax in lines 1002–1003, which bring epic and dramatic allusions together in the context of a verbal negation of the Persian men. This is a moment comparable to the place in the rongi in which Zeami composes a lyric line for Sanemori. Although Zeami adds a new line to the epic context while Aeschylus has recreated the original word from Phrynichus and explained it with an epic word, this particular difference is not essential: they both use allusions ingeniously and artfully in the theater. In terms of each work as a whole, the expression of pity for Sanemori is nowhere as intense as it is in the rongi, and the expression of lament and grief by the Persians is nowhere as intense as it is in the last part of the kommos. The nō is more narrowly focused in that the rongi pertains to the warrior only, whereas the kommos pertains to an entire people, the Persians. That is in the nature of the great degree of inwardness and "subjectivity" that we see again and again in nō.[127] And yet, it is relevant to an appreciation of both the *Persians* and *Sanemori* not only that Aeschylus

---

[127] In those nō which feature a poet or other artist as the chief character, the focus of the contributing parts is even more complete than it is in *Sanemori*.

and Zeami lead up to and prepare their audiences for dramatic peaks in the performance, but also that the climaxes of the plays as a whole, when the audiences are the most spellbound, have a "literary" dimension.

In culling material from Phrynichus, Aeschylus achieves an effect in the *Persians* that bears a resemblance to the effect gained by Zeami through his use of other literature in *Sanemori*. The epic and lyric relationship that Zeami creates between Sanemori and Yorimasa during the nō is brought to a climax at the end in a lyric line about a "crumpled tree," which Zeami adds to his version of the parts of the *Heike* specifically pertaining to *Sanemori*. In addition, Zeami brings together character and literary precedents in such a way that he converts the epic Sanemori into a dramatic character and presents him even nobler and more sympathetic than the audience expects before seeing the nō. Aeschylus associates Xerxes with Homeric warriors through his allusions to the *Iliad*, alters parts of history specifically related to the exploits of Xerxes, and creates a character who is more culpable than the historian Herodotus later suggests he was. In addition, since Xerxes could well have been the subject of the play *The Phoenician Women*, and since Aeschylus alludes repeatedly to the first line of that play, he may have presented a character different from what the members of the audience who have seen Phrynichus's play expect. The example of *Sanemori*, one out of many nō that could have been chosen for this study, is informative in that it illustrates how we can assess the dramatic implications of the use that Aeschylus makes of history, epic, proverbs, ethico-religious sayings, poetry, and even a single line from Phrynichus.

Coda

The works of Aeschylus and Zeami played similarly crucial and formative roles in the historical development of Greek tragedy and nō. For this reason, if for no other, a comparison of the two authors is important to the study of the history of drama in general. To be sure, there are obvious cultural differences between the early classical period in Greece and the middle Muromachi period in Japan; however, as demonstrated in the Introduction, the theatrical and cultural milieus in which Aeschylus and Zeami worked exhibit sufficient similarities to motivate and justify a comparative study of these particular playwrights. Moreover, because we have the opinions of Zeami, who was not only involved in writing about nō, but, like Aeschylus, was involved in almost every aspect of his theater, we can gain insights into how successful nō should be written, organized, and performed. I have argued here that in the absence of such documentation for Greek tragedy, these insights can be relevant and useful to an analysis of Aeschylus's work.

The intention of this comparative study has been to determine how what Zeami says about nō in his treatises and how the nō that he himself produced increase our understanding of character portrayal, structure, and the use of language in Aeschylean tragedy. I believe that the comparative method has in fact illuminated certain important features of Aeschylus's approach, especially in his early play, the *Persians*, a work that occupies a pivotal position in the history of Greek tragedy. Not only does this play involve a tragic event and scenes that feature discourse between two actors, thus containing the potential for dramatic tension so important to later tragedy, but simultaneously, like much of Aeschylus's other work, it is highly poetic, and it does not rely on a tragic event contemporaneous with the dramatic time frame for its effect, as does later tragedy. In these latter two respects it exhibits some structural and stylistic similiarities to most nō plays.

A grasp of Zeami's principle of jo-ha-kyū helps one not only to understand something of the appeal that the structure of the *Persians* and other works by Aeschylus could have had for a Greek audience, but also to gain some insights into the effective use of performance elements in later Greek tragedy. In Chapters One and Two I argued that although the emotions of pity and fear are not built into the Aeschylean plot in precisely the manner recommended by Aristotle, Aeschylean theater, like that of Zeami, creates a powerful emotional and aesthetic effect through the coherent organization of its different structural parts, such as songs, dialogue, and ritual enactment, and through a variety of other means as well: a gradual intensification of rhythmic effect in the lines spoken, recited, and sung by actors and chorus within both the individual sections and the play as a whole; an increase in the number and complexity of the actors' movements during the course of the play; the inclusion, at an appropriate point in the play's development, of a section drawing on the authority of traditional wisdom in order to set into relief the scenes that precede and the climax that follows; the carefully planned and fully functional use of costumes, masks, and props; and a progressive focusing of attention on the principal actor playing the role of the main character, achieved in part by means of an economical use of entrances and exits. A clear understanding of jo-ha-kyū and an examination of the structure of the *Persians* in the light of this organizing principle are equally illuminating about some of the many essential differences between nō and Aeschylean tragedy and between nō and Greek tragedy. The most obvious of these differences are the greater importance accorded in Greek tragedy to dramatic conflict and destructive and fatal acts, and the extent to which action dictates the unfolding of a tragic plot.

In style as well, Zeami's nō resemble certain Aeschylean works more closely than they do later tragedy because the nō and Aeschylean tragedy both bear many affinities with the nondramatic poetry of their respective cultures. In spite of the differences between the Greek and Japanese languages and their early "literary" traditions, the styles of Aeschylus and Zeami are analogous in the use they make of such verbal techniques as repetition, verbal elaboration, paronomasia, verbal interaction, and overlapping syntax, and even of allusions. Moreover, each dramatist brings these aspects of style to life in the theater by means of the actors' and choruses' careful articulation of the words and by such purely dramatic elements as costumes, masks, gestures, dance, and entrances and exits.

One could argue that the conclusions drawn here about Aeschylus's dramatic methods might have been reached without recourse to the comparative method or through comparison with an author other than Zeami. With the present approach, however, we have not only uncovered some hitherto unrecognized dimensions of Aeschylean style and performance but have also shown that these and features of style already known to students of Aeschylus, when they are like those of nō, can be examined from the perspective of a living theatrical tradition. Whether this comparative study has made positive contributions to the work of nō scholars remains to be seen; however, at the very least it can claim to have offered a fresh outlook. The method used here in explicating the structure of plays and the dynamics of the words to a certain degree reflects standard approaches to nō and to Greek tragedy. The method has also blended these approaches in the analysis of specific texts in such a way that the reader is guided past merely superficial similarities and differences between nō and Greek tragedy to those that are essential and significant. On the one hand, the intention of this study has been to enhance our appreciation of both nō and Greek tragedy. On the other, it is a challenge to students of the theater to broaden the definition of tragic drama and to include within it poetry that is enacted by a few actors and a chorus, and yet is not dramatic in the conventional sense of that word.

Appendix 1

A Comparison of Structural Parts in Nō

I. From the table below one can see at a glance how the deployment of shōdan varies and is similar in the four warrior nō and in *Takasago*, which through the first choral song in regular rhythm is like most other waki nō.

THE SHŌDAN IN THE MAEBA OF FIVE NŌ

	Takasago	*Sanemori*	*Atsumori*	*Tadanori*	*Yorimasa*
Dan 1	shidai	—	shidai	shidai	—
	nanori	nanori	nanori	nanori	nanori
	—	sashi	—	sashi	—
	ageuta	ageuta	ageuta & tsukizerifu	sageuta & ageuta (tsukizerifu)	ageuta & tsukizerifu
Dan 2	—	—	shidai	—	—
	issei & sashi	sashi	sashi	sashi & issei & sashi	—
		kotoba			
	sageuta	kakaru	sageuta	sageuta	—
	ageuta	—	ageuta	—	—
Dan 3	mondō	mondō	mondō & ageuta	mondō & ageuta	mondō & ageuta
	kakeai	kakeai	kakeai	mondō	mondō
	ageuta	ageuta	sageuta	rongi	ageuta

Near the beginning of each warrior play and *Takasago*, there is a nanori ("naming speech"); *Sanemori* is unique in that the kyōgen, rather than the

279

waki, delivers the speech. Both *Sanemori* and *Yorimasa* lack the shidai, a short introductory song following the five- and seven-syllable sequence of Japanese prosody, sung by the waki, which in the other three nō forms an appropriate lyrical introduction to plays that feature poets or characters connected with poetry.[1] In *Sanemori* and *Tadanori*, before the waki's and wakizure's songs, Zeami inserts recitative sashi. But dan one of these two nō, like the others, concludes in song.[2] Only the tsukizerifu ("arrival speeches"), at the end of dan one in *Atsumori* and *Yorimasa*, and in some performances of *Tadanori*, interrupt the flow from speech through recitative to song.[3] This is the progression that characterizes part of the definition of jo-ha-kyū as it applies to the majority of dan found in nō.

Dan two of all five nō begins with the entrance of the shite. In *Atsumori* only, the shite and the tsure sing a special introduction. Four of the nō then proceed with the recitative shōdan—issei (a short melodious and dignified song in free rhythm) or sashi or both—and build up to the melodic conclusions, the sageuta ("low-pitched song") and ageuta ("high-pitched song"). In *Sanemori*, although it does not end in melody that follows a beat, the dan does conclude with melody (*kakaru*) after an intermediate spoken section (*kotoba*). In *Yorimasa*, there are no shōdan in dan two.

In dan three, all five nō begin with a mondō ("dialogue") and continue with song. In *Sanemori* and *Takasago*, the kakeai, an epirrhematic type of exchange, follows and flows into the ageuta, a song that follows the beat. In *Atsumori*, there is a slight variation: the ageuta follows directly after the mondō, but then Zeami introduces a kakeai that, in turn, leads to the sageuta. In *Tadanori* and *Yorimasa*, there is a doubling of the series mondō and song—in the latter, the songs are both ageuta; in the former, the songs are an ageuta and a rongi, which itself is in a melody that follows a beat and, as is usual, is sung as an exchange, here between the shite and the chorus. Thus the third dan ends in melody before the shite exits in each of these nō, as indeed one might say it does in the maeba of every nō. The major difference between the warrior nō and *Takasago* lies in the addition

[1] On the tendency for shura nō to begin with shidai and the function of this shōdan, see Yasuda, "The Structure of *Hagoromo*," 37–38. Actually, if one takes into account all known nō, including those written by Zeami, over seventy percent have a shidai.

[2] The sageuta is in a lower pitch than the ageuta, but like it, a song.

[3] Perhaps it is better to think of them as interim speeches. Today they belong to the waki's script and are not properly a part of the shite's. This explains why, although the Shōgakkan edition publishes it and the Iwanami refers to it, the Kanze school texts do not include the tsukizerifu for *Tadanori*. My source is Shimazaki Chifumi, who remarked that in Zeami's day actors did not specialize in waki roles as they do today, but played these roles and had other functions connected with the performances to carry out as well. At that time, waki's speeches were included in the shite texts. However, since many actors could not read the texts, they learned them orally. Waki schools as such developed in the seventeenth century.

of shōdan in the latter: *Takasago* continues with dan four, in which there is the series kuri, sashi, kuse, and rongi, a series delayed, as Zeami advised, for the nochiba of the shura nō.

II. The differences between three warrior nō can be seen in the table below, which provides a general, although not a comprehensive, outline of shōdan:

THE SHŌDAN IN THE NOCHIBA OF THREE WARRIOR NŌ

	Sanemori	*Atsumori*	*Yorimasa*
Dan 4 and 5	kuri	kuri	*nanoriguri* (a kuri with the function of a nanori)
	sashi	sashi	sashi
	katari	kuse	kuse
	hyoshiai (a sageuta)	kakeai	kotoba
	ageuta	issei	chūnori
	kuse	dance	—
Dan 6	rongi	waka	rongi
	chūnori	ōnori	*jo no ei*
	—	*awazu*	uta
	—	chūnori	—

Kotoba is, like a katari, a spoken section. The waka and the awazu units of *Atsumori*, recited by the shite, do not follow the beat. The ōnori is like the chūnori in having a regular and insistent beat, but features one beat per syllable in a six- to eight-syllable line, rather than the two syllables per beat of chūnori. The jo no ei is like an issei. Of these three nō, *Atsumori* and *Yorimasa* follow the normal sequence of a kusemai scene, that is, kuri, sashi, kuse. *Sanemori* builds up the expectation of a kuse with the kuri and sashi at the beginning, but deflects the sequence away from the kuse, presents a katari, and then includes a song that replaces the kuse. (The kuse itself appears later.)

Appendix 2

A Comparative Translation of Sections of *Sanemori* and *The Tale of the Heike*

NOTE: Sections from *Sanemori* are my translations. Those from the *Heike* are translated by Kitagawa and Tsuchida in *The Tale of the Heike*, 414–416; however, I have not used all the names of persons as they appear in their translation but have used the other names of those same characters that agree with mine. Also, I do not use the first-person pronoun in the report of Sanemori's words. The spaces appearing between lines of the translation of the nō are provided so that the two accounts are aligned. Parentheses in the *Heike* version indicate those sections Zeami omitted from his account.

The katari begins with the following introduction: Now then, when the battle of Shinowara was lost, . . .

Katari	*Heike*
SHITE: Tezuka no Tarō Mitsumori, a Genji, came before Lord Kiso and said, "Mitsumori [I], fighting a strange character, has cut off his head.	Tezuka, having given Sanemori's head to one of his retainers to carry, galloped back to Lord Kiso's camp and said, "I have brought you, my lord, the head of a strange fellow whom I fought and killed.
He looks, he [I] said at the time, like a great leader, but he has not the forces behind him. And again, if you think he is an ordinary warrior, he	Though he wore a red brocade battle robe and he looked like a great leader, he had no retainer in attendance.

282

wears a brocade robe. He [I] insists that he name his name, but to the end he refuses to give it. His accent was that of the Kantō dialect." Lord Kiso said, "Ah, this must be Saitō Bettō Sanemori.

If so, his hair and beard should be white, but it is strange that they are black. Higuchi no Jirō should recognize him."

When he had Higuchi sent for, on arrival and with but one glance, Higuchi shed tears and said, "Alas, how pitiful! This is indeed Saitō Bettō!

Sanemori was accustomed to say that, if at sixty years of age or more one goes to battle, to compete with young warriors in order to advance first would be childish. And again, to be looked down upon by people as an old warrior would be mortifying. He would choose to dye his hair and beard with black ink and be killed fighting just like a young man. That is what he always said. Indeed he has dyed them. Have his head washed and look for yourselves."

When I asked his name, he demanded mine, but would not give his own. He spoke in Kantō dialect."
"Splendid!" exclaimed Lord Kiso. "This must be Sanemori. (I saw him once when I went to Kōzuke Province. At that time I was only a little boy, but I remember that he already had grizzled hair.) Now it must be white all over. But, strangely this hair and this beard are black. Higuchi no Jirō has been a friend of Sanemori for a long time, and so he must know him well. Summon Higuchi."
Higuchi answered the summons, and, after a glance at the head, he burst into tears, saying: "What a pity! It is the head of Sanemori." ("He must have been more than seventy," said Lord Kiso. "Why is his hair still so black?"
Higuchi, now repressing his tears, replied: "When I think of why it is, I am moved to tears. A man of the bow and the sword must leave some memorable words to the world.) Sanemori used to tell me: 'If I go to fight after I am past sixty years of age, I will dye my hair and beard black so that I may still look young. I would be considered impetuous if I had white hair flowing in disorder as I competed with younger men. Surely I would be scorned as an old fool.'

It is true that Sanemori dyed his hair and beard. My word will be proven if you have them washed."

Scarcely had he spoken when
holding the head. . . .

Kuse

CHORUS: And then, Sanemori's
wearing a brocade robe was not
taking liberties with his own wishes.
Sanemori, when he left the capital,
said to Lord Munemori [i.e., his
commanding officer],

"There is a saying in the classics,
'Wearing brocade one returns to his
birthplace.' Sanemori [I] was from
Echizen, but in recent years was
awarded a domain and took
residence in Nagai of Musashi. Now
if he leaves and goes North, he will
surely be killed in battle. In his old
age, nothing would make him
happier to remember than being
granted this permission [i.e., to wear
a brocade robe]." Since that was his
wish, Munemori bestowed upon
him a red brocade robe.

SHITE: Now, in an old poem as well
[there appear the words]—"Maple
leaves,"
CHORUS: "While brushing them
aside he returns home wearing

When Lord Kiso had the head
washed, indeed the hair and
beard turned white.

The reason Sanemori had worn a
red brocade robe is as follows.
When he took leave of
Munemori, the state minister, he
said: ("Last year when I went
down with our men to the
eastern provinces, I was startled
by the noise of the waterfowl and
fled in panic from Kambara in
Suruga without shooting a single
arrow against the enemy. There
were of course many others who
fled also, but the fact that I did is
a disgrace to me.) Now I am an
old man. I am going to the
northern provinces, where I am
determined to die. Echizen is the
province where I was born. It is
only in later years that I have
lived in Nagai in Musashi
Province, the domain that my
lord has bestowed upon me. The
proverb says, 'Wear a brocade
robe when you return to your
homeland.' Now I beg you to
grant me the right to wear a
brocade battle garb." (It is said
that Munemori was moved by
Sanemori's bravery and thus)
allowed him to wear a brocade
battle robe into his last battle.

brocade and the people see him."
That is what a poet wrote and it is
in the spirit of the original saying.
Shubaijin of old let his brocade
sleeves flutter [in the wind] on Mt.
Kaikei. Now, Sanemori has brought
fame to the four corners of the
Northern province and the
celebrated warrior's name has lasted
through generations, visible to all.

Long ago in China, Chu
Maich'en flaunted brocade
sleeves on Mount Hui-chi.
In the same manner Sanemori
raised his name in the northern
provinces. He left to this world
an illustrious name.

Rongi

SHITE: Kiso—He [I] intended to
grapple with him, but Tezuka came
between them [us]. Even now that
resentment persists.

One of Kiso's men, Tezuka, saw
him (and, because of his gorgeous
battle garb, thought that he
might be a warrior of great
fame).

CHORUS: Among Kiso's followers,
who one by one gave their names,
the first to advance was
SHITE: Tezuka no Tarō Mitsumori.

Riding forward,
Tezuka (exclaimed: "A brave
man! Your men are all running
away, but you have remained
here. How gallant you are! Let
me ask your name and title."
"Who is he that asks me who I
am?" replied Sanemori. "I am
Tezuka, a native of Shinano
Province." "If that is who you
are," said Sanemori, "your sword
deserves a fight with mine. I do
not mean to offend you, but I
have good reason for not
declaring my name. Come now,
Tezuka. On your guard!")
As he urged his horse alongside
Tezuka's, one of Tezuka's
retainers, fearing that his master
might be killed, rushed up and
thrust himself between them.
Now he grappled with Sanemori.

CHORUS: A retainer, fearing lest his
lord be killed,
SHITE: On his horse interceded. And
to the side of Sanemori
CHORUS: He came. And as he
grappled with him,

SHITE: Sanemori said, "Ah, you want to grapple with Japan's number-one warrior." Against the front of the saddle he pressed him and cut off and threw away his [the retainer's] head.

CHORUS: After that, Tezuka no Tarō circled around Sanemori on the left, pulled up the skirt of his armor, and stabbed him twice with his sword. They grappled at close quarters and between the two horses fell down with a crash.
SHITE: Alas, he was an old warrior
CHORUS: Exhausted from battle an old tree, beaten by the wind, whose strength is broken beneath Tezuka. As he fell, finally his head was cut off.

He became one with the earth at Shinowara.

"Splendid! You want to fight with the greatest warrior in Japan," cried Sanemori as he caught the retainer in his arm, pressed him hard against the pommel of his saddle, and cut off his head.
Tezuka, seeing his retainer fall, slipped around to the left side of his opponent and, lifting the skirts of Sanemori's armor, stabbed him twice.

Sanemori weakened. As they jumped from their horses, Tezuka fell upon him. Tough and valiant though he was, Sanemori was pressed down and beheaded, for he had already been exhausted by the long battle, too severe for a man well advanced in years.

Appendix 3

Japanese Passages Analyzed for Style in Chapters Three and Four

1. 実盛

名ノリ―　　　　アイ・かやうに候ふ者は，加賀の國篠原の里に住まひ仕る者にて候，さるほどにここに遊行の流れに，他阿弥上人と申して尊きおん方のござ候ふが，毎日法談をなさるる，それにつき不思議なることの候，いつも日中の前後ひとり言を仰せらるる，いづれもこれを不思議なりとの申しごとにて候，それがしは高座近う参る者のことなれば，いづれもこれを不審致せとの申しごとにて候ふ間，日中過ぎ候へばあれへ参り不審致さうずる間，皆々その分心得候へ心得候へ

サシ―　　　　ワキ・それ西方は十萬億土，遠く生まるる道ながら，ここも己心の弥陀の國，貴賤群集の称名の聲，

　　　　　ワキ連・日々夜々の法の場，

　　　　　ワキ・げにもまことに摂取不捨の，

　　　　　ワキ連・誓ひにたれか

　　　　　ワキ・残るべき

上ゲ哥―　ワキ/ワキ連・ひとりなほ，仏のみ名を　尋ね見ん，仏のみ名を　尋ね見ん，おのおの帰る　法の場，知るも知らぬも　心引く，誓ひの網に　洩るべきや。知る人も，知らぬ人をも　渡さばや，かの國へ行く　法の舟，浮かむも易き　道とかや，浮かむも易き道とかや。

サシ―　　　　シテ・笙歌遙かに聞こゆ孤雲の上，聖衆来迎す落日の前，あら尊やけふもまた紫雲の立つて候ふぞや。

詞　　　　　・鉦の音念仏の聲の聞こえ候，さては聴聞も今なるべし，さなきだに　立ち居苦しき老いの波の，寄りも付かずは法の場に，よそながらもや聴聞せん，

節　　　　　　　・一念称名の聲のうちには，摂取の光明曇らねども，老眼の通
　　　　　　　　路なほもつて明きらかならず，よしよしすこしは遅くとも，
　　　　　　　　ここを去ること遠かるまじや南無阿弥陀仏。

問答—　　　　ワキ・いかに翁，さても毎日の称名に怠ることなし，されば志しの
　　　　　　　　者と見るところに，おことの姿餘人の目に見ることなし，た
　　　　　　　　れに向かひてなにごとを申すぞと皆人不審しあへり，けふは
　　　　　　　　おことの名を名のり候へ

　　　　　　　シテ・これは思ひもよらぬ仰せかな，もとより所は天離がる，鄙人
　　　　　　　　なれば人がましやな，名もあらばこそ名のりもせめ，ただ上
　　　　　　　　人のおん下向，ひとへに弥陀の来迎なれば，

　　　　　　　　・かしこうぞ長生きして，

　　　　　　　　・この称名の時節に逢ふこと，

　　　　　　　　・盲亀の浮木優曇華の，花待ち得たるここちして，老いの幸ひ
　　　　　　　　身に越え，喜びの涙袂に餘る，さればこの身ながら，安楽國
　　　　　　　　に生まるるかと，無比の歓喜をなすところに，輪回妄執の閻
　　　　　　　　浮の名を，また改めて名のらんこと　口惜しうこそ候へとよ。

　　　　　　　ワキ・げにげに翁の申す所理至極せり，さりながらひとつは懺悔の
　　　　　　　　回心ともなるべし，ただおことの名を名のり候へ

　　　　　　　シテ・さては名のらではかなひ候ふまじきか

　　　　　　　ワキ・なかなかのこと急いで名のり候へ

　　　　　　　シテ・さらばおん前なる人を退けられ候へ近う参りて名のり候ふ
　　　　　　　　べし

　　　　　　　ワキ・もとより翁の姿餘人の目に見ゆることはなけれども，所望な
　　　　　　　　らば人をば退くべし，近う寄つて名を名のり候へ

　　　　　　　シテ・昔長井の斎藤別当実盛は，この篠原の合戦に討たれぬ，聞こ
　　　　　　　　しめし及ばれてこそ候ふらめ

　　　　　　　ワキ・それは平家の侍，弓取つての名将，その戦物語りは無益，た
　　　　　　　　だおことの名を名のり候へ

　　　　　　　シテ・いやさればその実盛は，このおん前の池水にて鬢鬚を洗はれ
　　　　　　　　しとなり，さればその執心残りけるか，今もこのあたりの人
　　　　　　　　には幻のごとく見ゆると申し候

　　　　　　　ワキ・さては今も人に見え候ふか

　　　　　　　シテ・深山木の，その梢とは見えざりし，桜は花に現はれたる，老
　　　　　　　　い木をそれとご覧ぜよ

　　　　　　　ワキ・不思議やさては実盛の，昔を聞きつる物語り，人の上ぞと思
　　　　　　　　ひしに，身の上なりける不思議さよ，さてはおことは実盛の，
　　　　　　　　その幽霊にてましますか

　　　　　　　シテ・われ実盛が幽霊なるが，魂は善所にありながら，魄はこの世
　　　　　　　　に留まりて，

　　　　　　　ワキ・なほ執心の閻浮の世に，

　　　　　　　シテ・二百餘歳の程は経れども，

　　　　　　　ワキ・浮かみもやらで篠原の，

シテ・池の徒波夜となく，
ワキ・昼とも分かで心の闇の，
シテ・夢ともなく，
ワキ・現ともなき
シテ・思ひをのみ

上ゲ哥— シテ・篠原の，草葉の霜の　翁さび，
地・草葉の霜の　翁さび，人な咎めそ　假そめに，現はれ—出で
たる　実盛が，名を洩らし　給ふなよ，亡き世語りも　恥づか
しとて，おん前を　立ち去りて，行くかと見れば　篠原の，
池のほとりにて　姿は，幻となりて　失せにけり，幻となり
て失せにけり。

〔アイの語〕

ワキ・いざや別時の称名にて，かの幽霊を弔はんと

上ゲ哥— ワキ/ワキ連・篠原の，池のほとりの　法の水，池のほとりの　法の水，深
くぞ頼む　称名の，聲澄み渡る　弔ひの。初夜より後夜に
至るまで，心も西へ　行く月の，光とともに　曇りなき，鉦
を鳴らして　夜もすがら

ワキ・南無阿弥陀仏南無阿弥陀仏。

シテ・極楽世界に行きぬれば，永く苦海を越え過ぎて，輪回の古里
隔たりぬ，歓喜の心いくばくぞや。所は不退の所，命は無量
寿仏とのう頼もしや。

—セイ— シテ・念々相続　する人は，
地・念々ごとに　往生す。

ノリ地— シテ・南無と言つぱ，
地・即ちこれ帰命，
シテ・阿弥陀と言つぱ，
地・その行この義を，以つてのゆゑに，
シテ・必ず往生を得べしとなり，
地・有難や。

掛ケ合— ワキ・不思議やな　白みあひたる池の面に，幽かに浮かみ寄る者を，
見ればありつる翁なるが，甲冑を帯する不思議さよ
シテ・埋れ木の　人知れぬ身と沈めども，心の池の言ひ難き，修羅
の苦患の数々を，浮かめて賜ばせ給へとよ
ワキ・これほどに　目のあたりなる姿言葉を，餘人はさらに見も聞
きもせで，

詞　シテ・ただ上人のみ明らかに，
節　ワキ・見るや姿も残りの雪の，
シテ・鬢鬚白き老武者なれども，
ワキ・その出立は花やかなる，
シテ・よそほひことに曇りなき，
ワキ・月の光
シテ・ともし火の影

289

上ゲ哥—　　　　　地・暗からぬ，夜の錦の　直垂に，夜の錦の　直垂に，萌葱匂ひ
　　　　　　　　　　の　鎧着て，金作りの　太刀刀，今の一身にては　それとて
　　　　　　　　　　も，なにか宝の，池の　蓮の，臺こそ宝　なるべけれ。げにや
　　　　　　　　　　疑はぬ，法の教へは　朽ちもせぬ，金の言葉　重くせば，な
　　　　　　　　　　どかは至ら　ざるべき，などかは至ら　ざるべき。

詞—　　　　　　　ワキ・見申せばなほも輪回の姿なり，その執心を振り捨てて，弥陀
　　　　　　　　　　即滅の臺に至り給ふべし

クリ—　　　　　　シテ・それ一念弥陀仏即滅無量罪，
　　　　　　　　　　地・すなはち廻向発願心，心を残すことなかれ。

サシ—　　　　　　シテ・時至つて今宵逢ひ難きみ法を受け，
　　　　　　　　　　地・慚愧懺悔の物語り，なほも昔を忘れかねて，忍ぶに似たる篠
　　　　　　　　　　原の，草の蔭野の露と消えし，有様語り申すべし

語り—　　　　　　シテ・さても篠原の合戦敗れしかば，源氏の方に手塚の太郎光盛，
　　　　　　　　　　木曾殿のおん前に参り申すやう，光盛こそ奇異の曲者と組ん
　　　　　　　　　　で首取つて候へ，大将かと見れば続く勢もなし，また侍かと
　　　　　　　　　　思へば錦の直垂を着たり，名のれ名のれと責むれども終に名
　　　　　　　　　　のらず，聲は坂東聲にて候ふと申す，木曾殿あつぱれ斎藤別
　　　　　　　　　　当実盛にてやあるらん，然らば鬢鬚白髪たるべきが，黒きこ
　　　　　　　　　　そ不審なれ，樋口の二郎は見知りたるらんとて召されしかば，
　　　　　　　　　　樋口参りただひと目見て涙をはらはらと流いて，

節　　　　　　　　・あな無慚やな斎藤別当にて候ひけるぞや，実盛常に申せしは，
　　　　　　　　　　六十に餘つて戦をせば，若殿ばらと争ひて，先を駈けんも大
　　　　　　　　　　人気なし，また老武者とて人びとに，侮られんも口惜しかる
　　　　　　　　　　べし，鬢鬚を墨に染め，若やぎ討ち死にすべきよし，常づね
　　　　　　　　　　申し候ひしが，まことに染めて候。洗はせてご覧候へと，申
　　　　　　　　　　しもあへず首を持ち，

下ゲ哥—　　　　　地・おん前を立つてあたりなる，この池波の岸に臨みて，水の緑
　　　　　　　　　　も影映る，柳の糸の　枝垂れて

上ゲ哥—　　　　　地・気霽れては，風新柳の　髪を梳り，氷消えては，波舊苔の，
　　　　　　　　　　鬚を　洗ひて見れば，墨は　流れ落ちて，元の一白髪と　なり
　　　　　　　　　　にけり，げに名を惜しむ　弓取りは，たれもかくこそ　ある
　　　　　　　　　　べけれや，あら　優しやとて，皆感涙をぞ　流しける。

クセ—　　　　　　地・また　実盛が，錦の一直垂を　着ること，私ならぬ　望みな
　　　　　　　　　　り，実盛一都を　出でし時，宗盛公に　申すやう，故郷へは
　　　　　　　　　　錦を着て，帰るといへる　本文あり，実盛　生国は，越前
　　　　　　　　　　の一者にて　候ひしが，近年一ご領に　付けられて，武蔵の
　　　　　　　　　　長井に，居住つかまつり　候ひき。このたび　北國に，罷り
　　　　　　　　　　下りて　候はば，定めて一討ち死に　つかまつるべし，老後
　　　　　　　　　　の一思ひ出　これに過ぎじ，ご免あれと　望みしかば，赤地
　　　　　　　　　　の　錦の，直垂を下し　賜はりぬ。
　　　　　　　　　　シテ・しかれば一古歌にも　もみぢ葉を，

地・分けつつ行けば　錦着て，家に帰ると，人や―見るらんと
　　詠みしも，この本文の　心なり，されば　いにしへの，朱買
　　臣は，錦の　袂を，會稽山に　飜し，今の　実盛は，名を北
　　國の　巷にあげ，隠れなかりし　弓取りの，名は末代に　有
　　明の，月の　夜すがら，懺悔物語り　申さん。

ロンギー　　地・げにや懺悔の　物語り，心の水の　底清く，濁りを残し　給
　　ふなよ，

シテ・その妄執の　修羅の道，巡り巡りて　またここに，木曾と―
　　組まんと　たくみしを，手塚めに　隔てられし，無念は　今
　　にあり，

地・続く兵　たれたれと，名のる中にも　まづ進む，

シテ・手塚の太郎　光盛，

地・郎等は主を　討たせじと，

シテ・駈け隔たりて　実盛と，

地・押し並べて　組むところを，

シテ・あつぱれ―おのれは　日本一の，剛の者と　組んでうずよとて，
　　鞍の―前輪に　押し付けて，首―搔き切つて　捨ててんげり

中ノリー　　地・その後　手塚の太郎，実盛が　弓手に回りて，草摺りを　畳
　　み上げて，ふた刀　刺すところを，むずと組んで　二匹が間
　　に，どうど　落ちけるが。

シテ・老武者の　悲しさは，

地・戦には　為疲れたり，風に縮める，枯木の　力も折れて，手
　　塚が下に　なるところを，郎等は　落ち合ひて，終に首をば
　　搔き落とされて，篠原の　土となつて，影も形も　亡き跡の，
　　影も形も　南無阿弥陀仏，弔ひて　賜び給へ，跡弔ひて　賜
　　び給へ。

2. 松風

ロンギー　　地・運ぶは遠き　陸奥の，その名や千賀の　塩竈，

シテ・賤が塩木を　運びしは，阿漕が浦に　退く潮，

地・その伊勢の海の　二見の浦，ふたたび世にも　出でばや，

シテ・松の叢立ち　霞む日に，潮路や遠く　鳴海潟，

地・それは　鳴海潟，ここは鳴尾の　松蔭に，月こそ障はれ　芦
　　の屋，

シテ・灘の―潮汲む　憂き身ぞと，人にやたれも　黄楊の櫛，

地・さし来る潮を　汲み分けて，見れば月こそ　桶にあれ，

シテ・これにも月の　入りたるや，

地・嬉しやこれも　月あり，

シテ・月はひとつ

地・影はふたつ，満つ　潮の，夜の車に　月を載せて，憂しとも
　　思はぬ，潮路　かなや。

3. 江口

クセ―　　　　地・紅花の春の　あした，紅錦　繡の山，装ほひをなすと　見え
　　　　　　　しも，夕べの風に　誘はれ，黄葉の秋の　夕べ，黄纐纈の
　　　　　　　はやし，色を含むと　いへども，朝の霜に　うつろふ。秋風
　　　　　　　蘿月に，言葉を交はす　賓客も，去つて来る　こともなし，
　　　　　　　翠帳　紅閨に，枕を並べし　妹背も，いつの間にかは　隔つ
　　　　　　　らん，およそ一心なき　草木,情ある　人倫，いづれあはれを
　　　　　　　逃がるべき，かくは思ひ　知りながら。

4. 頼政ヽ

中ノリ―　　　地・衙を揃へ　川水に，すこしも　ためらはず，群れ居る一群ら
　　　　　　　鳥の　翼を並ぶる，羽音もかくやと　白波に，ざっざっと
　　　　　　　うち入れて，

5. 井筒

サシ―　　　　ワキ・風吹けば　沖つ白波竜田山

サシ―　　　　シテ・風吹けば　沖つ白波竜田山,
　　　　　　　地・夜半にや君がひとり行くらんと

ロンギ―　　　シテ・白波の　竜田山，夜半に...

6. 姨捨

問答―　　　　シテ・わが心慰めかねつ更科や，「姨捨山に照る月を見て」

Appendix 4
Greek Passages Analyzed for Style in Chapters Three and Four

1. *Agamemnon*   ΧΟ. ἥκω σεβίζων σόν, Κλυταιμήστρα, κράτος·
258–316

                    δίκη γάρ ἐστι φωτὸς ἀρχηγοῦ τίειν
                    γυναῖκ᾽, ἐρημωθέντος ἄρσενος θρόνου.   260
                    σὺ δ᾽ εἴ τι κεδνὸν εἴτε μὴ πεπυσμένη
                    εὐαγγέλοισιν ἐλπίσιν θυηπολεῖς,
                    κλύοιμ᾽ ἂν εὔφρων· οὐδὲ σιγώσῃ φθόνος.

ΚΛ. εὐάγγελος μέν, ὥσπερ ἡ παροιμία,
                    ἕως γένοιτο μητρὸς εὐφρόνης πάρα·   265
                    πεύσῃ δὲ χάρμα μεῖζον ἐλπίδος κλύειν·
                    Πριάμου γὰρ ᾑρήκασιν Ἀργεῖοι πόλιν.

ΧΟ. πῶς φῄς; πέφευγε τοὔπος ἐξ ἀπιστίας.

ΚΛ. Τροίαν Ἀχαιῶν οὖσαν· ἦ τορῶς λέγω;

ΧΟ. χαρά μ᾽ ὑφέρπει δάκρυον ἐκκαλουμένη.   270

ΚΛ. εὖ γὰρ φρονοῦντος ὄμμα σοῦ κατηγορεῖ.

ΧΟ. τί γὰρ τὸ πιστόν; ἔστι τῶνδέ σοι τέκμαρ;

ΚΛ. ἔστιν, τί δ᾽ οὐχί; μὴ δολώσαντος θεοῦ.

ΧΟ. πότερα δ᾽ ὀνείρων φάσματ᾽ εὐπιθῆ
                     σέβεις;

ΚΛ. οὐ δόξαν ἂν λάβοιμι βριζούσης φρενός.   275

ΧΟ. ἀλλ᾽ ἦ σ᾽ ἐπίανέν τις ἄπτερος φάτις;

ΚΛ. παιδὸς νέας ὣς κάρτ᾽ ἐμωμήσω φρένας.

ΧΟ. ποίου χρόνου δὲ καὶ πεπόρθηται πόλις;

ΚΛ. τῆς νῦν τεκούσης φῶς τόδ᾽ εὐφρόνης λέγω.

ΧΟ. καὶ τίς τόδ᾽ ἐξίκοιτ᾽ ἂν ἀγγέλων τάχος;   280

ΚΛ.　Ἥφαιστος, Ἴδης λαμπρὸν ἐκπέμπων
　　　σέλας·
　　φρυκτὸς δὲ φρυκτὸν δεῦρ᾽ ἀπ᾽ ἀγγάρου
　　　πυρὸς
　　ἔπεμπεν. Ἴδη μὲν πρὸς Ἑρμαῖον λέπας
　　Λήμνου, μέγαν δὲ πανὸν ἐκ νήσου τρίτον
　　Ἀθῷον αἶπος Ζηνὸς ἐξεδέξατο·　　　　　　285
　　ὑπερτελὴς δὲ πόντον ὥστε νωτίσαι
　　ἰσχὺς πορευτοῦ λαμπάδος πρὸς ἡδονὴν
　　〈　　　　　　　　　　　　　　　　　　〉
　　πεύκη τὸ χρυσοφεγγὲς ὥς τις ἥλιος
　　σέλας παραγγείλασα Μακίστου σκοπαῖς.
　　ὁ δ᾽ οὔτι μέλλων οὐδ᾽ ἀφρασμόνως ὕπνῳ　　290
　　νικώμενος παρῆκεν ἀγγέλου μέρος,
　　ἑκὰς δὲ φρυκτοῦ φῶς ἐπ᾽ Εὐρίπου ῥοὰς
　　Μεσσαπίου φύλαξι σημαίνει μολόν.
　　οἱ δ᾽ ἀντέλαμψαν καὶ παρήγγειλαν πρόσω
　　γραίας ἐρείκης θωμὸν ἅψαντες πυρί.　　　　295
　　σθένουσα λαμπὰς δ᾽ οὐδέ πω μαυρουμένη,
　　ὑπερθοροῦσα πεδίον Ἀσωποῦ, δίκην
　　φαιδρᾶς σελήνης, πρὸς Κιθαιρῶνος λέπας
　　ἤγειρεν ἄλλην ἐκδοχὴν πομποῦ πυρός.
　　φάος δὲ τηλέπομπον οὐκ ἠναίνετο　　　　　300
　　φρουρά, πλέον καίουσα τῶν εἰρημένων·
　　λίμνην δ᾽ ὑπὲρ γοργῶπιν ἔσκηψεν φάος,
　　ὄρος τ᾽ ἐπ᾽ αἰγίπλαγκτον ἐξικνούμενον
　　ὤτρυνε θεσμὸν †μὴ χαρίζεσθαι† πυρός·
　　πέμπουσι δ᾽ ἀνδαίοντες ἀφθόνῳ μένει　　　305
　　φλογὸς μέγαν πώγωνα †καὶ Σαρωνικοῦ
　　πορθμοῦ κάτοπτον πρῶν᾽ ὑπερβάλλειν
　　　πρόσω
　　φλέγουσαν†· εἶτ᾽ ἔσκηψεν, εἶτ᾽ ἀφίκετο
　　Ἀραχναῖον αἶπος, ἀστυγείτονας σκοπάς,
　　κἄπειτ᾽ Ἀτρειδῶν ἐς τόδε σκήπτει　　　　　310
　　　στέγος
　　φάος τόδ᾽ οὐκ ἄπαππον Ἰδαίου πυρός.
　　τοιοίδε τοί μοι λαμπαδηφόρων νόμοι,
　　ἄλλος παρ᾽ ἄλλου διαδοχαῖς πληρούμενοι·
　　νικᾷ δ᾽ ὁ πρῶτος καὶ τελευταῖος δραμών.
　　τέκμαρ τοιοῦτον σύμβολόν τέ σοι λέγω　　　315
　　ἀνδρὸς παραγγείλαντος ἐκ Τροίας ἐμοί.

2. *Agamemnon*　XO.　Δίκα δὲ τοῖς μὲν παθοῦ-
　250–251　　　　　σιν μαθεῖν ἐπιρρέπει.

3. *Agamemnon*　XO.　μεγάλ᾽ ἐκ θυμοῦ κλάζοντες Ἄρη,
　48–59　　　　　τρόπον αἰγυπιῶν οἵτ᾽ ἐκπατίοις
　　　　　　　　　ἄλγεσι παίδων ὕπατοι λεχέων　　　　　50
　　　　　　　　　στροφοδινοῦνται
　　　　　　　　　πτερύγων ἐρετμοῖσιν ἐρεσσόμενοι,
　　　　　　　　　δεμνιοτήρη
　　　　　　　　　πόνον ὀρταλίχων ὀλέσαντες·
　　　　　　　　　ὕπατος δ᾽ ἀίων ἤ τις Ἀπόλλων　　　　　55
　　　　　　　　　ἢ Πὰν ἢ Ζεὺς οἰωνόθροον
　　　　　　　　　γόον ὀξυβόαν τῶνδε μετοίκων,
　　　　　　　　　ὑστερόποινον
　　　　　　　　　πέμπει παραβᾶσιν Ἐρινύν.

4. *Agamemnon*　XO.　δαιμόνων δέ που χάρις βίαιος
　182–183　　　　σέλμα σεμνὸν ἡμένων.

5. *Agamemnon*　XO.　Ἰλίῳ δὲ κῆδος ὀρ-　　　　　　[ἀντ. α
　699–731　　　　θώνυμον τελεσσίφρων　　　　　　　700
　　　　　　　　　Μῆνις ἤλασεν, τραπέζας ἀτί-
　　　　　　　　　μωσιν ὑστέρῳ χρόνῳ
　　　　　　　　　καὶ ξυνεστίου Διὸς
　　　　　　　　　πρασσομένα τὸ νυμφότι-　　　　　　705
　　　　　　　　　μον μέλος ἐκφάτως τίοντας,
　　　　　　　　　ὑμέναιον ὃς τότ᾽ ἐπέρ-
　　　　　　　　　ρεπε γαμβροῖσιν ἀείδειν.
　　　　　　　　　μεταμανθάνουσα δ᾽ ὕμνον
　　　　　　　　　Πριάμου πόλις γεραιὰ　　　　　　710
　　　　　　　　　πολύθρηνον μέγα που στένει, κικλήσκου-
　　　　　　　　　σα Πάριν τὸν αἰνόλεκτρον
　　　　　　　　　†παμπρόσθη πολύθρηνον
　　　　　　　　　αἰῶν᾽ ἀμφὶ πολιτᾶν†　　　　　　715
　　　　　　　　　μέλεον αἷμ᾽ ἀνατλᾶσα.

　　　　　　　　　ἔθρεψεν δὲ λέοντος ἶ-　　　　　　[στρ. β
　　　　　　　　　νιν δόμοις ἀγάλακτον οὕ-
　　　　　　　　　τως ἀνὴρ φιλόμαστον,
　　　　　　　　　ἐν βιότου προτελείοις　　　　　　720
　　　　　　　　　ἄμερον, εὐφιλόπαιδα,
　　　　　　　　　καὶ γεραροῖς ἐπίχαρτον·

πολέα δ' ἔσχ' ἐν ἀγκάλαις
νεοτρόφου τέκνου δίκαν,
φαιδρωπὸς ποτὶ χεῖρα σαί-   725
    νων τε γαστρὸς ἀνάγκαις.

χρονισθεὶς δ' ἀπέδειξεν ἦ-   [ἀντ. β
θος τὸ πρὸς τοκέων· χάριν
    γὰρ τροφεῦσιν ἀμείβων
μηλοφόνοισι σὺν ἄταις   730
δαῖτ' ἀκέλευστος ἔτευξεν·

6. *Agamemnon* XO. "τόσον περ εὔφρων ἁ καλὰ   [ἐπῳδ. 140
   140–155   δρόσοις ἀέπτοις μαλερῶν λεόντων
πάντων τ' ἀγρονόμων φιλομάστοις
θηρῶν ὀβρικάλοισι τερπνά,
τούτων αἰτεῖ ξύμβολα κρᾶναι,
δεξιὰ μὲν κατάμομφα δὲ φάσματα   145
ἱήιον δὲ καλέω Παιᾶνα,
μή τινας ἀντιπνόους Δαναοῖς χρονί-
    ας ἐχενῇδας ἀπλοίας
τεύξῃ σπευδομένα θυσίαν ἑτέραν ἄνομόν 150
    τιν' ἄδαιτον,
νεικέων τέκτονα σύμφυτον, οὐ δει-
    σήνορα· μίμνει γὰρ φοβερὰ παλίνορτος
οἰκονόμος δολία, μνάμων Μῆνις
    τεκνόποινος."   155

7. *Agamemnon* KA. καὶ μὴν ὁ χρησμὸς οὐκέτ' ἐκ καλυμμάτων
   1178–1183.   ἔσται δεδορκὼς νεογάμου νύμφης δίκην,
λαμπρὸς δ' ἔοικεν ἡλίου πρὸς ἀντολὰς   1180
πνέων ἐφήξειν, ὥστε κύματος δίκην
κλύζειν πρὸς αὐγὰς τοῦδε πήματος πολὺ
μεῖζον.

8. *Agamemnon* XO. πολλὰ γοῦν θιγγάνει πρὸς ἧπαρ·
   432–444   οὓς μὲν γὰρ ⟨τις⟩ ἔπεμψεν
οἶδεν, ἀντὶ δὲ φωτῶν
τεύχη καὶ σποδὸς εἰς ἑκά-   435
    στου δόμους ἀφικνεῖται.

ὁ χρυσαμοιβὸς δ' Ἄρης σωμάτων   [στρ. γ
καὶ ταλαντοῦχος ἐν μάχῃ δορὸς

πυρωθὲν ἐξ Ἰλίου   440
φίλοισι πέμπει βαρὺ
ψῆγμα δυσδάκρυτον ἀντ-
ήνορος σποδοῦ γεμί-
ζων λέβητας εὐθέτους.

9. *Agamemnon*   ΧΟ. . . . οἴκτῳ γὰρ ἐπίφθονος Ἄρτεμις ἁγνὰ
   134—136   πτανοῖσιν κυσὶ πατρὸς   135
                     αὐτότοκον πρὸ λόχου μογερὰν πτάκα
                     θυομένοισιν.

10. *Suppliants*   ΧΟ. νῦν δ᾽ ἐπικεκλομένα   [στρ. α   40
   40—49   Δῖον πόρτιν, ὑπερπόντιον τιμάορ᾽, ἷνιν γ᾽
                     ἀνθονομούσας προγόνου βοὸς ἐξ
                     ἐπιπνοίας
                     Ζηνός· ἔφαψιν ἐπωνυμίαν δ᾽ ἐπεκραίνετο
                     μόρσιμος αἰὼν   45
                     εὐλόχως, Ἔπαφον δ᾽ ἐγέννασεν·

                     ὅν τ᾽ ἐπιλεξαμένα   [ἀντ. α

11. *Libation*   ΧΟ. ἔμολε μὲν Δίκα Πριαμίδαις χρόνῳ,   [στρ. αω 935
  Bearers   βαρύδικος ποινά·
  935—938   ἔμολε δ᾽ ἐς δόμον τὸν Ἀγαμέμνονος
                     διπλοῦς λέων, διπλοῦς Ἄρης·

12. *Libation*   ΧΟ. ἔμολε δ᾽ ᾇ μέλει κρυπταδίου μάχας [ἀντ. α
  Bearers   δολιόφρων Ποινά,
  946—950   ἔθιγε δ᾽ ἐν μάχᾳ χερὸς ἐτήτυμος
                     Διὸς κόρα, Δίκαν δέ νιν
                     προσαγορεύομεν   950

13. *Suppliants*   ΔΑ. ὄρνιθος ὄρνις πῶς ἂν ἁγνεύοι φαγών;
  226—228   πῶς δ᾽ ἂν γαμῶν ἄκουσαν ἄκοντος πάρα
                     ἁγνὸς γένοιτ᾽ ἄν;

14. *Persians*   ΒΑ. ἐπεὶ δ᾽ ἀνέστην καὶ χεροῖν καλλιρρόου
  201-206   ἔψαυσα πηγῆς, σὺν θυηπόλῳ χερὶ
                     βωμὸν προσέστην, ἀποτρόποισι δαίμοσιν
                     θέλουσα θῦσαι πελανόν, ὧν τέλη τάδε·
                     ὁρῶ δὲ φεύγοντ᾽ αἰετὸν πρὸς ἐσχάραν   205
                     Φοίβου, φόβῳ δ᾽ ἄφθογγος ἐστάθην, φίλοι·

297

15. *Agamemnon* ΧΟ. μάλα †γὰρ τοι τᾶς πολλᾶς ὑγιείας† [στρ.β
    1001-1017   ἀκόρεστον τέρμα· νόσος γὰρ
                    γείτων ὁμότοιχος ἐρείδει.
              〈   〉
              καὶ πότμος εὐθυπορῶν   1005
              ἀνδρὸς ἔπαισεν ἄφαντον ἕρμα.
              καὶ τὸ μὲν πρὸ χρημάτων
              κτησίων ὄκνος βαλὼν
              σφενδόνας ἀπ᾽ εὐμέτρου,   1010
              οὐκ ἔδυ πρόπας δόμος
              πλησμονᾶς γέμων ἄγαν,
              οὐδ᾽ ἐπόντισε σκάφος.
              πολλά τοι δόσις ἐκ Διὸς ἀμφιλα-   1015
                  φής τε καὶ ἐξ ἀλόκων ἐπετειᾶν
              νῆστιν ὤλεσεν νόσον.

16. *Agamemnon* ΧΟ. τό θ᾽ ὑπέργηρων φυλλάδος ἤδη
    79–82   κατακαρφομένης τρίποδας μὲν ὁδοὺς   80
              στείχει, παιδὸς δ᾽ οὐδὲν ἀρείων
              ὄναρ ἡμερόφαντον ἀλαίνει.

17. *Persians*   ΒΑ. ὧδ᾽ ἔχει, γνώμης δέ πού τις δαιμόνων
    724–726   ξυνήψατο.
          ΔΑ. φεῦ μέγας τις ἦλθε δαίμων ὥστε μή
                φρονεῖν καλῶς.   725
          ΒΑ. ὡς ἰδεῖν τέλος πάρεστιν οἷον ἤνυσεν
                κακόν.

18. *Persians*   ΧΟ. λαοπαθέα σέβων ἀλίτυπά τε βάρη
    945

19. *Persians*   ΧΟ. ἐχυροῖς ἕρκεσιν εἴργειν ἄμαχον κῦμα
    90–91   θαλάσσας·
              ἀπρόσοιστος γὰρ ὁ Περσᾶν στρατὸς
              ἀλκίφρων τε λαός.

20. *Persians*   ΞΕ. βοᾷ βοᾷ 〈μοι〉 μελέων ἔντοσθεν ἦτορ.
    991

21. *Persians*   ΞΕ. ὅδ᾽ ἐγὼν οἰοῖ αἰακτός,   [στρ. α
    931–932   μέλεος. . . .

22. *Persians*   XO. γᾶ δ᾽ αἰάζει τὰν ἐγγαίαν
    922–923   ἥβαν. . . .

23. *Agamemnon* ΚΛ. ῥίζης γὰρ οὔσης φυλλὰς ἵκετ᾽ ἐς δόμους
    966–974   σκιὰν ὑπερτείνασα σειρίου κυνός·
                καὶ σοῦ μολόντος δωματῖτιν ἑστίαν,
                θάλπος μὲν ἐν χειμῶνι σημαίνεις μολόν·
                ὅταν δὲ τεύχῃ Ζεὺς ἀπ᾽ ὄμφακος πικρᾶς   970
                οἶνον, τότ᾽ ἤδη ψῦχος ἐν δόμοις πέλει,
                ἀνδρὸς τελείου δῶμ᾽ ἐπιστρωφωμένου.
                Ζεῦ Ζεῦ τέλειε, τὰς ἐμὰς εὐχὰς τέλει·
                μέλοι δέ τοί σοι τῶνπερ ἂν μέλλῃς
                    τελεῖν.

24. *Persians*   ΒΑ. ταῦτά μοι διπλῆ μέριμν᾽ ἄφραστός ἐστιν ἐν
    165–169   φρεσίν,   165
                μήτε χρημάτων ἀνάνδρων πλῆθος ἐν τιμῇ
                    σέβειν
                μήτ᾽ ἀχρημάτοισι λάμπειν φῶς ὅσον
                    σθένος πάρα·
                ἔστι γὰρ πλοῦτός γ᾽ ἀμεμφής, ἀμφὶ δ᾽
                    ὀφθαλμῷ φόβος·
                ὄμμα γὰρ δόμων νομίζω δεσπότου
                    παρουσίαν.

25. *Persians*   ΑΓΓ. Ξέρξης μὲν αὐτὸς ζῆ τε καὶ φάος βλέπει.
    299–301   ΒΑ. ἐμοῖς μὲν εἶπας δώμασιν φάος μέγα   300
                καὶ λευκὸν ἦμαρ νυκτὸς ἐκ μελαγχίμου.

26. *Persians*   ΞΕ. ὁρᾷς τὸ λοιπὸν τόδε τᾶς ἐμᾶς στολᾶς;
    1017–1018 ΧΟ. ὁρῶ ὁρῶ.

27. *Persians*   ΧΟ. πεπέρακεν μὲν ὁ περσέπτολις ἤδη   [στρ. α 65
    65–132   βασίλειος στρατὸς εἰς ἀντίπορον
                    γείτονα χώραν,
                λινοδέσμῳ σχεδίᾳ πορθμὸν ἀμείψας
                    Ἀθαμαντίδος Ἕλλας,   70
                πολύγομφον ὅδισμα ζυγὸν ἀμφιβαλὼν
                    αὐχένι πόντου.

                πολυάνδρου δ᾽ Ἀσίας θούριος ἄρχων [ἀντ. α
                ἐπὶ πᾶσαν χθόνα ποιμανόριον θεῖον
                    ἐλαύνει   75

διχόθεν, πεζονόμοις ἔκ τε θαλάσσας
   ἐχυροῖσι πεποιθὼς
στυφελοῖς ἐφέταις, χρυσονόμου γενεᾶς
   ἰσόθεος φώς.   80

κυάνεον δ᾽ ὄμμασι λεύσσων φονίου   [στρ. β
   δέργμα δράκοντος
πολύχειρ καὶ πολυναύτας Σύριόν θ᾽ ἅρμα
   διώκων
ἐπάγει δουρικλύτοις ἀνδράσι τοξόδαμνον
   Ἄρη.   85

δόκιμος δ᾽ οὔτις ὑποστὰς μεγάλῳ   [ἀντ. β
   ῥεύματι φωτῶν
ἐχυροῖς ἕρκεσιν εἴργειν ἄμαχον κῦμα
   θαλάσσας·   90
ἀπρόσοιστος γὰρ ὁ Περσᾶν στρατὸς
   ἀλκίφρων τε λαός.

δολόμητιν δ᾽ ἀπάταν θεοῦ τίς ἀνὴρ   [μεσῳδ.
   θνατὸς ἀλύξει;
τίς ὁ κραιπνῷ ποδὶ πηδήματος εὐπετέος
   ἀνάσσων;   95
φιλόφρων γὰρ ποτισαίνουσα τὸ πρῶτον
   παράγει
βροτὸν εἰς ἄρκυας Ἄτα,
τόθεν οὐκ ἔστιν ὑπὲρ θνατὸν ἀλύξαντα
   φυγεῖν.   100

θεόθεν γὰρ κατὰ Μοῖρ᾽ ἐκράτησεν   [στρ. γ
τὸ παλαιόν, ἐπέσκηψε δὲ Πέρσαις
πολέμους πυργοδαΐκτους
διέπειν ἱππιοχάρμας τε κλόνους πόλεων
   τ᾽ ἀναστάσεις·   105

ἔμαθον δ᾽ εὐρυπόροιο θαλάσσας   [ἀντ. γ
πολιαινομένας πνεύματι λάβρῳ   110
ἐσορᾶν πόντιον ἄλσος,
πίσυνοι λεπτοτόνοις πείσμασι λαοπόροις
   τε μηχαναῖς.   114

ταῦτά μου μελαγχίτων φρὴν   [στρ. δ
   ἀμύσσεται φόβῳ.

ὀᾶ, Περσικοῦ στρατεύματος, τοῦδε μὴ
   πόλις πύθη-   117
ται κένανδρον μέγ' ἄστυ Σουσίδος·

καὶ τὸ Κισσίων πόλισμ' ἀντίδουπον   [ἀντ. δ
   ᾄσεται,
ὀᾶ, τοῦτ' ἔπος γυναικοπληθὴς ὅμιλος
   ἀπύων,   122
βυσσίνοις δ' ἐν πέπλοις πέσῃ λακίς.   125

πᾶς γὰρ ἱππηλάτας καὶ πεδοστιβὴς   [στρ. ε
   λεὼς
σμῆνος ὣς ἐκλέλοιπεν μελισσᾶν σὺν
   ὀρχάμῳ στρατοῦ,
τὸν ἀμφίζευκτον ἐξαμείψας ἀμφοτέρας
   ἅλιον   131
πρῶνα κοινὸν αἴας.

28. Persians   ΑΓΓ. . . . οἰμωγὴ δ' ὁμοῦ
426–434   κωκύμασιν κατεῖχε πελαγίαν ἅλα,
              ἕως κελαινῆς νυκτὸς ὄμμ' ἀφείλετο.
              κακῶν δὲ πλῆθος, οὐδ' ἂν εἰ δέκ' ἤματα
              στοιχηγοροίην, οὐκ ἂν ἐκπλήσαιμί σοι.   430
              εὖ γὰρ τόδ' ἴσθι, μηδάμ' ἡμέρᾳ μιᾷ
              πλῆθος τοσουτάριθμον ἀνθρώπων θανεῖν.

         ΒΑ.   αἰαῖ, κακῶν δὴ πέλαγος ἔρρωγεν μέγα
              Πέρσαις τε καὶ πρόπαντι βαρβάρων γένει.

29. Persians   ΧΟ.   Ξέρξης μὲν ἄγαγεν, ποποῖ,   550
550–553   Ξέρξης δ' ἀπώλεσεν, τοτοῖ,
              Ξέρξης δὲ πάντ' ἐπέσπε δυσφρόνως
              βαρίδεσσι ποντίαις.

30. Persians   ΧΟ.   νᾶες μὲν ἄγαγον, ποποῖ,   560
560–564   νᾶες δ' ἀπώλεσαν, τοτοῖ,
              νᾶες πανωλέθροισιν ἐμβολαῖς·
              διὰ δ' Ἰαόνων χέρας

31. Persians   ΒΑ.   φίλοι, κακῶν μὲν ὅστις ἔμπειρος κυρεῖ,
598–602   ἐπίσταται βροτοῖσιν ὡς, ὅταν κλύδων
              κακῶν ἐπέλθῃ, πάντα δειμαίνειν φιλεῖ,   600

ὅταν δ᾽ ὁ δαίμων εὐροῇ, πεποιθέναι
τὸν αὐτὸν αἰὲν ἄνεμον οὐριεῖν τύχης.

32. *Persians*   ΔΑ. Ζεὺς ἀπέσκηψεν τελευτὴν θεσφάτων· ἐγώ
   740–751   δέ που   740
                       διὰ μακροῦ χρόνου τάδ᾽ ηὔχουν
                       ἐκτελευτήσειν θεούς·
                       ἀλλ᾽, ὅταν σπεύδῃ τις αὐτός, χὠ θεὸς
                       συνάπτεται·
                       νῦν κακῶν ἔοικε πηγὴ πᾶσιν ηὑρῆσθαι
                       φίλοις·
                       παῖς δ᾽ ἐμὸς τάδ᾽ οὐ κατειδὼς ἤνυσεν νέῳ
                       θράσει,
                       ὅστις Ἑλλήσποντον ἱρὸν δοῦλον ὣς
                       δεσμώμασιν   745
                       ἤλπισε σχήσειν ῥέοντα, Βόσπορον ῥόον
                       θεοῦ,
                       καὶ πόρον μετερρύθμιζε καὶ πέδαις
                       σφυρηλάτοις
                       περιβαλὼν πολλὴν κέλευθον ἤνυσεν πολλῷ
                       στρατῷ,
                       θνητὸς ὢν θεῶν δὲ πάντων ᾤετ᾽ οὐκ
                       εὐβουλίᾳ
                       καὶ Ποσειδῶνος κρατήσειν. πῶς τάδ᾽ οὐ
                       νόσος φρενῶν   750
                       εἶχε παῖδ᾽ ἐμόν;

33. *Persians*   ΔΑ. μίμνουσι δ᾽ ἔνθα πεδίον Ἀσωπὸς ῥοαῖς   805
   805–808   ἄρδει, φίλον πίασμα Βοιωτῶν χθονί,
                       οὗ σφιν κακῶν ὕψιστ᾽ ἐπαμμένει παθεῖν
                       ὕβρεως ἄποινα κἀθέων φρονημάτων·

34. *Persians*   ΔΑ. πάσχουσι, τὰ δὲ μέλλουσι, κοὐδέπω κακῶν
   814–815   κρηνὶς ἀπέσβηκ᾽, ἀλλ᾽ ἔτ᾽ ἐκπιδύεται.   815

35. *Persians*   ΔΑ. θῖνες νεκρῶν δὲ καὶ τριτοσπόρῳ γονῇ
   818–828   ἄφωνα σημανοῦσιν ὄμμασιν βροτῶν
                       ὡς οὐχ ὑπέρφευ θνητὸν ὄντα χρὴ φρονεῖν·   820
                       ὕβρις γὰρ ἐξανθοῦσ᾽ ἐκάρπωσε στάχυν
                       ἄτης, ὅθεν πάγκλαυτον ἐξαμᾷ θέρος.
                       τοιαῦθ᾽ ὁρῶντες τῶνδε τἀπιτίμια
                       μέμνησθ᾽ Ἀθηνῶν Ἑλλάδος τε,
                         μηδέ τις

ὑπερφρονήσας τὸν παρόντα δαίμονα 825
ἄλλων ἐρασθεὶς ὄλβον ἐκχέῃ μέγαν.
Ζεύς τοι κολαστὴς τῶν ὑπερκόμπων ἄγαν
φρονημάτων ἔπεστιν, εὔθυνος βαρύς.

36. *Persians*   ΧΟ. νῦν δ᾽οὐκ ἀμφιλόγως Θεότρεπτα τάδ᾽ αὖ
905–906   φέρομεν πολέμοισι,
                  δμαθέντες μεγάλως πλαγαῖσι ποντίαισιν.

37. *Persians*   ΧΟ. . . . ἀνδρῶν, 920
920–930   οὓς νῦν δαίμων ἐπέκειρεν.
                  γᾶ δ᾽ αἰάζει τὰν ἐγγαίαν
                  ἥβαν Ξέρξᾳ κταμέναν, Ἄιδου
                  σάκτορι Περσᾶν· †ἀγδαβάται† γὰρ
                  πολλοὶ φῶτες, χώρας ἄνθος, 925
                  τοξοδάμαντες, πάνυ ταρφύς τις
                  μυριὰς ἀνδρῶν, ἐξέφθινται.
                  αἰαῖ ⟨αἰαῖ⟩ κεδνᾶς ἀλκᾶς·
                  Ἀσία δὲ χθών, βασιλεῦ γαίας,
                  αἰνῶς αἰνῶς ἐπὶ γόνυ κέκλιται. 930

38. *Persians*   ΞΕ. Ἰάων ναύφαρκτος Ἄρης ἑτεραλκὴς
951–952   νυχίαν πλάκα κερσάμενος δυσδαίμονά
                     τ᾽ ἀκτάν.

39. *Persians*   ΞΕ. Τυρίας ἐκ ναὸς ἔρροντας ἐπ᾽ ἀκταῖς
964–965   Σαλαμινιάσι, στυφελοῦ θείνοντας ἐπ᾽
                     ἀκτᾶς.

40. *Persians*   ΞΕ. στυγνὰς Ἀθάνας πάντες ἐνὶ πιτύλῳ,
976–977   ἐῆ ἐῆ, τλάμονες ἀσπαίρουσι χέρσῳ.

41. *Persians*   ΧΟ. ἰὼ ἰώ, δαίμονες 1005
1005–1007   ἔθεντ᾽ ἀέλπτον κακὸν
                  διαπρέπον, οἷον δέδορκεν Ἄτα.

42. *Persians*   ΧΟ. τί δ᾽ οὐκ ὄλωλεν, μεγάλατε Περσᾶν;
1016

43. *Persians*   ΧΟ. φίλων ἄταισι ποντίαισιν.
1037

44. *Persians*   ΞΕ. βόα νυν ἀντίδουπά μοι.   1040
    1040–1042 ΧΟ. δόσιν κακὰν κακῶν κακοῖς.
                ΞΕ. ἴυζε μέλος ὁμοῦ τιθείς.

45. *Persians*   ΧΟ. κακόμαντις ἄγαν ὀρσολοπεῖται   10
    10–11   θυμὸς ἔσωθεν

46. *Persians*   ΧΟ. τάδε μὲν Περσῶν τῶν οἰχομένων
    1

47. Phrynichus fr. 5   τάδ' ἐστὶ Περσῶν τῶν πάλαι βεβηκότων.
The Phoenician Women

48. *Persians*   ΧΟ. πᾶσα γὰρ ἰσχὺς Ἀσιατογενὴς
    12–13   ᾤχωκεν,

49. *Persians*   ΧΟ. τοιόνδ' ἄνθος Περσίδος αἴας
    59–60   οἴχεται ἀνδρῶν,   60

50. *Persians*   ΒΑ. [παῖς ἐμὸς] Ἰαόνων γῆν οἴχεται πέρσαι
    178   θέλων,

51. *Persians*   ΑΓΓ. ὄλβος, τὸ Περσῶν δ' ἄνθος οἴχεται πεσόν.
    252

52. *Persians*   ΞΕ. εἴθ' ὄφελε, Ζεῦ, κἀμὲ μετ' ἀνδρῶν   915
    915–916   τῶν οἰχομένων

53. *Persians*   ΞΕ. βεβᾶσι γὰρ τοίπερ ἀγρέται   [στρ. δ
    1002–1003   στρατοῦ.
              ΧΟ. βεβᾶσιν οἳ νώνυμοι.

Glossary of Japanese Terms

ageuta: A high-pitched song in a regular prosodic rhythm that follows the beat and often functions as the musical conclusion to a *dan*.

ai-kyōgen: The interlude scene in nō during which the *kyōgen* tells the background of the main character's story.

chūnori: A rhythm in which there are two syllables to each musical beat in a six- to eight-syllable line.

dan: Divisions of nō comparable to episodes and attendant odes in Greek tragedy.

dengaku: Originally field and harvest dances and songs.

engo: A rhetorical device in which an author uses the relationship between words associated in meaning to enhance the tone or significance of a passage.

enken: A stylistic device whereby an author creates a geographical perspective.

ha: Literally meaning "break open," the middle and developmental section of part of a nō, a nō play as a whole, or a nō program.

hashigakari: A bridge by which actors enter the nō stage.

Heike monogatari: (Abbreviated as *Heike*.) *The Tale of the Heike*, an epic account of the wars between the Heike and the Genji that was recited by bards in narrative prose to the accompaniment of the biwa lute and written down by Zeami's day.

hiranori: Regular musical rhythm in which a twelve-syllable line of a song is divided into eight beats as in the following example. The beats are numbered:

$$\begin{array}{cccccccc} \text{hi/-/to/na/to/-/ga/me/so/-/ka/ri/so/me/ni/-.} \\ 1 \quad 2 \quad 3 \quad 4 \quad 5 \quad 6 \quad 7 \quad 8 \end{array}$$

issei: A short, melodious, but dignified song that does not follow the regular prosodic rhythm.

jo: The quiet opening section of part of a nō, a nō play, or a nō program.

305

jo-ha-kyū: An aesthetic principle and the basis for the arrangement of parts in nō.

joshi or *jo*: An introductory phrase, often a formal poetic phrase, that prepares for the words that follow it.

kakaru: A melodic section in nō, in the style of a *sashi*, which occurs when there is a change from speech to song.

kakeai: An exchange in which there is some alternation between spoken and sung lines, as in an epirrhematic exchange.

kakekotoba: Pivot on a word or syllable by which an author takes advantage of its two or more meanings simultaneously.

kanjin nō: Subscription nō, that is, performances of nō staged to raise money.

katari: A long epic-like narrative speech.

kotoba: A spoken section in nō.

kuri: A high-pitched and melodious short song in a free prosodic rhythm that does not follow the beat.

kuse: An especially important *shōdan* of musical, rhythmic, thematic, and often kinetic interest that tends to deviate from the formal prosodic rhythm of Japanese verse. It is sung by the chorus, and begins on a low pitch and rises to a high pitch. Usually in the middle of a *kuse* the main actor (the *shite*, sometimes the *tsure* or child actor) sings a line or two. The *kuse* sometimes involves a dance by the *shite*, in which case it is called a *kusemai*. Zeami uses the term *kusemai* also to mean a sequence of six *shōdan* that includes a *kuri*, *sashi*, and *kuse*, in that order. The playwright of nō includes some of the most important thematic material in the *kuse*, which is either near or a part of the climax of a play.

kusemai: See *kuse*.

kyōgen: An actor who often, but not always, plays the role of an ordinary and nameless inhabitant of the place in which the nō is set. The word *kyōgen* is also used for the comic-relief plays found on a program of nō, in which all the actors are *kyōgen*.

kyū: The final and climactic, quickened section of part of a nō, a nō play, or a nō program.

machiutai: A type of *ageuta* sung by the *waki* and *wakizure* as they wait for the arrival of the *shite* in the *nochiba*.

maeba: The first half of a nō.

maejite: *Shite* of the *maeba*.

makurakotoba: A conventional epithet or attributive of a word that raises the tone of the word or line that follows; "pillow" word.

michiyuki: Literally, a "travel" song, a type of *ageuta*.

mondō: A question-and-answer dialogue, especially between the *shite* and the *waki* when they first meet in the *maeba* and the *nochiba*.

nanori: A "naming speech," delivered in informal prose near the beginning of a nō.

nochiba: The second half of a nō.

nochijite: *Shite* of the *nochiba*.

odori nembutsu: Special religious services of the Ji sect of Amidism, which
 include music, song, and dance.

Okina: The religious piece in song and dance with which programs of nō may
 begin.

ōnori: A rhythm in which there is one musical beat to each syllable of a six- to
 eight-syllable line.

rongi: A sung exchange between the chorus and an actor, or between two actors, in a melody that follows the beat, like an *ageuta*.

sageuta: A low-pitched song.

saku: The word that Zeami uses to refer to the construction of a nō; structure.

sanbanmemono: "The third-category nō," highly lyrical nō in which a woman
 is featured as the main character. It is so called because it is placed third
 on the standard program of five nō.

sarugaku: One meaning is "monkey songs and dances," an early name for nō.

sashi: A song that does not follow a beat or the regular prosodic rhythm and
 is delivered in a smooth recitative style.

shidai: Short introductory song following the formal prosodic rhythm and
 found most often at the beginning of nō.

shite: The main actor.

sho: The term used by Zeami to refer to the writing of the words in the composition of nō.

shōdan: A unit of a nō; a part of a *dan*.

shu: The term used by Zeami to refer to the choice of subject in the composition of nō.

shūgen nō: A congratulatory nō play.

shura nō: A nō about warriors, especially those suffering the agonies of *shura*
 "hell," and thus called warrior nō. These are often found in the second
 position on a program of nō plays.

taiko: A large drum.

tsukizerifu: An arrival speech, which usually follows a *michiyuki*.

tsure: Actor or actors "attendant" upon the *shite* or the *waki*. They are called
 simply *tsure* when they attend the *shite*; *wakizure* when they attend the
 waki.

waka: A Japanese poem consisting of a five-syllable, a seven-syllable, a five-
 syllable, and two seven-syllable lines.

waki: The second actor.

waki nō: Literally meaning "adjacent nō," the congratulatory and auspicious
 nō usually found after *Okina* at the beginning of a program of nō. It is
 often called a "god play."

wakizure: See *tsure*.

yūgen: An aesthetic ideal of half-revealed or suggested grace, tinged with wistful sadness.

Glossary of Greek Terms

anagnōrisis: According to Aristotle, an important component of complex plots. A dramatic character's recognition of the identity of some person or of the truth of a given situation previously unknown.

anaklēsis: An incantation to evoke a ghost; a "calling-up" hymn.

anapaest: Metrical foot consisting of two short syllables followed by one long. In anapaestic dimeters (four anapaestic feet) and in anapaestic recitatives, spondees and other appropriate metrical substitutions occur. This meter is used in the *parodos* by the chorus as it marches into the *orkhēstra* and in transitional passages of tragedy.

antistrophe: See *stasimon*.

choriamb: A metrical pattern that consists of two long syllables on either side of two short syllables or an appropriate variation of the same scheme.

dactyl: A metrical foot consisting of one long syllable followed by two short syllables.

desis: Aristotle's word for the "tying up" of a plot.

dianoia: "Thought." One of Aristotle's six elements of tragedy.

dochmiac: A metrical scheme especially suited to the expression of despair in Greek tragedy. One form the dochmiac takes is a short syllable followed by two long, one short and another long syllable. However, there are many variations on this scheme.

epirrhēma: An exchange in which one party, an actor or the chorus, speaks and the other party, another actor or the chorus, sings.

ēthos: "Character." One of Aristotle's six elements of tragedy.

exodos: A name given to the section with which a tragedy ends.

hypokritēs: An actor.

iambic trimeter: A metrical line composed of six iambs (a foot consisting of a short and a long syllable). A spondaic substitution (two long syllables) or a metrical resolution is allowed in some feet. This meter sounds the most like prose speech in ancient Greek.

308

ionic: A metrical foot consisting of two short followed by two long syllables or an appropriate variation of this scheme.

kommos: A sung exchange between the chorus and one or more actors, often a lament.

lexis: "Diction." One of Aristotle's six elements of tragedy.

lusis: Aristotle's word for the "untying" of a plot.

melopoiia: "Composition of music." One of Aristotle's six elements of tragedy.

muthos: "Plot." One of Aristotle's six elements of tragedy.

opsis: "Visual effects." One of Aristotle's six elements of tragedy.

orkhēstra: A name given to the circular (or rectangular) area in front of the *skēnē* around which the audience is seated and in which the chorus and often the actors perform in the Greek theater.

parodos: Both the passageway leading from "backstage" into the *orkhēstra* of the Greek theater and the song sung by the chorus as it enters the *orkhēstra* at or near the beginning of a tragic performance. The lyric *parodos* is the choral song that immediately follows the *parodos*.

pathos: A destructive or painful act; a tragic event.

peripeteia: An unexpected reversal in the action during the development of the plot of a Greek tragedy.

proskēnion: The stage or front part of the *skēnē*.

rhēsis: A speech given by an actor.

skēnē: A term used for the stage building in the Greek theater.

spondee: A metrical foot consisting of two long syllables.

stasimon: A choral song consisting of stanzas called strophes and antistrophes. An antistrophe is the stanza that repeats the meter of a strophe, with different words. The first choral song immediately following the *parodos*, although it can be a strophic ode, is called a lyric *parodos*.

stichomythy: A spoken dialogue between two actors or an actor and the chorus in which the speeches of each tend to be only one or two lines in length.

strophe: See *stasimon*.

thrēnos: A lament.

trochee: A metrical foot, consisting of one long syllable and one short, found in lyric and recited sections of tragedy. The trochaic tetrameter, consisting of eight trochees or the appropriate metrical substitutions, is the common form of the latter. This meter is faster moving and more excited than the iambic trimeter. It may have been accompanied by music. The *lekythion*, a trochaic dimeter catalectic (often difficult to distinguish from an iambic line), is found in lyric passages.

Works Cited

WORKS ON GREEK TRAGEDY AND RELATED SUBJECTS

Aichele, Klaus. "Das Epeisodion." In *Die Bauformen der griechischen Tragö-die*, ed. Walter Jens, 47–83. Munich: 1971.

Alexiou, M. *The Ritual Lament in Greek Tradition*. Cambridge: 1974.

Allen, Thomas W., ed. *Homeri opera* (Odyssey). Oxford: 1917.

Anderson, Michael. "The Imagery of *The Persians*." *Greece and Rome* 19 (1972): 166–174.

Arnott, Peter. *Greek Scenic Conventions in the Fifth Century B.C.* Oxford: 1962.

Avery, Harry C. "Dramatic Devices in Aeschylus' *Persians*." *American Journal of Philology* 85, no. 2 (April 1964): 173–184.

Barner, Wilfried. "Die Monodie." In *Die Bauformen der griechischen Tragö-die*, ed. Walter Jens, 277–320. Munich: 1971.

Becker, Heinrich Theodor. *Aischylos in der griechischen Komödie*. Darmstadt: 1915.

Becker, Ottfried. *Das Bild des Weges und verwandte Vorstellungen im frühgriechischen Denken. Hermes*, Einzelschriften 4. Berlin: 1937.

Bergk, T. *Griechische Literaturgeschichte*. 3 vols. Berlin: 1884.

Broadhead, H. D. *The Persae of Aeschylus*. Cambridge: 1960.

Bury, J. B. "Two Literary Compliments." *Classical Review* 19 (1905): 10–11.

Cameron, H. D. "Word Power in 'Seven Against Thebes.'" *Transactions and Proceedings of the American Philological Association* 101 (1970): 95–118.

Citti, Vittorio. *Il linguaggio religioso e liturgico nelle tragedie di Eschilo*. Bologna: 1962.

Conacher, D. J. "Aeschylus' *Persae*: A Literary Commentary." *Serta Turyniana, Studies in Greek Literature and Palaeography in honor of Alexander Turyn*, ed. John L. Heller, 143–168. Urbana, Ill.: 1974.

Couch, H. N. "Three Puns on the Root of *perthō* in the Persae of Aeschylus." *American Journal of Philology* 52 (1931): 270–273.

311

Croiset, Maurice. *Eschyle: Études sur l'invention dramatique dans son théâtre.* Paris: 1928.

Dale, A. M. "Seen and Unseen on the Greek Stage: A Study in Scenic Conventions." In *Collected Papers*, 119–129. Cambridge: 1969.

Dawe, R. D. "Inconsistency of Plot and Character in Aeschylus." *Proceedings of the Cambridge Philological Society* 189, n.s. 9 (1963): 21–62.

Deichgräber, K. "Die Perser des Aischylos." *Nachrichten der Akademie der Wissenschaften in Göttingen* (1941): 155–202.

Denniston, J. D. *The Greek Particles.* Oxford: 1954.

Denniston, J. D., and D. Page. *Aeschylus Agamemnon.* Oxford: 1957.

De Propris, Americo. *Eschilo nella critica dei Greci. Studio filologico ed estetico.* Turin: 1941.

Detscheff, Demetrius. *De tragoediarum Graecarum conformatione scaenica ac dramatica.* Diss., Göttingen: 1904.

Di Gregorio, Lamberto. *Le scene d'annuncio nella tragedia greca.* Milan: 1967.

Di Virgilio, Raffaele. *Il vero volto dei Persiani di Eschilo.* Bibliotheca Athena 13. Rome: 1973.

Dobson, Marcia Dunbar-Soule. "Oracular Language: Its Style and Intent in the Delphic Oracles and in Aeschylus' *Oresteia.*" Diss., Harvard University: 1976.

Dörrie, H. "Leid und Erfahrung, die Wort-und Sinn-Verbindung *patheinmathein* im griechischen Denken." *Akad. der Wiss. und der Lit. in Mainz, geist.- und soz.-wiss. Klasse* nr. 5 (1956).

Doyle, Richard E., S.J. "The Objective Concept of ATĒ in Aeschylean Tragedy." *Traditio* 28 (1972): 1–28.

Duchemin, Jacqueline. "Du lyrisme à la tragédie: Réflexions sur l'Agamemnon et les Perses d'Eschyle." In *Serta Turyniana*, ed. John L. Heller, 122–142. Urbana, Ill.: 1974.

Dworacki, Sylwester. "Atossa's Absence in the Final Scene of the Persae of Aeschylus." In *Arktouros: Hellenic Studies Presented to Bernard M. W. Knox on the Occasion of His Sixty-fifth Birthday*, ed. G. W. Bowersock, W. Burkert, and M.C.J. Putnam, 101–108. Berlin and New York: 1979.

Earp, F. R. *The Style of Aeschylus.* Cambridge: 1948.

Easterling, P. E. "Notes on Tragedy and Epic." *Papers Given at a Colloquium on Greek Drama in Honour of R. P. Winnington-Ingram.* The Society for the Promotion of Hellenic Studies. Suppl. Paper 15. (1987): 52–62.

———. "Presentation of Character in Aeschylus." *Greece and Rome* 20 (1973): 3–19.

Edinger, H. G. "Vocabulary and Imagery in Aeschylus' 'Persians.' " Diss., Princeton University: 1961.

Edwards, Mark W. "Agamemnon's Decision: Freedom and Folly in Aeschylus." *California Studies in Classical Antiquity* 10 (1977): 17–38.

Egan, Rory B. "The Calchas Quotation and the Hymn to Zeus." *Eranos* 77 (1979): 1–9.

Eitrem, S. "The Necromancy in the Persai of Aeschylus." *Symbolae Osloenses* 6 (1928): 1–16.

Else, Gerald F. *Aristotle's Poetics: The Argument*. Cambridge, Mass.: 1963.

———. "The Case of the Third Actor." *Transactions and Proceedings of the American Philological Association* 76 (1945): 1–10.

———. *The Origin and Early Form of Greek Tragedy*. Cambridge, Mass.: 1965.

———. "HYPOKRITĒS." *Wiener Studien* 72 (1959): 75–107.

Fontenrose, J. *The Delphic Oracle*. Berkeley, Los Angeles, and London: 1978.

Fowler, B. Hughes. "Aeschylus' Imagery." *Classica et Mediaevalia* 28 (1967): 1–74.

Fraenkel, E. *Aeschylus Agamemnon*. 3 vols. Oxford: 1962.

———. "Zum Schluss der 'Sieben gegen Theben.' " *Museum Helveticum* 21 (1964): 58–64.

Franklin, Susan B. "Traces of Epic Influence in the Tragedies of Aeschylus." Diss., Bryn Mawr College: 1895.

Furley, William D. "Motivation in the Parodos of Aeschylus' *Agamemnon*." *Classical Philology* 81, no. 2 (April 1986): 109–121.

Gagarin, Michael. *Aeschylean Drama*. Berkeley: 1976.

Garvie, A. F. "Aeschylus' Simple Plots." *Dionysiaca: Nine Studies in Greek Poetry by Former Pupils, Presented to Sir Denys Page on his Seventieth Birthday*, ed. R. D. Dawe, H. Diggle, and P. E. Easterling, 63–86. Cambridge: 1978.

———. *Aeschylus' Supplices: Play and Trilogy*. Cambridge: 1969.

Gigli, Matelda. "Dell'imitazione omerica di Eschilo." *Rivista Indo-Greco-Italica* 12 (1928): 43–59.

Goodell, Thomas D. "Structural Variety in Attic Tragedy." *Transactions and Proceedings of the American Philological Association* 41 (1910): 75–76.

Gould, John. "Dramatic Character and 'Human Intelligibility' in Greek Tragedy." *Proceedings of the Cambridge Philological Society*, n.s. 24, no. 204 (1978): 43–67.

Gow, A.S.F. "Notes on the *Persae* of Aeschylus." *Journal of Hellenic Studies* 48 (1928): 133–159.

Griffith, Mark. *The Authenticity of "Prometheus Bound."* Cambridge: 1970.

Groeneboom, P. *Aeschylus' Persae*. Amsterdam: 1966.

Hamilton, Richard. "Announced Entrances in Greek Tragedy." *Harvard Studies in Classical Philology* 82 (1978): 63–82.

Hammond, N.G.L. "The Conditions of Dramatic Production to the Death of Aeschylus." *Greek, Roman and Byzantine Studies* 13 (1972): 387–450.

———. "The Battle of Salamis." *Journal of Hellenic Studies* 76 (1956): 32–54.

Hansen, Jens. *Bildhafte Sprache des Aischylos: See und Schiffahrt in metaphorischer Verwendung*. Kiel: 1955.

Headlam, Walter G. *On Editing Aeschylus: A Criticism*. London: 1891.

Herington, John. *Aeschylus*. New Haven and London: 1986.

Herington, John. *Poetry into Drama: Early Tragedy and the Greek Poetic Tradition.* Berkeley: 1985.

Hermann, Gottfried. *De Aeschyli Persis dissertatio, Opuscula* 2. Leipzig: 1827–1877; reprinted, New York and Hildesheim: 1970.

Hiltbrunner, O. *Wiederholungs- und Motivtechnik bei Aischylos.* Bern: 1950.

Hölzle, R. "Zum Aufbau der lyrischen Partien des Aischylos." Diss., Freiburg: 1934.

Holtsmark, Erling B. "Ring Composition and the *Persae* of Aeschylus." *Symbolae Osloenses* 45 (1970): 5–23.

Janko, Richard. "Aeschylus' *Oresteia* and Archilochus." *Classical Quarterly* 30, no. 2 (1980): 291–293.

———. *Aristotle on Comedy: Towards a Reconstruction of Poetics II.* Berkeley: 1984.

Johansen, Holger Friis. "Some Features of Sentence-Structure in Aeschylus' Suppliants." *Classica et Mediaevalia* 15 (1954): 1–59.

Kaimio, Maarit. "The Chorus of Greek Drama within the Light of the Person and Number Used." *Commentiones Humanarum Litterarum* 46. Helsinki: 1970.

Kahlenberg, Guilelmus. "De paraphrasis Homericae apud tragicos poetas Graecos vestigiis quaestiones selectae." Diss., Strasburg: 1903.

Kassell, Rudolf, ed. *Aristotelis de arte poetica liber.* Oxford: 1965.

Keller, Joachim. *Struktur und dramatische Funktion des Botenberichtes bei Aischylos und Sophokles.* Tübingen: 1959.

Kierdorf, Wilhelm. "Erlebnis und Darstellung der Perserkriege." *Hypomnemata* 16. Göttingen: 1966.

Kitto, H.D.F. *Greek Tragedy.* London: 1950.

———. *Poiesis: Structure and Thought.* Berkeley: 1966.

Knox, Bernard M. W. "The Lion in the House." *Classical Philology* 47 (January 1952): 17–25.

———. "Traditional Structure and Formula in the Tragic Narrative Speech." Diss., Yale University: 1948.

Korzeniewski, Dietmar. "Studien zu den Persern des Aischylos." *Helikon* 6 (1966): 548–596 and 7 (1967): 29–62.

Kranz, Walther. *Stasimon: Untersuchungen zu Form und Gehalt der griechischen Tragödie.* Berlin: 1933.

Kubo Masaaki. "Perushanohitobito" (The Persians). In *Girishahigeki zenshū* (The Complete Greek Tragedies), ed. Kure Shigeichi, vol. 1. Tokyo: 1979.

Kumaniecki, Casmirus Felix. *De elocutionis Aeschyleae natura.* Cracow: 1935.

Lattimore, Richmond. "Aeschylus on the Defeat of Xerxes." In *Classical Studies in Honor of Wm. Abbott Oldfather*, 82–93. Urbana, Ill.: 1943.

Lawler, Lillian B. *The Dance of the Ancient Greek Theatre.* Iowa City: 1964.

———. "The Dance of the Ancient Mariners." *Transactions and Proceedings of the American Philological Association* 75 (1944): 20–33.

Lebeck, A. *The Oresteia: A Study in Language and Structure.* Washington, D.C.: 1971.

Lechner, Max. "De Aeschyli studio Homerico." *Jahresbericht von der königlichen Studienanstalt zu Erlangen in Mittelfranken* (1862): 3–28.

Lefkowitz, Mary R. *The Lives of the Greek Poets.* Baltimore: 1981.

Lembke, Janet, and C. J. Herington, trans. *Aeschylus: Persians.* New York and London: 1981.

Lesky, Albin. "Decision and Responsibility in the Tragedy of Aeschylus." *Journal of Hellenic Studies* 86 (1966): 78–85.

———. *Die griechische Tragödie.* Stuttgart and Leipzig: 1938. *Greek Tragedy,* trans. H. A. Frankfort. London: 1967.

Lloyd-Jones, Hugh. "The End of the *Seven against Thebes.*" *Classical Quarterly,* n.s. 9 (1959): 80–115.

———. *The Justice of Zeus.* Berkeley: 1971.

———, trans. and comm. *Aeschylus: Agamemnon, Aeschylus: The Libation Bearers,* and *Aeschylus: The Eumenides.* Englewood Cliffs: 1970.

Macleod, C. W. "Clothing in the Oresteia." *Maia,* n.s. 3, no. 27 (1975): 201–203.

Marx, F. "Der tragiker Phrynichus." *Rheinische Museum für Philologie* 77 (1928): 337–360.

Meyer, Jørgen. "Recognizing What When and Why? The Recognition Scene in Aeschylus' Choephori." In *Arktouros: Hellenic Studies Presented to Bernard M.W. Knox,* 115–121. Berlin: 1979.

Michelini, Ann N. *Tradition and Dramatic Form in the Persians of Aeschylus.* Cincinnati Classical Studies, n.s., vol. 4. Leiden: 1982.

Monro, David B., and Thomas W. Allen, ed. *Homeri opera* (Iliad). Oxford: 1920.

Moreau, Alain. "L'attelage et le navire: la rencontre de deux thèmes dans l'œuvre d'Eschyle." *Revue de philologie de littérature et d'histoire anciennes* 53, fasc. 1 (1979): 98–115.

Moritz, Helen. "Refrain in Aeschylus: Literary Adaptation of Traditional Form." *Classical Philology* 74, no. 3 (July 1979): 187–213.

Nes, D. van. *Die maritime Bildersprache des Aischylos.* Groningen: 1963.

Nestle, W. *Die Struktur des Eingangs in der attischen Tragödie.* Stuttgart: 1930.

Otterlo, W.A.A. van. *Beschouwingen over het archaïsche Element in den Stijl van Aeschylus.* Utrecht: 1937.

Paduano, Guido. *Sui Persiani di Eschilo problemi di focalizzazione drammatica.* Filologia e Critica 27. Rome: 1978.

Page, Denys. *Aeschyli septem quae supersunt tragoediae.* Oxford: 1972.

Paley, F. A. *The Tragedies of Aeschylus.* 2nd ed. London: 1855.

Pearson, A. C. *The Fragments of Sophocles,* vol. 1. Amsterdam: 1963.

Péron, Jacques. "Réalité et au-delà dans les Perses d'Eschyle." *Bulletin de l'Association Guillaume Budé* 1 (1982): 3–40.

Petrounias, Evangelos. *Funktion und Thematik der Bilder bei Aischylos. Hypomnemata* 48. Göttingen: 1976.

Pfeufer, Hedwig. "Die Gnomik in der Tragödie des Aischylos." Diss., Munich: 1940.

Pickard-Cambridge, A. *The Theatre of Dionysus at Athens.* Oxford: 1946.

——. *The Dramatic Festivals of Athens.* 2nd ed., rev. John Gould and D. M. Lewis. Oxford: 1968.

Podlecki, A. J. *Aeschylus: The Persians.* Englewood Cliffs: 1970.

——. *The Political Background of Aeschylean Tragedy.* Ann Arbor: 1966.

——. "Three Passages in Persae." *Antichthon* 9 (1975): 1–3.

Pöhlmann, E. "Die Proedrie des Dionysostheaters im 5. Jahrhundert und das Bühnenspiel der Klassik." *Museum Helveticum* 38, fasc. 3 (1981): 129–146.

Popp, Hansjürgen. "Das Amoibaion." In *Die Bauformen der griechischen Tragödie*, ed. Walter Jens, 221–276. Munich: 1971.

Quincey, J. H. "The Beacon-Sites in the *Agamemnon.*" *Journal of Hellenic Studies* 83 (1963): 118–132.

Richardson, L.J.D. "The Inner Conflict in the *Persae*: Athenian Dramatist and Persian Characters." In *Studies in Honor of Gilbert Norwood*, ed. Mary E. White, 55–67. *The Phoenix*, suppl. vol. 1. Toronto: 1952.

Rode, Jürgen. *Untersuchungen zur Form des aischyleischen Chorliedes.* Diss., Tübingen: 1965.

Rose, H. J. *A Commentary on the Surviving Plays of Aeschylus.* Verhandelingen der Koninklijke Nederlandse Akademie van Wetenschappen, afd. Letterkunde, n.s. 64, no. 2. Amsterdam: 1958.

——. "Ghost Ritual in Aeschylus." *Harvard Theological Review* 43 (1950): 257–280.

Rosenmeyer, Thomas G. *The Art of Aeschylus.* Berkeley: 1982.

Scott, William C. "The Mesode at *Persae* 93–100." *Greek, Roman and Byzantine Studies* 9, no. 3 (1968): 259–266.

——. *Musical Design in Aeschylean Theater.* Hanover, N.H. and London: 1984.

——. "Wind Imagery in the *Oresteia.*" *Transactions and Proceedings of the American Philological Association* 97 (1966): 459–471.

Schuursma, J. A. *De poetica vocabulorum abusione apud Aeschylum.* Paris: 1932.

Seeck, G. A. *Dramatische Strukturen der griechischen Tragödie: Untersuchungen zu Aischylos. Zetemata* 8. Munich: 1984.

Seewald, Johannes. *Untersuchungen zu Stil und Komposition der aischyleischen Tragödie.* Greifswald: 1936.

Segal, Charles. *Interpreting Greek Tragedy: Myth, Poetry, Text.* Ithaca, N.Y. and London: 1986.

——. "Visual Symbolism and Visual Effects in Sophocles." *Classical World* 74, no. 2 (1980/81): 125–142.

Seidensticker, Bernd. "Die Stichomythie." In *Die Bauformen der griechischen Tragödie*, ed. Walter Jens, 183–220. Munich: 1971.

Shisler, Famee Lorene. "The Technique of the Portrayal of Joy in Greek Trag-edy." *Transactions and Proceedings of the American Philological Associa-tion* 73 (1942): 277–292.

Sideras, Alexander. *Aeschylus Homericus: Untersuchungen zu den Homeris-men der aischyleischen Sprache. Hypomnemata* 31. Göttingen: 1971.

Silk, M. S. *Interaction in Poetic Imagery with Special Reference to Early Greek Poetry.* Cambridge: 1974.

Smith, Ole. "Some Observations on the Structure of Imagery in Aeschylus." *Classica et Mediaevalia* 26 (1965): 10–72.

Smith, Peter M. *On the Hymn to Zeus in Aeschylus' Agamemnon.* American Classical Studies 5. Ann Arbor: 1980.

Smyth, H. W. *Aeschylus.* Cambridge, Mass.: 1963.

———, trans. and ed. *Aeschylus.* 2 vols. 2nd ed., ed. Hugh Lloyd-Jones. Cam-bridge, Mass.: 1963.

Solmsen, Friedrich. *Hesiod and Aeschylus.* Ithaca, N.Y.: 1949.

Srebrny, S. *Critica et exegetica in Aeschylum.* Turin: 1950.

Stanford, William Bedell. *Aeschylus in His Style.* Dublin: 1942.

———. *Greek Metaphor: Studies in Theory and Practice.* New York and Lon-don: 1936.

Stössl, Franz. "Die Phoenissen des Phrynichos und die Perser des Aischylos." *Museum Helveticum* 2 (1945): 148–165.

Talcott, Lucy. "Kourimos Parthenos." *Hesperia* 8 (1939): 267–273.

Taplin, Oliver. *Greek Tragedy in Action.* Berkeley and Los Angeles: 1978.

———. *The Stagecraft of Aeschylus.* Oxford: 1977.

Thalmann, W. G. "Xerxes' Rags: Some Problems in Aeschylus' *Persians*." *American Journal of Philology* 101 (1980): 260–282.

Thomson, George. *The Oresteia of Aeschylus.* 2 vols. Amsterdam: 1966.

Trendall, A. D., and T.B.L. Webster. *Illustrations of Greek Drama.* London: 1971.

Tucker, T. G. *The "Supplices" of Aeschylus.* London: 1889.

Vellacott, Philip. *Aeschylus: Prometheus Bound and Other Plays.* Harmonds-worth: 1961.

Verrall, A. W. *The "Agamemnon" of Aeschylus.* London and New York: 1889.

———. "The Part of Phrynichus in the *Persae* of Aeschylus." *Proceedings of the Cambridge Philological Society* 79 (1908): 13–15.

Webster, T.B.L. *An Introduction to Sophocles.* Oxford: 1936.

———. *Greek Theatre Production.* 2nd ed. London: 1970.

———. *The Tragedies of Euripides.* London: 1967.

West, M. L. "The Parodos of the *Agamemnon*." *Classical Quarterly* 29, no. 1 (1979): 1–6.

Wilamowitz-Möllendorff, U. v. *Aeschyli tragoediae.* Berlin: 1958.

———. *Aischylos Interpretationen.* Dublin and Zürich: 1966.

———. "Die Perser des Aischylos." *Hermes* 32 (1897): 382–398.

Winnington-Ingram, R. P. "A Word in the Persae." *Bulletin of the Institute of Classical Studies* 20 (1973): 38.

———. "Zeus in the Persae." *Journal of Hellenic Studies* 93 (1973): 210–219. Reprinted in *Studies in Aeschylus*. Cambridge: 1983.

WORKS ON NŌ AND RELATED SUBJECTS

Arnott, Peter. *The Theatres of Japan*. London: 1969.

Bethe, Monica, and Karen Brazell. *Dance in the Nō Theatre*. Cornell University East Asia Papers, no. 29. Ithaca, N.Y.: 1982.

———. *Nō as Performance: An Analysis of the Kuse Scene of "Yamamba."* Cornell University East Asia Papers, no. 16. Ithaca, N.Y.: 1978.

Brower, Robert H., and Earl Miner. *Japanese Court Poetry*. London: 1962.

Butler, Kenneth D. "The Textual Evolution of the 'Heike Monogatari.' " *Harvard Journal of Asiatic Studies* 26 (1966): 5–51.

Chamberlain, H. B. *Things Japanese*. 5th ed. London and Yokohama: 1905.

Ernst, Earle. *The Kabuki Theatre*. New York: 1956.

Hare, Thomas B. *Zeami's Style: The Noh Plays of Zeami Motokiyo*. Stanford: 1986.

Hoff, Frank. "Zeami on Jo-Ha-Kyū Theory." *Proceedings of the Fourth ISCRCP* (1981): 217–228.

Hoff, Frank, and Willi Flindt. "The Life Structure of Noh." *Concerned Theatre Japan* 2, nos. 3 and 4 (1973): 210–256.

Hoff, Frank, and Jean Hoff. "Staging Epic: Theory and Practice, A Study of *Sanemori*." Unpublished article: 1976.

Itō Masayoshi. *Yōkyokushū*. 2 vols. In *Shinchō Nihon koten shūsei*. Tokyo: 1986.

Kanai Kiyomitsu. "Zeami to shuramono." *Kokugo to kokubungaku* 31, no. 9 (September 1954): 27–36.

Katayama Kuroemon, ed. *Kanzeke denrai nōmenshū*. Tokyo: 1954.

Keene, Donald. *Nō: The Classical Theatre of Japan*. 1st paperback ed. Palo Alto: 1973.

———. *20 Plays of the Nō Theatre*. New York and London: 1970.

Kitagawa Hiroshi, and Bruce T. Tsuchida, trans. *The Tale of the Heike*. 2 vols. Tokyo: 1977.

Kobayashi Yasuji. "Heike monogatari to shura nō: Yōkyoku Tadanori, Sanemori o chūshin ni." In *Gunkimono to sono shūhen*. Tokyo: 1969.

Komparu, Kunio. *The Noh Theater: Principles and Perspectives*. Trans. Jane Corddry and Stephen Comee. Tokyo and New York: 1983.

Kōsai Tsutomu. "Sakuhin kenkyū: Sanemori." *Kanze* (January 1970): 3–9. Also in *Nōyōshinkō: Zeami ni terasu*, 274–282. Tokyo: 1972; reprinted 1980.

Koyama Hiroshi, Satō Kikuo, and Satō Ken'ichirō, ed. *Yōkyokushū*, vol. 1. *Nihon koten bungaku zenshū*, vol. 33. Tokyo: Shōgakkan, 1973.

LaFleur, William R. *The Karma of Words: Buddhism and the Literary Arts in Medieval Japan.* Berkeley and Los Angeles: 1983.

Levy, Ian Hideo. *Hitomaro and the Birth of Japanese Lyricism.* Princeton: 1984.

McKinnon, Richard N. "Zeami on the Nō: A Study of Fifteenth-Century Japanese Dramatic Criticism." Diss., Harvard University: 1951.

———. "The Nō and Zeami." *Far Eastern Quarterly* 11, no. 3 (May 1952): 355–361.

Malm, William P. *Six Hidden Views of Japanese Music.* Berkeley: 1986.

Miner, E., H. Odagiri, and R. E. Morrell. *The Princeton Companion to Classical Japanese Literature.* Princeton: 1985.

Nearman, Mark J. "Feeling in Relation to Acting: An Outline of Zeami's Views." *Asian Theatre Journal* 1, no. 1 (Spring 1984): 40–51.

———. "Kakyō: Zeami's Fundamental Principles of Acting." *Monumenta Nipponica* 37, no. 3 (1982): 332–374; no. 4 (1982): 461–496; 38, no. 1 (1983): 49–71.

Nippon Gakujutsu Shinkōkai. *The Noh Drama.* 3 vols. Tokyo and Vermont: 1955–1960.

Nishio Minoru, ed. *Nōgakuronshū. Nihon koten bungaku taikei,* vol. 65. Tokyo: Iwanami, 1961.

Nogami Toyoichirō. *Kaichū yōkyoku zenshū.* vol. 2. Tokyo: Chuōkōron, 1935.

———. "Nō no shuyaku ichinin shugi." In *Nō: kenkyū to hakken.* Tokyo: 1930. Translated in part by Chieko Irie Mulhern, "The Monodramatic Principle of the Noh Theatre," *Journal of the Association of Teachers of Japanese* 16, no. 1 (April 1981): 72–86.

———, ed. *Nōgaku zensho.* 7 vols. Rev. by Nishino Haruo and Matsumoto Yasushi. Tokyo: 1984.

———. *Yōkyoku geijutsu.* Tokyo: 1936.

Omote Akira, and Katō Shūichi, eds. *Zeami: Zenchiku. Nihon shisō taikei,* vol. 24. Tokyo: Iwanami, 1974.

O'Neill, P.G. *Early Nō Drama: Its Background, Character and Development 1300–1450.* London: 1958.

———. "Translations: The Nô Plays Koi no Omoni and Yuya." *Monumenta Nipponica* 10, nos. 1–2 (1954): 203–226.

Peri, Noël. *Le Nô.* Tokyo: 1944.

Pigeot, Jacqueline. *Michiyuki-bun: Poétique de l'itineraire dans la littérature du Japon ancien.* Paris: 1982.

Raz, Jacob. *Audience and Actors: A Study of Their Interaction in the Japanese Traditional Theatre.* Leiden: 1983.

Renondeau, G. *Le bouddhisme dans les Nô.* Tokyo: 1950.

Rimer, J. Thomas, and Masakazu Yamazaki, trans. *On the Art of the Nō Drama: The Major Treatises of Zeami.* Princeton: 1984.

Sanari Kentarō. *Yōkyoku taikan.* 7 vols. Tokyo: Meiji Shoin, 1931; reprinted, 1983.

Sekine, Masaru. *Ze-ami and His Theories of Noh Drama*. Gerrards Cross: 1985.

Shimazaki Chifumi. *The Noh*. vols. I and III. *God Noh*, book I, and *Woman Noh*, books 1–3. Tokyo: Hinoki, 1972–1981.

Sieffert, René, trans. *La tradition secrète du Nô*. Paris: 1960.

———. *Nô et kyôgen: Théâtre du moyen âge*. 2 vols. Paris: 1979.

Takagi Ichinosuke, ed. *Heike monogatari*. vol. 2. In *Nihon koten bungaku taikei*, vol. 33. Tokyo: Iwanami, 1960.

Tamba, Akira. *La structure musicale du Nô: Théâtre traditionnel japonais*. Paris: 1974.

Tsubaki, Andrew A. "Zeami and the Transition of the Concept of Yūgen: A Note on Japanese Aesthetics." *The Journal of Aesthetics and Art Criticism* 30, no. I (Fall 1971): 55–67.

Waley, Arthur. *The Nō Plays of Japan*. London: 1921.

Watsuji Tetsurō. "Yōkyoku ni arawareta rinri shisō." Trans. David A. Dilworth. *Monumenta Nipponica* 24, no. 4 (1969): 467–498.

Wilson, William Ritchie. "Two Shuramono *Ebira* and *Michimori*." *Monumenta Nipponica* 24, no. 4 (1969): 415–465.

Yamazaki Masakazu. "The Aesthetics of Transformation: Zeami's Dramatic Theories." Trans. Susan Matisoff. *Journal of Japanese Studies* 7 (1981): 218–257.

Yashima Masaharu. "Sanemorikan no hensen: shudai ishiki kara mita nōsaku no suii." In *Zeami no nō to geiron*. Tokyo: 1985.

———. "Zeami ni okeru shura no keifu." In *Geinōshi kenkyū* 43 (1973): 14–26.

Yasuda, Kenneth K. "On the *Nonomiya* of Zeami." In *Asien Tradition und Fortschritt: Festschrift für Horst Hammitzsch*. Wiesbaden: 1971.

———. "The Structure of *Hagoromo*, a Nō Play." *Harvard Journal of Asiatic Studies* 33 (1973): 8–11.

Yokomichi Mario. "Sanemori no hanashi." In *Yōkyoku kyōgen, Nihon bungaku kenkyū shiryōhankōkai*. Tokyo: 1981.

Yokomichi Mario, and Omote Akira, eds. *Yōkyokushū*. 2 vols. *Nihon koten bungaku taikei*, vols. 40 and 41. Tokyo: Iwanami, 1960 and 1963.

WORKS ON THE COMPARISON OF GREEK TRAGEDY AND NŌ

Johnson, Martha Bancroft. "The Mask in Ancient Greek Tragedy: A Reexamination Based on the Principles and Practices of the Noh Theater of Japan." Diss., University of Wisconsin: 1984.

Lesky, Albin. "Noh-Bühne und griechische Theatre." *Maia*, n.s. 15 (1963): 38–44.

Nogami Toyoichirō. "Gasshōka no higikyokuteki seishitsu: Nō to girishageki to no hikaku." In *Nō no saisei*, 120–146. Tokyo: 1935.

———. "Nō to girishageki." In *Shisō*, 31–44. Tokyo: October 1938.

Ono, Shinichi. "A Comparative Study of Some Aspects of Greek Theatre and Nō Theatre: Aesthetic Values Arising from the Quest for the Meaning of Life." Diss., University of Texas: 1975.

Roussos, Jason. "Ancient Greek Tragedy and Noh." *Diotima* 13 (1985): 121–128.

Smethurst, Mae J. "Breaking Down the Barriers Between Text and Audience in Noh and Aeschylean Drama." In *Ancient and Modern: Essays in Honor of Gerald F. Else*, ed. John H. D'Arms and John W. Eadie, 11–30. Ann Arbor: 1977.

Takebe, Rinsyo. "Die griechische Tragödie und das japanische Noh-Drama." *Wiener humanistische Blätter* 3, 2nd ser., no. 5 (1960): 25–31.

Index

Furu Myōjin, 151
Fūshikaden, see treatises
Futami no Ura, in *Matsukaze*, 155-156, 163

Garvie, A. F., 84n
Gempei jōsuiki (Gempei seisuiki), 26n
gender: in Greek language, 224-225, 228; in Japanese language, 224, 227
Genji (Minamoto), 26, 40n, 42, 305; in *Atsumori*, 138n; in *Sanemori*, 58, 60n, 70-71, 119n, 282; in *Yorimasa*, 242-243
Genji monogatari (The Tale of Genji), 149n
genzaimono, 32-33, 53n, 149n; defined, 32
gesture: in nō and tragedy, 12-14, 166, 233-234, 277; in nō, 6, 28-29, 33; in *Matsukaze*, 158-159, 165; in *Sanemori*, 52, 67, 71-73, 76-79, 133, 148, 200-201, 256n; in tragedy, 147n; in *Agamemnon*, 160; in *Persians*, 94, 101, 130, 146, 148, 255-257; in *Suppliants*, 203n
ghost nō, *see* mugen nō
ghosts and spirits, in nō, 19-20, 31-33, 38, 239, 249n; in *Kiyotsune*, 42n, 94n, 249n; in *Nonomiya*, 32; in *Obasute*, 272; in *Sanemori*, 45-77 passim, 85, 94-95, 98-99, 112, 118, 125, 128, 180-204 passim, 238-239; in *Tadanori*, 71n; in *Takasago*, 40; in *Yorimasa*, 55n, 190, 257n; in tragedy, in *Eumenides*, 35; in *Persians*, 90, 98, 112, 129-131, 138-140, 238, 246n, 252. *See also* Sanemori
Glaucus, 36
Glaucus of Rhegium, 258n, 269n
god(s) and deities, 10n, 11, 24, 26, 34; in *Iliad*, 263; in tragedy, 19-20; in *Agamemnon*, 62, 160-161, 164, 196-198; in *Eumenides*, 188; in *Persians*, 99, 101, 105-106, 109-110, 113-114, 119-126, 130-131, 134-143, 145, 147-148, 225, 238-239, 243, 246-256, 265-267; in waki nō, 31; in *Furu*, 152; in *Takasago*, 40. *See also names of specific gods and deities*
god play, *see* waki nō
Goodell, Thomas D., 96n
Gosenshū, 191n, 200n; transl., 191
Greek language, 150, 178, 220, 224
Groeneboom, P., 112n

ha, 27-29, 31-38, 41, 69; defined, 305; in

Sanemori, 49, 55, 63, 69, 70, 74, 76, 134, 134n; in *Takasago*, 40
Hagoromo, 280n
Hajitomi, 112
hana, 28n
Hare, Thomas B., 39n, 78n
hashigakari, 48-50, 56, 65; defined, 9, 305
Hecabe, 108n
Hecataeus, 258n
Hector, in *Iliad*, 261-262, 268, 269n
Heike monogatari (The Tale of the Heike), 305; sections, book 1, chapter 1: 138n; book 1, chapter 15: 54n, 179n; book 4, chapter 12: 188n; book 4, chapter 14: 189n; book 7, chapter 8: 41n, 198; book 9, chapter 16, 43n, transl., 282-286; as source of shura nō, 260; *Atsumori*, 25, 43; *Sanemori*, 26, 40-41, 43, 68-80, 102, 119n, 137-138, 189-191, 198-204, 256-257, 260, 269, 275; *Yorimasa*, 25
Heike (Taira), 26, 26n, 40n, 42, 190n, 305; in shura nō, 40; in *Atsumori*, 138n; in *Kiyotsune*, 42n; in *Sanemori*, 41, 53, 58-59, 60n, 70, 119n, 201; in *Shunkan*, 32; in *Yorimasa*, 119n, 242
Helen, in *Agamemnon*, 173, 181-182, 186-187, 191n, 219
Hephaestus, in *Agamemnon*, 160, 164
Heraclitus, 19
Heracles, 32
herald and herald scene: in *Agamemnon*, 60-62, 88-91, 92n, 93, 116, 166; in *Seven against Thebes*, 86n
Herington, John, 20, 20n, 21n, 258
Hermes, in *Agamemnon*, 160
Herodotus, 41n, 122, 124, 137, 165, 236n, 264n, 275
Hesiod, 41n, 224n, 251n
Higuchi: in *Heike*, 199, 283; in *Sanemori*, 70-72, 74, 85, 122-123, 199-200, 283
hiranori, 40n, 79; defined, 305
Hitomaro, 217n; in *Kayoi Komachi*, 211-212
Holtsmark, Erling B., 96n, 110n
Homer, 41n, 43, 198, 217n, 224; influence on *Agamemnon*, 35, 190, 191n; on *Persians*, 119, 143, 212, 217n, 219, 240, 245, 256-275 passim. *See also Iliad; Odyssey*
homonym: in *Eguchi*, 214; in *Yorimasa*, 243
honkadori, 149n. *See also* allusion
honmon, 201n; defined, 200n

Index locorum

Aeschylus
Agamemnon
    39: 46
    40-1068: 92n
    41: 177n
    47: 177n
    48-49: 190
    48-59: Greek text, 295; transl., 172-173
    49: 268n
    51-52: 173
    52: 256n
    57: 177n, 217; transl., 173
    66-67: 190
    72: 102n
    74: 102n
    75: 102n
    79-82: 224; Greek text, 298; transl., 224
    83-1068: 92n
    84: 103n
    104: 102n
    104-106: 169
    105: 175n
    134-136: Greek text, 297; transl., 197
    140-155: 186; Greek text, 296
    147: 175n
    177: 47
    182-183: 174; Greek text, 295
    184-185: 175
    184-247: 171
    187: 175n
    187-192: 176n
    192: 175n, 176n
    219: 175n
    223: 176n
    237-238: 226n
    250-251: Greek text, 295; transl., 170
    251: 225
    258: 103n
    258-280: Greek text, 293
    261: 162
    261-262: transl., 162
    264: 150n, 162
    264-265: transl., 162
    265: 162, 163
    266: 162
    271: 162
    276-278: 162n
    279: 162
    281: 160; transl., 163
    281-316: Greek text, 294
    282: 164
    282-283: 165
    283: 160; transl., 164
    285: 160
    288: 165
    289: 160
    292: 160
    295: 165
    299: 164
    300: 160
    303: 161
    304: 164
    306: 161
    309: 160, 161n
    310: 160
    311: 160, 165; transl., 164